A COMPANION TO
FIFTEENTH-CENTURY ENGLISH POETRY

D1477461

A COMPANION TO FIFTEENTH-CENTURY ENGLISH POETRY

Edited by Julia Boffey
and
A. S. G. Edwards

D. S. BREWER

First published 2013
D. S. Brewer, Cambridge
Paperback edition 2016

ISBN 978 1 84384 353 5 hardback
ISBN 978 1 84384 430 3 paperback

D. S. Brewer is an imprint of Boydell & Brewer Ltd
PO Box 9, Woodbridge, Suffolk IP12 3DF, UK
and of Boydell & Brewer Inc.
668 Mt Hope Avenue, Rochester, NY 14620–2731, USA
website: www.boydellandbrewer.co.uk

A CIP catalogue record for this book is available
from the British Library

The publisher has no responsibility for the continued existence or accuracy
of URLs for external or third-party internet websites referred to in this book,
and does not guarantee that any content on such websites is,
or will remain, accurate or appropriate

This publication is printed on acid-free paper

Contents

Contributors

Anthony Bale is Professor of Medieval Studies in the Department of English and Humanities at Birkbeck, University of London.

Julia Boffey is Professor of Medieval Studies in the English Department, Queen Mary, University of London.

A. S. G. Edwards is Professor of Medieval Manuscripts in the School of English, University of Kent, Canterbury.

Susanna Fein is Professor of English in the English Department, Kent State University.

Alfred Hiatt is Reader in the English Department, Queen Mary, University of London.

Simon Horobin is Professor of English Language and Literature at the University of Oxford.

Sarah James is Lecturer in the School of English, University of Kent, Canterbury.

Andrew King is Lecturer in Medieval and Renaissance English Literature at University College, Cork.

Sheila Lindenbaum is Professor Emerita in the English Department at Indiana University, Bloomington.

Joanna Martin is Lecturer in the School of English, University of Nottingham.

Carol Meale is Senior Research Fellow in the Department of English, University of Bristol.

Robert Meyer-Lee is Associate Professor of English in the English Department at Indiana University, South Bend.

Ad Putter is Professor of Medieval English Literature in the Department of English, University of Bristol.

John Scattergood is Professor Emeritus of Medieval and Renaissance English Literature at Trinity College, Dublin and Pro-Chancellor of the University of Dublin.

Anke Timmermann is Postdoctoral Fellow in the Max Plank Research Group, 'Art and Knowledge in the Pre-Modern Europe' at the Max Plank Institute for the History of Science, Berlin

Daniel Wakelin is Jeremy Griffiths Professor of Medieval English Palaeography at the University of Oxford.

David Watt is Associate Professor in the Department of English, Film and Theatre at the University of Manitoba.

Abbreviations

Add.	Additional (manuscript)
BL	British Library
Bodl.	Bodleian Library, Oxford
c.	circa
CT	Chaucer, *Canterbury Tales*
CUL	Cambridge University Library
EETS	Early English Text Society
e. s.	extra series (of EETS)
fol./fols	folio(s)
HEH	Huntington Library, San Marino, California
MED	Robert Lewis (gen. ed.), *The Middle English Dictionary* (1953–2001), from *The Middle English Compendium* (University of Michigan Digital Library Production Service, 2001): http://quod.lib.umich.edu/m/med/
MS/MSS	manuscript(s)
NIMEV	Julia Boffey & A. S. G. Edwards, A *New Index of Middle English Verse* (London, 2005); cited by entry number.
NLS	National Library of Scotland
NLW	National Library of Wales
OED	*Oxford English Dictionary*, 2nd edn (Oxford, 1994), *Oxford English Dictionary Online* (Oxford University Press, 2009), http://www.oed.com/
o. s.	ordinary series (of EETS)
PRO	The Public Record Office
s. s.	supplementary series (of EETS)
STC	*A Short-Title Catalogue of Books Printed in England, Scotland, & Ireland and of English Books Printed Abroad 1465–1640*, 2nd edn, Katherine Pantzer et al., 3 vols (London, 1976–90); cited by entry number.
TC	Chaucer, *Troilus & Criseyde*
TNA	The National Archives

Conventions

All references to Chaucer's works are to *The Riverside Chaucer*, general ed. Larry D. Benson (Boston, 1987); cited by work, book (where appropriate) and line. For abbreviated forms of Chaucer's works see above.

Individual primary works are cited parenthetically in the text by author (as appropriate) and / or title and line(s), and (where appropriate) by book or chapter divisions. These citations are keyed to the list of 'Works Cited' at the end of the appropriate chapter.

Short forms of citation for secondary works are generally given parenthetically in the text to author, citing author's surname and page of work. Where more than one work by an author appears in the list of works cited, the appropriate year of publication precedes page references; works published by one author within the same one year are distinguished thus: '1971a', '1971b', etc.

Introduction

JULIA BOFFEY AND A. S. G. EDWARDS

The scholarly study of fifteenth-century English verse is very much a late twentieth-century phenomenon. A number of the writings associated with the fifteenth-century authors covered in this collection of essays were not accessible in usable editions until some point in the twentieth century, and the critical tendency to overlook fifteenth-century poetry was in part an inevitable result of its simple unavailability. But the early decades of the twentieth century saw significant changes in the landscape of fifteenth-century verse, attributable largely to the efforts of dedicated individuals working in isolation. Henry Bergen, most significantly, produced in the first two decades of the twentieth century notable editions of the two longest poetic works of the fifteenth century, John Lydgate's *Troy Book* and *Fall of Princes*, each over 30,000 lines (Bergen 1906–35 and 1924-27). The work of Eleanor Hammond on fifteenth-century manuscript and textual culture in England generated partial editions and an important survey of fifteenth-century poetry in the form of *English Verse between Chaucer and Surrey* (1927). And Walter Schirmer's study of John Lydgate, published originally in German in 1952 and translated into English in 1961, offered a *Kulturbild*, a historical and cultural analysis of the most prolific poet of the century that has still not been superseded. These figures stand apart from a general tendency to see the verse of the period between Chaucer and the early sixteenth century as largely unrewarding.

By the closing decades of the twentieth century a perceptible reassessment of fifteenth-century verse was under way. In 1970 Derek Pearsall published *John Lydgate*, a book that is considerably more than a critical reappraisal of the major poet of the fifteenth century. In the opening chapters Pearsall sets Lydgate in cultural and literary contexts, exploring in particular detail the long shadow of Chaucerian influence and the imputation of 'dullness' so frequently ascribed to the verse of this period. While the claims Pearsall makes for Lydgate's poetic art are carefully limited, his sense of the contexts in which Lydgate's verse was composed has provided fertile ground for a variety of sympathetic lines of approach taken in subsequent scholarship.

Other studies continued the process of reappraisal that Pearsall's book had initiated. John Scattergood's *Politics and Poetry in the Fifteenth Century* (1971), for example, was the first modern attempt to consider the contemporary historical contexts in which much fifteenth-century verse was created. Such an appreciation of the dynamic relationship between literature and history at this time was to become an important factor in reshaping understanding of the verse of the period.

Together these studies signalled the start of new kinds of interest in fifteenth-century verse. They have laid the groundwork for a still expanding range of assessments of such verse and its various practitioners, forms and genres, and their cultural and literary importance, challenging earlier views that saw fifteenth-century poetry as unworthy of serious consideration, either ignored or dismissed as banal tedium or feeble dilution of the 'master' Chaucer. Critical interest in reception and response of the kinds pursued in A. C. Spearing's *Medieval to Renaissance in English Poetry* (1985) or Seth Lerer's *Chaucer and his Readers* (1993) has led to a deeper understanding of the shapes of literary influence as it was channelled after 1400. The last two decades have seen the publication of numerous studies of Lydgate, some extensive; Hoccleve's perceived individuality has excited much comment; figures such as John Audelay have become the focus for considerable enquiry. There has been a much broader appreciation than hitherto of both the generic diversity and the historical circumstances that inform verse of this period, with the effect that such figures as John Hardyng, John Capgrave, Osbern Bokenham and Charles of Orléans have come to achieve a prominence that would have been inconceivable to literary historians even half a century ago.

An important factor in the development of modern work on fifteenth-century verse has been a recognition of the significance of the implications of manuscript study in its various forms. In 1981 Derek Pearsall organised a conference on this topic, which led to two books he subsequently edited: *Manuscripts and Readers in Fifteenth-Century England* (1983) and (with Jeremy Griffiths) *Book Production and Publishing in Britain, 1375–1475* (1989). Both books are collections of essays that examine various aspects of fifteenth-century manuscript culture: patronage, art history, book ownership, textual transmission and various aspects of codicology, and which explore, *inter alia*, the relationships between material form and literary analysis. These books have in their turn become the stimulus for much wider study of the textual and material forms of verse in this period and the contexts that surround its creation and transmission.

This *Companion* is an attempt to respond to these new and diverse interests in fifteenth-century English verse. Certain categories of material have been excluded, notably Scottish poetry and (to a degree) the lyric, since these subjects are explored in other Companion volumes published by Boydell & Brewer (Bawcutt and Hadley-Williams 2007; Duncan 2005). Otherwise the volume examines the writings of the most significant individual figures and genres and includes some chapters that offer broader perspectives and contexts in which verse of this period can be fruitfully situated. It is our hope that this collection will provide an overview of the state of scholarship in the field and of the significant issues that have emerged over recent decades when study of fifteenth-century verse has undergone such an extraordinary expansion.

We would like to thank the authors of these essays for their patience and goodwill; and Caroline Palmer and her team at Boydell and Brewer for their encouragement of this undertaking, and efficient production of the book.

Works cited

Bawcutt, Priscilla, and Janet Hadley-Williams, eds, *A Companion to Early Scottish Poetry* (Cambridge, 2007)

Duncan, Thomas, ed., *A Companion to the Middle English Lyric* (Cambridge, 2005)

Lerer, Seth, *Chaucer and his Readers: Imagining the Author in Late Medieval England* (Princeton, NJ, 1993)

Hammond, Eleanor Prescott, ed., *English Verse between Chaucer and Surrey* (Durham, NC, 1927)

Lydgate, John, *Lydgate's Troy Book*, ed. Henry Bergen, 4 vols, EETS, e. s. 97, 103, 106, 126 (London, 1906, 1908, 1910, 1935)

——, *Lydgate's Fall of Princes*, ed. Henry Bergen, 4 vols, EETS, e. s. 121–4 (London, 1924-27)

Pearsall, Derek, *John Lydgate* (London, 1970)

——, ed., *Manuscripts and Readers in Fifteenth-Century England: The Literary Implications of Manuscript Study* (Cambridge, 1983)

——, and Jeremy Griffiths, eds, *Book Production and Publishing in Britain, 1375–1475* (Cambridge, 1989)

Scattergood, V. J., *Politics and Poetry in the Fifteenth Century* (London, 1971)

Schirmer, Walter, *John Lydgate: ein Kulturbild aus dem 15. Jahrhundert* (Tübingen, 1952); trans. by Ann E. Keep as *John Lydgate: A Study in the Culture of the XVth Century* (Berkeley, CA, 1961)

Spearing, A. C., *Medieval to Renaissance in English Poetry* (Cambridge, 1985)

PART I

BACKGROUND AND CONTEXT

1

The Patronage of Poetry

CAROL M. MEALE

In 1445, when Isabel Bourchier, Countess of Eu, commissioned the Augustinian friar, Osbern Bokenham, to write a life of Mary Magdalene for her, she used a phrase in relation to her patronage that seems to be a gracious request, apparently leaving Bokenham a choice in the matter: 'If ye liked þe labour to take' (Bokenham, ed. Serjeantson 1938: line 5074).[1] Bokenham is, however, open about the quandary in which she places him. Further on in the 'Prolocutorye' to the Legend, following the conventional rehearsal of the modesty topos, doubting, he ruminates:

> I thowt how hard it is to denye
> A-statys preyer, wych aftyr þe entent
> Of þe poete is a myhty comaundement. (lines 5082–4)

Isabel consents that he should visit the shrine of St James, as was his wish, before he begins his task, but Bokenham then writes again of his 'ladyis wyl & hir comaundement' (line 5118), which overrides a commission he had already undertaken, to write of the life of St Elizabeth of Hungary:

> At request of hyr to whom sey nay
> I neyther kan, ne wyl, ne may,
> So mych am I bounden to hyr goodnesse,
> I mene of Oxenforthe þe countesse,
> Dame Elyzabeth ver. (lines 5051–5)

Political considerations almost certainly underlay this postponement of Elizabeth de Vere's request: Bokenham's friary of Clare, Suffolk, was beholden to Isabel Bourchier's brother, Richard, Duke of York, for patronage, and the 1445 translation of Claudian's *De Consulatu Stilichonis* (BL, Add. MS 11814, made in the house) contains a fulsome dedication to him. In addition, although the Duke's political fortunes were at a low ebb at this point in the decade, the de Vere family were allies in Richard's later claim to the throne of England, rather than protagonists in their own advancement (Edwards 2001).

The tensions and anxiety evident in Bokenham's work, together with a

---

[1] The sole extant manuscript of this version of Bokenham's saints' lives, dated to 1447, is now BL, MS Arundel 327.

reminder of the possible political ramifications of patronage for both parties involved, alert us to the fact that there can be no easy definition of the term. It carries implications of power held by one party, of superior and inferior, and of some degree of protection, as well as encouragement and material support (Lucas 1997). These factors should be borne in mind as bases for analysis, but, as this chapter will make clear, the conditions of patronage were rarely so straight-forward.

A preliminary observation is that a surprisingly small number of fifteenth-century authors availed themselves of the supportive framework of patronage. The authors whose works I shall be documenting, whilst at times giving the impression of dependency (as in the case of John Lydgate), in the main had other, more regular forms of employment or sustenance that provided them with a living, and there is no sense of there being professional writers, whose sole or primary income came from the generosity of patrons. (Such, of course, is the case with Chaucer, who died in the year that this study begins.) In spite of numerous scholars over the years referring to the Benedictine Lydgate as 'laureate' (Pearsall 1970), the earliest laureate figure appears to have been the now little-regarded John Kay, writing in the latter part of Edward IV's reign, whose prose account of the siege of Rhodes by the Turks in 1480 survives in two manuscripts and in one print by an unknown publisher (Gray 2004). No poems by him are known to survive. It was not until the title of laureate (apparently a form of degree) was bestowed on John Skelton by the University of Oxford c.1488, followed by a career largely in royal service, that the concept of poet laureateship, with an accompanying notion of preferment, seems to have been recognised by the crown (Skelton, ed. Scattergood 1983: 15–16), although its manifestations were anything but consistent – as in the example of Skelton himself. The post did not become institutionalised until 1670, in the person of John Dryden.

Lydgate arguably remains the best known of the writers working within systems of patronage, and especially for his relationships with royal patrons, for whom he composed his longest texts. Henry of Monmouth, later Henry V, commissioned *The Troy Book* in October 1412. It was finished, at 30,117 lines, in 1420 (Lydgate, ed. Bergen 1906–35). Henry himself, in typically loquacious and discursive Lydgatean fashion, is not mentioned until line 74 of the Prologue where Lydgate, protesting his lack of 'pride and presumpcioun' in the under-taking, writes that he is obeying 'with-oute variaunce/ My lordes byddyng' in his retelling of the Trojan history, and in the emphasis on 'the prowesse of olde chiualrie' (line 78). All ninety-one lines of the 'Lenvoye' are devoted to praise of the 'Most worþi prince of kny3thod sours & welle', with a plea from the author to the effect that:

> Lowly I praie, with a dredful face,
> Disdeyne nat benyngely to se
> Vp-on þis boke rudly made by me. (lines 59–61)

Whether or not Lydgate received any financial recompense for this, or for any other of the poems that he wrote during this period, we do not know for certain (Pearsall 1970, 1997). Once he is translating – and expanding – Laurent de Premier-fait's French translation of Boccaccio's *De casibus virorum illustrium*, a poem, or rather, more accurately, a series of exempla, in 36,365 lines, written during seven or eight years from 1431 onwards, he makes it clear that he is dependent upon the generosity of Humfrey, Duke of Gloucester, younger brother of Henry V, under whose aegis, or 'comaundement' (line 430) he is working (Mortimer 2005). There exists, separately from the *Fall*, a 'Letter to Gloucester', lamenting the emptiness of his purse through the conceit of starvation ('Lynyng outward, his guttes wer oute shake' (Lydgate, ed. McCracken 1911, 1934: II, 665–7, line 7), whilst in the *Fall* itself, Lydgate brings up his parlous financial state in the Prologue to Book III and 'A chapitle of þe gouernaunce of Poetis', which he inserts near the ending of the same book. In the former he tells how 'Support was non my dulnesse for to giue;/ Pouert approchid; in stal crokid age' (Lydgate, ed. Bergen 1924, 1927: III, 64–5) until his 'Lordis fredam and bounteous largesse' ensured that 'Fals Indigence list me no mor menace' (III, 74, 77). In the latter he complains:

> But poor Poetis (God sheld hem fro myschaunce!)
> May now-adaies for ther impotence,
> For lakke of support go begge ther dispence. (III, 3855–7)

It was shortly after beginning the poem that Lydgate returned permanently to the abbey at Bury, so we may assume that his money troubles ended. This is not the place to discuss Duke Humfrey's pursuit of humanist scholarship (Weiss 1967; Sammut 1980): suffice it to say that for his own reading he apparently preferred texts in French rather than Latin (Barker-Benfield 1982), and unlike his elder brother he seems not to have held the English language in high esteem (Lindenbaum 1999: 296). By commissioning the undoubtedly fashionable Lydgate, however, and in lending him books from his library, he was possibly, in Jennifer Summit's words, advancing his 'self-fashioning as a scholar prince' (Summit 2006: 221). It has been suggested that the commissioning by Humfrey of the de luxe copy of the English translation of Palladius' *De Re Rustica* by an unknown author, probably in the early 1440s, to those in his affinity signalled 'a retreat from the active life to one focused on rural concerns', which view, given the sad state of Humfrey's political position at this time, makes sense of what otherwise might appear as a rather baffling act of patronage, highlighted by overly fulsome praise: 'Serenous prince! Or thus: O princis flour!/ Or this: O prince in pees and duc in were!' (I, 1186–7), and by Humfrey's active involvement as critic (Edwards 2003: 75). The author wrote (somewhat incongruously) in the courtly rhyme royal stanza, versifying the text from the original Latin prose, in the process at times forcing an awkwardly expressed Latinate syntactic construction into an inappropriate verse form.

To return to Lydgate, he stands apart from his contemporaries not merely by virtue of his prolific output, but also in its generic variety and the social diversity of his audience.[2] Members of the monastic orders, unsurprisingly, formed part of this public. Lydgate's home abbey of Bury, in the person of abbot William Curteys, commissioned his composition of the *Lives of Saints Edmund and Fremund*, for the royal visit of the young Henry VI from Christmas 1433 until

---

[2] For his audience see the now unjustly little-considered Walter Schirmer.

Easter 1434 (Edwards 2004); a record of payment survives for his *Life of St Albon and St Amphibal*, written for abbot John Whethamstede of St Alban's, a member of Humfrey of Gloucester's circle, the earliest such record to survive. The Register of Abbots John Whethamstede and Thomas Ramryge reads (fol. 67r): 'Item, cuidam monacho de Burgo Sancti Edmundi, Propter translacionem vite sancti Albani in nostrum vulgare/ iij.li.vi.s.viii.d.' (Pearsall 1997: 59; Lydgate, ed. van der Westhuizen 1974). Women, too, acted as patrons, despite the misogynistic attitude that has sometimes been attributed to Lydgate (Boffey 1995; Renoir 1961; Edwards 1970). We are chiefly reliant, however, upon the annotations of the London book collector and scribe John Shirley (c.1366–1456) for information about the majority of the activities of these women, either from manuscripts he actually copied, or from those that derived from Shirleian exemplars (Connolly 1998; Boffey and Thompson 1989). For Anne, Countess of Stafford, he composed the *Invocation to St Anne* (Lydgate, ed. McCracken: I, 130–3; Bodl., MS Ashmole 59); and for her daughter, also Anne (Mortimer, Lady March), he says that he wrote, again under 'commaundement' (line 70), the *Legend of St Margaret* (Lydgate, ed. McCracken: I, 173–92; Cambridge, Trinity College R.3.20; the intended recipient was both widowed and then herself dead by the time the headnote to the poem was written [Connolly 1998: 78–9]). The *lyff off Guy of Warwyk* was composed for Margaret Talbot, Countess of Shrewsbury, who was daughter to Richard Beauchamp, 5th Earl of Warwick – it was presumably commissioned by way of demonstrating the ancestral myth of the descent of the Beauchamps from the romance hero of that name (Lydgate, ed. McCracken: II, 516–38; BL, Harley MS 7333; Harvard University, Houghton Library, MS Eng. 530). The final stanza states that it was 'compiled vnder correccyoun' (line 585). Isabel, the third wife of this same earl of Warwick, was apparently patron of *The Fifteen Joys of Our Lady* (Lydgate, ed. McCracken: I, 260–7; BL, Cotton Titus MS A.XXVI), whilst to Alice Chaucer, Countess of Suffolk, is attributed the doctrinal *Virtues of the Mass* (Lydgate, ed. McCracken: I, 87–115; Oxford, St John's College, MS 56).[3] The seventeen-stanza reflection on worldly transience known as 'That Now is Hay Sometime was Grase' was supposedly written at 'þe commaundement of þe Quene Kateryn as in here sportes she wallkyd by the medowes that were late mowen in the monthe of julij' (Lydgate, ed. McCracken: II, 809–13; BL, Add. MS 29729, a sixteenth-century volume compiled by John Stow). Until recently no literary critic has found much to write about Lady Sibille Boys, of the gentry family of Holm Hale in Norfolk, to whom Lydgate's *Epistle to Sibille*, a reworking of Proverbs 31: 10–31, was probably addressed (Lydgate, ed. McCracken: I, 14–8; Bodl., MS Ashmole 59). She was, though, a neighbour of William Paston (she gave him a recipe for ale-making) and Colin Richmond and Anthony Bale have detailed what is known of her life and contacts with the Paston family, so a far rounder picture of her emerges (Richmond 1990, 1996; Bale 2009). The attribution to her of the commissioning of *The Treatise for Launderesses*, though, rests on more shaky grounds (Boffey 1995).[4] Whilst it is satisfying to see so many women playing an active role in patronising the most prolific author of the fifteenth century, a

---

3   This is not a Shirley codex and the attribution is written in Latin.
4   For an account of the poem, which rereads the subject matter as a spiritual metaphor,

cautionary note should be added: it is only the shorter pieces with which women can be associated – *Guy of Warwick* is the longest of them, extending to 502 lines. It should also be observed that neither in the body of the texts, nor in Shirley's headnotes to them, is there any of the obsequiousness with which patrons are addressed, which may be seen in the long(er) poems written at the behest of men.

Critical interest has also been concentrated in recent years on what may be termed Lydgate's 'civic' poetry, that is, poems written for more public consumption within the city of London (Nolan 2005; Benson 2006). Despite this renewed interest, there are grounds for asserting that only two of the poems generally placed in this group are by Lydgate. One is his translation of the French *Danse Macabre*, requested by both 'frensshe clerkis' (line 22) and, according to Shirley, John Carpenter, clerk of London from 1417–38, who in 1430 stated a wish for Lydgate's verses to accompany the painting of the subject in Pardon churchyard, near St Paul's (Lydgate 1931, ed. Warren and White). 'King Henry VI's Triumphal Entry into London, 21 Feb., 1432' (Lydgate, ed. McCracken: II, 630–48), the second example, reached a genuinely wide audience: commissioned by the 'noble Meir', at that time John Wells (line 531), and the other governors of the city, the original 'devises' would have been witnessed by the citizens crowding the route of Henry's procession before being turned into a work of literature. Such a broad public would not have been in evidence for the remainder of Lydgate's mummings, or his *Legend of St George*, made, as a note by Shirley in Cambridge, Trinity College, MS R.3.20 tells us, for the armourers of London to celebrate their feast of St George (Floyd 2008).[5] His mummings, for the royal court, for the mercers, the goldsmiths and, in *The Mumming at Bishopswood*, for the city's officials, were, by contrast, intended for different types of elite audiences (Lydgate, ed. McCracken: II, 668–701; Lindenbaum 1999; Sponsler 2008). What is about this last text, and those intended for citizens rather than royalty, is their general lack of any modesty topos. In *Bishopswood*, for example, Lydgate virtually admonishes his public:

> Beo faythfull founde in al [vertu],
> Mayre, provost, shirreff, eche in his substaunce;
> And aldermen, whiche haue þe governaunce
> Over þe people by vertue may avayle,
> Þat noone oppression beo done to þe pourayle. (lines 59–63)

The absence of the deference found in his poems for royalty (excepting his pleas to Humfrey of Gloucester for monetary relief, and even these are respectful in tone) align these works with those for women.

Class, then, as well as gender, is an important determinant in the language of patronage. There is a hierarchy of address. This is true even of Osbern Bokenham: aside from his two aristocratic patrons for his *Legendys of Hooly Wummen*, he refers to 'my frende DENSTON KATERYNE' (line 1466) in the prologue to the

---

see Nolan (2008). The poem survives uniquely in CUL, MS Ff.1.6, the so-called Findern Manuscript (fol. 164r), which famously circulated amongst a group of women in Derbyshire.

[5]   It is argued here that the verses were painted on cloths, accompanying a visual representation of the saint's life.

life of St Anne (Katherine's daughter was her namesake) and at the end of this text he prays to God that He will grant her and her husband a son 'Of her body [...] or they hens pace' (line 2095). At the conclusion of the 'Lyf of S. Dorothye' he offers up a prayer for John Hunt and Isobel his wife, although the wording does not make clear whether the translation was made at the request of the couple or of Isabel acting by herself (lines 4976–81). Katherine Howard and Katherine Denston are joint dedicatees of the legend of Saint Katherine (Prologue, lines 6365–7) and the text ends with a prayer that both women and Bokenham himself, through the intercession of the saint may enter heaven (lines 7363–75); whilst the Life of St Agatha begins with a lengthy definition of the name's derivation and moves to an equally diffuse conclusion that 'þe deuyl with non enpechemente' Agatha Flegge 'mow lette from þe souereyn blys' (lines 8348–9). This phrasing would not seem to be categorisable as unequivocal evidence of patronage, but elsewhere, in the first chapter of a prose work that he wrote, the *Mappula Angliae*, he refers to the *Legendys* that he had composed 'at the instaunce of my specialle frendis and for edificacioun and comfort of alle tho þe whiche shuld redden hit or here it' (Bokenham, ed. Serjeantson 1938: xvi–xvii).[6] This almost relaxed approach to the issue suggests that, largely, he felt himself on a par with those for whom he was writing. In relation to Bokenham it should be noted that the surviving codex, including the Life of St Margaret, was written out under the direction of Friar Thomas Burgh in Cambridge, and given by him to an unnamed convent, possibly the house of Franciscan nuns at Denney (ibid.: 175–222 and epilogue; Doyle 1958). Bokenham's text(s), however, survived in different forms: it has been suggested that individual legends could have been in independent circulation (Edwards 1993), whilst a recently discovered manuscript shows that he was author of a far larger collection, lacking the commentaries of patronage in BL, MS Arundel 327, though it may, perhaps, have been destined to be a 'gift' for Cecily, duchess of York (Horobin 2005, 2007, 2008).

Another cleric and another female patron are John Walton and Elizabeth Berkeley, first wife of Richard Beauchamp, 5th Earl of Warwick. Although the evidence for her patronage of Walton's 1410 verse translation of Boethius' *Consolation of Philosophy* comes only in an acrostic of her name in the conclusion to Thomas Richard's of Tavistock 1525 edition (Walton, ed. Science 1927: xlii–xl), and although there is debate about which John Walton was the author, the milieu in which she lived both as daughter and wife would appear to have encouraged her own, independent activities and, further, links her with Lydgate's female patrons (Hanna 1989; Johnson 1996). Yet another canon, this time the Augustinian John Capgrave of Bishop's Lynn in Norfolk (c.1393–1464), wrote for women as well as men, in the production of the manuscripts of his work establishing what has been termed 'publication' (Lucas). Dedicating works to royalty can be attributed to flattery on the part of the writer rather than reliable evidence of patronage, yet he did write for specific patrons as well as for kings, princes, and even on one occasion for local gentry. He wrote comparatively little verse, and women do not figure amongst the patrons for it, although a copy of his *Life of St Katherine* came

---

6   This is a translation of Higden's geographical account of England from the latter's *Polychronicon* in BL, MS Harley 4011.

into the possession in the fifteenth century of the Augustinian sub-prioress of Campsey in Suffolk, Katherine Babington. By contrast, Sir Thomas Tuddenham of Oxburgh in Norfolk paid for Capgrave to visit Rome, probably in 1450, and in the resulting *Solace of Pilgrimes*, verses intersperse the prose; his *Life of St Norbert* of c. 1420 was composed for John Wygenhale, abbot of the Premonstratensian house at West Dereham.

An older contemporary of Capgrave's, Thomas Hoccleve, had to work harder for any patronage he received. Born in 1366/7, he worked as a clerk of the Privy Seal in London until shortly before his death in 1426 (Burrow 1994, 1995; Hoccleve, ed. Furnivall and Gollancz 1970: li–lxiii). He was, in his career, dependent on the whim of royalty to supplement his income, but what grants he received seem to be unconnected to his literary activities. In 1399, for instance, Henry IV, on his accession, granted him an annuity of £10 for life, which was raised to twenty marks in 1409. In addition he had board and lodging at the Privy Seal hostel, money for robes at Christmas, two corrodies, and fees from Privy Seal clients. Despite this apparent security, Hoccleve wrote 'balades' to Henry IV, to the dukes of York and Bedford, the Subtreasurer, Henry Somer, and other men of influence in which he bemoaned the state of his finances. In one poem addressed to Henry V he begged the sovereign 'Tendre pitee haue on our sharp distresse' (line 4), invoking the debtors' gaol of Newgate as his likely destination (Hoccleve, ed. Furnivall and Gollancz: 62). The work for which Hoccleve is, and probably was, best-known is his *Regiment of Princes*, composed c. 1411 and dedicated to Henry of Monmouth, soon to be Henry V (Hoccleve, ed. Furnivall 1970). It is extant in forty-six manuscripts, of which some are de luxe, featuring a prefatory miniature that shows either Hoccleve presenting Henry with a copy of his work (the original does not survive), or conversely, perhaps, Henry himself, in turn, acting as donor (McKendrick et al. 2011: cat. 64, 65). In the case of Hoccleve, we are presented with a completely different concept of patronage, one in which reward was anticipated, or hoped for, after composition. This is as true of what is now known as the *Series* as it is of the *Regiment of Princes*.

This collection of materials begins with the 'Complaint' of Hoccleve, in which he describes his mental breakdown in extraordinarily vivid terms, recalling how 'the substaunce // of my memorie/ Went to pleye' (Hoccleve, ed. Furnivall and Gollancz 1970: lines 50–1; Burrow and Doyle 2002: intro.). This is followed by the 'Dialogue' with a friend; the story of 'Jereslaus' Wife', a text entitled 'Learn to Die' and the story of 'Jonathas and Fellicula'. All three of the latter poems conclude with prose moralisations. The *Series*, with its integral references to Humfrey, Duke of Gloucester, would seem to indicate the source of patronage for which Hoccleve was hoping. However, the majority of these texts (excepting the 'Complaint' and the first thirty-six stanzas of the 'Dialogue', copied out later by John Stow) survive in Hoccleve's hand in Durham University Library, MS Cosin V.iii.9, which bears an envoy to Joan, Countess of Westmoreland, daughter of John of Gaunt and Katherine Swynford, thus aunt to both Henry V and Humfrey. Hoccleve directs his 'small book' 'looke thow // in all manere weye/ To plese hir wommanhede // do thy might', signing it 'humble seruant // to your gracious // noblesse // T. hoccleue.' (fol. 95r). Whether or not this dedicated copy (or the one Hoccleve presumably made for Humfrey) served their purpose in prompting an equally noble response, is not known. He may, however, have been encouraged to give, or at least prepare for Joan, a presentation copy because of a reputation for ownership of books on her part (Meale 1996).

Another poet, and composer, who was associated with the royal court – this time that of the Yorkists – was Gilbert Banester (Banester, ed. Wright 1937; Hall and Williamson 2004). He was the earliest translator of Boccaccio's cautionary tale of *Guiscardo and Ghismonda* from the *Decameron* and, although perhaps better known as a composer of plainsong and polyphony, because of his literary work he occupies a significant role in the history of English literature.[7] He was possibly the wealthiest of the authors considered in this essay, describing himself in his will as 'gentilman' of 'Est Grenewich in the Counte of kent' (18 August 1487: TNA: PRO Prob 11/8). By 1469 he had become a lay clerk in Edward IV's Chapel Royal and ten years later he was formally confirmed in the post of Master of the Choristers, being granted an additional forty marks a year to train the boy singers. His dwelling had a wharf, meaning that it was situated on the bank of the Thames and he owned eleven tenements in East Greenwich and neighbouring Kidbrooke. His material possessions – gowns, eating and drinking utensils, hangings and furniture – suggest a prosperous and easeful existence.

The earliest of the two manuscripts in which the text, based on a French version of the Latin adaptation by Leonardo Bruni in 1436 or 1438, survives is BL, Add. MS 12524, which can be dated to c.1450 (Banester, ed. Wright 1937: frontispiece). This manuscript has a corrupted text, but contains an important envoy that is lacking in the other, later, extant codex, Bodl., MS Rawlinson C.86 (which is a London production [Boffey and Meale]). The second stanza of the envoy contains the following lines:

> [...] if here be fawte or offens,
> Speke to Gilbert banester, whiche at the mocioune
> Off Iohn Raynere this made aftir þe sentence.
>   Explicit legenda Sismond (lines 623–5)

Presumably this envoy has been dropped from the Rawlinson copy (if, of course, it had been there in the exemplar) because it is a much later codex, and neither of the names carried the resonance they once had. John Raynere was an emissary of the Duke of Milan (Seymour 1995), so this commission of a translation of a text by Boccaccio may be seen as eminently appropriate. There is no hint that Banester was seeking a financial reward for his efforts and the phrase 'at the mocioune/ Off' broadens the terminology of patronage, eliminating questions of necessity, urgency, or obligation on the part of the author. It is worthy of note that the *MED* cites only one other occurrence of the word 'mocioune', and this has a different meaning, unsurprisingly connected with movement, and can be found in the tale of *Beryn*, dating from c.1400. Banester's social circle is one that is deserving of further investigation for what it may reveal of literary networks in late-medieval London. The executors of his will were two London citizens, John Wheteley,

---

[7]   Stevens 1961: 325 n.76 suggests that Banester may also have written an interlude, in 1482.

grocer, and John Combe, tailor, whilst the supervisor was 'henry Colett Maier of the Cite of London', a mercer, and father of the great educationist, John Colet.

A London merchant who was a producer, and not just consumer, of texts was the citizen and skinner Henry Lovelich. Early in the fifteenth century he translated, and versified, texts from the French Vulgate cycle, namely *Merlin* and the *Holy Grail*, both of which survive uniquely in Cambridge, Corpus Christi College, MS 80 (Lovelich, ed. Kock 1975; Lovelich, ed. Furnivall 1973). A note on fol. 127r, in the hand of John Cok, a brother of St Bartholomew's Hospital (situated outside London's city walls) and a prolific scribe in his own right, explains the genesis of the translations, stating that the work was undertaken 'at þe instaunce of harry barton', also a skinner, and twice mayor of London. Leaves are missing from both the beginning and ending of the text so any dedication or additional information about the commissioning of the romances that there may have been is lost. John Cok was also a friend of John Shirley (Doyle 1961; Connolly 1998), which complicates any interpretation, perhaps raising the implication that the phrase 'at þe instaunce of' may have had commercial overtones (Meale 1994).[8] Professional production is certainly in evidence both in the manner in which corrections were carried out and in the decorated ascenders of some top lines. Also, a considerable number of spaces were left within the texts, recalling in size and positioning both French manuscripts of the Arthurian Vulgate cycle, which were lavishly illustrated and, within England, the much-mutilated Auchinleck manuscript of romances and allied texts (NLS, Advocates 19.2.1, aesthetically a poor relation of its continental predecessors); Cambridge, Corpus Christi College, MS 61, the de luxe version of Chaucer's *Troilus and Criseyde*, in which, famously, only the frontispiece was ever completed; and, to a lesser extent, in that illustrations were fewer, and later, manuscripts of Lydgate's *Troy Book* (Pearsall and Cunningham 1979: intro.; Parkes and Salter 1978: intro.; Lawton 1983). That the spaces in Lovelich's text were intended to be filled with pictures would seem to be confirmed by the occurrence of notes such as 'A pagent' (fol. 154r) and 'pagent' (fol. 159r). In the case of Corpus Christi 61 it may have been lack of an exemplar, the sudden death of a patron (perhaps Henry, 3rd Baron Scrope of Masham, who was executed for treason in 1415 [Harris 2000]), or unexpectedly straitened circumstances (as in the case of the French royal captive Charles, Duc d'Orléans [Scott 2000]), which occasioned the incompleteness. The lack of an exemplar, since Lovelich's texts were translations from the French, seems unlikely to be the explanation for the gaps in the codex of his work. Perhaps cost came into the equation: illustration on such a scale would have been an expensive investment, and may have proved a breaking point for the patron. Paper, after all, rather than parchment or vellum, was used in its production.

Only one more romance, out of the hundred and more that survive, is known to have been written for particular individuals and this is John Metham's *Amoryus and Cleopes*, composed for Sir Miles and Lady Katherine Stapleton of Ingham in

---

8   For observations on glossing in the manuscript, and the occurrence of a female name in a
    margin, see Meale 1996: 141. Warren (2008), stresses, rather, 'the craft context of the work's
    patronage and intended audience'.

Norfolk, in 1448/9 (Metham, ed. Page 1999). The romance survives in only one manuscript, dating from at least two decades later, now in Princeton University Library, MS Garrett 141, and contains an elaborate encomium of Metham's patrons, who died in 1466 and 1488 respectively, stretching to ten rhyme royal stanzas (lines 2115–84).[9] The Stapletons', or perhaps just Katherine's, investment in the romance, and its accompanying treatises by John Metham, is signalled by the elaborate coats of arms of the couple, which open both the romance and its preceding text, a treatise on palmistry (Metham, ed. Craig 1916). These are: argent, a lion rampant for Stapleton, impaling azure, on a fess between three leopards or, a mullet sable, for de la Pole. (Katherine was cousin to William de la Pole, in later life Duke of Suffolk.) Originally it would seem that Metham, a devoted, if somewhat inept, follower of Chaucer and Lydgate, was actively seeking patronage, for he writes:

> Go now, lytyle boke; and with alle obeychauns,
> Enterly me comende to my lord and mastyr eke,
> And to hys right reverend lady; with alle plesauns,
> Enformyng them how feythfully I hem beseke
> Of supportacioun of the rude endytyng owte of Greke.
> For alle this wrytyng ys sayd undyr correccion,
> Bothe of thi rymyng and eke of thi translacion.
>
> (Metham, ed. Page, lines 2178–84)

The latter two lines may be an example of the modesty topos, but the heartfelt pleas of those preceding them expand the language of patronage still further.[10] Metham, writing a treatise on palmistry in the 'xxvti winter of his age', as a 'sympul scoler of philosophye' (Metham, ed. Craig: 84), adding further elsewhere that he was a 'scolere off Cambrygg' (ibid.: 145; although no record of his education there survives), was probably a distant relative to the Stapletons (Metham, ed. Page: 2–3, 99).

The texts that I have considered in this essay vary enormously both in subject-matter and in the skill of their authors. Patronage was important to their writers, yet the support of even arguably the greatest man of letters of his time, Humfrey of Gloucester, was neither assured nor unconditional. Patronage took many shapes, and was informed by class and gender, status and wealth. And the language in which it was expressed was just as complex as the factors that determined it.

---

[9]   On the dating of the manuscript and its patronage (as opposed to that of the text), see Meale, forthcoming.

[10] Vines does not make any distinction between the writing of the text and the production of the manuscript.

Works cited

Bale, Anthony, 'A Norfolk Gentlewoman and Lydgatian Patronage: Lady Sibylle Boys and her Cultural Environment', *Medium Aevum*, 78 (2009), 394–413

Banester, Gilbert et al., *Early English Versions of the Tales of Guiscardo and Ghismonda and Titus and Gisippus from the Decameron*, ed. Herbert G. Wright, EETS, o. s. 205 (London, 1937)

Barker-Benfield, B., 'Review: Alfonso Sammut, *Unfredo Duca di Gloucester e gli Umanisti Italiani*', *The Library*, 6th series, 4 (1982), 191–4.

Benson, C. David, 'Civic Lydgate: The Poet and London', in Scanlon and Simpson, eds, *John Lydgate*, pp. 147–68

Boffey, Julia, 'Lydgate's Lyrics and Women Readers', in *Women, the Book and the Worldly*, eds Lesley Smith and Jane Taylor (Cambridge, 1995), pp. 139–49

——, and John J. Thompson, 'Anthologies and Miscellanies: Production and Choice of Texts', in *Book Production and Publishing in England, 1375–1475*, eds Jeremy Griffiths and Derek Pearsall (Cambridge, 1989), pp. 279–315

——, and Carol M. Meale, 'Selecting the Text: Rawlinson C.86 and some other Books for London Readers', in Riddy, ed., *Regionalism*, pp. 143–69

Bokenham, Osbern, *Bokenham's Legendys of Hooly Wummen*, ed. Mary S. Serjeantson, EETS, o. s. 206 (London, 1938)

Burrow, J. A., *Thomas Hoccleve*, Authors of the Middle Ages, 4, (Aldershot, 1994)

——, 'Thomas Hoccleve: Some Redatings', *Review of English Studies*, n.s. 46 (1995), 366–72

——, and A. I. Doyle, intro., *Thomas Hoccleve: A Facsimile of the Autograph Verse Manuscripts*, EETS, s. s. 19 (Oxford, 2002)

Connolly, Margaret, *John Shirley: Book Production and the Noble Household in Fifteenth-Century England* (Aldershot, 1998)

Cooper, Lisa H., and Andrea Denny-Brown, eds, *Lydgate Matters: Poetry and Material Culture in the Fifteenth Century* (New York, 2008)

Doyle, A. I., 'Books Connected with the Vere family and Barking Abbey', *Transactions of the Essex Archaeological Society*, n. s. 5 (1958), 222–43

——, 'More Light on John Shirley', *Medium Aevum*, 30 (1961), 93–101

Edwards, A. S. G., 'Lydgate's Attitudes to Women', *English Studies*, 51 (1970), 436–7

——, 'The Transmission and Audience of Osbern Bokenham's *Legendys of Hooly Wummen*', in *Late-Medieval Religious Texts and their Transmission: Essays in Honour of A. I. Doyle*, ed. A. J. Minnis (Cambridge, 1993), pp. 157–67

——, 'The Middle English Translation of Claudian's *De Consulatu Stilichonis*', in *Middle English Poetry: Texts and Traditions: Essays in Honour of Derek Pearsall*, ed. A. J. Minnis (York, 2001), pp. 267–78

——, 'Duke Humfrey's Middle English Palladius Manuscript', in *The Lancastrian Court: Proceedings of the 2001 Harlaxton Symposium*, ed. Jenny Stratford (Donington, 2003), pp. 68–77

——, intro., *The Life of St Edmund King and Martyr: John Lydgate's Illustrated Verse Life Presented to Henry VI: A Facsimile of British Library MS Harley 2278* (London, 2004)

Floyd, Jennifer, 'St George and the "Steyned Halle": Lydgate's Verse for the London Armourers', in Cooper and Denny-Brown, eds, *Lydgate Matters*, pp. 139–64

Gray, Douglas, 'Kay, John (*fl.* c.1482)', *Oxford Dictionary of National Biography* (Oxford, 2004) <http://www.oxforddnb.com/view/article/4350> [accessed 12 Jan 2011]

Hall, Jonathan, and Magnus Williamson, 'Banestre, Gilbert (*d.* 1487)', *Oxford Dictionary of National Biography* (Oxford, 2004) <http://www.oxforddnb.com/view/article1266> [accessed 2 Jan 2011]

Hanna III, Ralph, 'Sir Thomas Berkeley and his Patronage', *Speculum*, 64 (1989), 878–916

Harris, Kate, 'The Patronage and Dating of Longleat House MS 24, a Prestige Copy of the *Pupilla Oculi* Illuminated by the Master of the *Troilus* Frontispiece', in Riddy, ed., *Prestige*, pp. 35–54

Hoccleve, Thomas, *Hoccleve's Works: The Minor Poems*, eds Frederick J. Furnivall and I. Gollancz, rev. by Jerome Mitchell and A. I. Doyle, 2 vols, EETS, e. s. 61, 73 (London, 1892, 1925; repr. in one volume, 1970)

——, *Hoccleve's Works, III: The Regement of Princes*, ed. Frederick J. Furnivall, EETS e. s. 72 (London, 1897)

Horobin, Simon, 'The angle of oblivioun: A lost Medieval MS Discovered in Walter Scott's Collection', *Times Literary Supplement*, 11 November 2005, 12–13

——, 'Politics, Patronage, and Piety in the Work of Osbern Bokenham', *Speculum*, 82 (2007), 932–49

——, 'A Manuscript Found in the Library of Abbotsford House and the Lost Legendary of Osbern Bokenham', *English Manuscript Studies 1100–1700*, 14 (2008), 130–62

Johnson, I. R., 'New Evidence for the Authorship of Walton's *Boethius*', *Notes and Queries*, 241 (1996), 19–21

Lawton, Lesley, 'The Illustration of Late Medieval Secular Texts, with Special Reference to Lydgate's *Troy Book*', in *Manuscripts and Readers in Fifteenth-Century England: The Literary Implications of Manuscript Study*, ed. Derek Pearsall (Cambridge, 1983), pp. 41–69

Lindenbaum, Sheila, 'London Texts and Literate Practices', in *The Cambridge History of Medieval English Literature*, ed. David Wallace (Cambridge, 1999), pp. 284–309

Lovelich, Henry, *The History of the Holy Grail by Henry Lovelich*, ed. Frederick J. Furnivall, 5 vols, EETS, e. s. 20, 24 (London, 1874, 1875; repr. as one volume, 1973) and 28, 30, 95 (London, 1877, 1878, 1905; repr. as one volume, 1973)

——, *Henry Lovelich's Merlin*, ed. E. A. Kock, 3 vols, EETS, e. s. 93, 112; o. s. 185 (London, 1904, 1913, 1932; repr. as one volume, 1975)

Lucas, Peter J., *From Author to Audience: John Capgrave and Medieval Publication* (Dublin, 1997)

Lydgate, John, *Lydgate's Troy Book*, ed. Henry Bergen, 4 vols, EETS, e. s. 97, 103, 106, 126 (London, 1906, 1908, 1910, 1935)

——, *The Minor Poems of John Lydgate*, ed. Henry Noble McCracken, 2 vols, EETS, e. s. 107 and o. s. 192 (London, 1911, 1934)

——, *Lydgate's Fall of Princes*, ed. Henry Bergen, 4 vols EETS, e. s. 121–4 (London, 1924, 1927)

——, *The Dance of Death*, eds Florence Warren and Beatrice White, EETS, o. s. 181 (London, 1931)

——, *John Lydgate: The Life of Saint Alban and Saint Amphibal*, ed. J. E. Van der Westhuizen (Leiden, 1974)

McKendrick, Scot et al., *Royal Manuscripts: The Genius of Illumination* (London, 2011)

Meale, Carol M., '"gode men / Wiues maydnes and alle men": Romance and its Audiences', in *Readings in Medieval English Romance*, ed. Carol M. Meale (Cambridge, 1994), pp. 209–25

——, '". . . alle the bokes that I haue of latyn, englisch and frensch": Laywomen and their Books in Late Medieval England', in *Women and Literature in Britain 1150–1500*, ed. Carol M. Meale, 2nd edn (Cambridge, 1996), pp. 128–58

——, 'Katherine de la Pole and East Anglian Manuscript Production in the Fifteenth Century: An Unrecognised Patron?', forthcoming

Metham, John, *The Works of John Metham*, ed. Hardin Craig, EETS, o. s. 132 (London, 1916)

——, *Amoryus and Cleopes*, ed. Stephen F. Page (Kalamazoo, MI, 1999)

Mortimer, Nigel, *John Lydgate's Fall of Princes: Narrative Tragedy in its Literary and Political Contexts* (Oxford, 2005)

Nolan, Maura, *John Lydgate and the Making of Public Culture* (Cambridge, 2005)

——, 'The Performance of the Literary: Lydgate's Mummings', in Scanlon and Simpson, eds, *John Lydgate*, pp. 169–206

——, 'Lydgate's Worst Poem', in Cooper and Denny-Brown, eds, *Lydgate Matters*, pp. 71–87

Parkes, M. B., and Elizabeth Salter, intro., *'Troilus and Criseyde', Geoffrey Chaucer: A Facsimile of Corpus Christi College Cambridge MS 61* (Cambridge, 1978)

Pearsall, Derek, *John Lydgate* (London, 1970)

——, *John Lydgate (1371–1449): A Bio-Bibliography* (Victoria, 1997)

——, and I. C. Cunningham, intro., *The Auchinleck Manuscript: Edinburgh, National Library of Scotland Advocates' MS 19.2.1* (London, 1979)

Renoir, Alan, 'Attitudes toward Women in Lydgate's Poetry', *English Studies*, 42 (1961), 1–14

Richmond, Colin, *The Paston Family in the Fifteenth Century: The First Phase* (Cambridge, 1990)

——, *The Paston Family in the Fifteenth Century: Fastolf's Will* (Cambridge, 1996)

Riddy, Felicity, ed., *Regionalism in Late Medieval Manuscripts and Texts* (Cambridge, 1991)

——, ed., *Prestige, Authority and Power in Late-Medieval Manuscripts and Texts* (Cambridge, 2000)

Sammut, Alfonso, *Unfredo Duca di Gloucester e gli Umanisti Italiani*, Medioevo e Umanesimo, 41 (Padua, 1980)

Scanlon, Larry and James Simpson, eds, *John Lydgate: Poetry, Culture and Lancastrian England* (Notre Dame, IN, 2006)

Schirmer, Walter F., *John Lydgate: A Study in the Culture of the XVth Century*, trans. Ann E. Keep (London, 1961)

Scott, Kathleen L., 'Limner-Power: A Book Artist in England *c.* 1420', in Riddy, ed., *Prestige*, pp. 55–75

Seymour, M. C., *A Catalogue of Chaucer Manuscripts, vol. 1, Works Before the Canterbury Tales* (Aldershot, 1995)

Skelton, John, *John Skelton: The Complete English Poems*, ed. John Scattergood (Harmondsworth, 1983)

Sponsler, Claire, 'Lydgate and London's Public Culture', in Cooper and Denny-Brown, eds, *Lydgate Matters*, pp. 13–33

Stevens, John, *Music and Poetry at the Early Tudor Court* (London, 1961)

Summit, Jennifer, '"Stable in study": Lydgate's *Fall of Princes* and Duke Humphrey's Library', in Scanlon and Simpson, eds, *John Lydgate*, pp. 207–31

Vines, Amy N., 'Fictions of Patronage: The Romance Heroine as Sponsor in John Metham's *Amoryus and Cleopes*', *Journal of the Early Book Society*, 13 (2010), 139–68

Walton, John, *Boethius: De Consolatione Philosophiae Translated by John Walton Canon of Oseney*, ed. Mark Science, EETS, o. s. 170 (London, 1927)

Warren, Michelle R., 'Lydgate, Lovelich and London Letters', in Cooper and Denny-Brown, eds, *Lydgate Matters*, pp. 113–38

Weiss, Roberto, *Humanism in England during the Fifteenth Century*, 3rd edn (Oxford, 1967)

2

Forms of Circulation

SIMON HOROBIN

Just as the verse of fifteenth-century poets such as Lydgate and Hoccleve was heavily indebted to Chaucer's model for its themes, subjects and forms, so too were its modes of circulation influenced by Chaucerian texts and manuscripts. An important model for the format and layout of the verse manuscripts of his followers was the Ellesmere manuscript of the *Canterbury Tales* (HEH, MS EL 26.C.9), a de luxe and authoritative copy of the work, produced in London in the first decade of the fifteenth century. In addition to its expansive use of white space, illuminated initials and the provision of a series of pilgrim miniatures at the beginnings of tales, the Ellesmere manuscript gives prominence to a body of Latin marginal source glosses and references that contribute to the presentation of Chaucer as a learned *auctor* (Parkes 1976; Doyle and Parkes 1979). The influence of the Ellesmere manuscript is most apparent in the layout and appearance of the earliest copies of Hoccleve's major work, *Regiment of Princes*. Hoccleve's *Regiment* survives in a total of forty-six manuscripts; the two earliest and textually most authoritative copies, BL, MSS Harley 4866 and Arundel 38, were both produced in London in the early fifteenth century and employ very similar features of layout. Individual stanzas are separated by blank lines, with decorated paragraph marks indicating their beginnings, and Latin glosses have been added within the margins; new sections of text are accompanied by decorated borders. In addition to similarities in the layout of the text and apparatus, these two manuscripts are linked by a shared programme of illustration, although this relationship has been disrupted as a result of later losses. The Arundel manuscript contains a presentation miniature, in which a young man, perhaps the commissioner of the book, John Mowbray, Duke of Norfolk, offers the book to Hoccleve's patron, Prince Henry, later Henry V (Scott 1996: II, 158–60). This image was probably originally present in the Harley manuscript, but has since been removed. The Harley manuscript has an illustration no longer found in Arundel, in which Chaucer himself appears, gesturing towards the moment in the text where Hoccleve remembers the poet with a pointing finger (Scott 1996: II, 160–2). The placement of the Chaucer portrait in the margin alongside this textual reference recalls the marginal pilgrim portraits in the Ellesmere manuscript, while the similarities in facial expression, clothing and gesture demonstrate a close relationship with the image of 'Chaucer the pilgrim' in Ellesmere, with the clever decision to swap the horse's reins for rosary beads. The similarities suggest that one was copied from another, or perhaps the existence of a common exemplar

from which both derive.[1] The visual appearance of the two Hoccleve manuscripts seems deliberately designed to recall the Ellesmere manuscript, and thus
the model of Hoccleve's illustrious predecessor and literary father figure. It has
been suggested that Hoccleve was involved in the production of the Ellesmere
manuscript itself (Pearsall 1992: 289; Bowers 2007: 192). The evidence for this is
circumstantial, but suggestive: Hoccleve was himself a scribe and contributed to
a manuscript of Gower's *Confessio Amantis* along with four other copyists, one
of whom was the scribe of the Ellesmere manuscript. There may be more direct
evidence of his involvement in the production of an earlier copy of Chaucer's
Canterbury Tales, the Hengwrt manuscript (NLW, MS Peniarth 392D), copied by
the same scribe as Ellesmere. In this manuscript the original scribe left several
blank lines, subsequently filled by another copyist whose writing closely resembles that of Hoccleve (Doyle and Parkes 1979).

The continued influence of Chaucer's model is also reflected in the circulation
of Lydgate's most overtly Chaucerian work, *The Siege of Thebes*, a continuation of
Chaucer's *Canterbury Tales* in which the poet meets the pilgrims in Canterbury
and tells his own tale on the homeward journey. Responding to this framework,
five manuscripts append the *Siege of Thebes* to a copy of *Canterbury Tales*.[2] But
even where the two texts are not together in the same codex, the relationship
between the two was often emphasised. One important manuscript of the *Siege of
Thebes*, now BL, MS Arundel 119, employs a familiar pattern of textual *ordinatio*,
including the provision of illuminated initials, decorated borders, and marginal
Latin glosses, that seems explicitly intended to recall that of the Ellesmere manuscript of Chaucer's work. In addition to its visual echo of the Ellesmere manuscript, Arundel 119 has genuine Chaucerian pedigree. Its opening folio contains
an armorial badge painted with the arms of William de la Pole, Duke of Suffolk,
who was married to Chaucer's granddaughter Alice in 1430, who herself had
patronage connections with Lydgate; it has been suggested that the volume may
have been commissioned specifically to commemorate their marriage (Hanna
and Edwards 1996: 16–17). The Ellesmere manuscript was owned by families
with Suffolk connections in the early fifteenth century and so may have been
directly available to those responsible for Arundel 119.

As the fifteenth century progressed, a new style of vernacular verse manuscript emerged, which extended the model of the Ellesmere manuscript, and that
of Cambridge, Corpus Christi College, MS 61 of Chaucer's *Troilus and Criseyde*,
in which an ambitious series of planned miniatures was never completed, to the
production of magisterial, de luxe codices accompanied by extensive cycles of
illustration. This format is particularly associated with copies of Lydgate's major
works, *Troy Book* and *The Fall of Princes*, which circulated in some of the most
impressive and expensive manuscripts of medieval vernacular verse (Lawton

---

[1] Derek Pearsall has argued that the awkward proportions of the Ellesmere image, in which
    the poet's upper body towers over the horse on which he is seated, suggest that it is the result
    of an attempt to adapt a three-quarter-length portrait such as that found in Harley 4866 to a
    figure on horseback. See Pearsall 1992: 285–91.
[2] These manuscripts are BL, Add. MS 5140, BL, MS Egerton 2864, Oxford, Christ Church, MS
    152, Longleat House, MS 257, University of Texas, MS 143.

1983). The most de luxe of these is a copy of *Troy Book*, Manchester, John Rylands Library, MS English 1, which has half-page miniatures at the beginning of each of the books, as well as a further sixty-four marginal illustrations. In addition to a miniature depicting Lydgate presenting the work to Henry V, the manuscript includes the coat of arms of the Carent family, a prominent Somerset family with Lancastrian political connections (Scott 1996: II, 259–63). Another manuscript that was conceived on a similarly lavish scale is BL, MS Royal 18.D.II, containing both *Troy Book* and *Siege of Thebes*. The manuscript contains an opening miniature depicting its patrons, Sir William Herbert and his wife Anne Devereux, kneeling before a king. Although numerous gaps were left for the inclusion of further miniatures, many were left unexecuted and only completed for a later owner in the early sixteenth century; the volume may never have been presented to the king for whom it was intended (Scott 1996: II, 282–5).

The increased demand for copies of these lengthy works is attested by a group of manuscripts of the works of Chaucer, Gower and Lydgate, copied by professional scribes employing similar handwriting and layouts and drawing upon identical exemplars. A copyist known as the 'hooked-g' scribe, because of his distinctive formation of that letter, contributed to a large group of up to fifteen manuscripts, including five of Lydgate's *Fall of Princes* and two of his *Troy Book* (Edwards and Pearsall 1989: 265–6; Mooney and Mosser 2004). While some of these are comparatively de luxe productions, others have gaps left for decorated initials that were never filled in, perhaps indicative of attempts to supply copies to a wider range of readers with varying budgets.

Just as Lydgate and Hoccleve's longer poems depended in part upon Chaucer's works for their models of transmission, their shorter poems frequently circulated within Chaucerian anthologies. This is particularly evident in the manuscripts of the so-called Oxford group, which place Hoccleve's *Letter of Cupid* and Lydgate's *Complaint of a Lover's Life* alongside Chaucer's shorter poems. These three manuscripts, all now in the Bodleian Library in Oxford, include a large number of shared items, probably copied from a series of independent booklets circulating within the London book trade (Robinson 1980, 1982; Norton-Smith 1979). Possibly the earliest of these manuscripts, Bodl., MS Tanner 346, copied c.1440, has just two items not found in either Bodl., MS Fairfax 16 or Bodl., MS Bodley 638, and 12 items that are present in both. Despite their overlapping contents, these three manuscripts did not use identical exemplars, but seem rather to have drawn independently upon similar collections of texts, circulating in unbound sets of booklets. The first booklet in Tanner 346 places Chaucer's *Legend of Good Women*, *Anelida and Arcite*, *Complaints of Mars*, *Venus* and *Pity* alongside Hoccleve's *Letter of Cupid* and Lydgate's *Complaint of a Lover's Life*. All of these items recur in the two later collections, although not in the same order. Tanner 346 also includes Chaucer's *Book of the Duchess*, *Parliament of Fowls*, and *Legend of Good Women*, as well as Lydgate's *Temple of Glass*, although these are all copied into separate booklets. These poems are also found in Fairfax 16 and Bodley 638, but in these manuscripts the text and arrangement of these items suggest the existence of a single booklet exemplar from which both scribes drew. This evidence suggests that these individual works by Chaucer, Hoccleve and Lydgate originally circulated in independent booklets amongst interested readers, who gradually incorporated similar poems; these expanded collections subsequently served as exemplars for larger anthologies. Unsurprisingly, these original individual booklets do not survive, but the physical make-up of these larger and more durable collections is important testimony to this otherwise unrecorded mode of transmission.

Unfortunately, we know little of the original patrons for whom these collections were made. The exception is Fairfax 16, the most de luxe of the three Oxford manuscripts, which includes a full-page frontispiece depicting Mars, Venus and Jupiter, designed to accompany the *Complaint of Mars* and painted by a prominent London artist (Scott 1996: II, 281). The frontispiece contains a coat of arms belonging to John Stanley of Hooton (d.1469), a prominent member of Henry VI's court and presumably the person responsible for commissioning the manuscript. Tanner 346 was owned by John Greystoke (d.1501), but he could not have been its original owner, nor is there any indication of from whom he acquired it. Bodley 638 differs from the other two in having been written later in the fifteenth century, by an amateur scribe who signed himself 'Lyty' and who may have been compiling the volume for his own enjoyment.

Another verse collection of the fifteenth century owned by a gentry family is Cambridge, Magdalene College, MS Pepys 2006, which shares ten items with the Oxford group, alongside the more unusual pairing of 'The Tale of Melibee' and 'Parson's Tale' (Edwards 1985). Inscribed within the Pepys manuscript in fifteenth-century hands are the names John Kyriell, a member of a prominent Kentish family, and William Fettyplace, a prosperous London merchant. Both families combined business interests in the capital with property in Kent, so that the manuscript could have changed hands in either location (Erler 2004). Another anthology that provides a rare glimpse of the process by which such collections were transmitted to Scotland, is Bodl., MS Arch. Selden. B.24. The Selden manuscript began life as a copy of Chaucer's *Troilus and Criseyde*, but subsequent stages of copying led to the addition of a familiar selection of poems by Lydgate, Hoccleve, Walton and Clanvowe, as well as the unique surviving copy of James I's *Kingis Quair* (Boffey and Edwards 1997). The Selden manuscript is a comparatively high-grade production, which opens with a historiated initial depicting a scene from *Troilus and Criseyde*. The inclusion of the arms of Henry, Lord Sinclair (d.1513), suggests that the manuscript was made at his commission. Selden. B.24 was copied by a professional scribe, whose hand has been identified in three further manuscripts, all of which have connections with the Sinclair family. The Selden manuscript differs from the earlier anthologies we have considered in that it contains a wider selection of verse, including many items of exclusively Scottish provenance. But, while Selden attests to the widening of the tradition of the 'Chaucerian' anthology, the importance of Chaucer's own authority continues to be affirmed. Not only are Chaucer's poems grouped together at the beginning of the Selden manuscript, but many of those by his followers are wrongly attributed to him. Of the nine texts that are attributed to Chaucer in Selden, five are incorrectly associated with him. Hoccleve's *Mother of God* is wrongly titled 'Oracio galfridi Chaucere', the ascription 'quod Chaucer' is appended to an extract from John Walton's verse translation of Boethius, and Lydgate's *Complaint of the Black Knight* is given the title: 'The Maying and disport of Chaucer'. These three instances attest to a peculiarly Scottish tradition of misattribution; all are found in other manuscripts of Scottish provenance.

An important group of anthologies containing works by Chaucer and Lydgate, as well as a range of didactic and historical works, are the three miscellaneous collections copied by John Shirley between 1420 and 1440 (Connolly 1998). Having spent much of his life in the retinue of Richard Beauchamp, Earl of Warwick, Shirley spent the latter years of his life in the close of St Bartholomew's Hospital, Smithfield, from which he rented four shops. This location, close to the centre of the metropolitan book trade, may imply commercial motives, a theory supported in part by verse prologues added at the beginnings of his manuscripts. In these prologues Shirley makes clear that his volumes were designed for circulation, perhaps in the form of booklets, although they were apparently intended to be returned: 'So whan ye had thes storyes rede [...] sendeth this boke to me agayne/shirley I meane' (Connolly 1998: 210; Hanna 1996). Was Shirley operating some form of lending-library, or was this a means of advertising his wares in anticipation of subsequent commissions?

Shirley's copies of these texts are well known for the 'gossipy' headings that he supplied, which situated Chaucer's and Lydgate's verse within a supposed biographical context. Thus, according to Shirley, Chaucer's poem *Truth* was composed on the poet's death bed, and *Lak of Stedfastnesse* during 'hees laste yeeres'. Lydgate's *That now is Hay sometyme was Grase* is headed with the following detailed account of its commission: 'Here begyneth a balade whych John Lydgate the Monke of Bery wrott and made at þe commaundement of þe Quene Kateryn as in here sportes she wallkyd by the medowes that were late mowen in the monthe of Julii'. Shirley also added marginal responses to antifeminist extracts from the *Fall of Princes*, urging Lydgate to 'Be stille daun Iohan. Suche is youre fortune', and issuing threats: 'Be pees or I wil rende this leef out of your booke' (Pearsall 1970: 74–5; Connolly 1998: 180). The audience envisaged for Shirley's comparatively plain collections of courtly verse, with their name-dropping headings and hints at familiarity with the poets themselves, may have included noble households like that of the Earl of Warwick, as well as a more diverse group with social aspirations and literary pretensions (Connolly 1998: 190–5; Edwards 1997).

Shirley's manuscripts, and the exemplars from which they were copied, continued to circulate within the London book trade long after his death. They formed the basis for subsequent verse miscellanies copied by a prolific London copyist, the 'Hammond' scribe, whose hand has been identified in a total of fifteen manuscripts, including two copies of the *Canterbury Tales* and two of Hoccleve's *Regiment of Princes*, as well as other works concerned with governance and heraldry (Mooney 2000). Two manuscripts written by the Hammond scribe, BL, Add. MS 34360 and MS Harley 2251, were copied directly from two of Shirley's anthologies: Cambridge, Trinity College, MS R.3.20 and Bodl., MS Ashmole 59 (Connolly 1998: 178–82). Shirley's manuscripts were also important in supplying regional centres of production; BL, MS Harley 7333, a compilation of works by Chaucer, Gower, Lydgate and Hoccleve, was copied at the Augustinian Priory of St Mary de Pratis, Leicestershire, from Shirley exemplars, including a copy of the *Canterbury Tales* no longer extant (Connolly 1998: 173–5; Mooney 2003). Shirley's volumes were also central to the sixteenth-century reception of

Chaucerian and Lydgatean works; the antiquarian and editor John Stow wrote of Shirley's books: 'I haue seene them, and partly do possesse them'. Several Shirley manuscripts contain annotations in Stow's hand, and parts of them were transcribed by Stow into BL Add. MS 29729 and MS Harley 367 (Connolly 1998: 182–5; Edwards 2004a: 115–16).

Despite the widespread practice of anthologising individual shorter works within larger collections, the fifteenth century saw little movement towards the production of collections of works by a single author. Perhaps the closest gesture to a 'Collected Works' of a single author are the three surviving manuscripts that gather together Hoccleve's shorter poems. It has been suggested that two of these, HEH, MSS HM 111 and 744, which together contain twenty-eight poems by Hoccleve, with only a single text, *Lerne to Die*, appearing twice, were originally a single codex, designed to function as a 'Collected Shorter Poems' (Bowers 1989). But this argument is difficult to sustain, given differences in size and ruling, and it is safer to assume that they were intended to be compatible partners rather than a single volume (Burrow and Doyle 2003). The intended function of the three Hoccleve manuscripts is also difficult to determine; the fact that they were copied by the author himself, towards the end of his life, may imply a personal concern for the preservation of his literary oeuvre, rather than the response to a demand for such a volume from a third party. The third holograph collection, Durham University Library, MS Cosin V.iii.9, includes an envoy on its final leaf, directing the 'smal book' to Joan Neville (d.1440), daughter of John of Gaunt and second wife of Ralph Neville, first Earl of Westmorland (d.1425). The Durham manuscript was decorated to a higher standard than the two Huntington manuscripts; this additional expense may be a reflection of the status of the dedicatee, although the parchment is of poor quality and it is unclear whether the volume was ever presented to Joan Neville, Countess of Westmorland. The Hoccleve holograph collections are unusual in their focus on the work of a single author; it is not until the printed editions of Chaucer, beginning with William Thynne's of 1532, that we see the inception of a tradition of offering single-volume collections of an author's works (Gillespie 2006).

Although London became increasingly seen as the centre of the book trade throughout the fifteenth century, Middle English verse continued to be copied and circulated in regional centres. Monastic houses produced manuscripts of Middle English verse texts, especially orthodox religious works with a local appeal. The earliest surviving copy of Lydgate's lives of the East Anglian saints Edmund and Fremund, a text originally composed for Henry VI, was produced at the abbey in Bury St Edmunds for presentation to the king. This manuscript, BL, MS Harley 2278, contains an impressive cycle of illustrations and has a claim to being one of the most de luxe of all manuscripts of Middle English verse (Edwards 2004b; Scott 1996: II, 225–9). The illustrations devised for that copy later formed the basis for a picture cycle employed by a group of manuscripts copied in the 1460s by a professional scribe who has been named the 'Lydgate' scribe for his apparent specialisation in Lydgate's works (Edwards 1983; Scott 1982). A total of eleven manuscripts have been attributed to this scribe, all but one containing works by Lydgate. Four are copies of the *Lives of Saints Edmund and Fremund*; two are copies of the *Fall of Princes* (one of these now only a fragment);

two preserve the *Secrees of Old Philisoffres*, left unfinished by Lydgate at his death in 1449 and subsequently completed by Benedict Burgh; another is a copy of *Troy Book*. This scribe also copied at least part of BL, MS Harley 2255, an anthology of Lydgate's minor verse, perhaps a deliberate attempt to create an authorial collection (Edwards 2000).[3] The only manuscripts copied by this scribe to contain work by another author are BL, MS Harley 4826, which adds Hoccleve's *Regiment of Princes* to the more predictable combination of the *Lives of Saints Edmund and Fremund* and the *Secrees*, and a fragmentary copy of the *Canterbury Tales* (Horobin 2009). The focus on the works of Lydgate, and particularly his lives of the East Anglian saints Edmund and Fremund, suggests that the scribe was based in the poet's home town of Bury St Edmunds, more likely in a commercial workshop than in a scriptorium based at the abbey itself (Scott 1982: 365–6). As well as presenting de luxe illustrated copies of Lydgate's work, these manuscripts are also textually important, in preserving variant or supplementary texts. Three of the copies of the *Lives of Saints Edmund and Fremund* contain additional stanzas describing miracles of St Edmund that took place in London and Bury in 1441 and 1444, while BL, MS Harley 1766 and Montreal, McGill University Library, MS 143, witness to an abbreviated version of Lydgate's *Fall of Princes*, with the text compressed into eight rather than nine books, and supplemented with additional material (Edwards 1974).

Another Suffolk writer who also translated Latin saints' lives into Middle English verse was Osbern Bokenham, a member of the house of Augustinian friars at Clare. Bokenham's works were copied at the convent in Clare under the author's supervision, possibly even by Bokenham himself (Horobin 2008). As with some of Lydgate's shorter hagiographical works, Bokenham was responding to commissions from members of local gentry families and religious houses. The prologue to Bokenham's life of St Mary Magdalen recounts how Dame Isabel Bourchier, sister to Richard Duke of York, requested that Bokenham compose a life of Mary Magdalen, a saint for whom she had a particular devotion. Other noblewomen commissioned lives of their patron saints: Elizabeth de Vere, wife of the 12th Earl of Oxford, requested a life of St Elizabeth of Hungary. Bokenham's verse saints' lives survive predominantly in two substantial collections, although the make-up of one of these, BL, MS Arundel 327, suggests that it may comprise smaller sections originally designed for independent circulation (Edwards 1994). The other is a more de luxe production, clearly intended for a noble patron, perhaps Isabel Bourchier for whom the Magdalen legend was composed (Horobin 2007). Bokenham also wrote a verse translation of part of Claudian's *De Consulatu Stilichonis*, which survives in a single copy, now BL, Add. MS 11814, with a colophon recording that it was translated and written at Clare Priory in 1445. The opening of each section of the manuscript is accompanied by a badge associated with the House of York, suggesting that it was intended as a presentation copy for Richard Duke of York. The layout of the Claudian manu-

---

[3]   The manuscripts attributed to this scribe are: Arundel Castle, Duke of Norfolk's MS; BL MSS Arundel 99, Harley 1766, Harley 2255, Harley 4826, Sloane 2464, Yates Thompson 47; Montreal, McGill University, 143; Bodl., MSS Ashmole 46, Laud Misc 673. See Scott 1982 and Edwards 1983.

script is unusual in presenting both the English translation and Latin original on facing pages in a parallel text format, with the two texts closely aligned, thereby allowing the reader to consult both texts in tandem (Edwards 2001). While the parallel text format of the Claudian manuscript has no obvious English models, alternating Latin and English layouts are found in copies of Benedict Burgh's translation of the *Parvus* and *Magnus Cato*, in which Latin and English stanzas often alternate with each other, with the Latin stanzas distinguished by red ink.

Manuscripts containing the works of the Augustinian Friar John Capgrave were also copied under the author's own supervision, sometimes in his own hand, at Lynn Priory in Norfolk, where Capgrave himself was prior. Capgrave wrote chronicles in Latin and English, and vernacular saints' lives, two of which are in verse. Capgrave's verse life of St Norbert survives in just one manuscript, HEH, MS HM 55, an autograph copy, while his verse life of St Katherine, despite Bokenham's claim that it was 'rare and straunge to get', seems to have enjoyed a wider distribution. It now survives in four manuscripts, none of which is holograph, although the provenance of these copies suggests a predominantly East Anglian focus to its distribution. One surviving copy, BL, MS Arundel 396, was donated to the Augustinian nunnery of St Mary, Campsey, Suffolk, by its former prioress, Katherine Babbington. Another, Bodl., MS Rawlinson Poetry 118, was copied by William Gybbe, chaplain and then vicar of the parish church of Wisbech, Cambridgeshire, for pastoral use among his parishioners (Lucas 1997: 127–65).

Provincial book production was also carried out in private houses belonging to gentry families, by local clerks or members of the family themselves, as in the case of the 'Findern' manuscript, CUL, MS Ff.1.6, a diverse collection of romances, lyrics, devotional and historical prose copied by up to thirty different members of a prominent Derbyshire family and friends (Beadle and Owen 1977). A surviving list of books owned by John Paston II, of the Norfolk Paston family, includes a volume whose contents recall the Chaucerian anthologies described above: Chaucer's *Legend of Good Women* and *Parliament of Fowls*, and Lydgate's *Temple of Glass* (*Paston Letters*, ed. Davis: 516–8). But, determining whether a book was produced in the provinces or in London is not straightforward; books and scribes were peripatetic, while provincial patrons frequently drew upon their London connections to commission scribes and other book artisans (Hanna 1989). John Paston's *Grete Boke* (BL, MS Lansdowne 285), a diverse collection of texts relating to knighthood and tournaments, including poems by Lydgate, Burgh and Scrope, was copied by William Ebesham, a freelance London scribe who worked within the close of Westminster Abbey (Doyle 1957). Such instances must warn us against attempting to draw too fine a distinction between 'metropolitan' and 'provincial' manuscripts during this period before the emergence of the professional bookshop.

Works cited

Beadle, Richard, and A. E. B. Owen, intro., *The Findern Anthology, Cambridge University Library MS Ff.1.6* (London, 1977)

Boffey, Julia, and A. S. G. Edwards, intro., *The Works of Geoffrey Chaucer and 'The Kingis Quair': A Facsimile of Bodleian Library, Oxford, MS Arch. Selden. B.24* (Cambridge, 1997)

Bowers, John M., 'Hoccleve's Huntington Holographs: The First "Collected Poems" in English', *Fifteenth-Century Studies*, 15 (1989), 27–51

——, *Chaucer and Langland: The Antagonistic Tradition* (Notre Dame, IN, 2007)

Burrow, J. A., and A. I. Doyle, intro., *Thomas Hoccleve: A Facsimile of the Autograph Verse Manuscripts*, EETS, s. s. 19 (Oxford, 2003)

Connolly, Margaret, *John Shirley: Book Production and the Noble Household in Fifteenth-Century England* (Aldershot, 1998)

Doyle, A. I., 'The Work of a Late Fifteenth-Century English Scribe, William Ebesham', *Bulletin of the John Rylands Library*, 39 (1957), 298–325

——, and M. B. Parkes, 'Paleographical Introduction', in *The Canterbury Tales: A Facsimile and Transcription of the Hengwrt Manuscript, with Variants from the Ellesmere Manuscript*, ed. Paul G. Ruggiers (Norman, OK, 1979), pp. xix–xlix

Edwards, A. S. G., 'The McGill Fragment of Lydgate's *Fall of Princes*', *Scriptorium*, 28 (1974), 75–7

——, 'Lydgate Manuscripts: Some Directions for Future Research', in *Manuscripts and Readers in Fifteenth-Century England: The Literary Implications of Manuscript Study*, ed. Derek Pearsall (Cambridge, 1983), pp. 15–26

——, intro., *Magdalene College, Cambridge MS. Pepys 2006: A Facsimile* (Norman, OK, 1985)

——, 'The Transmission and Audience of Osbern Bokenham's *Legendys of Hooly Wummen*', in *Late Medieval Religious Texts and their Transmission: Essays in Honour of A. I. Doyle*, ed. A. J. Minnis (Cambridge, 1994), pp. 157–67

——, 'John Shirley and the Emulation of Courtly Culture', in *The Court and Cultural Diversity*, eds Evelyn Mullally and John Thompson (Cambridge, 1997), pp. 309–17

——, 'Fifteenth-Century Middle English Verse Author Collections', in *The English Medieval Book: Studies in Memory of Jeremy Griffiths*, eds A. S. G. Edwards, Vincent Gillespie and Ralph Hanna (London, 2000), pp. 101–12

——, 'The Middle English Translation of Claudian's *De Consulatu Stilichonis*', in *Middle English Poetry: Texts and Traditions: Essays in Honour of Derek Pearsall*, ed. A. J. Minnis (York, 2001), pp. 267–78

——, 2004a. 'John Stow and Middle English Literature', in *John Stow (1525–1605) and the Making of the English Past*, eds Ian Gadd and Alexandra Gillespie (London, 2004), pp. 109–118

——, intro., 2004b. *The Life of St. Edmund, King and Martyr: John Lydgate's Illustrated Verse Life Presented to Henry VI: A Facsimile of British Library MS Harley 2278* (London, 2004)

——, and Derek Pearsall, 'The Manuscripts of the Major English Poetic Texts', in

Book Production and Publishing in Britain, 1375–1475, eds Jeremy Griffiths and Derek Pearsall (Cambridge, 1989), pp. 257–78

Erler, Mary C., 'Fifteenth-Century Owners of Chaucer's Work: Cambridge, Magdalene College MS Pepys 2006', *Chaucer Review*, 38 (2004), 401–14

Gillespie, Alexandra, *Print Culture and the Medieval Author: Chaucer, Lydgate, and their Books, 1473–1557* (Oxford, 2006)

Hanna III, Ralph, 'Sir Thomas Berkeley and his Patronage', *Speculum*, 64 (1989), 878–916

——, 'John Shirley and British Library, MS Additional 16165', *Studies in Bibliography*, 49 (1996), 95–105

——, and A. S. G. Edwards, 'Rotheley, the De Vere Circle, and the Ellesmere Chaucer', *Huntington Library Quarterly*, 58 (1996), 11–35

Horobin, Simon, 'A Manuscript Found in the Library of Abbotsford House and the Lost Legendary of Osbern Bokenham', *English Manuscript Studies 1100–1700*, 14 (2008), 132–164

——, 'The Edmund-Fremund Scribe Copying Chaucer', *Journal of the Early Book Society*, 12 (2009), 191–201

Lawton, Lesley, 'The Illustration of Late Medieval Secular Texts, with Special Reference to Lydgate's *Troy Book*', in *Manuscripts and Readers in Fifteenth-Century England: The Literary Implications of Manuscript Study*, ed. Derek Pearsall (Cambridge, 1983), pp. 41–69

Lucas, Peter J., *From Author to Audience: John Capgrave and Medieval Publication* (Dublin, 1997)

Mooney, Linne R., 'A New Manuscript by the Hammond Scribe Discovered by Jeremy Griffiths', in *The English Medieval Book: Studies in Memory of Jeremy Griffiths*, eds A. S. G. Edwards, Vincent Gillespie and Ralph Hanna (London, 2000), pp. 113–23

——, 'John Shirley's Heirs: The Scribes of Manuscript Literary Miscellanies Produced in London in the Second Half of the Fifteenth Century', *Yearbook of English Studies*, 33 (2003), 182–98

——, and Daniel W. Mosser, 'The Hooked-g Scribes and Takamiya Manuscripts', in *The Medieval Book and a Modern Collector: Essays in Honour of Toshiyuki Takamiya*, eds Takami Matsuda, Richard A. Linenthal and John Scahill (Cambridge, 2004), pp. 179–96

Norton-Smith, John, intro., *Bodleian Library MS Fairfax 16* (London, 1979)

Parkes, M. B., 'The Influence of the Concepts of *Ordinatio* and *Compilatio* on the Development of the Book', in *Medieval Learning and Literature: Essays Presented to Richard William Hunt*, eds J. J. G. Alexander and M. T. Gibson (Oxford, 1976), pp. 115–41

Paston Letters and Papers of the Fifteenth Century, Part I, ed. Norman Davis, EETS, s. s. 20 (Oxford, 2004)

Pearsall, Derek, *John Lydgate* (London, 1970)

——, *The Life of Geoffrey Chaucer* (Oxford, 1992)

Robinson, P. R., intro., *Manuscript Tanner 346: A Facsimile* (Norman, OK, 1980)

——, intro., *Manuscript Bodley 638: A Facsimile* (Norman, OK, 1982)

Scott, Kathleen L., 'Lydgate's Lives of Saints Edmund and Fremund: A Newly-Located Manuscript in Arundel Castle', *Viator*, 13 (1982), 335–66

——, *Later Gothic Manuscripts, 1390–1490*, 2 vols (London, 1996)

Woodward, Daniel, and Martin Stevens, intro., *The New Ellesmere Chaucer Monochromatic Facsimile* (San Marino, CA, 1997)

PART II

AUTHORS

3

Thomas Hoccleve

SHEILA LINDENBAUM

Thomas Hoccleve began the practice of poetry at a crucial juncture, just at the start of the Lancastrian era, when poets were attempting to adapt the achievements of their late fourteenth-century predecessors to a new set of cultural conditions. As a clerk of the Privy Seal, Hoccleve himself was professionally well placed to negotiate this transition. Although he lacked the social rank and learning of his poetic 'masters', Chaucer and Gower, his employment in the world of London's elite clerks, where these authors were well known, enabled him to absorb and perpetuate their example, while he also had first-hand knowledge of the administrative crises and dynastic projects that would define the new regime (for biography, see Burrow 1994; Mooney 2007; Richardson 1986). A position so close to the heart of the king's government was not without its challenges, however, and recent accounts of Hoccleve's writings have explored his troubled engagement with the approved narratives of Lancastrian rule (Strohm 1998, 1999; Patterson 2001; Meyer-Lee 2007; Cole 2008).

Hoccleve's poetry is distinctive in its preference for two structuring principles: first, a compelling authorial presence, often the engagingly real, quasi-autobiographical persona ('Thomas' or 'Occleve') whose personal afflictions mirror the larger problems of the realm; second, a narrative that examines the origin of political selfhood and poetic authority. In this narrative, which Hoccleve repeats in various forms, an anguished figure moves from a state of profound disorientation, through dialogic encounters that serve to expose and cure his deficiencies, to a recognised position within the social order, where he is authorised by a sovereign power to engage in poetic discourse. (On Hoccleve's persona see further Tolmie 2007; Kerby-Fulton 1997; on the basic narrative, Hasler 1990; Simpson 1991: 18; Knapp 2001: 36).

Structured in these ways, the poetry Hoccleve produced over a period of nearly twenty years has a remarkable coherence. Just as remarkable, however, is his persistent ability to discover these shaping principles anew in the various materials of his poetry, whether they be the actualities of political and social life, the forms of documentary culture, or his chosen literary genres. In the successive phases of his career, we can observe Hoccleve adapting his poetic project to changes in the political environment and the audience he intends to address. We see him first as a court poet, a clerk in Henry IV's service, producing sophisticated verse for the entertainment of the royal household and his literary-minded fellow professionals. He then moves on, under Henry V, to address a wider political community in public poetry, before discovering the diverse audience for spiritually edifying literature that was opening up through the London book trade.

It was as a royal servant, a clerk of the Privy Seal, that Hoccleve began his known poetic career. Both of his principal early poems, *L'epistre de Cupide* (1402) and *La Male Regle* (1405–06), allude to the work of that office and its documentary forms, and both propose to extend the clerk's professional service to the king into the literary realm. These poems are witty productions, approaching political matters through playful indirection, and displaying highly developed poetic skills. Although they would later circulate more widely, they seem to have been addressed initially to a small audience consisting of Henry IV and his house-hold, the inner circles of his government, and Hoccleve's own professional associates (Thompson 2000) – readers who would appreciate the sophisticated use of literary precedent, French and English, and the poet's insight into current affairs.

The main work of the Privy Seal was to write up the king's responses to peti-tions from his subjects as formal instructions, which would then go to the appro-priate government office to be put into effect (Brown 1971; Catto 1985: 79–81; Dodd 2008: 109–13). The surviving examples of Privy Seal writing in a formulary compiled by Hoccleve himself are richly suggestive of how this documentary practice influenced his poetry (Knapp 2001: ch. 1), most obviously in the basic process of petitioning. In his early poems, Hoccleve uses the petition to model the relationship between subject and sovereign, and to imagine playful literary solutions to the most pressing problems of Henry IV's reign: the incessant rebel-lions that plagued the regime, and the financial crises created by the king's exces-sive largesse to members of his affinity.

Hoccleve's earliest datable poem, *L'epistre de Cupide*, addresses the problem of rebellious subjects. A translation, with deletions and additions, of a poem by Christine de Pizan, it purports to be a courtly 'game' written to celebrate 'the lusty monthe of May'; but it nevertheless refers to the sphere of royal admin-istration where real problems must be solved. As it begins, the God of Love is hearing a complaint from ladies of his court against men who have betrayed and defamed them. In this early version of Hoccleve's characteristic narra-tive, Cupid deals with the petition by exposing to public view the ladies' abject misery and shame, citing disturbing examples of male betrayal, and quoting the men's misogynist opinions, against which he cites his own examples of women's 'constaunce'. By the time his formal 'letter' of response finally banishes the offending men, however, we realise that the real issue is not the nature of women but the stability and unity of the god's court. The poem redefines the ladies as loyal political subjects, and the banished lovers as the god's 'reble foon', men who have betrayed not women but 'realmes grete, and kynges', in the manner of Henry IV's own rebellious subjects (XIX: lines 447, 466, 85).[1]

Hoccleve offers this engaging poem as a gift of service to the king, an exten-sion of the service he performs every day writing up the king's actual responses

---

[1]   References are to Hoccleve, ed. Furnivall, rev. edn (with roman numerals for item numbers, arabic for line numbers), except for the *Complaint* and *Dialogue* from the *Series*, which are quoted from Hoccleve, ed. Burrow.

to petitions. But the gift also has serious literary implications, in that it contains a strong endorsement of poetry in English. Although it is based on a French poem, *L'epistre de Cupide* seeks to further the claims of its own literary vernacular. This is not to say that Hoccleve finds the French tradition old fashioned or alien; to the end of his life, he authenticated his poems as productions of cosmopolitan court culture by giving them French titles and headings, and he was of course fluent in French, the primary language of the Privy Seal. His debt to French poetry can be seen in his other translations from that language (I, XVIII), his numerous 'begging' poems (Burrow 1997: 45–9), and his extensive use of the ballade form. His collections of his own verse and the story of his own bookmaking in the *Series* follow precedents set by French poets (Burrow 1997: 40–5). But when he moves the location of Cupid's court to 'Albioun', Hoccleve absorbs his French original within the native literary tradition. He makes it clear that his true foundational text is not Christine de Pizan's poem, or even the *Roman de la rose* or *Ovide moralisé*, both of which Cupid rejects as sources of reliable information about women. It is 'our legende of martirs' (line 316): that is, Chaucer's *Legend of Good Women*, one of the English texts, including Clanvowe's *Book of Cupid* and Gower's *Confessio Amantis*, that had already treated the God of Love in English with relevance to English politics. Although Hoccleve reserves the right to participate in international court culture, the literary lineage he proposes to honour is distinctly English and Chaucerian.

Chaucer is also the primary reference point for changing Christine's couplets to rhyme royal: here, as later, Hoccleve prefers to use a stanzaic form, the better to expand small segments of his translated material or organise blocks of dialogue. And Chaucer is the source of Hoccleve's impressive vocal effects. Like the narrators of the *Canterbury Tales*, Hoccleve's Cupid can access a range of styles, from regal rhetoric to racy proverbial expressions that are only to be found 'in Englissh' (XIX: line 183). Like them, his voice can carry several levels of irony. He can betray his own limitations, naively thinking that banishment will rid him of his political foes, or he can approximate the poet's own voice, as he does when he speaks out of character to praise the purity of virgin saints. This display of Chaucerian skill gains in significance if we recall that just a year or two earlier, Henry IV was attempting to recruit Christine de Pizan herself as his court poet (Fenster and Erler 1990: 171). In *L'epistre de Cupide*, Hoccleve urges the king to support native literary talent, and the writing of Chaucerian poetry in the English language, instead.

As if in response to his own invitation, the poet puts himself at the centre of his next major poem, *La Male Regle*. This is a highly complex begging poem, a masterpiece of the genre, written at a time of acute financial crisis when the king was forced to cancel the payment of annuities, including those of his clerks. Like *L'epistre de Cupide* it is offered to the king as a witty form of service (it is often assumed that the poem is addressed to Lord Furnival, but he is the minister responsible for executing the king's response to the petition). The poem turns on the poet's willingness to take upon himself, in the disguised form of his own immoderate behaviour, the sins of excessive expenditure by which the king brought about the crisis. Thus, in his anguished autobiographical persona, the poet confesses to all the sordid sins of 'excesse' (the 'misrule' of the title) that he committed as a young clerk of the Privy Seal, haunting the Paul's Head tavern in the Strand. By serving the poem's sovereign, the glorious God of Health, in this obscure and tortured way, he earns the right to petition for his delayed annuity, while preserving the sovereign's unblemished authority to honour his request.

In this initial appearance of Hoccleve's autobiographical persona, we can see in all its troubled intensity the preoccupation with selfhood and self-examination for which Hoccleve is best known. Modern readers have often discovered in Hoccleve a hidden kernel of personality that resists the sovereign's designs (Hasler 1990; Patterson 2001; Tolmie 2007), a truly private self, and there is certainly something akin to that form of interiority in the anguished and needy clerk who introduces *La Male Regle* and Hoccleve's other autobiographical poems. In the dialogue that inevitably follows, however, such as the confessional segment of *La Male Regle*, the poet's persona is motivated to cure that condition by remapping the self according to external categories devised by the social order, or in this case the Church. In *La Male Regle*, he speaks to himself like a priest in the confessional questioning a penitent youth, enumerating his sins of 'excesse' according to the paradigm of the seven deadly sins. It is this process of socialisation, we understand, that enables him to do the king a further service, by speaking as his adviser and truth-teller towards the end of the poem.

The truthtelling in *La Male Regle* links Hoccleve to the Langlandian poets of Henry IV's reign (Bowers 2002: 361–3). Much like the author of *Mum and the Sothsegger*, for example, Hoccleve attacks flatterers at court and warns that a king's failure to heed his subjects' needs is a dangerous invitation to rebellion (a point on which Henry IV doubtless agreed, as it is what motivated his excessive grants to the nobility). Unlike these other poets, however, Hoccleve, as we have seen, uses his recognised position as the king's servant to authorise his truth-telling. This means of validating his work is a distinctive move that eventually earns him the right not just to speak truth to the king, a long-standing prerogative of English poets, but to speak on behalf of the regime as its public voice.

From about 1409, with the rise of the future Henry V to political power, Hoccleve began to write his poetry with the apparent support of that prince. We do not know the precise terms of their relationship, but it is clear that Hoccleve sought to contribute to the prince's extensive public relations initiatives, and as a consequence to address a larger audience than he had done under Henry IV. In their concerns and mode of address, therefore, the poems of this period speak to a political community beyond the king's inner circle, extending to other governing elites, as well as to prominent merchants and churchmen. In this phase of his career, we can think of Hoccleve participating in public culture or in what has been called the 'public sphere', setting an example that his more prolific and prosperous rival, John Lydgate, would follow to greater acclaim.

Hoccleve's great work of this period is the *Regiment of Princes*, written for the prince and his partisans in 1410–11 (see Chapter 4). Following the prince's accession to the throne, however, Hoccleve also produced an important group of short poems – three ballades commemorating ceremonial occasions (1413–16) and the *Address to Sir John Oldcastle* (1415) – which familiarise the elite political community with the ideological language of the new regime. All of these poems use the vocabulary of religious controversy to associate the king with divine authority and stigmatise any opposition to his policies, and they all develop his chosen identity as Champion of the Christian faith, a role designed as much to sanctify his military campaigns in France as to discourage dissent at home.

As might be expected of public poetry, these new productions take the entire realm ('this land', 'this yle') as their purview. They are particularly relevant, however, to the city of London and its governing elite, a prime target of Henry's public relations campaign. The political issues raised in the poems – the king's military leadership and the Lollard threat – speak to the major concerns of the city, whose merchants were heavily involved in financing and provisioning the king's armies, as well as hunting down the heretics (including John Oldcastle) in their midst. It was probably through these poems, then, that Hoccleve began to cultivate a readership among the civic elite, a crucial segment of the political community, and one that could be counted on to take an interest in the court cere-monies to which the ballades refer. We know that Hoccleve had a highly influ-ential London patron in the former mayor and royal financier Robert Chichele, a brother of Archbishop Henry Chichele, for whom he translated a French poem on the Virgin's intercessory powers (XVIII). Another prominent patron, John Carpenter, to whom Hoccleve later addressed a begging poem (XVI), was an active member of the Guildhall secretariat at this time, just prior to beginning his illustrious career as the city's Common Clerk. The longtime chancellor of the exchequer, Henry Somer, to whom Hoccleve wrote a poem from the Court of Good Company, a dining club to which they both belonged (XVII, XIII), also moved in this milieu. Given these associations, the Henrician ballades, together with the Oldcastle poem, can be placed with other London texts that promoted Henry's chosen public image: London chronicles, the correspondence between Henry and the city concerning his campaigns in France, public proclamations on Lollardy and the French campaigns, and the great civic spectacle marking the king's victory at Agincourt.

Like most of these other texts, Hoccleve's poems for Henry V are highly conscious of the 'eloquence' required in the public sphere. They have been linked stylistically to the diplomatic letters Hoccleve composed in the Privy Seal (Catto 1985: 80), and, in this phase of his poetry, Hoccleve frequently refers to the stylistic eloquence characteristic of both kinds of writing. Offering a 'pamfilet' of his poems to the Duke of York after a meeting 'at London', he speaks of his imper-fect use of rhetorical 'colours' and other failures of 'eloquence' – his disclaimers, of course, calling attention to his considerable mastery of these skills (IX: lines 51, 25; see also XI; IV: lines 36–7). More broadly, he is concerned with the art of public eloquence expounded by Giles of Rome, a main source for the *Regiment of Princes*, and by one of his own poetic 'maisters', John Gower. This is a branch of rhet-oric that lends moral authority to its practitioners, enabling postures of ethical advice and commentary even as it serves the special interests of noble patrons. It often uses persuasive examples of virtuous and vicious behavior to translate those special interests into ethical terms, and its voice is that of the pulpit orator, passionately committed to a cause.

In keeping with this model, the Henrician ballades engage in a Lancastrian poetics of praise and blame. They laud the king for the Christian piety and military prowess that inspire 'constance' and unity in his subjects, while they use the Lollards to embody the forces of darkness and all forms of religious or political 'variaunce'. They also support the ever increasing scope of Henry's political ambitions. In the verses on Henry's accession to the throne in March 1413, the poet simply advises the king to become 'holy chirches Champion [...] chacyng away/ Therror which sones of iniquitee/ Han sow[n] ageyn the faith' (IV: lines 22, 25–7). By the time of Richard II's reburial in December of the same year, Henry has become the saviour who has intervened between Albion and the fiend, reversing the entire country's fall into the 'confusioun' of heresy (VIII: lines 2, 12). Finally, in the double ballade for the Order of the Garter, probably written for the induction of Emperor Sigismund in 1416, Henry carries on the fight not only as King of England but also as King of France and successor to the Christian emperors Constantine and Justinian (V, VI). As always in Hoccleve, there is something excessive in each of these poems – the gratuitous spectre of a Lollard king, for example (VIII: lines 25–32) – that threatens to destabilise its ethical polarities, but the emotion generated by such passages is eventually recuperated for the main cause.

Hoccleve's major achievement in this genre, the *Address to Sir John Oldcastle*, is a more complex exercise in praise and blame than the ballades, and one that has been subject to a greater range of interpretations (Bowers 2002: 354; Knapp 2001: 138–46; Patterson 2001: 460–1; Cole 2008: 106–14). It was written, Hoccleve notes, while Henry was at Southampton in August 1415, waiting to embark on his first French campaign, and thus while Oldcastle, formerly a Lancastrian captain, but then a convicted heretic and rebel leader, was still at large. Once again Henry is the guarantor of unity in the land and defender of 'all hem that stande in the cleernesse/ Of good byleeue', and the Lollards are 'cursid caitiffs, heires of darknesse' (II: lines 13–15), but this time the poem is addressed to one of the latter in the hope of his reform.

To show how this reform can be accomplished, Hoccleve returns to the world of documentary culture that grounded his earlier poems. Assuming the role of a priestly inquisitor, he examines Oldcastle on the very points made in the official report of his trial that Archbishop Arundel circulated to Parliament and parish priests for 'exposition' in the native tongue (Cole 2008: 107). He also revives the confessional technique employed in *La Male Regle*, engaging in dialogue with the absent rebel by quoting his erroneous opinions on the sacraments, and, in an inspired addition to the trial record, beseeching him to return to the religious conformity required of a Christian knight, as exemplified by the king himself ('Obeie, obeie!').

Given the unlikelihood that Oldcastle, obdurate at his trial, would respond to this appeal, even if he somehow heard of it while in hiding, we might ask what this poem was meant to accomplish for the readers it was more likely to reach. Conceptually, it attempts to clarify the essential points of orthodox belief, as they were currently being codified by the Lancastrian church: a matter of some interest to those in ecclesiastical or civil authority. It also provides a surprising amount of argument on points of doctrine, suited to lay readers with a taste for vernacular theology, and it takes up a number of weighty issues of concern in the public sphere, such as papal supremacy and the right to hereditary titles and property – though not without the rhetorician's obvious suppression of inconvenient detail, such as the three current claimants to the papacy or the Lancastrians' notorious violation of hereditary rights. Moreover, on the affective level, the poet's emotional appeal to the rebel knight addresses every Lancastrian subject, each one being asked to suppress whatever inner stirrings of resistance he may feel in order to find safety in the social whole. It is this relevance to 'everyman' that the poet will develop further in the next phase of his poetry, when he turns from the public sphere to the welfare of the soul.

In his last major work, the *Series* (1419–21), Hoccleve resumes his autobiographical persona in order to describe a catastrophic mental breakdown. It was a 'wylde infirmitee', he tells us, which reduced him to a bestial state and left him shunned by everyone, including his former friends (*Complaint*: lines 40, 120–34). Although he has been recovered for five years, the impulse to write poetry has 'lurkid … in ydilnesse' since that time, and he hints that he has lost his royal patron: 'cloudy hath bene the fauour / That shoon on me ful bright in tymes past' (*Complaint*: lines 23–4).

We do not know how closely this account reflects Hoccleve's actual experience, but when he resumes the writing of poetry with the *Series*, whatever 'infirmitee' he suffered has taken his work in a new direction, from political verse in the public sphere to works of moral self-cultivation for a more socially diverse group of readers. There is a weakening of the implied contract between the poet and sovereign that underwrote his public poetry, and a corresponding shift of emphasis from the sovereign to God as the guarantor of personal identity and wellbeing. While the *Series* remains well within the orbit of Lancastrian influence, especially in its orthodox religious views, the Lancastrian patron within the poem, Duke Humfrey, has only a slight relationship to the overall project. Instead, Hoccleve authorises his work by asserting its spiritual benefits for himself and his readers, and by citing his own literary achievement as grounds for a new endeavour.

As a basis for the new project, Hoccleve looks back to his earlier work. Indeed, the *Series* is, in part, one of the exercises in retrospection and consolidation that Hoccleve undertook in his last years, the others being the formulary of documents from the Privy Seal, which he completed just before his death (BL, Add. MS 24062), and the collected poems from all phases of his career that he copied between 1422 and 1426 (Huntington Library, MSS 111 and 744; Burrow and Doyle 2002, intro.: pp. xx–xxi). The narrative that underlies the *Series* thus treads familiar ground. In his opening *Complaint*, the troubled poet recounts the humiliations of his illness; he then engages in a recuperative *Dialogue* with a Friend, whom he convinces that he is sane and capable of writing again, before launching into the work of translating and compiling three texts: *Learn to Die* (a chapter of Heinrich Suso's *Horologium sapientie*, to which he adds a prose description of the New Jerusalem) and two tales from the *Gesta romanorum*: *Jereslaus's Wife* and *Jonathas and Fellicula*, accompanied by their prose moralisations.

This assembly of texts is in itself a reprise of the poet's career. The *Gesta* tales restage the opposing views of women in his debut poem, *L'epistre de Cupide*: the virtuous queen of the first tale is countered by the diabolical seductress Fellicula in the second. The stories of youthful dissipation in *Learn to Die* and *Jonathas and Fellicula* recapitulate the poet's own indiscretions in *La Male Regle*, and the Young

Man's disclosures to the Disciple in *Learn to Die* follow from the confessional dialogues in *La Male Regle* and the Oldcastle poem. Of the *Series'* recycled materials, however, all but the digression on Duke Humfrey's military exploits, which refers back to the Henrician ballades (*Dialogue*: lines 551, 554–616), are reoriented to Hoccleve's new preoccupation with the welfare of the soul. The poet translates *Learn to Die* in order to cleanse his own soul and teach 'Many another wight' the doctrine of its salvation (*Dialogue*: lines 216, 219), and the *Gesta* tales are moralised as allegories of the soul. As before, the self represented by the soul is cultivated in a climate of socialisation, but this climate too is redefined. The sovereign who earlier stabilised the world now tends to be distant or unavailable, like the absent ruler in *Jereslaus's Wife* (a likely reference to Henry V's frequent absences in France). The soul aspires instead to the sight of God, the king of 'inestimable' majesty and brightness reigning over the New Jerusalem (XXIII: 214), while for present reassurance in the world, it looks to loyal friends.

In addition to reorienting his poetry in these ways, Hoccleve uses the *Series* to give it a new kind of validation. This is centred on his own achievement. The reprise of his own *oeuvre*, for example, is a self-authorising strategy, an empowering reference to his personal accomplishment similar to Chaucer's list of his own works in the *Legend of Good Women*. Even more significantly for his current project, Hoccleve represents himself as a successful member of the London book trade. Thus he tells us in the course of the *Series* the story of how it came to be compiled: how what was first 'purposid, cast & ment' as a small book consisting of the *Complaint* and *Learn to Die* (*Dialogue*: line 641) gradually became a more complex assembly of texts through his able deployment of the trade's working methods and professional resources.

Though much of this account is probably fictitious, it is nevertheless a convincing representation of the poet at home in his chamber, busily working in concert with patrons, the owners of exemplars, prospective readers, and a supervisor of the trade. This is the Hoccleve who may have helped to organise and edit the early manuscripts of the *Canterbury Tales* after Chaucer's death, as well as engaging fellow members of the trade to make presentation copies of his *Regiment of Princes*, and assisting four other well-known scribes to make a copy of Gower's *Confessio Amantis* (Doyle and Parkes 1978). As we see him in the *Series*, he procures copies of texts from a friend and a 'devout' patron, presumably in booklet form, then translates and copies them, as well as supplying the finished segments with the prologues and links that bring them together, as was done for the *Canterbury Tales*. The Friend, who represents various kinds of professional expertise, helps when another hand is needed: he advises on the choice of texts and then reads or listens to each one as it is produced, in each case suggesting additional items and supplying copies of them from his own store of exemplars. The Friend is also a censor of sorts, determined to 'ouersee' the entire operation (*Dialogue*: lines 795–6), perhaps to reflect the intensified civic regulation of the book trade at this time.

The readership envisioned for this new book, though presumed to be entirely orthodox in religion, is more diverse than the implied audiences of Hoccleve's earlier poems. It includes his former readers: high-ranking Lancastrian patrons (in this case Duke Humfrey and the Countess of Westmoreland, who is mentioned only in a dedicatory stanza); the courtly 'ladyes' who disapproved of *L'epistre de Cupide*, whose favour he hopes to regain (*Dialogue*: line 806); and the professional friends in London and Westminster who used to call him 'to conpaignie' prior to his illness. But there are new London readers as well, ranging from the 'deuout man' at whose 'excitynge and monicioun' he translates *Learn to Die* to the Friend's 'sauage' and 'wylde' 15-year old son, for whom he is asked to translate *Jonathas and Fellicula* (*Complaint*: lines 75–6; *Dialogue*: lines 234–5). And there are also 'the peple' to whom the Friend imagines Hoccleve releasing his work, a more amorphous group than the political community addressed in the public poems, though it would seem to include the latter as one of its components (*Dialogue*: lines 23–4). The diversity of this imagined readership testifies to Hoccleve's awareness of the developing audience for religious writing in English, as well as to the growing opportunities within the metropolitan book trade for alternative forms of commission and distribution, the building of an audience by circulation to multiple coteries, and eventual circulation to readers beyond those initially envisioned.

For this diverse audience, Hoccleve chooses uncontroversial religious texts with a high entertainment value. He tells us that he translates *Learn to Die* as an act of personal piety, to commemorate God's goodness in bringing him out of his illness, but the texts in the *Series* are distinct from his devotional poems: the prayers and Marian lyrics he collected in his autograph manuscripts, and the miracle of the Virgin that he translated for the London stationer Thomas Marlburgh (later incorporated into one of the manuscripts of Chaucer's *Canterbury Tales*, Oxford, Christ Church, MS 152; Hoccleve, ed. Ellis: 88–92). They are the kind of imaginative material that a skilled preacher might draw upon to teach the way to eternal salvation, and they are made the more engaging, in Hoccleve's hands, by a return to Chaucerian style. Thus he translates Latin sources into colloquial English dialogue, adds ironic commentary to the *Gesta*'s romance narratives (the exiled queen, the three gifts), and produces expert vocal effects in *Learn to Die*, where the Young Man conveys the 'woful waymentacions' of his heart in tones 'horrible of deeth sownynge' (XXIII: lines 274, 129).

In this final phase of his career, Hoccleve's poetry resonates strongly with other imaginative religious writing of the 1420s. As moral literature on the Soul, the three translations in the *Series* inhabit the same textual environment as the Deguileville translations that appeared in the 1420s as sequels to that author's *Pilgrimage of the Soul*, which was translated in 1413 with a poem of Hoccleve's (I). *Learn to Die* can also be grouped with visionary texts of the 1420s inspired by the Lancastrian cult of St Birgitta, notably the *Revelation of Purgatory* by a Winchester nun.

Hoccleve is far less sensational than the *Revelation* author in representing the bodily torments of purgatory; although his alter-ego, the Disciple, presumes to converse with the deity (Divine Sapience) in *Learn to Die*, Hoccleve does not venture into the ecstatic forms of religious experience chronicled by his close contemporary, Margery Kempe. Nevertheless, once one realises that Hoccleve and Kempe shared a patron, the Countess of Westmoreland, and that their paths may well have crossed in London around 1417, it is striking how much their quasi-autobiographical works have in common. Most significantly for the *Series*, they both use an urban setting to stage the abjection and ostracism they suffer and their obsessive need to be acknowledged by figures of authority. As we have seen, these have been Hoccleve's preoccupations throughout his career, from his earliest efforts at court poetry. Their development in the *Series*, in a context of urban labour and spirituality that recalls Margery's world, shows how far he can expand his range of social reference, while still remaining focused on Lancastrian unease.

Works cited

Bowers, John M., 'Thomas Hoccleve and the Politics of Tradition', *Chaucer Review*, 36 (2002), 352–69

Brown, A. L., 'The Privy Seal Clerks in the Early Fifteenth Century', in *The Study of Medieval Records: Essays in Honour of Kathleen Major*, eds D. A. Bullough and R. L. Storey (Oxford, 1971), pp. 260–81

Burrow, J. A., *Thomas Hoccleve*, Authors of the Middle Ages, 4 (Aldershot, 1994)

——, 'Hoccleve and the Middle French Poets', in *The Long Fifteenth Century: Essays for Douglas Gray*, eds Helen Cooper and Sally Mapstone (Oxford, 1997), pp. 35–49

——, and A. I. Doyle, intro., *Thomas Hoccleve: A Facsimile of the Autograph Verse Manuscripts*, EETS, s. s. 19 (Oxford, 2002)

Catto, Jeremy, 'The King's Servants', in *King Henry V: The Practice of Kingship*, ed. G. L. Harriss (Oxford, 1985), pp. 75–96

Cole, Andrew, 'Thomas Hoccleve's Heretics', in his *Literature and Heresy in the Age of Chaucer* (Cambridge, 2008), pp. 103–30

Dodd, Gwilym, 'Patronage, Petitions and Grace: The "Chamberlains' Bills" of Henry IV's Reign', in *The Reign of Henry IV: Rebellion and Survival, 1403–13*, eds Gwilym Dodd and Douglas Biggs (Woodbridge, 2008), pp. 105–35

Doyle, A. I., and M. B. Parkes, 'The Production of Copies of the *Canterbury Tales* and the *Confessio Amantis* in the Early Fifteenth Century', in *Medieval Scribes, Manuscripts and Libraries: Essays Presented to N. R. Ker*, eds M. B. Parkes and Andrew G. Watson (London, 1978), pp. 163–210

Fenster, Thelma S., and Mary Carpenter Erler, eds and trans., *Poems of Cupid, God of Love* (Leiden, 1990)

Hasler, Antony, 'Hoccleve's Unregimented Body', *Paragraph*, 13 (1990), 164–83

Hoccleve, Thomas, *Hoccleve's Works, I: The Minor Poems*, ed. F. J. Furnivall, EETS, e. s. 61 (London, 1892), rev. by A. I. Doyle and J. Mitchell (London, 1970)

——, *Thomas Hoccleve's Complaint and Dialogue*, ed. J. A. Burrow, EETS, o. s. 313 (Oxford, 1999)

——, *'My Compleinte' and other Poems*, ed. Roger Ellis (Exeter, 2001)

Kerby-Fulton, Kathryn, 'Langland and the Bibliographical Ego', in *Written Work: Langland, Labor, and Authorship*, eds Steven Justice and Kathryn Kerby-Fulton (Philadelphia, PA, 1997), pp. 67–143

Knapp, Ethan, *The Bureaucratic Muse: Thomas Hoccleve and the Literature of Late Medieval England* (Philadelphia, PA, 2001)

Meyer-Lee, Robert J., 'Thomas Hoccleve: Beggar Laureate', in his *Poets and Power from Chaucer to Wyatt* (Cambridge, 2007), pp. 88–124

Mooney, Linne R., 'Some New Light on Thomas Hoccleve', *Studies in the Age of Chaucer*, 29 (2007), 293–340

Patterson, Lee, '"What is Me?": Self and Society in the Poetry of Thomas Hoccleve', *Studies in the Age of Chaucer*, 23 (2001), 437–70

Richardson, Malcolm, 'Hoccleve in his Social Context', *Chaucer Review*, 20 (1986), 313–22

Simpson, James, 'Madness and Texts: Hoccleve's *Series*', in *Chaucer and Fifteenth-Century Poetry*, eds Julia Boffey and Janet Cowen (London, 1991), pp. 15–29

Strohm, Paul, *England's Empty Throne: Usurpation and the Language of Legitimation 1399–1422* (New Haven, CT, 1998)

——, 'Hoccleve, Lydgate and the Lancastrian Court', in *The Cambridge History of Medieval English Literature*, ed. David Wallace (Cambridge, 1999), pp. 640–61

Thompson, John J., 'A Poet's Contacts with the Great and the Good: Further Consideration of Thomas Hoccleve's Texts and Manuscripts', in *Prestige, Authority and Power in Late Medieval Manuscripts and Texts*, ed. Felicity Riddy (Woodbridge, 2000), pp. 77–101

Tolmie, Sarah, 'The Professional: Thomas Hoccleve', *Studies in the Age of Chaucer*, 29 (2007), 341–73

4

Thomas Hoccleve's *Regiment of Princes*

DAVID WATT

To judge by the number of surviving manuscripts, the *Regiment of Princes* was not only Thomas Hoccleve's most popular poem but also, arguably, among the most popular poems written in Middle English in the fifteenth century. The *Regiment* survives in forty-six copies that seem to have been designed to be substantial or complete (Edwards 1971; Seymour 1974; Green 1978).[1] In comparison, John Lydgate's *Fall of Princes* survives in thirty-nine copies that initially seem to have been complete, though selections of it survive in many other manuscripts. The number of surviving *Regiment* manuscripts also compares favourably with the number of witnesses to the major fourteenth-century Middle English poems: Chaucer's *Canterbury Tales* survives in fifty-five manuscripts in addition to twenty-eight selected or fragmentary copies; Langland's *Piers Plowman* survives in fifty-four more or less complete manuscripts plus fragments and extracts; Gower's *Confessio Amantis* survives in forty-eight complete manuscripts plus fragments and extracts. The *Regiment of Princes* seems to have been highly regarded by fifteenth-century readers, and it merits the sustained attention that these other significant Middle English poems have been given.

Hoccleve completed the *Regiment* after March 1410, when John Badby (mentioned in lines 281 ff.) was burned at the stake for heresy, and before March 1413, when Prince Henry, its dedicatee, became Henry V. The poem was most likely written in 1410–11 while the Prince was head of the council and thus effectively responsible for England's governance during Henry IV's illness (for this and further detail of Hoccleve's biography see Burrow 1994). While many critics consider the poem to be propaganda written on behalf of a governing Prince keen to represent himself 'as a sound ruler who would be open to wise counsel' (Knapp 2001: 80), others have argued that it critiques the realm's governance. Lawton (1987), Ferster (1996) and Tolmie (2000) draw particular attention to the contrast the *Regiment* establishes between the Prince and Henry IV. For Lawton and Ferster, this suggests that the poem may have been completed after 30 November 1411, when the King had recovered sufficiently to dismiss the Prince as head of the council (McNiven 1980). The lack of agreement about dating and the revisions that Hoccleve made in 1412 (Burrow 1994: 41; Mooney 2011a) remind us that the *Regiment* might have been read very differently at different stages of its circulation.

---

[1] For surviving manuscripts of the *Regiment* and other works mentioned here, see *NIMEV*.

The *Regiment* circulated widely in the fifteenth century, and Prince Henry's association with the poem likely contributed to its dissemination. The presentation scene in one of the *Regiment*'s most authoritative manuscripts, BL, MS Arundel 38, can help to explain this. Critics agree that the standing figure is the Prince, but disagree about the identity of the kneeling figure. Nicholas Perkins persuasively argues that it is Hoccleve (2001: 116–17; cf. Seymour 1982). In his view, this scene is similar to other fifteenth-century presentation scenes in which the humble poet displays loyalty and goodwill by presenting his book to the Prince, who shows grace and wisdom by accepting it. Yet this particular copy was not made for Prince Henry. It was made for John, Lord Mowbray and Segrave, Earl Marshall and (after 1425) 2nd Duke of Norfolk; his family arms appear in the initial below the presentation scene as well as in the initials on folios 1 and 71. This has led some critics to believe that the miniature depicts Prince Henry's presentation of the book to Mowbray (Harris 1984; Scott 1996). In their view, the scene implies that the Prince sanctions the advice it collects and wants to encourage others to read it, perhaps by paying for lavish copies such as the one in which the presentation scene appears (Pearsall 1994: 393–5).

Copies of the *Regiment* were made for readers of various social classes throughout the fifteenth century. Hoccleve made a copy of the *Regiment* in his own hand for the Prince's brother, John, Duke of Bedford (Mooney 2011b: 197–8). Linne Mooney identifies this book as BL, MS Royal 17 D.xviii (Mooney 2011a). Bodl., MS Selden supra 53 preserves a copy of Hoccleve's *Regiment* followed by his *Series* and John Lydgate's *Danse Macabre*. This manuscript does not contain any family arms, yet its standard of production indicates that it was made for someone with considerable means (Watt 2011: 17–18). In contrast, two later fifteenth-century manuscripts seem to have been produced for readers of less substantial means, though they contain the same texts as MS Selden supra 53. Bodl., MS Laud misc. 735 and Beinecke Library, New Haven, CT, MS 493, written by one scribe using the same paper stock (Burrow 1999: xv, xvii), may have been commercially produced: testimony to the *Regiment*'s appeal to a broad spectrum of readers.

The *Regiment* survives mainly in manuscripts that either present or were designed to present its 5,463 lines as a whole. The manuscripts also divide the poem into the two parts recognised today as the Prologue and the *Regiment* proper. Most of the manuscripts also subdivide these parts. The first section of the Prologue (lines 1–2016) frames the text as a whole by reflecting on Hoccleve's manner of living, his need for writing, and his reasons for addressing it to the Prince. The Prologue's second section (lines 2017–56) identifies the *Regiment*'s three main sources for the poem, examples of the *Fürstenspiegel* or 'mirror for princes' genre. The *Regiment* proper follows (lines 2057–5439). In many manuscripts this is subdivided into fifteen (sometimes fourteen) sections under topical headings. The final twenty-four lines, the 'Words of the Compiler to the Book', are written in eight-line ballade stanzas rather than the seven-line rhyme royal form used in the rest of the work. Most manuscripts record some version of these lines. Some treat them as a final section of the *Regiment* proper while others present them as an envoy.

The structural relationship between the *Regiment*'s two main parts has been a focus for critical enquiry. Anna Torti (1986, 1991) argues that both main parts are mirrors and that they also mirror each other. In Hoccleve's dialogue with the old man, he learns the lesson the Old Man teaches through his account of personal misgovernance, and from exempla and proverbs. Hoccleve, in turn, provides an account of his personal misregulation that bears remarkable similarities to his other ostensibly autobiographical poems, *La Male Regle* (1405–06) and the *Series* (1419–21). He then recounts further exempla and tales in the *Regiment* proper. The text as a whole thus functions as an instructive mirror, for readers are encouraged to learn from Hoccleve's personal experience as well as from the other materials the narrative presents. The *Regiment* draws upon the mirror tradition for its source material, invokes the mirror as a genre, and employs Hoccleve's narrative persona structurally in order to hold up a mirror to fifteenth-century English society.

The *Regiment*'s three main sources are all popular mirrors for princes. The first is the *Secretum secretorum*, a book that Hoccleve identifies as 'epistles' sent by Aristotle 'to Alisaundre' (line 2039). Full of proverbial advice and exemplary stories, the *Secretum secretorum* was widely disseminated throughout the later Middle Ages, as was the view that it was by Aristotle. It survives in over six hundred Latin manuscripts from across Europe; a dozen English translations of it were made in the fifteenth century besides Hoccleve's (Hoccleve, ed. Blyth 1999: 9). Hoccleve identifies his second source as 'Gyles of Regiment / Of Princes' (lines 2052–3). Giles of Rome's *De regimine principium* is also a compilation of proverbial wisdom and stories organised to offer advice on governing the individual, domestic and political realms. It survives in over 300 manuscripts and had been translated into English by John Trevisa at the beginning of the fifteenth century (see Briggs 1999). After briefly describing how he will translate and compile his *Regiment* 'plotmeel' [piecemeal] (line 2060) from these two sources, Hoccleve names his third source, Jacob de Cessolis' *De ludo scaccorum* or 'Ches Moralysed' (line 2111). This text frames its collection of advice about governing the self and the realm as allegorical instructions about succeeding at chess.

Hoccleve acknowledges that Prince Henry would already have read all three of his sources (lines 2129–30), yet he hopes to serve some purpose by compiling the 'sentence' (line 2132) of these texts 'that in hem thre is scatered fer in brede' (line 2135). Marginal notes in many manuscripts indicate that Hoccleve also drew material from a variety of other texts. These notes indicate that many fifteenth-century readers valued the *Regiment*, in Perkins' words, 'as a store of wisdom on subjects of moral or political value' (Perkins 2001: 189). Hoccleve's *Regiment* seems to have met widespread demand for a compilation of advice translated into English, compiled from a variety of sources, and 'so organized that its sections are easily found and read' (Hoccleve, ed. Seymour 1981: xxviii). The twenty-six manuscripts that preserve the *Regiment* alone suggest that some readers felt it was compendious enough to meet their needs. Yet the *Regiment* also likely appealed to readers because it was relatively compact. This becomes clear when the *Regiment* is compared with Trevisa's translation of *De regimine principium*, a lengthy book that survives in only one copy (Bodl., MS Digby 233). The *Regiment* may have been so widely disseminated in the fifteenth century because it is a relatively small book – a 'pamfilet' (line 2060) – that translates and compiles the 'sentence' (line 2132) of widely dispersed exemplary materials and organises them in an accessible format.

In order to provide an account of why the work was written, and a model for how it might be read, the first section of the Prologue integrates a number of contemporary genres. At first, the *Regiment* invites comparison with Boethius' *Consolation of Philosophy*, and manuscript notes suggest that many readers saw parallels between the two texts (Perkins 2001: 146, 181). Like Boethius' narrator, Hoccleve describes enduring a sleepless night on his own before encountering a spiritual guide: Boethius encounters Lady Philosophy; Hoccleve encounters an old man in the fields surrounding London. The old man assures Hoccleve that he can overcome his grief by revealing the cause of his illness and then amending his governance (lines 260–6). As the dialogue proceeds, it looks increasingly like a confession. Little (2006) notes that confession in the early fifteenth century could be seen as both a traditional genre and a contested practice. The old man establishes his orthodoxy by encouraging the narrator to confess his beliefs, partly in order to assure himself that the narrator is not afflicted with heretical ideas such as the perilous thought that led John Badby to be burned at the stake. The old man then turns his attention to newfangled fashions, and the dialogue takes on the characteristics of the complaint, another prominent genre in the late fourteenth and early fifteenth centuries. The old man laments how difficult it is to distinguish between lords and others who simply dress lavishly (lines 443–8) and complains about the way retainers fail to defend their lords because their sleeves are too long (lines 463–9). These issues were pertinent, to judge by the pointing finger sketched alongside this passage in BL, MS Harley 4866 and by similar passages in contemporary texts (Nuttall 2007: 33–4, 66–8). The old man ends his complaint by recounting his misspent youth and thanking God for letting him live – and thus allowing him to amend his wickedness. He says he could go on complaining but he wants to hear the narrator's tale of grief.

The narrator's tale begins as a specific complaint about his delayed annuity – he is still owed six marks (lines 935, 974) – then becomes a general complaint about life as a scribe in the office of the Privy Seal, where Hoccleve worked from Easter 1387 until just before his death in 1426. According to Burrow, most of the petitions Hoccleve wrote begin 'with a complaint of some wrong or lack, followed by a petition for remedy addressed either to the potential benefactor or else to some third party who could act as an intercessor, broker, or "mean" in the matter' (Burrow 1994: 6). The old man proposes that Hoccleve can only achieve a remedy for his grief by complaining to the Prince: 'Endite in Frenssh or Latyn thy greef cleer,/ And for to wryte it wel do thy poweer' (lines 1849–50). At this stage it appears as though Hoccleve will write a begging poem or even a petition, for the bureaucratic languages of the Privy Seal were French and Latin. (Hoccleve's Formulary, BL, Add. MS 24062, is written in French and Latin.) Yet once the old man has heard Hoccleve's tale, his 'formal statement of cause or complaint' (*MED*, s.v. 'tale'), he convinces him to write other kinds of tales for the Prince: 'Wryte to him a goodly tale or two/ On which he may desporten him by nyght' (lines 1902–3). The dialogue ends when the narrator claims to have recorded in his mind the lesson that the old man teaches him through proverbs and exemplary stories.

The *Regiment* invites comparison with similar compilations. It resembles Gower's *Confessio Amantis,* which is also a story collection framed by a confessional dialogue, dedicated to a noble reader, and includes a Mirror for Princes (Blyth 1993). Hoccleve knew the *Confessio*: his hand appears in a copy of it in Cambridge, Trinity College, MS R. 3. 2 (Doyle and Parkes 1978: 182). The *Regiment* also laments Gower's death alongside Chaucer's (line 1975 ff.). Hoccleve's dialogue with the old man evokes the *Canterbury Tales* in the old man's advice that the poet should write improving tales for the Prince: 'Wryte him nothing that sowneth into vice' (line 1947). His words echo Chaucer's retraction of those *Canterbury Tales* 'that sownen into synne' (X (I) 1085). Although the range of stories told within the *Regiment* proper is on a much smaller scale than those told by Chaucer's pilgrims, a number of its stories exemplify the genre Chaucer introduced into English in the 'Monk's Tale', partly modelled on Boccaccio's *De casibus virorum illustrium,* concerning the falls of famous men.

The *Regiment*'s admixture of genres can be understood as a sophisticated means of commenting indirectly on political events and avoiding the 'gret disese' that the stories of the 'Monk's Tale' occasion in the fictional audience of Canterbury pilgrims. For example, the story of a judge in Persia that appears under the heading *De justicia* [Of Justice] can be read as a *de casibus* narrative that invites direct questions about heredity and legitimate governance, though it also encourages readers to interpret it as a general moral *ensample* to help the Prince to embrace virtue and eschew vice. In two stanzas, Hoccleve describes how there was once a man who was wrongly condemned by an unscrupulous judge (lines 2675–8). When the King heard about the false sentence, he ordered the judge to be flayed alive out of his skin (lines 2679–82), which was then used to cover the judge's seat (line 2683). The judge's son took his father's place and was made to sit on the seat covered with his father's skin so 'that he/ Sholde be waar how he his doomes gaf,/ And lene always to rightwisnesse staf' (lines 2686–8). The account of the judge and his son might be interpreted as a commentary on the political tension between Henry IV and the Prince in 1412. As Nuttall argues (2007: 32), *de casibus* narratives enabled contemporary writers to comment on contemporary questions about succession and legitimacy, and as a *de casibus* narrative, this tale seems explicitly to critique justice in Henry IV's realm. Yet the marginal gloss to line 2675 in most manuscripts directs attention away from the judge and his son and towards the King: 'Nota de justitia cuiusdam regis qui quendam judicem excoriari fecit quia falsum reddidit judicium' [Note the justice of a certain king who caused a certain judge to be flayed because he rendered false justice]. The gloss encourages readers to understand the tale as an *ensample* that establishes the standard by which virtuous justice is to be measured. Though the *ensample* initially seems concerned with justice as an ideal, it can also be understood as an indirect critique of England's governance. By implicitly inviting the ruler to contrast the ideal exemplified by the king in the tale with the manifestation of justice in his realm, this tale suggests a gap between the ideal and reality. Hoccleve's combination of genres in this tale is one of several strategies adopted in order to work around the constraints on plain speaking felt by a number of early fifteenth-century writers.

One of the most innovative ways in which Hoccleve manages his audience's expectations in the *Regiment* is through his persona. Early studies of Hoccleve's persona focused on its historical rather than its poetic significance. Scholars in the early twentieth century such as T. F. Tout valued Hoccleve's apparently candid account of London's bureaucracy in the *Regiment* and in other works, and H. S. Bennett found Hoccleve's accounts of the London of his day to be of interest for social but not poetic reasons (146–7). This line of thought shifted when Penelope Doob argued that Hoccleve's autobiographical accounts of mental instability are primarily conventional, and Burrow subsequently questioned the basis of readings where 'convention and autobiographical truth are in general to be taken as alternatives' (1982: 393). Lawton (1987) then pointed out that Hoccleve's dull and ignorant persona, long taken to be an accurate self-representation of a poet who could not hope to match Chaucer, is actually a fifteenth-century trope developed in a turbulent time by authors who wished to offer advice and even criticism on a range of contentious topics. Seminal studies by Greetham (1989) and Hasler (1990) have helped to consolidate the shift in Hoccleve studies from personality to persona. Calin (1994) and Burrow (1997) have pointed out that Hoccleve's complex persona and use of genre owe a great deal to his French predecessors, and further work remains to be done to trace these connections.

The role of money in the *Regiment*, especially the account of a delayed annuity payment (line 1411), can help to explain why the critical shift from personality to persona is an important one. Early critics felt that Hoccleve was being indiscreet by drawing attention to his financial need; recent critics have argued that this aspect of his persona enhances his authority as a poet and as an advisor. Robert Meyer-Lee argues that Hoccleve's begging is the sign of his authenticity (2007: 98) and that 'mendicancy and counsel are mutually affirming' (ibid.: 113). Judith Ferster explains that Hoccleve's personal appeal for funds may have been aligned with the Prince's policy at this time, 'since enabling the government to honour its debts was exactly his project' (1996: 145). Tolmie (2000) argues that Hoccleve criticises the Lancastrian regime directly, warning the Prince that if he fails to pay the patents he has granted to the Crown's servants, especially those among the bureaucratic ranks, he will exile 'þe peples beneuolence, / And kyndeleþ hate vndir priue scilence' (lines 4789–95). By withholding promised funds, the Prince will engender resentment among those in the Privy Seal and elsewhere.

Tolmie contends that future scholarship should re-evaluate Hoccleve's self-representation as a poet (2007: 342), but the poetry itself is equally promising. We might begin with Hoccleve's use of rhyme royal (explored by Mitchell 1968), which is indebted to Gower, who employs the form in a couple of poems, including *To Henry the Fourth in Praise of Peace*, and to Chaucer, who employs it in *The Parliament of Fowls, Troilus and Criseyde*, and several *Canterbury Tales*. As Perkins points out, Hoccleve 'exploits the organizing potential of his rhyme royal stanzas' (2001: 103) in the *Regiment* when translating a story from *De ludo scaccorum*. Elsewhere, Hoccleve aligns his unit of thought with the stanza form in order to emphasise the need to control speech. The old man rambles about the danger of saying too much, before eventually acknowledging: 'Unbrydlid wordes ofte man byweepith' (line 2433). In the following stanza, he develops the *Regiment*'s leitmotif of beast imagery by asserting that all wild beasts can be tamed but the tongue cannot. The old man makes this point by means of a self-contained rhyme royal stanza, ironically suggesting that the tongue – a metonym for speech – can be bridled by poetic form.

Like unbridled speech, ungoverned thought can be unsettling. Hoccleve suggests this in the opening stanza of the *Regiment*:

> Musynge upon the restlees bysynesse
> Which that this troubly world hath ay on honde,
> That other thing than fruyt of bittirnesse
> Ne yildith naght, as I can undirstonde,
> At Chestres In, right faste by the Stronde,
> As I lay in my bed upon a nyght,
> Thoght me byrefte of sleep the force and might. (lines 1–7)

Thought is here characterised by means of the 'small scale personification' that Spearing (1985: 119) describes as one of the hallmarks of Hoccleve's style. Person-ification functions synecdochically in this stanza in order to establish the *Regiment*'s major theme: if one does not govern each part of oneself effectively, then the ungoverned part – thought, in this instance – will govern the whole. Thought, ungoverned, prevents Hoccleve from sleeping peacefully in his bed at night. Later in the Prologue, Hoccleve reverts to the topic of thought when the old man asks him if he has succumbed to the kind of thought that led John Badby to heretical belief. The old man points out that this kind of thought – again personi-fied – leads people to anxiety and possesses outrageous violence (lines 268–9); it lurks within people and pursues their confusion (lines 274–5). Retrospectively, the personified thought that disrupts Hoccleve's sleep at the beginning of the *Regiment* can be interpreted as an unruly subject who disrupts the metaphorical sleep that political and religious peace have to offer. Hoccleve underlines the figurative relationship between sleep and peace in the realm late in the *Regiment* proper by shifting registers from metaphor to simile. In the final section of the poem, Hoccleve argues that three things lead to peace: conformity to God's will, humility and tranquillity of thought. He explains 'for as a wight [person]' cannot sleep in a bed of thorns, 'right so' someone afflicted with grievous thought cannot find peace with himself or others (lines 5055–60). He augments the connection between sleep and peace in the next stanza by repeating diction in the structure of the simile but shifting the tenor from political to religious peace, asserting that 'even as' it is easy to rest on a soft pillow, 'right so' Christ can more easily enter the heart of one whose heart is open to peace. The relationship between sleep as a metaphor in the Prologue and a simile in the *Regiment* proper encourages readers to reconsider its figurative significance in the Prologue.

Hoccleve's representation of himself also shifts registers, moving from persona to personification. The Prologue implies that Hoccleve will be able to sleep peacefully only once he has learned to subject his thought to a regiment; the *Regiment* proper insists that peaceful sleep will be possible in the realm only if subjects themselves are regimented. As Torti (1986, 1991) and Hasler (1990) argue, Hoccleve's body becomes the microcosm that mirrors the macrocosm: he personifies misregulation in the realm. Hoccleve turns to poetry in order to represent thought on a personal and political plane as well as to regiment it. In the penultimate section of the *Regiment* proper, on taking counsel in all actions,

Hoccleve invokes a more traditional representation of thought when he encourages the prince to 'impresse' good counsel 'in the cheste/ Of your memorie and executith it' (lines 4988–9). He then points out that the Prince should remember good counsel because it 'may wel be likned to a brydil/ Which that an hors up keeptih fro fallyng' if it is followed (lines 4929–30). This imagery establishes a parallel between the poet as advisor, who must bridle his words if he hopes to offer advice, and the Prince, who must avoid pursuing his 'lust bestial' (line 3303) by accepting the bridle of good counsel for himself and the realm offered by the poem.

The exemplary proverbs and tales that the *Regiment* offers to the Prince can be understood more broadly as ideals against which other readers might measure themselves. The *Regiment*'s focus on moral edification is the main reason why the author of Caxton's *Book of Courtesy* recommends 'Oclyff in his translacion' for his 'goodly langage and sentence passing wyse' (Caxton, ed. Furnivall 1868: 361), and this view provides one insight into its fifteenth-century popularity. While the establishment of ideal moral values might seem to be fairly innocuous, princes might not always want all of their practices to be measured against a standard that they cannot always – if ever – meet. The *Regiment* has returned to prominence as critics have recognised the way that it invites readers to judge the realm's governance most acutely when it appears to be concerned with more general concepts such as financial responsibility and personal governance. Recent studies have tended to concentrate on the challenges of Hoccleve's role as Lancastrian apologist (Strohm 1998: 379–88), but the *Regiment*'s range is such that it has much to contribute to our understanding of other important aspects of fifteenth-century culture, including conceptions of gender (Batt 1996; Nissé 1999; Yeager 2004; Davis 2007: 138–67) and religious orthodoxy (Little 2006; Cole 2008; Gayk 2010).

Works cited

Batt, Catherine, 'Hoccleve and … Feminism? Negotiating Meaning in *The Regiment of Princes*', in *Essays on Thomas Hoccleve* (London, 1996), pp. 55–84

Bennett, H. S., *Chaucer and the Fifteenth Century* (Oxford, 1948)

Blyth, Charles, 'Thomas Hoccleve's Other Master', *Medievalia* 16 (1993 for 1990), 349–59

Briggs, Charles F., *Giles of Rome's 'De Regimine Principum': Reading and Writing Politics at Court and University, c.1275–c.1525* (Cambridge, 1999)

Burrow, John, 'Autobiographical Poetry in the Middle Ages: The Case of Thomas Hoccleve', *Proceedings of the British Academy*, 68 (1982), 389–412

——, *Thomas Hoccleve*, Authors of the Middle Ages, 4 (Aldershot, 1994)

——, 'Hoccleve and the Middle French Poets', in *The Long Fifteenth Century: Essays for Douglas Gray*, eds Helen Cooper and Sally Mapstone (Oxford, 1997), pp. 35–49

——, 'Introduction', in *Thomas Hoccleve's Complaint and Dialogue*, ed. John Burrow, EETS, o. s. 313 (Oxford, 1999), pp. ix–lxv

Calin, William, *The French Tradition and the Literature of Medieval England* (Toronto, 1994)

Carlson, David R., 'Thomas Hoccleve and the Chaucer Portrait', *Huntington Library Quarterly*, 54 (1991), 283–300

Caxton, William, *Caxton's Book of Courtesy*, ed. Frederick J. Furnivall, EETS, e. s. 3 (London, 1868)

Cole, Andrew, *Literacy and Heresy in the Age of Chaucer* (Cambridge, 2008)

Davis, Isabel, *Writing Masculinity in the Later Middle Ages* (Cambridge, 2007)

Dean, James, 'Gower, Chaucer, and Rhyme Royal', *Studies in Philology*, 88 (1991), 251–275

Doob, Penelope B. R., *Nebuchadnezzar's Children: Conventions of Madness in Middle English Literature* (New Haven, CT, 1974)

Doyle, A. I., and Malcolm B. Parkes, 'The Production of Copies of the *Canterbury Tales* and the *Confessio Amantis* in the Early Fifteenth Century', in *Medieval Scribes, Manuscripts and Libraries: Essays Presented to N. R. Ker*, eds M. B. Parkes and A. G. Watson (London, 1978), pp. 163–210

Edwards, A. S. G., 'Hoccleve's *Regiment of Princes*: A Further Manuscript', *Edinburgh Bibliographical Society Transactions*, 5 (1971), 32

——, 'The Chaucer Portraits in the Harley and Rosenbach Manuscripts', *English Manuscript Studies*, 4 (1993), 268–71

Ferster, Judith, *Fictions of Advice: The Literature and Politics of Counsel in Late Medieval England* (Philadelphia, PA, 1996)

Gayk, Shannon, *Image, Text, and Religious Reform in Fifteenth-Century England* (Cambridge, 2010)

Green, R. F., 'Notes on Some Manuscripts of Hoccleve's *Regiment of Princes*', *British Library Journal*, 4 (1978), 37–41

——, *Poets and Princepleasers: Literature and the English Court in the Late Middle Ages* (Toronto, 1980)

Greetham, D. C., 'Self-Referential Artifacts; Hoccleve's Persona as Literary Device', *Modern Philology*, 86 (1989), 242–51

Harris, Kate, 'The Patron of British Library MS Arundel 38', *Notes and Queries*, n.s. 31 (1984), 462–3

Hasler, Antony, 'Hoccleve's Unregimented Body', *Paragraph*, 13 (1990), 164–83

Hoccleve, Thomas, *Hoccleve's Works, III: The Regement of Princes*, ed. F. J. Furnivall, EETS, e. s. 72 (London, 1897)

——, *Selections from Hoccleve*, ed. M. C. Seymour (Oxford, 1981)

——, *Thomas Hoccleve: The Regiment of Princes*, ed. Charles R. Blyth (Kalamazoo, MI, 1999)

Knapp, Ethan, *The Bureaucratic Muse: Thomas Hoccleve and the Literature of Late Medieval England* (University Park, PA, 2001)

——, 'Thomas Hoccleve' in *The Cambridge Companion to Medieval English Literature, 1100–1500*, ed. Larry Scanlon (Cambridge, 2009), pp. 191–203

Lawton, David, 'Dullness and the Fifteenth Century', *English Literary History*, 54 (1987), 761–99

Little, Katherine C., *Confession and Resistance: Defining the Self in Late Medieval England* (Notre Dame, IN, 2006)

Marzec, Marcia Smith, 'The Latin Marginalia of the *Regiment of Princes* as an Aid to Stemmatic Analysis', *Text*, 3 (1987), 269–84

McMillan, Douglas J., 'The Single Most Popular of Thomas Hoccleve's Poems: The *Regement of Princes*', *Neuphilologische Mitteilungen*, 89 (1988), 63–71

McNiven, Peter, 'Prince Henry and the English Political Crisis of 1412,' *History*, 65 (1980), 1–16

Meyer-Lee, Robert J., *Poets and Power from Chaucer to Wyatt* (Cambridge, 2007)

Mitchell, Jerome, *Thomas Hoccleve: A Study in Early Fifteenth Century Poetic* (Urbana, IL, 1968)

Mooney, Linne R., 2011a. 'A Holograph Copy of Thomas Hoccleve's *Regiment of Princes*', *Studies in the Age of Chaucer*, 33 (2011), 263–96

——, 2011b. 'Vernacular Literary Manuscripts and their Scribes', in *The Production of Books in England, 1350–1500*, eds Alexandra Gillespie and Daniel Wakelin (Cambridge, 2011), pp. 192–211

Nissé, Ruth, '"Oure Fadres Olde and Modres": Gender, Heresy, and Hoccleve's Literary Politics', *Studies in the Age of Chaucer*, 21 (1999), 275–99

Nuttall, Jenni, *The Creation of Lancastrian Kingship* (Cambridge, 2007)

Pearsall, Derek, 'Hoccleve's *Regement of Princes*: The Poetics of Royal Self-Representation', *Speculum*, 69 (1994), 386–410

Perkins, Nicholas, *Hoccleve's 'Regiment of Princes': Counsel and Constraint* (Cambridge, 2001)

Scanlon, Larry, *Narrative, Authority, and Power: The Medieval Exemplum and the Chaucerian Tradition* (Cambridge, 1994)

Scott, Kathleen, *Later Gothic Manuscripts, 1390–1490*, 2 vols (London, 1996)

Seymour, M. C, 'The Manuscripts of Hoccleve's *Regiment of Princes*,' *Edinburgh Bibliographical Society Transactions*, 4 (1974), 255–97

——, 'Manuscript Portraits of Chaucer and Hoccleve', *Burlington Magazine*, 124, no. 955 (1982), 618–23

Simpson, James, 'Nobody's Man: Thomas Hoccleve's *Regement of Princes*', in *London and Europe in the Later Middle Ages,* eds Julia Boffey and Pamela King (London, 1995), pp. 149–80

Spearing, A. C., *Medieval to Renaissance in English Poetry* (Cambridge, 1985)

Strohm, Paul, *England's Empty Throne: Usurpation and the Language of Legitimation, 1399–1422* (New Haven, CT, 1998)

Tolmie, Sarah, 'The *Prive Scilence* of Thomas Hoccleve', *Studies in the Age of Chaucer*, 22 (2000), 281–309

——, 'The Professional: Thomas Hoccleve', *Studies in the Age of Chaucer*, 29 (2007), 341–373

Anna Torti, 'Mirroring in Hoccleve's *Regement of Princes*', *Poetica*, 24 (1986), 39–57

——, *The Glass of Form: Mirroring Structures from Chaucer to Skelton* (Cambridge, 1991)

Tout, T.F., *Chapters in the Administrative History of Medieval England*, 6 vols (Manchester, 1920–35)

Trevisa, John, *The Governance of Kings and Princes: John Trevisa's Middle English*

Translation of the 'De Regimine Principum' of Aegidius Romanus, eds David C. Fowler, Charles F. Briggs and Paul G. Remley (New York, 1997)

Watt, David, 'Compilation and Contemplation: Beholding Thomas Hoccleve's *Series* in Oxford, Bodleian Library, MS Selden Supra 53', *Journal of the Early Book Society*, 14 (2011), 1–30

Yeager, R. F., 'Death is a Lady: *The Regement of Princes* as Gendered Political Commentary', *Studies in the Age of Chaucer*, 26 (2004), 147–93

5

John Lydgate's Major Poems

ROBERT J. MEYER-LEE

John Lydgate (c.1370–1449) was a Benedictine monk of the abbey of Bury St Edmunds, who entered the novitiate at age 15 and in his forties served for several years as prior of Hatfield Broad Oak (Hatfield Regis) in Essex. He was also indisputably the most prominent vernacular poet in England in the first half of the fifteenth century. Over the course of his writing career, he produced an astonishing amount of verse – in the order of 145,000 lines (Pearsall 1970: 4). He wrote in a wide array of genres, ranging from secular accounts of ancient military conflicts, such as two of the major poems considered here, to sophisticated and accomplished devotional works, such as *The Life of Our Lady*, to proto-dramatic pieces such as *The Mumming at Windsor*, to the popular courtesy poem *Stans puer ad mensam*. Correspondingly broad is the social scope of his recorded patrons, which ranges from royalty to ecclesiastical leaders, to London guilds and country gentry. And manuscripts of his works, which survive in the hundreds, enjoyed high circulation in his own lifetime, unlike those of his Ricardian predecessors; hence it is also no surprise that his characteristic aureate style was markedly influential, adopted by poets throughout the century, some of whom explicitly cite him as a poetic authority.

Against the backdrop of Lydgate's remarkable poetic output, what one first notices about his major poems is, inevitably, their staggering individual sizes: at 30,117 and 36,365 lines, respectively, *Troy Book* (begun 1412, completed 1420) and *Fall of Princes* (begun 1431, completed c.1439) account for nearly half of his verse. In comparison, his *Siege of Thebes* (c.1421–22), at 4,716 lines, may seem compact, although, since he stages this work as his contribution to the *Canterbury Tales*, the fact that it more than doubles the longest of those (the 'Knight's Tale', to which the *Siege* forms a kind of response) maintains the imposing sense of scale. These works also rank among the most copied of any medieval poetic texts in English: *Troy Book* survives in twenty-three manuscripts and fragments, *Siege* in thirty-one, and *Fall of Princes* in thirty-nine (as well as appearing in extract in dozens more), and many of these are quite lavishly produced. While more famous vernacular literary works such as the *Canterbury Tales* and *Piers Plowman* survive in more copies, one may fairly gauge the contemporary prominence of these three Lydgate poems by comparison with the sixteen surviving manuscripts of Chaucer's 8,239-line *Troilus and Criseyde*, to which these Lydgate poems possess generic affinity and a similar implied audience.

A comparison with *Troilus*, however, makes evident that literary efforts do not garner the epithet 'major' by the strength of mere numbers. Ambition, and historical and literary significance, are essential considerations in this regard, but these qualities are, of course, notoriously subject to tendentious determination. Fortunately, in these particular poems Lydgate himself displays unusual self-consciousness – and consistency – about his ambitions, and thus a brief glance at one of his own comments in this respect in the earliest of the three works, *Troy Book*, may serve as a basis for understanding the multifaceted significance of all three.

In the prologue to *Troy Book*, after a complex invocation to a series of deities, Lydgate details the royal commissioning of the work by Prince Henry of Monmouth, 'eldest sone of the noble kyng,/ Henri the firþe' (and King Henry V by the time Lydgate completed the work). As Lydgate describes, the Prince:

> [...] me comaunded the drery pitus fate
> Of hem of Troye in englysche to translate,
> The sege also and the destruccioun,
> Lyche as the latyn maketh mencioun,
> For to compyle, and after Guydo make,
> So as I coude, and write it for his sake,
> By-cause he wolde that to hyʒe and lowe
> The noble story openly wer knowe
> In oure tonge, aboute in euery age,
> And y-writen as wel in oure langage
> As in latyn and in frensche it is;
> That of the story þe trouthe we nat mys
> No more than doth eche other nacioun:
> This was the fyn of his entencioun.
> The whyche emprise anoon I gynne schal
> In his worschip for a memorial.
>   (Lydgate, ed. Bergen 1906–35, pro. lines 95–6, 105–20)

These lines have understandably been the focus of much scholarly attention, especially in recent decades, as they have suggested to many readers an incipient English nationalism linked closely with a conscious elevation of the status of the English language, a nascent sense of a high-culture English literary tradition, and, more subtly, Henry's imperial aspirations (see Fisher 1992; Ambrisco and Strohm 1995). Although the particularities of *Troy Book* bear on many of these considerations, here I wish to unpack the more general import of the final sentence of the passage, in which Lydgate defines quite concisely what he seeks to construct through the poetic 'emprise' he has undertaken: namely, 'a memorial'. Since he uses the term in a very similar context in the prologue to *Fall of Princes* (Lydgate, ed. Bergen 1924–27: Book 1, lines 64–77), and since *Siege of Thebes*, while it does not contain the term, is so similar to *Troy Book* in genre, method and style, we may fairly assume that this term denotes essential aspects of the common project of all three major poems.

In Lydgate's hands, the semantic range of 'memorial' covers a spectrum from the faculty of memory (as in *Troy Book*, 1.113, referring to the feeble 'mynde and memorial' of Eson) to a meaning very close to its modern sense of a monument intended as a sociocultural preservation of a memory of a specific event or person (as in *Troy Book*, 4.6915–17, referring to 'Þe riche toumbe, costful and royal,/ Þere set and made for a memorial /Of Eccuba, whilom of grete fame'). His uses of 'memorial' to refer to literary composition appear to be as much metaphorical extensions of the latter meaning as specialisations of the former, as evident in his use of the term to refer, on the one hand, to the 'pilers' Hercules erects to mark a particular 'conquest royal' (*Troy Book*, 2.7439–40), and, on the other, to Ovid's literary recording of Hercules' 'famus dedis twelue' in *Metamorphoses*, 'Whiche ben remembrid ther in special,/ In his honour for a memorial' (*Troy Book*, 1.568–70). Indeed, that other poems of Lydgate's became, in his day, elements of actual physical spectacles – such as *The Danse Macabre*, which accompanied a mural painted on the cloister walls of Pardon Churchyard near St Paul's Cathedral in London (see Schirmer 1961: 126–9), or *The Legend of St George*, which accompanied wall hangings in the London Armourer's Hall (Floyd) – suggests that the idea of a textual memorial would have been a natural one to him, scarcely even metaphorical.

Memorial monuments, then as now, are complex, multifunctional public objects. They are strategically designed signifying edifices that seek to impel negotiations between the present and a typically violent, deadly, traumatic moment in the past. They usually have didactic intentions, serving as interpretive gateways that aim to direct the viewing individual's negotiation with the past towards civic and ethical ends; yet, especially when the memorialised events were – as in the case of these three Lydgate poems – disastrous rather than victorious, a memorial's didactic intentions can be acutely polysemic, underdetermined, or ambivalent. As Françoise Choay has suggested, memorials stand at once as a claim to have transcended the trauma that they memorialise, evidence that the polity in which they exist continues to thrive, and a warning of the ongoing possibility of like trauma. As spectacular physical objects and points of collective visitation, they have a range of social, cultural and economic functions beyond their immediate aim of memorialisation; they may be totems of cultural identity, emblems of civic pride and generators of economic value. And as self-consciously constructed aesthetic objects, they participate in a tradition of high art whose claim to timelessness serves as the essential, but uneasy, counterforce to the corrosive march of history to which they testify. As textual memorials, then, Lydgate's major poems exhibit nothing less than his ambition to fuse verbal art and public service in an attempt to transcend history by constructing, in these instances, monuments to historical catastrophe. In this light, we may understand that the sheer bulk of Lydgate's major poems helps to create the aura of grandiosity that is typically a crucial feature of the memorial aesthetic; likewise, the lavish production of the manuscripts serves as a material equivalent to the social salience and physicality of the monument.

Derek Pearsall, the most influential Lydgate scholar of the second half of the twentieth century, pointed the way towards this understanding of Lydgate's major poems when he remarked that, for Lydgate, 'poetry is public art, its existence conditioned and determined by outer needs and pressures, not by inner ones. In this sense, all his poetry is occasional poetry' (Pearsall 1970: 5). Subsequently, the historicist trends in literary criticism that came to the fore in the 1980s did much to adumbrate the multivalent complexity of this 'public art'. De-emphasising, if not really dismissing, the question of relative literary value (in regard to which Lydgate will never escape the shadow of Chaucer, especially since he himself so often offers self-deprecating comparisons with his poetic predecessor) in favour of explorations of literature's social, political and economic significances, critics such as David Lawton, Lois Ebin, Paul Strohm, James Simpson, Larry Scanlon and Lee Patterson led the way to a new appreciation of the nature of Lydgate's public poetic interventions (a trend that Pearsall [2005] in fact finds cause for concern). Although not formulating this nature precisely as that of a memorial, they and a number of others have in effect explored many of the implications and ramifications of the memorial functionality of Lydgate's major poems. In the rest of this chapter, I will focus on three of the most crucial dimensions of this functionality, ones that have occupied much of the scholarship on these poems over the last thirty years or so, but which still beckon further inquiry: the memorial's political didacticism and the relation of this to the established political powers at the time of its construction; the memorial's self-conscious participation in a tradition of high art, which for these poems means in particular Lydgate's relation to his sources and to Chaucer; the memorial's social, cultural and economic currency, which, for this chapter's purposes, I will narrow to a consideration of the material vehicles of this currency, the surviving manuscripts of the poems. Of course, in practice these dimensions function not independently but in concert, each interacting with the others to create the powerful individual experience and social phenomenon of these three textual memorials; indeed, it is the mechanisms and effects of these interactions (especially between the third dimension, the manuscripts, and the other two) that most demand further study.

The implied audience of all three of Lydgate's major poems is the secular, martial aristocracy and, more specifically, the Lancastrian ruling class of the time of the poems' composition. (The poems' *actual* audience was notably broader, extending through the lesser gentility and the merchant class.) Two of the poems, as they themselves testify, had royal patrons and hence also primary implied readers: the future Henry V for *Troy Book*, and Henry's brother, Duke Humfrey of Gloucester, for *Fall of Princes*. (The patron of *Siege*, if it had one, cannot be identified.) All three possess a historical narrative infrastructure: *Troy Book* tells the story of the fall of Troy, from Jason and the Golden Fleece through the death of Ulysses, long after the war, at the hand of his son Telegonus; *Siege* tells the story of the fall of Thebes from the raising of the city walls by King Amphion to Theseus' climactic total destruction of the city, then ruled by King Creon after the mutual slaughter of the brothers and competing kings Eteocles and Polyneices; *Fall of Princes* consists of a vast sequence of tales of the ruin and death of the great, notable and (typically) powerful, beginning with Adam and Eve and ending with King John of France. Yet all three works, as has often been observed, are also deeply and pervasively infused with advisory, moralising matter, with their narratives always on the verge of being subsumed into exempla (or, in *Fall of Princes*, playing that role outright) and thus the poems, considered in their entirety, becoming more a species of *Fürstenspiegel*, or mirror for princes, than an epic or encyclopaedic recounting of ancient history. Each of the poems therefore turns its gaze into the far reaches of the past in order to intervene in the political present.

The exact nature of this intervention, however, has been a matter of some debate, one that has been driven by the curious fact that, in each case, what these poems memorialise is the destruction – and, often, brutally violent self-destruction – of the very martial aristocracy that forms the poems' implied audience, and whose values the poems also celebrate (albeit typically in such strategic places as prologues and envoys). All three poems contain numerous examples of stark juxtapositions between implicit and sometimes explicit condemnations of aristocratic martial values, and celebrations of the manhood and prowess of the narratives' warrior heroes and their contemporary Lancastrian doppelgangers. To give just one instance, near the end of *Siege of Thebes*, Lydgate introduces Theseus as the ideal warrior king, 'the noble worthy knyght' and 'worthy conquerour' who achieves the final, cataclysmic destruction of Thebes and its people:

> He bete it downe and the howsys brente,
> The puple slough for al her crying loude,
> Maad her wallys and her towrys proude
> Rounde aboute, euene vpon a rowe,
> with the Soyle to be laide ful lowe
> That nou3t was left / but the soyle al bare.
> (Lydgate, ed. Erdmann and Ekwall 1911, 1930: lines 4506, 4535, 4556–61

After this virtual genocide, Theseus leaves for Athens, 'laurer crownyd in signe of victorye', where he performs 'his honur duely to marte' (lines 4597–9). But shortly after this apparently positive depiction of Theseus' homage to Mars, Lydgate turns from the end of his narrative and offers a blistering anti-Martian tirade of some sixty-two lines (lines 4628–89), which begins, 'lo her the fyn of contek and debat / Lo her the myght of Mars the froward sterre' (lines 4628–9); he associates the origin of war with 'Lucyfer, fader of Envie' (line 4662), and asserts that the:

> Ground and cause why that men so stryve,
> Is coveytise and fals Ambicioun
> That euerich wold han domynacioun
> Ouer other, and trede hym vndyr foote:
> Which of al sorowe gynnyng is and Roote. (lines 4674–8)

Then, to conclude the poem, he imagines a future of universal peace, when 'Martys swerd shal no more manace' and boldly associates this apocalyptic vision with his political present and the recently (and temporarily, as it turned out) achieved end of the war with France:

> But loue and pees in hertys shal awake,
> And charite […]
> Thorgh grace only in dyuers naciouns,
> Forto reforme a-twixe Regyouns
> Pees and quyet[,] concord and vnyte. (lines 4698–703)

As Axel Erdmann points out in his edition, the final two lines of this passage echo the terms of the twenty-fourth paragraph of the Treaty of Troyes ('Item, ut Concordia, Pax, & Tranquilitas inter praedicta Franciae & Angliae Regna perpetuo furturis temporibus observentur'), which in May 1420 marked the culmination of the great martial ambitions of England's contemporary Theseus, Henry V. Whatever one makes of this series of juxtapositions, one must admit that, on close inspection, they remain highly ambiguous, and they foreground the question of the contemporary political valence of the poem's depiction of past trauma.

A number of critics, contextualising Lydgate's celebrations of his warrior heroes and royal patrons within the political turbulence of the Lancastrian era, have taken Lydgate's patronage by Lancastrian princes – and his panegyrical reports of this patronage – as evidence of a Lancastrian project to shore up dynastic authority (and legitimacy) by displays of high culture. For critics such as Paul Strohm, the tension between the implications of the disastrous narratives and the gestures towards complicity with power that frame those narratives is the inevitable product of the incoherence of Lancastrian authority itself (see for example Strohm 1999). Others, similarly understanding Lydgate as attempting to shore up this self-contradictory authority, are more willing to grant the poet awareness of the pitfalls that this project entails. Lee Patterson, for example, writes that 'we can recognize [in *Siege*] anxiety and even the intuition of failure'; we can detect 'Lydgate's own skepticism toward his identity as spokesman for Lancastrian interests, and perhaps even an acknowledgment that poetry and power can never be brought to a perfect identity of purpose' (Patterson 1993: 93). Still others have argued for a more independent and even critical role for the poet, as one who wishes to check the militarism of the Lancastrians and who advocates, above all, prudence as the primary personal virtue required to avoid the calamities of history that he recounts – though views of this role range from a cautiously optimistic (or naive) advocate of peace to a pessimistic prophet of doom (as in Simpson 1997). At stake in this debate is not merely the question of whether one wishes to grant Lydgate the competency to possess genuine political insight or the will to exercise genuine political agency. Rather, the debate raises the questions of the nature and efficacy of late medieval public poetry more generally, especially within the parameters of Lancastrian governance, and of the nature and efficacy of the unstable practical middle ground between the competing ideologies of clerisy and aristocracy in fifteenth-century England. (And, in this latter regard, Richard Kaeuper's nuanced analyses [1999, 2009] of these competing ideologies in chivalric romance could be profitably adapted to these and others of Lydgate's poems.)

This critical debate, moreover, perhaps reflects an intransigent indeterminacy and ambivalence in the major poems themselves, in their function as complex public memorials. As with some actual, physical memorials, the events they memorialise – say, the apocalyptic calamity of *Siege of Thebes*, as apprehended in the contemporary context of Henry's conquest of France – do not lend themselves to a straightforward, unproblematic exemplarity. Rather, in their depiction of such 'negative events' they encode 'moral traumas', as these events 'not only result in loss or failure but also evoke disagreement and inspire censure' and yet nonetheless 'cannot always be ignored without denying their noble side, without forgetting commitments and sacrifices that would be considered heroic in the service of other ends' (Wagner-Pacifici and Schwartz 1991: 384). Similarly, the copresence in *Fall of Princes* of diametrically opposing explanations for the ruinous ends of the powerful (for example, as the result of moral or spiritual failure, or the senseless whim of fortune) is akin to those physical memorials that have been termed a *coincidentia oppositorum,* 'an agency that brings [...] opposed meanings together without resolving them' (ibid.: 392). Instead of choosing among competing critical opinions about these poems, therefore, we might profitably explore how those views collectively illuminate those poems' peculiar aesthetic project.

However one wishes to characterise the relation between poet and political power in Lydgate's major poems, an important consequence of the very prominence of this relation is a rather pronounced emphasis on the public authority of the poet (what I have elsewhere [Meyer-Lee] called 'laureate authority'), and the necessary distinction – whether superficial or not – between this authority and that of the poet's royal patrons and aristocratic audience. And one of the crucial distinguishing grounds for the public authority of the poet is the tradition of high-culture literature that, for the English language, these very poems were in fact instrumental in constituting. The complex, ambivalent relation between poet and power in these works demands a new sort of English poetry, but one whose novelty necessarily involves, somewhat paradoxically, the appearance of following in a pre-existing authoritative tradition.

Each of the major poems begins with a prologue that, beneath the sheen of Lydgate's self-derogation, indirectly but nonetheless quite plainly registers the poem's participation in a high- culture literary tradition. *Troy Book* speaks at length about the role of writers as preservers of the past and sculptors of fame, and it provides a critical account of the literary tradition of the Troy story. *Fall of Princes* begins by reflecting on Lydgate's methods of translation and then provides a rather extensive eulogy of Chaucer, which includes a virtually comprehensive bibliography; it then remarks that 'these poetis [...] Were by old tyme had in gret deynte,/ With kyngis, pryncis in euery regioun' (1.358–60). And in the prologue to *Siege*, in place of such explicit metaliterary commentary, Lydgate offers a self-conscious adaption of the General Prologue to the *Canterbury Tales*, resetting the scene in Canterbury before the journey home. In each case, the effect is to depict Lydgate as an author among authors, the latter of whom either carry august, long-established cultural authority, or, in the case of Chaucer, is granted such authority by analogy to the others. At their outsets, then, Lydgate's major poems, by so signalling a tradition of high art, stake their claim to possessing this tradition's cultural authority, from which vantage point they can address political matters to their aristocratic audiences.

Between their prologues and their concluding matter, each of the major poems carries forward this authority through their canny use of intertexts and, in particular, primary sources, minor sources and allusions to Chaucer. (*Fall of Princes* also contains a great deal of additional metaliterary commentary.) The primary source for *Troy Book* is Guido delle Colonne's *Historia destructionis Troiae*, a comprehensive Latin prose account of the Troy story completed in the late thirteenth century. In Lydgate's day, this was the most authoritative version of the story, believed to be a historically rigorous recounting based on ancient, first-hand sources (even though it was in fact an adaption of Benoît de Sainte-Maure's *Roman de Troie*, a mid-twelfth-century Old French verse romance). Taking advantage of his source's prestige, Lydgate foregrounds his negotiations with the source, referring quite frequently to 'Guydo', sometimes citing Guido's own supposedly ancient sources, and sometimes even contesting Guido's authority (as in the several instances of Lydgate's ironic complaints about Guido's antifeminism). The impression this creates is that of one author in conversation with another, rather than of a translator before a text.

Fall of Princes takes a very similar strategy by means of its ongoing dialogue with 'Bochas' or Giovanni Boccaccio, a strategy all the more visible to us because we know that Lydgate's actual source is not Boccaccio's mid-fourteenth-century Latin *De casibus virorum illustrium*, but rather Laurent de Premierfait's early-fifteenth-century French prose translation of Boccaccio, *Des cas des nobles hommes et femmes*. While Lydgate admits early on to his use of the latter, references to Premierfait are very rare, while those to 'Bochas' are ubiquitous, which creates the impression of a direct dialogue with his more prestigious precursor – even though, as his editor Henry Bergen persuasively demonstrates, Lydgate nowhere evidences actual knowledge of Boccaccio's Latin.

In contrast with *Fall of Princes* and *Troy Book,* in *Siege* Lydgate does not name a source, almost certainly because he knew that his actual primary source – a late French prose redaction of the mid-twelfth-century Old French verse romance *Roman de Thèbes* (see Battles 2004) – carried little prestige in comparison to, say, Statius' *Thebaid*, which Lydgate mentions in *Troy Book*. Instead, as we have seen, by staging his Theban narrative as a continuation of the *Canterbury Tales*, Lydgate figures the latter as the primary precursor text. In addition, when he departs from his actual primary source to add material from a more prestigious minor source – such as Boccaccio's *Genealogiae deorum gentilium* – he does not hesitate to cite the latter.

Lydgate's pose as an author among authors is not merely a pose. In all three major poems, the primary source remains Lydgate's guide throughout, and yet, as many have shown, Lydgate is never a slavish translator. He does not hesitate to expand or compress his source; he regularly deletes, reorders and supplements material. For this reason, close systematic analysis of Lydgate's use of his primary sources has been a fruitful interpretive method, and, given the vastness of these poems, remains a fertile one (see for example Keller 2008; Battles 2004; Mortimer 2005). Similarly productive has been detailed analysis of the manner in which Lydgate makes use of Chaucer, both as a minor textual source and as authoritative English poetic precedent and touchstone. Indeed, much of the criticism on the major poems focuses on one or both of these methods of analysis, and the study of Lydgate's relation to Chaucer has in particular yielded readings of great nuance, in which Lydgate's apparently anxious laudatory stance towards his predecessor has been characterised as more subtly critical, usurpative, aggressive, self-inflating and strategically canonising (see for example Spearing 1985; Lerer 1993; Baswell 1997; Straker 2001).

Significantly less studied, but also quite important, is Lydgate's use of minor sources other than Chaucer. Recent work in this area helps to show how meaning-laden Lydgate's decisions to turn to an alternative source can be, as in, for example, Stephanie A. V. G. Kamath's study of Lydgate's use of *Roman de la rose* in *Troy Book*, and Maura Nolan's work on Lydgate's use of Ovid and Gower in *Fall of Princes* (Nolan 2004, 2005). Even a brief allusion can be freighted with meaning, as in the opening invocation of *Troy Book*, in which one of the several deities Lydgate addresses is 'Othea, goddesse of prudence' (pro. 38). Since Christine de Pizan invented this particular goddess for her *Epistre Othea* (c.1400), Lydgate's allusion is specifically to this latter work and, as I have argued (Meyer-Lee 2007: 61–8), serves as both a nod to his patron Henry V (who was likely Lydgate's source for the manuscript containing *Epistre*) and a signal of the nature of the ensuing work (like *Epistre* a mirror for princes). In a nutshell, this allusion illustrates how Lydgate, through his shrewd use of intertexts, fashions a poetic authority that, by appearing as less contingent and less interested than political discourse, underwrites his textual memorials' political significance. Hence, while the study of Lydgate's use of intertexts obviously helps us understand what his own texts mean at local and global levels, it also sheds light on the specific ways in which his cultivation of a sense of participation in a high literary tradition serves the larger purposes of his major poems.

It has been my contention that not merely are Lydgate's major poems textual memorials in an abstract metaphorical sense, but they also functioned as real social analogues of memorials in fifteenth-century England. If this is so, then the physical experience and hence social reality of these textual memorials lay, of course, with the manuscripts, which therefore also serve for us, in all their individual particularities, as the historical record of this social reality. This record is an incredibly rich one: most of the manuscripts of all three major poems are highly decorated prestige items, meant for display, which suggests that their viewership was likely much broader than their readership. Many manuscripts have illustrations, and a few them possess elaborate sequences of miniatures. The evidence of ownership indicates that they circulated among the elite but also gained a wide audience. The poems' manuscript contexts – in particular, the high frequency with which a major poem formed the sole contents, and typical accompanying texts such as Thomas Hoccleve's *Regiment of Princes* (c.1411) – underscore both their individual social saliency and the ready recognition of their contemporary political relevance. And the numbers of manuscripts suggest that the poems were in high demand, despite (or perhaps because of) the evident costliness of their production. Altogether, the evidence points towards broad social recognition of Lydgate's major poems as status objects and cultural artefacts of *gravitas*. Although actual acquaintance with the texts was likely the privilege of a few, the poems must have figured in the elite social imaginary as sites where one may experience lavish, expensive, beautifully rendered accounts of past cataclysms as meditations on the political present.

The manuscripts of Lydgate's major poems have not, however, received much study in this vein – that is, in the approach that D. F. McKenzie (1999) has termed the 'sociology of texts'. To be sure, solid bibliographical groundwork was laid by the EETS editors Bergen, and Erdmann and Ekwall, and this scholarship has been expertly supplemented since, especially in an illuminating series of studies by A. S. G. Edwards (for example, Edwards 1983, 1984; Edwards and Pearsall 1989; and see also Pearsall 1997 for a convenient bibliographical catalogue).

Furthermore, Lydgate's important role in the history of the English book – as, for example, a key agent in the evolution towards the authorcentric literary codex and the commercial viability of vernacular poetic books – has received apt attention, especially in the work of Edwards, in studies of Lydgate's role in the early years of English print culture (for example Gillespie 2006; Kuskin 2008), and in accounts of the activities of scribe and proto-literary-impresario John Shirley (for example Connolly 1998). Yet – given the evident high and pervasive social currency of the manuscripts of these major poems – the brimming repositories of social and cultural history that individual manuscripts represent, while having received some notice, are far from fully tapped.

Here I will simply mention two rather remarkable manuscripts that would repay further inquiry from a sociology-of-the-text vantage point: Manchester University, John Rylands Library, MS English 1; BL, MS Harley 1766. The Rylands manuscript, which dates from the middle of the fifteenth century, is an exquisite production of *Troy Book*. It is beautifully illuminated and copiously illustrated, containing sixty-nine miniatures in all: four half-page miniatures, one column miniature and sixty-four marginal illustrations, many of which, according to Kathleen Scott, render 'landscapes on a scale scarcely known elsewhere in English book illustration of the period' (Scott 1996: II, 261). There has been some study of these illustrations in their manuscript context (notably, by Lawton 1983), and some investigation of the manuscript's social circulation (see Warner 1999). But the sociocultural valences of the interactions between image and text in the multimedia spectacle that is this manuscript would certainly repay in-depth attention akin to, if not necessarily as sustained as, that which Jessica Brantley has given to the devotional manuscript BL, Add. MS 37049. Such attention would shed light not just on the contemporary social experience of this particular instance of *Troy Book* memorial, but also, as Edwards (1983) has suggested, more generally on secular manuscript culture in the upper reaches of English society.

Harley 1766 contains a carefully and coherently abridged and restructured version of *Fall of Princes*, about three-fifths as long as the full version. At the same time, the manuscript is an even more spectacular multimedia production than the Rylands *Troy Book*, containing a sequence of 158 miniatures, about which Edwards remarks, 'I am not aware of any English poetic text of the fifteenth century containing so many miniatures nor in such a striking style' (Edwards 1983: 18). Given the existence of a manuscript fragment that testifies to another copy of this elaborately produced abridgement (Montreal, McGill University Library, MS 143; for which, see Edwards 1974) and the fact that the same scribe copied both manuscripts as well as seven other Lydgate ones (including an early and finely produced copy of *Troy Book*, BL, MS Arundel 99), Edwards has argued that Harley 1766 does not represent, as Bergen supposes, a scribal redaction created after Lydgate's death. He rather explains the 'discrepancy between elaborateness of format and textual aberrancy' as evidence of Lydgate's own involvement in the creation of this version, which was 'either an early version or a later "compact" version for presentation to some patron' (Edwards 1983: 18). If this is so, then Harley 1766 testifies to the existence of a quasi-workshop or community of manuscript artisans in the Bury area that was at least in part directed by Lydgate and consciously concerned with the intricacy of the design of the manuscript spectacles they forged for their elite customers. Like Rylands, Harley 1766 would repay intensive study of the sociocultural valences of the relation of its text and images; it further may help to illuminate the socioeconomic circumstances of, and motivations behind, the production of material iterations of Lydgatean textual memorials.

There are, of course, many other dimensions to the study of Lydgate's major poems than the three I have chosen to discuss here. For example, the role of female characters and Lydgate's attitude towards them – and Lydgate's probable expectation of female readers – have been fruitful areas of inquiry, and the gender dynamics in the poems could bear further study. In addition, as some of the best recent Lydgate criticism has shown, the traditional divisions of Lydgate's oeuvre into sacred and secular compositions does not well correspond to the monastic vantage point – and specifically that of the Benedictine community at Bury St Edmunds – from which he unfailingly wrote (see Cole 2008; Gayk 2010). Hence, studies that explore the common concerns and social significances of these two putative categories of poems would help illuminate the nature and cultural impact of Lydgate's poetic project more generally. Nonetheless, despite its topical selectivity, I hope that this chapter has made the case that *Troy Book*, *Siege of Thebes* and *Fall of Princes* do indeed merit the epithet 'major' for reasons other than their massive size. They are each literary achievements in several respects, but, beyond this, their status as textual memorials with broad social currency makes them collectively one of the most important cultural phenomena of fifteenth-century England.

Works cited

Ambrisco, Alan S., and Paul Strohm, 'Succession and Sovereignty in Lydgate's Prologue to *The Troy Book*', *Chaucer Review*, 30 (1995), 40–57

Baswell, Christopher, '*Troy Book*: How Lydgate Translates Chaucer into Latin', in *Translation Theory and Practice in the Middle Ages*, ed. Jeanette Beer (Kalamazoo, MI, 1997), pp. 215–37

Battles, Dominique, *The Medieval Tradition of Thebes: History and Narrative in the OF 'Roman de Thèbes', Boccaccio, Chaucer, and Lydgate* (New York, 2004)

Brantley, Jessica, *Reading in the Wilderness: Private Devotion and Public Performance in Late Medieval England* (Chicago, IL, 2007)

Choay, Françoise, *The Invention of the Historic Monument* (Cambridge, 2001)

Cole, Andrew, *Literature and Heresy in the Age of Chaucer* (Cambridge, 2008)

Connolly, Margaret, *John Shirley: Book Production and the Noble Household in Fifteenth-Century England* (Aldershot, 1998)

Ebin, Lois A., *Illuminator, Makar, Vates: Visions of Poetry in the Fifteenth Century* (Lincoln, NE, 1988)

Edwards, A. S. G., 'The McGill Fragment of Lydgate's *Fall of Princes*', *Scriptorium*, 28 (1974), 75–7

——, 'Lydgate Manuscripts: Some Directions for Future Research', in Pearsall, ed., *Manuscripts and Readers*, pp. 15–26

——, 'Lydgate Scholarship: Progress and Prospects', in *Fifteenth-Century Studies: Recent Essays*, ed. Robert F. Yeager (Hamden, CT, 1984), pp. 29–47

——, and Derek Pearsall, 'The Manuscripts of the Major English Poetic Texts', in *Book Production and Publishing in Britain, 1375–1475*, eds Jeremy Griffiths and Derek Pearsall (Cambridge, 1989), pp. 257–78

Fisher, John H., 'A Language Policy for Lancastrian England', *PMLA*, 107 (1992), 1168–80

——, *The Emergence of Standard English* (Lexington, KY, 1996)

Floyd, Jennifer, 'St. George and the "Steyned Halle": Lydgate's Verse for the London Armourers', in *Lydgate Matters: Poetry and Material Culture in the Fifteenth Century*, eds Lisa H. Cooper and Andrea Denny-Brown (New York, 2008), pp. 139–64

Gayk, Shannon, *Image, Text, and Religious Reform in Fifteenth-Century England* (Cambridge, 2010)

Gillespie, Alexandra, *Print Culture and the Medieval Author: Chaucer, Lydgate, and their Books, 1473–1557* (Oxford, 2006)

Kaeuper, Richard W., *Chivalry and Violence in Medieval Europe* (Oxford, 1999)

——, *Holy Warriors: The Religious Ideology of Chivalry* (Philadelphia, PA, 2009)

Kamath, Stephanie A. Viereck Gibbs, 'John Lydgate and the Curse of Genius', *Chaucer Review*, 45 (2010), 32–58

Keller, Wolfram R., *Selves and Nations: The Troy Story from Sicily to England in the Middle Ages* (Heidelberg, 2008)

Kuskin, William, *Symbolic Caxton: Literary Culture and Print Capitalism* (Notre Dame, IN, 2008)

Lawton, David, 'Dullness and the Fifteenth Century', *English Literary History*, 54 (1987), 761–99

Lawton, Lesley, 'The Illustration of Late Medieval Secular Texts, with Special Reference to Lydgate's *Troy Book*,' in Pearsall, ed., *Manuscripts and Readers*, pp. 41–69

Lerer, Seth, *Chaucer and his Readers: Imagining the Author in Late-Medieval England* (Princeton, NJ, 1993)

Lydgate, John, *Lydgate's Troy Book*, ed. Henry Bergen, 4 vols, EETS, e. s. 97, 103, 106, 126 (London, 1906, 1908, 1910, 1935)

——, *Lydgate's Siege of Thebes*, eds Axel Erdmann and Eilert Ekwall, 2 vols, EETS, e. s. 118, 125 (London, 1911, 1930)

——, *Lydgate's Fall of Princes*, ed. Henry Bergen, 4 vols, EETS, e. s. 121–4 (London, 1924, 1927).

McKenzie, D. F., *Bibliography and the Sociology of Texts* (Cambridge, 1999)

Meyer-Lee, Robert J., *Poets and Power from Chaucer to Wyatt* (Cambridge, 2007)

Mortimer, Nigel, *John Lydgate's 'Fall of Princes': Narrative Tragedy in its Literary and Political Contexts* (Oxford, 2005)

Nolan, Maura, '"Now wo, now gladnesse"': Ovidianism in the *Fall of Princes*', *English Literary History*, 71 (2004), 531–58

——, 'Lydgate's Literary History: Chaucer, Gower, and Canacee', *Studies in the Age of Chaucer*, 27 (2005), 59–92

Patterson, Lee, 'Making Identities in Fifteenth-Century England: Henry V and John Lydgate', in *New Historical Literary Study: Essays on Reproducing Texts,*

Representing History, eds Jeffrey N. Cox and Larry J. Reynolds (Princeton, NJ, 1993), pp. 69–107

Pearsall, Derek, *John Lydgate* (London, 1970)

——, ed., *Manuscripts and Readers in Fifteenth-Century England: The Literary Implications of Manuscript Study* (Cambridge, 1983)

——, *John Lydgate (1371–1449): A Bio-Bibliography* (Victoria, BC, 1997)

——, 'The Apotheosis of John Lydgate', *Journal of Medieval and Early Modern Studies*, 35 (2005), 25–38

Scanlon, Larry, *Narrative, Authority, and Power: The Medieval Exemplum and the Chaucerian Tradition* (Cambridge, 1994)

Schirmer, Walter F., *John Lydgate: A Study in the Culture of the XVth Century*, trans. Ann E. Keep (Berkeley, CA, 1961)

Scott, Kathleen L., *Later Gothic Manuscripts, 1390–1490*, 2 vols (London, 1996)

Simpson, James, '"Dysemol daies and fatal houres"': Lydgate's *Destruction of Thebes* and Chaucer's *Knight's Tale*', in *The Long Fifteenth Century: Essays for Douglas Gray*, eds Helen Cooper and Sally Mapstone (Oxford, 1997), pp. 15–33

——, *Reform and Cultural Revolution* (Oxford, 2002)

Spearing, A. C., *Medieval to Renaissance in English Poetry* (Cambridge, 1985)

Straker, Scott-Morgan, 'Deference and Difference: Lydgate, Chaucer, and the *Siege of Thebes*', *Review of English Studies*, n.s. 52 (2001), 1–21

Strohm, Paul, *England's Empty Throne: Usurpation and the Language of Legitimation, 1399–1422* (New Haven, CT, 1998)

——, 'Hoccleve, Lydgate and the Lancastrian Court', in *The Cambridge History of Medieval English Literature*, ed. David Wallace (Cambridge, 1999), pp. 640–61

Wagner-Pacifici, Robin, and Barry Schwartz, 'The Vietnam Veterans Memorial: Commemorating a Difficult Past', *American Journal of Sociology*, 97 (1991), 376–420

Warner, Kathryn, 'The Provenance and Early Ownership of John Rylands MS English 1', *Bulletin of the John Rylands Library*, 81 (1999), 127–40

6

John Lydgate's Religious Poetry

ANTHONY BALE

In the fervent, contentious, and sometimes ostentatious religious culture of fifteenth-century England, one writer stands out as a particularly prolific and versatile author of devotional texts: the monk of Bury St Edmunds, John Lydgate (c.1370–1449). Lydgate wrote thousands of lines of religious poetry for a wide range of patrons, both individual and institutional, and his poetry provides a comprehensive picture of orthodox fifteenth-century English religious life and its concerns: highly sacramental, habitually influenced by meditative spirituality and *imitatio Christi*, defiantly anti-Lollard, and profoundly invested in the cults of the saints and of the Virgin. Perhaps more surprisingly, however, Lydgate's religious poetry is, like his more overtly political poems, often highly topical. Lydgate was long viewed as a repetitive monk, cloistered in self-indulgent rhetoric (Mortimer 2005: 2–20, summarises the relevant unflattering assessments and Lydgate's changing critical fortunes). Now, Lydgate is increasingly seen as a poet who innovated and experimented: he negotiated the vernacular translation of religious material, the incorporation of Chaucerian diction and themes, and the use of aureate language and humanist ideas all within the parameters of orthodoxy. Lydgate's poetry also inaugurates several new European traditions into English devotional culture: subjects such as the Dance of Death and visual-material forms such as mural poetry and the *pietà* or image of pity find early English expressions in Lydgate's poetry. In short, Lydgate provides us with a ready conspectus of religious literary forms, from short prayers to epic narratives, poised between cloistered monasticism and a vigorous patronage culture of 'pray and display'. However, recent criticism has tended to focus on Lydgate's 'secular' works, especially those in *de casibus* and *Fürstenspiegel* traditions of political, princely counsel. David Lawton's important reassessment of Lydgate's poetry, in which Lawton argued that Lydgate was a shrewd political operator hiding behind poses of servitude and gilded diction, opened up richly historicised readings of Lydgate's politics (Lawton 1987). Likewise, Derek Pearsall's critical position moved from largely mocking Lydgate's prolixity (Pearsall 1970) to – in an important later article (Pearsall 1992) – drawing attention to Lydgate's astuteness and originality. In particular, scholarship has focused on political controversy and anxieties over the Lancastrian cause in Lydgate's poetry (see Patterson 1993; Strohm 1998, 2005; Simpson 2001; Galloway 2008). Scholars have been less ready to engage with Lydgate's religious works, although the critical rediscovery of Lydgate in the last twenty years has yielded some productive studies of individual religious works and themes (for example Somerset 2005; Bale 2009a, 2009b; Lewis 2009; Gayk 2010: 85–122; Meyer-Lee 2010; Sisk 2010).

It would be impossible in a short essay to cover all of Lydgate's voluminous oeuvre, not only because of its extent: Lydgate's poetry repays close analysis, to pick out the tensions, fault lines and anxieties that sustain it. In this essay I will use a handful of Lydgate's texts to consider key themes and trends to which Lydgate repeatedly returns. I open with a discussion of Lydgate's narrative persona, the construction of his monastic, vernacular poetic voice, in *Life of Our Lady*, and his sense of devotional localism, in his *Lives of SS Edmund and Fremund*. I then explore a 'minor' and a 'major' work, the *Legend of St Austin at Compton* and *Lives of SS Alban and Amphibal*, which I consider 'representative' of much of Lydgate's writing produced under patronage and concerned with sanctity. Finally, I close with a brief consideration of the adaptation of his religious verse into material forms outside the codex, forms that often involve visual and mystical imagination.

Lydgate's religious background, his vocation and his abbey at Bury, which he had entered in his youth, are central to the speaking voice he established in his poetry. The abbey had extensive estates, known as the 'banleuca' of St Edmund, in which the abbot enjoyed all but royal powers: the abbot appointed his own justices there and, contentiously, the 'banleuca' was exempt from the jurisdiction of the bishops of Norwich, in whose diocese Bury was located. The 'banleuca' and the Liberty of St Edmund, a large part of Suffolk in which the abbot had vice-regal rights, formed a powerful physical space and image of belonging and exclusion based on reverence to St Edmund (Gransden 1985). It is in this context of fiercely guarded independence and privilege that Lydgate's monasticism was forged, in which religion was closely intertwined with a distinctive local, legal identity and a specific territory. Later, Lydgate travelled to Paris around 1426, he was often in London in the 1430s and 1440s, and he became prior of Hatfield Broad Oak (Hatfield Regis), Essex, one of Bury's dependent priories. Lydgate's background can be characterised as provincial (East Anglia and Bury are presences throughout his life and his poetry), monastic, pious and orthodox. In this way, Lydgate is typical of a number of fifteenth-century English religious poets, such as the Augustinians John Capgrave of Lynn, Norfolk (1393–1464) and Osbern Bokenham of Clare, Suffolk (c.1392–c.1464), the Cambridge scholar John Metham (*fl.* 1449), and the cleric of Colchester and Westminster Benedict Burgh (d.c.1483), all of whom were based in East Anglia, sustained and enabled by local patronage, and all of whom used vernacular poetry to bridge clerical vocation and secular engagement. Moreover, all showed considerable versatility in the range of audiences for whom they wrote.

One might expect the strongest image of Lydgate to be gained from the semi-autobiographical and confessional poem written towards the end of his life, his *Testament* (*NIMEV* 2464; quotations from *Testament* are taken from Lydgate, ed. MacCracken 1910: 329–62). It is from *Testament* that we learn the shape, if not the facts, of Lydgate's life: a self-described wild youth ('Ful geryssh, and voyde of all resoun', line 399), a bad student ('Loth toward skole', line 625), and a lazy Christian ('My pater noster, my crede, or my beleve/ Cast atte cok, lo, this was my maner!', lines 651–2). At some point he entered the monastery, but disregarded the Benedictine rule ('Of religioun I wered a blak habite,/ Only outward as be apparence', lines 691–2), until, apparently near the age of 15, he was converted to 'humble diligence' (line 751) and Christian reverence by a vision of Christ on a crucifix. *Testament* is a highly formulaic and conventional spiritual biography of conversion and revelation. Its formulae of pity and redemption and its long meditations on the name of Jesus, the facets of springtime, and the power of meditating on Christ's Passion all point to the conventional, rather than the individual. What is perhaps most surprising about *Testament* is its total lack of other characters: powerful patrons, abbots, kings – people we know to have been profoundly important in Lydgate's biography and career – are missing. *Testament* appeals instead, through petition, to Christ, and, through emulation, to sacred biographies of repentance. As Augustine describes his youthful theft of fruit from a pear tree, Lydgate describes how he too, in the Suffolk of his childhood, stole apples from local trees (*Testament*, lines 638–9). This image of illicit fruit-picking, ultimately taken from Genesis, was borrowed by Lydgate from Augustine as a symbol of youthful concupiscence. Likewise, the moment of young Lydgate's spiritual conversion – when he beholds a crucifix with the word 'vide' engraved on it (*Testament*, line 745) – may not be untrue, but it is startlingly similar to the popular account of the conversion of St Francis of Assisi (d.1226) (on this passage see Gayk 2010: 115–16). As is so often the case, what looks like individuating detail actually obscures historical fact behind the screen of the poet's conventional piety. In fact, Lydgate's poetic and monastic careers went hand-in-hand with, and were profoundly influenced by, three figures connected with his abbey at Bury: two kings of England, Henry V and Henry VI, and Lydgate's abbot William Curteys.

Henry V, who seems to have known Lydgate and taken an interest in his Oxford studies, proved catalytic in Lydgate's professional development as a poet and, especially, Lydgate's development of a religious poetics based around the translation of Latin texts into 'aureate' – that is, elaborately gilded – English. For Henry's use Lydgate probably wrote a translation of prayers by St Bernard of Clairvaux (*The Eight Verses of St Bernard*, NIMEV 2553) and a translation of Psalm 102, *Benedic anima mea domino* (NIMEV 2572; see Pearsall 1997: 17). More assuredly, Lydgate was developing his orthodox poetic voice in his short poem *A Defence of Holy Church* (NIMEV 2219; Lydgate ed. MacCracken 1910: 30–5), addressed to 'Most worthi prince, of whome the noble fame/ In virtue floureth' (lines 1–2), probably Henry V when he was Prince of Wales (see Lydgate, ed. Norton-Smith 1966: 151). This poem clearly addresses the Lollard controversies of the period 1404–15, the time of Archbishop Arundel's constitutions (which sought to regulate preaching, bible translation and religious education) and Oldcastle's Lollard rebellion (see Watson 1995). Lydgate presents Henry as like the saviour of Christ's Spouse, 'al bysett with enmyes envyroun' (line 11), 'constreyned' in Babylon, 'al solitaire and trist in compleynyng' (line 16). Her foes, 'mortall howndis' (line 29), are clearly akin to Lollards, 'hem that gan to threaten and manace/ The libertees of Cristys mansioun,/ And for to pynch att her fundacioun,/ In preyudice of the olde and new lawe,/ The Patrymony of Petir to withdrawe' (lines 38–42). Conventionally religious yet polemical in the charged atmosphere of early fifteenth-century England, the poem shows Lydgate developing his distinctive blend of flattery (or 'princepleasing') in a moral frame, with an explicit defence of papal authority (upholding 'the Patrymony of Petir'). 'O noble prynce! exaumple of rightwisnesse [...] Distroye hem to, that falsely now werrey/ Her own modir, to whom thai shulde obeye' (lines 122–6) he exhorts Henry, as religious poetry shades into political advice. Not for the last time in his career, Lydgate establishes himself as a flattering subject *and* wise, sometimes admonishing, counsellor: the servant of kings and the voice of faith. The question of Lydgate's engagement with his contemporary politics, and in particular his use of poetry against Lollardy, has yielded rich critical results in recent years (for example Horner 1990; Cole 2008), and is likely to continue to be an area for future exploration.

Also probably at Henry's instigation, Lydgate wrote his imposing *Life of Our Lady* (*NIMEV* 2574), a 6,000-line biography of the Virgin Mary heavily indebted to pseudo-Bonaventure's influential *Meditatationes vitae Christi* (c.1300). Lydgate's poem is in no way a 'simple' or direct translation from any Latin source, and much work remains to be done on the poem's literary background and its medieval reception. That Lydgate, around the same time, was also writing the 'secular' *Troy Book* (*NIMEV* 2516) for Henry should not surprise us, because Lydgate's vocation and identity as devout monk and princely mentor are thoroughly intertwined. *Life of Our Lady* was probably written in 1416, according to astrological clues in the poem, although it underwent significant revision and may be incomplete (see Schirmer 1961: 40; Parr 1971; Pearsall 1970: 285–6; Hardman 1996). The poem describes Mary's childhood and her role as mother of the young Jesus in memorable ekphrastic scenes of heightened emotion, in keeping with meditative spirituality fashionable in the fifteenth century. The poem is structured around the key liturgical feasts of the Virgin, from Nativity to Purification, possibly to reflect the religious festivals around Christmas (Norton-Smith: 155). Gail Gibson has argued that, by ending the poem at the Purification and the associated feast of Candlemas, Lydgate was making a distinctly parochial choice, given 'the local civic importance of the Candlemas guild at Bury' (Gibson 1981: 66). Alternatively, Phillipa Hardman, examining manuscript evidence, argues that the poem was 'in transition', as scribes made significant revisions to the poem: for instance, a poem on the Virgin's Assumption was added, to make her biography 'complete', from birth to death, whilst elsewhere prayers were excerpted, with Lydgate's text 'mined' for versatile prayers to be used outside the original narrative setting (Hardman 1996: 259–61; see also O'Sullivan 2005). Robert Meyer-Lee has recently argued that in *Life of Our Lady* we can discern the 'emergence of the literary' as, in this ostensibly devout poem, Lydgate eulogises Chaucer and creates a rhetorically sophisticated, aureate Marian poetic register; Meyer-Lee argues that 'Lydgate articulates a vernacular literary as a potential sacral power wielded by an authoritative English poet vis-à-vis Mariology and the threat of heresy, and marshaled in defense of his own and his religious order's position vis-à-vis the crown and alternative official vernacular theologies' (Meyer-Lee 2010: 324). So, far from being a messy translation produced at the king's command, Lydgate's poem can be seen to muster the English language and in particular Chaucerian diction in order to support Henry and defend Bury and orthodoxy. The poem was evidently widely read, with over forty surviving manuscripts, and can be seen as leading, rather than reflecting, late medieval Mariology. Rhapsodic, visionary and often infectiously joyful, *Life of Our Lady* demands to be taken seriously as a work both of spiritual intensity and literary creativity.

The themes of prince-pleasing and the defence of Bury became more acute during Henry VI's turbulent reign, during which the abbey at Bury took on a new importance as a place to which the troubled King retired and developed a distinctive spiritual atmosphere and culture. Henry VI was closely linked to Lydgate for many years, and for him Lydgate produced various kinds of poems, such as coronation ballades, poetic pedigrees, and verse mummings performed for the King. Lydgate's commissions for Henry VI are often secular in purpose or in character but one major religious poem by Lydgate for Henry VI demands sustained attention, as it knits royal poetry with Bury's traditions: that is, *Lives of SS Edmund and Fremund* (*NIMEV* 3440; quotations are taken from Lydgate, ed. Bale and Edwards). William Curteys (abbot 1429–46, d.1446) was the dynamic abbot at Bury who presided over the visit to St Edmund's abbey of the 12-year-old King Henry VI over the winter of 1433–34, a visit for which Lydgate wrote his accomplished poem. Curteys had considerably extended the prestige and wealth of Bury and, as A. S. G. Edwards has commented, 'was an adroit statesman who came to enjoy Henry VI's favour and steadfastly pursued the Abbey's larger political and economic interests' (Edwards 2009: 134; see also Sisk 2010). Curteys' abbacy, though splendid, was also markedly learned; under Curteys, book production and scholarship at Bury was encouraged, a new library was built there, and Curteys also made significant bequests to Gloucester College, Oxford (Gransden 2004). Book production at Bury in this period included many vernacular verse miscellanies and there seems to have been a vigorous production line for the dissemination of Lydgate's poetry (see Scott 1982; Rogers 1987).

Many of Lydgate's religious poems were a way of simultaneously upholding Bury's distinctive spiritual and political identity whilst thanking the English kings for their generosity and patronage. The relationship between Bury and the English throne seems to be secured in the manuscript (now BL, Harley MS 2278) of *Lives of SS Edmund and Fremund* produced for Henry VI's visit to Bury. It is a magnificent manuscript, richly detailed and sumptuously produced, illustrating Lydgate's poem and depicting, amongst other things, the young Henry VI kneeling in devotion at St Edmund's shrine. Lydgate describes the poem's occasion several times, and closes the poem with an address to the king:

> Souereyn lord, plese to your goodlyheed,
> And to your gracious royal magnificence,
> To take this tretys which atwen hope and dreed
> Presentyd ys to your hyh excellence.
> And for kyng Edmundis notable reuerence
> Beth to his chyrche dyffence and champion,
> Because yt ys off your ffundacion. (lines 3607–12)

The praise of Henry's 'royal magnyficence' is conventionally given by the abject subject-poet, 'atwen hope and dreed'; but the poet is not so anxious as to miss the opportunity to assert Edmund's 'notable reuerence' and remind Henry of his obligation to defend and champion his foundation at Bury. This was not only a reminder of the monarch's connections and duties to Bury, but also an advertisement, by Bury, of its royal associations and special status.

Lydgate describes his work as a 'translacion', but in fact his poem is an original combination of several sources (see further Lydgate, ed. Bale and Edwards 2009: 20–2). Lydgate's account of the poem's occasion also introduces the conventional praise of monarchy, reiterates Henry's claim to the French as well as English throne, and smuggles in praise of the young king's 'consail' (line 62) who ruled during his minority and a rather self-congratulatory reference to the 'ful gret habundance' (line 60) of Christian celebrations at the abbey. Uniquely, Lydgate paired Edmund with Fremund, and this is one of the major innovations of his poem, reflecting an emerging fifteenth-century English trend for thematic pairs and groups of saints' lives. Whilst Edmund garnered other holy family-members elsewhere (a brother, St Edwold of Cerne Abbas, and a relative, St Ragener of Northampton), Fremund made a fitting companion for Edmund as both are of royal blood and both have a vengeful sense of justice against transgressors. Like Edmund, Fremund punishes those who 'trespace' on his sanctity, a 'transgressioun' of the saint's community (lines 2633–9). Both saints also stand for a potent sacral nationalism against 'mescreantis off Denmark' (line 2547) but this last element was invented by Lydgate: in the Latin source, Fremund's adversaries are named as pagans, whereas Lydgate identifies them as Danes, thereby drawing a more explicit parallel between the two saints' adversaries. Lydgate's changes to his sources show the agenda at work in the pairing of the saints. In his source, Lydgate would have read that Fremund's first shrine was at Cropredy, Oxfordshire, and that Fremund's martyrdom led to the evangelical works of St Birinus, named by Lydgate as merely being responsible for the translation of Fremund's body to Dunstable (line 2866); the Cropredy shrine and Birinus' works and miracles are missing from Lydgate's poem, diminishing the importance of Oxfordshire in Fremund's life and focusing instead on Dunstable. This allows Lydgate to return to Edmund's miraculous posthumous slaying of the Danish tyrant Sweyn, and thereby circle back to Bury and its patron saint's miracles.

A brief example from the poem will suffice to reveal the complicated attitude the poem has towards earthly and saintly power. Following his martyrdom, Edmund's head goes missing, and the distraught Christians, 'of hih deuocion', go in search of it (line 1909), once the Danish tyrants Hyngwar and Ubba have, 'in party', eased their persecution of Christians. The Christians are vividly depicted in crisis as 'they wanted and failed of the hed' (line 1914), which can be read both literally as a decapitated headless body and metaphorically as a body-politic without its head. This dual meaning is suggested by Lydgate in his description of the people 'serchyng al the boundys' (line 1918), 'boundys' being a key word at Bury to describe the extent of its territories, liberties and area in which St Edmund was patron. Lydgate describes the people as utterly bereft without their king, a portrait of a power-vacuum that must have been freighted with contemporary, as well as historical, symbolism during Henry VI's long minority and the wars with France: 'Wher is our confort, our consolacioun?', the people cry, 'Wher is allas! the hed now of our kyng?' (lines 1921–2). Eventually, the people are led to the king's head, which is miraculously guiding them by shouting 'Her! Her! Her!' (line 1944) and is guarded by a wolf, who is 'foryetyng his woodnesse' (line 1950). This detail is found in multiple sources and so is not at all original to Lydgate, but the passive image of kingship and the concomitant image of the tamed wolf (replying to Lydgate's description, cited above, of Lollards in the *Defence of Holy Church* as 'mortall howndis') can be read as an advertisement for, warning of, or resignation to passive kingship: it is, to be sure, an ambiguous choice of exemplum to a young king. The episode closes with the head miraculously joining the body and a characteristically Lydgatean account of anxiety and contraries:

> Thus was ther wepyng medlyd with gladnesse,
> And ther was gladnesse medlyd with wepyng,
> And hertly sobbyng meynt with ther swetnesse,
> And soote compleyntes medlyd with sobbyng. (lines 1975–9)

Lydgate's poetry, in blending politics with religion, is characterised throughout by a 'serene poetic surface [that] tolerates a number of deeply divisive implications', to use Paul Strohm's terms (Strohm 1998: 194). The *Lives of SS Edmund and Fremund* may warn against regicide, but it does so in a way that draws uncomfortable parallels with Henry VI's minority and presages his chaotic rule. As Jennifer Sisk has argued, '[a]n uncomplicated *passio* celebrating the passivity and political execution of the saintly King Edmund would have presented a problematic model for Henry, so Lydgate dwells on Edmund's life, drawing upon the conventions of literature of advice to princes to establish Edmund as the poem's chief exemplar' (Sisk 2010: 351). In doing so, Lydgate must rely on Edmund's spiritual and posthumous power, the ongoing litany of vengeful and exclusive marvels that comprises the third part of the poem.

As well as *Lives of SS Edmund and Fremund*, Lydgate wrote numerous other poems that glorify his monastery at Bury: *To St Robert of Bury* (*NIMEV* 2399), which commemorates a local boy-saint (Bale 2006: 105–43); *The Legende of St Petronilla* (*NIMEV* 3446), a saint for whom there was a chapel and hospital at Bury (Pearsall 1970: 277; Winstead 2000: 86); *The Legend of St Gyle* (*NIMEV* 2606), which has been called 'verse propaganda' for Bury's exemptions and liberties (Gibson 1989: 33); shorter prayers to St Edmund (*NIMEV* 915, 2445), the abbey's patron saint; *On De Profundis* (*NIMEV* 1130), written for abbot Curteys 'to hang it on the wal' (Pearsall 1970: 259); versified charters (*NIMEV* 1513, 3631.55), which made various claims – largely spurious – for Bury's historical privileges (Lowe 2006).

Lives of SS Edmund and Fremund reflects the important conjunction of patronage and hagiography in Lydgate's career. Whilst Lydgate had an assured audience and patron in the community at Bury, he appears to have been rather adroit at maintaining patrons' favour during turbulent political and religious periods and also maintaining his position from which to offer counsel. In the second quarter of the fifteenth century, Lydgate's commissions appear to have spread from Bury to other patrons. In the secular poetry, patrons include various Lancastrian nobility and gentry, and in the religious poetry, a range of religious institutions: religious guilds in London (*A Procession of Corpus Christi*, *NIMEV* 3606), craft guilds in the same city (*The Legend of St George*, *NIMEV* 2592, written for the Armourers'

Guild), possibly St Leonard's Benedictine priory in Norwich (*A Prayer to St Leonard*, *NIMEV* 2812), the archdeacon John Thornton (*The Image of Our Lady*, *NIMEV* 490), and two patrons I shall briefly consider here, the Augustinians at Canterbury (*Legend of St Austin at Compton*, *NIMEV* 1875) and the Benedictines at St Albans (*Lives of SS Alban and Amphibal*, *NIMEV* 3748).

Lydgate's highly readable *Legend of St Austin at Compton*, surviving in six manuscripts, describes a miracle of St Austin [Augustine] of Canterbury (d.604), in which a horrifying ghost appears out of his tomb at Long Compton, Warwickshire. The ghost has not been able to rest in peace because he was excommunicated for non-payment of his tithes; the sight of the ghost frightens a local knight into paying his own tithes. The ghost returns to the tomb, and harmony and social order are restored. The poem, which starts with a long preamble on the history and importance of tithes, has been called 'an unabashed effort to intimidate stubborn laypeople into making a ready and generous donation of tithes' (Delany 1998: 64), and this is, assuredly, part of the poem's purpose. It is also highly nationalistic (Austin is 'Cristes Apostil in Brutis Albioun', line 88) as Lydgate describes an early figure of the English church to consolidate an especially nationalistic kind of piety whilst offering a quick history of the early English Church. The poem can be read as a characteristically Lydgatean reminder of financial and hierarchical obligations, knitted with a celebration of devotional identity and elements of Chaucerian emulation (in particular, the formulaic envoy, 'Go litil tretys' (line 401), harking back to Chaucer's *Troilus and Criseyde* V. 1786) (see further Whatley 2001).

As is the case again and again, Lydgate here translated a Latin text in a specific and highly charged context, and thus made a widely disseminated text very topical. E. Gordon Whatley has comprehensively shown how Lydgate was engaging with a fierce controversy about tithing in the late 1420s, in particular the persecution and prosecution as a heretic of William Russell, a London Franciscan, who had argued against some elements of tithe obligations (Whatley 2001: 195). Whilst Russell was not a Lollard, he was prosecuted as a heretic and his preaching caused considerable alarm; likewise, Lydgate describes the knight who will not pay tithes as 'obstynat' (line 155), 'rebel' (line 288) and 'cursed' for 'rebellioun' (lines 159–60). Lydgate's poem might contain a more direct anti-Lollard message (lines 385–92), enjoining that 'no fals Cokkyl be medlyd with good corn' (line 388); as Paul Strohm has described, cockles (in Latin, *lollium*) in good corn 'had long provided an obvious, and highly suggestive, metaphorical vehicle for orthodox distress over invasive and unwelcome doctrines' (Strohm 2000: 21–2). In listing the biblical precedents for tithing in his poem, Lydgate might therefore be seen not so much as *repeating* orthodoxy and a praise of hierarchy but *defending* and *extending* orthodoxy and the importance of hierarchy through vernacular poetry. As Whatley notes, Lydgate's poem is filled with legalistic terminology and emphasises Austin's role as bringer of spiritual *and* financial rule (Whatley 2001: 201–2); this is a devotional realm in which the worldly obligations of giving money to the Church are paramount.

No specific patronage or occasion has been identified for Lydgate's composition of the poem, although one of Lydgate's favourite subjects is the precedents offered by early English martyrs. It is worth briefly noting the poem's later life, as *The Legend of St Austin* was printed, on the eve of the Reformation in the period 1530–52, at Canterbury, its original objective of ecclesiastical defence apparently deployed as the suppression of the monasteries was under way (Boffey 2004: 260; on Lydgate in print culture more generally, see Gillespie 2006).

Walter Schirmer tenuously connected the poem's occasion to John Whetham-stede (c.1392–1465), the abbot of the erudite and influential abbey at St Albans, as in 1433 the abbey was involved in legal disputes about tithing (Schirmer 1961: 160). Whethamstede, himself an accomplished Latin author and grammarian, was certainly the prime mover behind Lydgate's composition of *Lives of SS Alban and Amphibal*. The poem was translated at Whethamstede's request in 1439 and can be seen as a counterpart to *Lives of SS Edmund and Fremund* for St Albans, another royal Benedictine house. The abbey's payment of £3 6s 8d survives (see Pearsall 1970: 283) and cryptic (but hardly subtle) references in the poem point to Whethamstede's identity, the patron being referred to as 'Sayde of an hom or a stede of whete' and 'His name braidyng on a stede of whete' (lines 897, 2999; quotations from the poem are taken from Lydgate, ed. van der Westhuizen 1974). The genesis of *Lives of SS Alban and Amphibal* is similar to that of *Lives of SS Edmund and Fremund*: the canonical life of the martyr Alban, derived from the early historians Bede and Gildas, was joined to the later and more apocryphal life of his teacher, Amphibal, in the twelfth century. The saints' legends were energetically developed under the auspices of the abbey so that, by the later thirteenth century, St Albans had an 'official' version of the lives of Alban and Amphibal, as promulgated in Latin texts by Ralph of Dunstable and Matthew Paris, in the Anglo-Norman *Vie de Seint Auban* and, later, the lives of the saints by Lydgate and Capgrave. Lydgate's direct sources were the Latin *Interpretation Guilielmi*, written after 1178 at St Albans, and the *Tractatus de Nobilitate, Vita et Martirio Albani et Amphibali* produced at St Albans in the 1390s, probably taken from a devotional compendium held at St Albans (now BL, Cotton MS Claudius E.IV; Lydgate, ed. van der Westhuizen 1974, 45). As at Bury, Lydgate was there-fore responsible for the production of an institutionally sanctioned biography, in which monastic identity was directly confirmed and promoted in vernacular poetry. Like Bury, St Albans vigorously sought to develop a distinctive spiritual identity that justified and extended ecclesiastical lordship over land and people (see Carlson 2003; Clark 2004).

Given that Lydgate's poem was produced under the auspices of an institu-tion that may be regarded as at the apogee of late medieval monastic culture – a wealthy, royal abbey with impeccable learned credentials – and given that it was evidently a popular poem, surviving in six manuscripts and printed in 1534 (*STC* 17025), remarkably little scholarly work has been done on *Lives of SS Alban and Amphibal* in recent years (Pearsall 1970: 284, has a low opinion of the poem, ascribing to it 'a repetitiveness so limp and so pointless as to be noticeable even in Lydgate'). This is surprising, as both the political context of the poem's commission and the distinctively Lydgatean additions to the legend are of some interest. Lydgate again moves away from the traditional voice of the hagiogra-pher to adopt that of the princely advisor, repeatedly insisting on the importance of political, not clerical, harmony:

Make providence that no division
Fil vnwarly on hih or lowe estate,
Which causid hath gret dissolucion,
Made many a Reaume to be Infortunate;
For wher as striff contynueth or debate,
Bi experience of many gret Cite,
The liht enclipsid of thei felicite. (lines 393–9)

So, unlike other late medieval religious writers, for Lydgate poetic composition was not a withdrawal from the world, but rather a direct engagement with state-craft, class and political expedience. Throughout Lydgate's poetry, the political and the religious converge and reconverge, 'a union of religious imagery with more resolutely secular concerns' (Strohm 2005: 205).

To close, I want to consider one of Lydgate's significant innovations in religious poetry. The 'material turn' in criticism has been particularly beneficial in Lydgate studies, as so much of his religious poetry appeared in mediated spaces outside the codex. This awareness of the material contexts of Lydgate's poetry accompanies a growing awareness of the importance of Lydgate's audiences (whereas previous criticism focused on issues concerned with patronage and authorship).

Several shorter poems by Lydgate are designed for visual contemplation. *Testament*, with its account of Lydgate's conversion-by-vision, describes the normal mystical method, privileging devotional vision ('having in mind' and 'beholding'), exploiting what Shannon Gayk has called 'the affective potential of images' (Gayk 2010: 96). Extracts from *Testament* and other Lydgate verses appeared as part of the elaborate design of the Clopton family's chantry chapel at Long Melford (Suffolk), built about thirty years after Lydgate's death, painted on to wooden 'pages' to form a literary frieze in which the Clopton family were surrounded by Lydgate's poetry as they prayed (Trapp 1955: 1–11; Griffith 2011). Similarly, the *Legend of St George* is said to have been painted on wall-hangings at the Armourers' Hall in London (see Floyd 2008). A particularly potent example is furnished by the now-lost *Dance of Macabre* (*NIMEV* 2590, 2591; see Lydgate, ed. Warren 1931) by Lydgate at Old St Paul's, London.

Lydgate had visited Paris in 1426 and seen the *Danse Macabre* painted at the church of the Holy Innocents. He seems to have already translated it when in 1430 John Carpenter (c.1377–1442), Town Clerk of London 1417–38, requested Lydgate to have the verses of the *Danse Macabre* inscribed on the wall at the Pardon churchyard at St Paul's, London, where Carpenter had a chantry. Pearsall comments that Lydgate was 'particularly active in exploring this borderland of word and picture, though he did so quite unconsciously and would not have been aware of a borderland' (Pearsall 1970: 179; see also Appleford 2008). The varied mediated and performative spaces of Lydgate's poetry provide an important and exciting direction for Lydgate studies; as Lisa Cooper and Andrea Denny-Brown have argued, 'Lydgate's poetry considers the role of material goods and the material world in the formation of late-medieval identity and culture' (Cooper and Denny-Brown 2008: 1).

The poem closes in Lydgate's characteristic voice, poised between self-advertisement and conventional embarrassment:

Owte of the frensshe I drowe hit of entent
Not worde be worde but folwyng the substaunce
And fro Paris to Inglond hit sent
Oneli of purpose ȝow to do plesaunce
Rude of langage y was not borne yn fraunce
Haue me excused my name is Jon Lidgate
Of her tunge I haue no suffisaunce
Her corious metris In Inglissh to translate. Amen. (lines 665–72)

The public setting of the *Dance of Death* is concomitant with Lydgate's important contribution more generally to widening the literary audience, as described by Maura Nolan. Nolan argues that Lydgate 'sought to expand the audience for Chaucerian writing' but, paradoxically, did so in ways that represent, speak for and aspires to the ruling elite, both clerical and royal (Nolan 2005: 4). These lines resonate with Lydgate's self-advertisement, but they also point to his inexhaustible fascination with 'corious metris' and the registers of 'langage'. In the mural *Dance of Death*, Lydgate's poetry marked the physical aspect of London, a poetry of and on the cityscape, the vernacular word embodied in sacred space, showing how vernacular poetry had become one of the principal ways of describing and shaping the private self in the public sphere.

Works cited

Appleford, Amy, 'The Dance of Death in London: John Carpenter, John Lydgate, and the *Daunce of Poulys*', *Journal of Medieval and Early Modern Studies*, 38 (2008), 285–314

Bale, Anthony, *The Jew in the Medieval Book: English Antisemitisms 1350–1500* (Cambridge, 2006)

——, 2009a. 'A Norfolk Gentlewoman and Lydgatian Patronage: Lady Sibylle Boys and her Cultural Environment', *Medium Aevum*, 78 (2009), 394–413

——, 2009b. 'St Edmund in Fifteenth-Century London: The Lydgatian *Miracles of St Edmund*', in *St Edmund King and Martyr: Changing Images of a Medieval Saint*, ed. Anthony Bale (York, 2009), pp. 145–61

Boffey, Julia, 'John Mychell and the Printing of Lydgate in the 1530s', *Huntington Library Quarterly*, 67 (2004), 251–60

Carlson, David R., 'Whethamstede on Lollardy: Latin Styles and the Vernacular Cultures of Early Fifteenth-Century England', *Journal of English and Germanic Philology*, 102 (2003), 21–41

Clark, James G., *A Monastic Renaissance at St Albans: Thomas Walsingham and his Circle c.1350–1440* (Oxford, 2004)

Cole, Andrew, *Literature and Heresy in the Age of Chaucer* (Cambridge, 2008)

Cooper, Lisa H., and Andrea Denny-Brown, 'Introduction: Lydgate Matters', in *Lydgate Matters: Poetry and Material Culture in the Fifteenth Century*, eds Lisa H. Cooper and Andrea Denny-Brown (New York, 2008), pp. 1–11

Delany, Sheila, *Impolitic Bodies: Poetry, Saints, and Society in Fifteenth-Century England: The Work of Osbern Bokenham* (New York, 1998)

Edwards, A. S. G., 'John Lydgate's *Lives of Ss Edmund and Fremund*: Politics, Hagiography and Literature', in *St Edmund King and Martyr: Changing Images of a Medieval Saint*, ed. Anthony Bale (York, 2009), pp. 133–44

Floyd, Jennifer, 'St. George and the "Steyned Halle": Lydgate's Verse for the London Armourers' in *Lydgate Matters: Poetry and Material Culture in the Fifteenth Century*, eds Lisa H. Cooper and Andrea Denny-Brown, pp. 139–64

Galloway, Andrew, 'John Lydgate and the Origins of Vernacular Humanism', *Journal of English and Germanic Philology*, 107 (2008), 445–71

Gayk, Shannon, *Image, Text and Religious Reform in Fifteenth-Century England* (Cambridge, 2010)

Gibson, Gail McMurray, 'Bury St Edmunds, Lydgate, and the N-Town Cycle', *Speculum*, 56 (1981), 56–90

——, *Theater of Devotion: East Anglian Drama and Society in the Late Middle Ages* (Chicago, 1989)

Gillespie, Alexandra, *Print Culture and the Medieval Author: Chaucer, Lydgate and their Books, 1473–1557* (Oxford, 2006)

Gransden, Antonia, 'The Legends and Traditions Concerning the Origins of the Abbey of Bury St Edmunds', *English Historical Review*, 100 (1985), 1–24

——, 'Curteys, William (*d.* 1446)', *Oxford Dictionary of National Biography* (Oxford, 2004) <http://www.oxforddnb.com/view/article/54428> [accessed 2 Jan 2012]

Gray, Douglas, 'Lydgate, John (*c.*1370–1449/50?)', *Oxford Dictionary of National Biography* (Oxford, 2004) <http://www.oxforddnb.com/view/article/17238. [accessed 7 Jan 2012]

Griffith, David, 'A Newly Identified Verse Item by John Lydgate at Holy Trinity Church, Long Melford, Suffolk', *Notes and Queries*, 58 (2011), 364–7

Hardman, Phillipa, 'Lydgate's *Life of Our Lady*: A Text in Transition', *Medium Aevum*, 65 (1996), 248–68

Horner, Patrick J., 'The King Taught Us the Lesson': Benedictine Support for Henry V's Suppression of the Lollards', *Mediaeval Studies*, 52 (1990), 190–220

Lawton, David, 'Dullness and the Fifteenth Century', *English Literary History*, 54 (1987), 761–99

Lewis, Katherine J., 'Edmund of East Anglia, Henry VI and Ideals of Kingly Masculinity', in *Holiness and Masculinity in the Middle Ages*, eds P. H. Cullum and Katherine J. Lewis (Cardiff, 2009), pp. 158–73

Lowe, Kathryn A., 'The Poetry of Privilege: Lydgates *Cartae Versificatae*', *Nottingham Medieval Studies*, 50 (2006), 151–65

Lydgate, John, *The Minor Poems of John Lydgate, Part One: The Religious Poems*, ed. Henry Noble MacCracken, EETS, e. s. 107 (London, 1910)

——, *The Dance of Death*, ed. Florence Warren, EETS, o. s. 181 (London, 1931)

——, *John Lydgate: Poems*, ed. John Norton-Smith (Oxford, 1966)

——, *The Life of Saint Alban and Saint Amphibal*, ed. J. E. van der Westhuizen (Leiden, 1974)

——, *John Lydgate's Lives of SS Edmund and Fremund with the Extra Miracles of St Edmund*, eds Anthony Bale and A. S. G. Edwards (Heidelberg, 2009)

Meyer-Lee, Robert J., 'The Emergence of the Literary in John Lydgate's *Life of Our Lady*', *Journal of English and Germanic Philology*, 109 (2010), 322–48

Mortimer, Nigel, *John Lydgate's 'Fall of Princes': Narrative Tragedy in its Literary and Political Contexts* (Oxford, 2005)

Nolan, Maura, *John Lydgate and the Making of Public Culture* (Cambridge, 2005)

O'Sullivan, Katherine K., 'John Lydgate's *Lyf of Our Lady*: Translation and Authority in Fifteenth-Century England', *Mediaevalia*, 26 (2005), 169–201

Parr, J., 'The Astronomical Date of Lydgate's *Life of Our Lady*', *Philological Quarterly*, 50 (1971), 120–5

Patterson, Lee, 'Making Identities in Fifteenth-Century England: Henry V and John Lydgate', in *New Historical Literary Study: Essays on Reproducing Texts, Representing History*, eds Jeffrey N. Cox and Larry J. Reynolds (Princeton, NJ, 1993), pp. 67–107

Pearsall, Derek, *John Lydgate* (London, 1970)

——, 'Lydgate as Innovator', *Modern Language Quarterly*, 53 (1992), 5–22

——, *John Lydgate (1371–1449): A Bio-Bibliography* (Victoria, BC, 1997)

Rogers, Nicholas J., 'Fitzwilliam Museum MS 3–1979: A Bury St Edmunds Book of Hours and the Origins of the Bury Style', in *England in the Fifteenth Century: Proceedings of the 1986 Harlaxton Symposium*, ed. D. Williams (Woodbridge, 1987), pp. 229–43

Schirmer, Walter, *John Lydgate: A Study in the Culture of the XVth Century*, trans. Ann E. Keep (Westport, CT, 1961)

Scott, Kathleen L., 'Lydgate's Lives of Saints Edmund and Fremund: A Newly-Located Manuscript in Arundel Castle', *Viator*, 13 (1982), 335–66

Simpson, James, 'Bulldozing the Middle Ages: The Case of John Lydgate', *New Medieval Literatures*, 4 (2001), 213–42

Sisk, Jennifer, 'Lydgate's Problematic Commission: A Legend of St. Edmund for Henry VI', *Journal of English and Germanic Philology*, 109 (2010), 349–75

Somerset, Fiona, '"Hard is with seyntis for to make affray": Lydgate the "Poet-Propagandist" as Hagiographer', in *John Lydgate: Poetry, Culture, and Lancastrian England*, eds Larry Scanlon and James Simpson (Notre Dame, IN, 2005), pp. 258–78

Strohm, Paul, *England's Empty Throne: Usurpation and the Language of Legitimation, 1399–1422* (New Haven, CT, 1998)

——, *Theory and the Premodern Text* (Minneapolis, MN, 2000)

——, *Politique: Languages of Statecraft between Chaucer and Shakespeare* (Notre Dame, IN, 2005)

Trapp, J. B., 'Verses by Lydgate at Long Melford', *Review of English Studies*, 21 (1955), 1–11

Watson, Nicholas, 'Censorship and Cultural Change in Late-Medieval England: Vernacular Theology, the Oxford Translation Debate, and Arundel's Constitutions of 1409', *Speculum*, 70 (1995), 822–64

Whatley, E. Gordon, 'John Lydgate's *Saint Austin at Compton*: The Poem and its Sources', in *Anglo-Latin and its Heritage: Essays in Honour of A. G. Rigg on his 64th Birthday*, eds Siân Echard and Gernot R. Wieland (Turnhout, 2001), pp. 191–227

Winstead, Karen A., ed. and trans., *Chaste Passions: Medieval English Virgin Martyr Legends* (Ithaca, NY, 2000)

7

John Lydgate's Shorter Secular Poems

JOANNA MARTIN

The number of short secular poems associated reliably with John Lydgate (c.1370–1449) is considerable. However, despite the variety of Lydgate's shorter verse in style, subject matter and genre, its critical reception has been mixed and his shorter poems are often neglected in favour of his more ambitious works such as *Siege of Thebes*, *Troy Book* and *Fall of Princes*. The only critical edition of Lydgate's collected 'minor' poems, secular and religious, is that by Henry Noble MacCracken, made for the Early English Text Society in the early decades of the twentieth century (Lydgate, ed. MacCracken 1934; see also Lydgate, ed. Norton Smith 1966; Lydgate, ed. Sponsler 2010). The poems are not always accurately transcribed, there is no commentary, and MacCracken was unaware of some witnesses. Critical analysis of these poems has been intermittent apart from Pearsall (1970).

This critical and editorial neglect is surprising above all because Lydgate was immensely popular as a writer of short secular, as well as religious, verse during his lifetime and well into the sixteenth century. He seems to have had an eye for a bestseller in short-poem terms: he composed in all the popular forms of the time, including lyric complaint, parental advice literature, beast fable, historical narrative, debate, and estates and anti-feminist satire, and also wrote 'mummings' or 'disguisings' – important early dramatic texts usually intended for household performance (Dillon 2006: 39) – and poetic accounts of public celebrations. His patronage by the social and political elite of Lancastrian England was extensive, and his shorter poems, on the evidence of manuscripts and prints, also appealed to all of the reading public of fifteenth-century England: aristocrats, gentry, merchants, wealthy London citizens and guildsmen, clergy, men and women, are represented amongst his audience. Indeed, although a few of Lydgate's short poems survive in single witnesses, many were widely circulated: *A Dietary*, for example, survives in fifty-seven witnesses. The short poems lent themselves to anthologising in family or household miscellanies and anthologies, as is suggested by the appearances they make in the contents of collections such as the holster book, Bodl., MS Ashmole 61, the family-owned Findern Manuscript (CUL, MS Ff.1.6), compiled in Derbyshire, and Richard Hill's commonplace book (Oxford, Balliol College, MS 354), which was copied in the household of a merchant in Tudor London. Some of Lydgate's short poems were printed individually as inexpensive pamphlets by Wynkyn de Worde, William Caxton and William Copland, presumably both reflecting and increasing their popularity

(Boffey and Edwards 1999: 559, 566; Gillespie 2006: 46–7, 144–86). Some of the short poems had a life as inscriptional verse displayed on church walls or, as is apparently the case with the misogynistic beast fable *Bycorne and Chychevache*, on wall hangings or paintings in private houses (Lydgate, ed. Sponsler 2010).

Lydgate's preference for fashionable literary forms as a way of reaching his audiences has endeared him less to modern readers, resulting in accusations of conventionality (Pearsall 1970: 14). Yet, Lydgate's short poems engage with a range of themes and subjects in a way that is often subtle and challenging. Questions of governance, both royal and moral, preoccupy him in his lyric, short narrative and occasional poems, as suited his association with the Lancastrian political elite and the responsibilities bestowed on him by his monastic duties. Didacticism is important to his work, though is seldom delivered in a manner that makes it completely uncomplicated or unstimulating for the reader. He is also repeatedly concerned in his short poems with the role of the poet, both in political and societal, as well as literary terms. Only a few examples of his shorter verse can be discussed in this chapter; his treatment of the themes of governance and the role of poetry will be the focus of the following overview of this part of Lydgate's literary output.

The Complaint of the Black Knight (sometimes known by an early print title as 'A Complaint of a Lover's Life'), is usually dated, along with several short poems on courtly love themes, including *The Floure of Curtesy*, to the early part of Lydgate's career. It is one of the best known of the shorter poems and – given its connections to a literary past, its self-conscious literariness, and its interest in the poet's creative and moral role – it is a good place to begin. For modern readers, its attraction has resided in its connections with Chaucer's love visions to which it provides a response in its own exploration of the nature of love and the usefulness of literary complaint, themes that continued to occupy Lydgate, as more ambitious works such as *The Temple of Glass* illustrate. In the fifteenth and sixteenth centuries it also seems to have been relatively widely read, surviving in early printed versions, one a Scottish print (that by Chepman and Myllar, 1508, *STC* 17014.3), and one by Wynkyn de Worde (1531, *STC* 17014.7), a group of closely related English manuscripts, and three Scottish manuscripts that contain corrupt versions of the poem, which are nonetheless important because of the evidence they provide of the reception of Lydgate's work (Edwards 2010) beyond East Anglia, London and the south of England. In the Scottish witnesses the poem is attributed to Chaucer (and given the title 'The Maying and Disport of Chaucer'), but there are attributions to Lydgate in three earlier manuscript witnesses (Lydgate, ed. MacCracken 1934: 282).

The poem's setting is an idealised May landscape, described, after the introduction of the sorrowful first-person narrator, in aureate detail. The narrator walks into a wood to hear bird song, and finding an enclosed park enters it and pauses at 'a litel welle' (line 75). Refreshed, he retreats to 'an erber grene' (line 125). He finds he is not alone there for the arbour is already sanctuary to a pale, but distinguished-looking, individual, dressed in black. Observing him from a hiding place the narrator notices that 'To speke of manhod' he is 'oon the best on lyve' (line 158), but that he is afflicted by some kind of sickness. After protestations of his own dullness of wit, he offers to rehearse the 'ful high sentence' (line 213) of the man's lament 'as doth a skryuener' (line 194), appealing for the audience's patience. Over three hundred lines of complaint follow: the cold disdain of the complainer's lady is the cause of his grief, and in conventional allegorical terms he represents himself as a victim of envy and falsehood. When he has compared his plight to that of other faithful but rejected (male) lovers, the plaintiff departs for a lodge where it is his custom each May to lament his pain. We are left with the narrator who writes down what he has heard and, after a prayer to Venus for mercy on the knight, returns home. The poem concludes with a dedicatory envoy, which survives in two different versions (one addressed to a 'Princess') in the witnesses.

The main source for the poem's scenario is undoubtedly Chaucer's *The Book of the Duchess*, although other sources are also interwoven with the many references to this and other works by Chaucer (Edwards 1985: 175–82). However, Lydgate's poem is very far from being simply imitative of Chaucer and is distinguished from *The Book of the Duchess* in narrative and structure, as well as in the handling of certain themes. This reveals a response to Chaucer and an attempt to explore what it means to be a poet.

Lydgate's poem, unlike *The Book of the Duchess*, is not a dream vision. Sleep comes for the narrator after the act of writing down the knight's complaint has been completed (line 652), rather than, as in Chaucer's *The Book of the Duchess*, being shaken off in a renewed creative energy that allows the composition of the poem. In Chaucer's love visions, dreaming and the dream are metaphors for the act of composing and for the poem itself: dreams foreground important questions about interpretation and truth for Chaucer, who was well acquainted with and interested in medieval dream theory stemming from Macrobius. Lydgate chooses not to exploit the ambiguity or creativity of the dream form: such suffering is not the thing of dreams and neither its severity nor consequences are open to interpretation. Furthermore, his narrator, unlike Chaucer's, never interacts with the complainant. No attempt is made by the narrator to do anything but silently sympathise with the man from 'Amonge the bowes' (line 583). Consequently, no resolution is found within the poem for the man's suffering, but it is deferred to some future time dependent on the workings of a planetary deity. We are told that the man makes his complaint every May, and will presumably continue to do so, unless the narrator's appeal to Venus for mercy is efficacious: this, we as readers will never know.

The poem's view of love is deeply pessimistic. Unlike in *The Book of the Duchess*, where the man in Black has won his lady's love, albeit only to enjoy it for a short time before her death, there is no indication in Lydgate's poem that the complainer has ever made any progress in his affair, despite his assertion of his fidelity. All profitable human actions, the complainer insists, using figures from literary tradition to prove his point, are despised by love:

> Trwe menyng, awayte, or besynesse,
> Stil[le] port ne feythful attendaunce,
> Manhode ne myght in armes worthinesse,
> Pursute of wurschip, nor [no] high provesse
> [...]
> Ful lyte or noght in love dothe avayle. (lines 408–13)

There is misogyny here too, for while the knight claims that his lady is peer-less, his account of her as impressionable and unable to recognise faithful service is hardly flattering. This attitude is found in other short poems by Lydgate on the dangers of loving women, such as the catalogue of false women, *Examples Against Women*, or *The Pain and Sorrow of an Evil Marriage*, which celebrates the escape of its narrator from any lasting commitment to his beloved thanks to the numerous authorities who revealed to him the untrustworthiness of women. But ultimately, *The Complaint of the Black Knight* also leaves the reader with a sense that the lover's judgement is poor and his self-pity ill advised. Indeed, the poem's portrayal of human love is cautionary, urging the reader to consider the true nature of intemperate and uncontrolled desire and its consequences. The fact that the complaint is not heard by the narrator in a dream vision, but in his own waking world, seems to underpin the bleakness of this assessment.

The divergences in *The Complaint of the Black Knight* from Chaucer's *The Book of the Duchess* focus attention on individual morality in love, but also on literary matters. In literary terms, the poem suggests love lament to be highly claustro-phobic and unproductive as a literary form. The narrator's inability to engage directly with the complainant confirms this stasis: what can be said to comfort one so immersed in self pity? As well as reading like a rejection of love, the poem is an expression of doubt on the efficacy of writing in the comfort of lovers. And, as others have noted, the separateness of narrator and complainer is also part of Lydgate's exploration of the relationship between the 'master' (poet) and his pupil, and as such provides some insight into Lydgate's ambitions as a lyric poet following on from an august generation. As A. C. Spearing puts it: 'On the level of the poem's fiction, the master whom he copies is the knight, whose words he writes as he hears them [...] on the level of the image, the master is of course Chaucer' (Spearing 1993: 227). Perhaps more to the point, the narrator's inability to engage with the complainer and do anything but, in a dull-witted way (he claims), transcribe his words, reflects a feeling of distance between the writer and the 'origins' of the poetry (Chaucer's legacy) – a comment on the way in which recent tradition and current fashion force the new poet to write in a particular mode that is estranging and not morally enriching.

There are other literary, as well as moral, concerns reflected in the poem's nega-tive presentation of love. The knight's complaint is largely concerned with the disregard for truth and dangers of false accusation. Try as he might, complaining each May, the truth of his words is simply not heard by his lady and this figures the poet's frustration at the power of false tales ('Lesynges') and 'flaterye' (line 421) above his own attempts to present the truth on the subject of love. Even though the poet's complaint about the attractions of flattery and falsity, above truth, is a conventional one, Lydgate's dependence on patronage throughout his career gives it particular resonance as he subtly recasts fashionable Chaucerian devices to produce a sophisticated rather than dully imitative poem.

The literary tensions and the thematic austerity of *The Complaint of the Black Knight* in its handling of the subject of love and interrogation of love complaint, are made more apparent in comparison with Lydgate's *The Temple of Glass*, a dream vision indebted to Chaucer's *The House of Fame* as well as to *The Book of the Duchess*, which is also dominated by complaint – this time of a male and female plaintiff to a benign Venus – again overheard by a disconsolate narrator. *The Temple of Glass* is more structurally complex than the *Complaint*, consisting of a series of laments, supplications and inset ballades, and as such constructs an alternative narrative in which the despair of love complaint gives way, through the request for and receiving of advice, to self-knowledge, a degree of self governance, and the grateful acceptance of patient suffering in the hope of amelioration. The lady's complaint against the cruelty of 'jalousye' (line 342) is met by Venus' assurance that as she is 'voyde of al offence' (line 373), that her 'pacyent' (line 379) prayers will be answered in time. The goddess also indicates that no happiness comes without suffering: 'Thus ende of sorowe is joye, yvoyde of drede' (line 406). The 'lesson' (line 952) given by Venus to the man reminds him that, as his lady's 'cherisshing/ Shal be so grounded upon al honestee' (line 890), he must 'Lat resoun brydell lust' (line 898). His ensuing 'balade' indicates his willingness to accept and follow her counsel, and both are rewarded by the goddess' blessing on their unwavering love. The specifics of their situation are not disclosed (though an unhappy marriage from which the lady must await release before joining her beloved is hinted at) but the narrator emphasises throughout their virtue and growing self-restraint as they learn to love honestly. The ambig-uous ending to the vision, in which the waking narrator seems less able than the participants in his vision to embrace the virtues of patience and hope, serves to emphasise the hopelessness of stagnation and self-pity in contrast to the moral development of the complainants. It seems that in this poem, which is possibly later than the *Complaint* (*Fifteenth-Century English Dream Visions*, ed. Boffey 2003: 16), Lydgate has found a way of reconciling the need to write about love as a subject for fashionable (and commissioned) verse and, in the way he addresses his theme, his desire to distinguish his poetic voice from that of Chaucer. The poem also anticipates the concern with the methods and value of advice-giving, and the importance of self-reform, found in many of his later works.

Like *The Complaint of the Black Knight*, the less well-known poem *The Churl and the Bird* is concerned with the role of the poet and the relationship between the poet and reader. It was popular with early readers (Simpson 2006: 134), surviving in fifteen manuscripts, and was printed by Caxton in 1477 (*STC* 17008) and de Worde in 1510 (*STC* 17012). It is a fusion of the genres of beast fable and debate, rather like Lydgate's later poem, *The Debate of the Horse, Goose and Sheep*. The narrator claims to be translating from French (Wolfgang 1995; Cartlidge 1997), and he opens the poem by insisting on the 'fructuous […] sentence' (line 2) of 'liknessis' (line 29) – fables. He thus situates the poem within a tradition of didactic literature that is efficacious by virtue of being pleasurable to read – a tradition Lydgate also celebrated in the prologue to his *Isopes Fabules*. However, although the story appears simple, its teaching is elusive and the process of reading is complicated rather than pleasurable. The fable tells how a churl catches a bird in his garden but the bird convinces him to release her in return for the gift of 'Thre greete wisdames' (line 159). On her escape, she lectures the churl on his folly, telling him that he has just forfeited the possession of a precious stone that is to be found inside her, and provoking in him remorse and regret. Then she adds insult to injury by telling him that, in fact, there is no such precious stone after all, and he was even more of a fool to believe her words than he was when he let her go. She tells him that it is impossible 'To teche a cherl termys of gentilnesse' (line 343).

The first part of the fable – the bird's capture and release – reads as a discussion of the relationship between the poet and the patron or reader. The bird explains to the churl that her freedom is more important to her than any material luxury she might be able to enjoy in captivity, and if she is 'in distresse,/ [She] can-nat syng, nor make no gladnesse' (lines 90–1). Her words cast the relationship between the poet and reader/patron as one of negotiation: if the churl wants to enjoy her music he must do so by allowing it to flourish naturally rather than by trying to control it. In return for freedom to sing as she wishes, the bird promises advice and wisdom – something to be cherished by the reader, especially one in a position of power: 'Yiff thou wilt on-to my rede assesnt […] I shal the yeve a notable gret gwerdoun' (lines 155–9).

As Helen Barr points out, the diction of *The Churl and the Bird* frequently 'figures the relationship between patron and writer as ruler and ruled' (Barr 2001: 194). The fable form is introduced by the narrator as being a way in which poets explore political relationships: how 'Som […] haue lordship, & som […] obey' (line 21). However, this use of a language of power to describe the poet/reader relationship becomes more complex as the story unfolds. The fact that the patron/reader figure is a churl, albeit one who has a cultivated garden and can offer the bird a pretty cage, requires careful interpretation. This is no king or prince who wants the bird to sing in obedience to him. Indeed, the intellectual lordship resides with the bird for much of the poem. It seems that the association of the churl with uncouth ignorance is a sharp rebuke to those without the intelligence to appreciate poetry but who nonetheless want to make it subject to their whims (and wealth?) – an apparent challenge to the 'maistir' (line 380) to whom the envoy directs the poem. Yet poets don't come out of the poem well either. The bird as poet and teacher is problematic and unreliable, and despite her early negotiating skills clearly wants to have everything on her terms. On her release, the bird urges the churl to 'Trust' her (line 162) and yet she still subjects him to trickery and mockery. Her trickery is a test of sorts: once she has offered her gifts of wisdom, she tests the churl to see if he has learnt anything. She has told him to consider everything with reason and prudence, because 'Mong many talis is many grett lesyng' (line 200); to not wish for the impossible or to desire to climb above one's station; never to be sorrowful for things lost. When she pretends to have a jewel concealed in her body, he proves his lack of heed for her words by his hasty response, desire to be rich, and regret at having freed her. Although she is testing the churl, she does so with a 'grett lesyng', and the nature of her test certainly doesn't help him to learn anything. Her parting shot – that you can't teach 'gentilnesse' to a churl – potentially turns the lesson into a matter of class conduct rather than morality, although 'gentilnesse' is complicated in its polysemy (*MED*, s.v. 'gentilesse, n.'). The bird presents herself as the one who learns from her experience: on her release she notes that 'now that I sich daungers am askapid,/ I wole bewar' (lines 190–1). In conclusion she acknowledges the hopelessness of everything she has just done: 'Whoo serveth a cherl hath many a carful day' (line 361). The reader in the text has many shortcomings, but the poet appears to be engaging in a didactic project that is of no help to the audience but merely of benefit to himself.

These poems show Lydgate examining the role of the poet and the poet's relationship to literary tradition and to the demands of readers and patrons. His poems with clearer links to a particular individual must allow for expressions of deference and support for the patron or distinguished subject. However, it would be wrong to assume that such poems are only sycophantic. One interesting example is his often-neglected *Guy of Warwick* (c.1425?). According to the rubrics in BL, MS Harley 7333 and Harvard, Houghton, MS Eng. 530 (both derived from copies made by the scribe John Shirley), Lydgate wrote the poem for Margaret, daughter of the Earl of Warwick, whose ancestor the poem commemorates. The poem makes no effort to praise Margaret's father, Richard Beauchamp, Earl of Warwick, even though he was a distinguished soldier, an important figure in the minority of Henry VI, and commissioned other works by Lydgate. Instead, all emphasis is on the historical exemplum provided by Guy of Warwick for his living descendants, subtly reminding them of the ideals they must aspire to. This chronicle-based account of Guy's combat with a Danish champion during the Viking attacks of Athelstan's reign is highly topical. The story is of God's intervention in a political crisis, which cannot be solved by the desperate king or his councillors. As his instrument, God uses the ageing and pious Guy, who has just returned to England after a pilgrimage. Guy's identity is hidden from the king until after his triumph, and even then is only revealed in private. Guy refuses reward, and retires to a hermitage, rejecting further involvement in public life: he exemplifies loyal service without concern for personal gain in terms of money or power. Thus the poem sets high standards for those engaged in service of king and country and is highly relevant to England's predicament in the years after Henry V's death (Edwards 2007: 86–93).

Neither are Lydgate's occasional poems merely dutiful. The poem on Thomas Chaucer's departure to France on ambassadorial duties in 1417 belongs to an established tradition of propemticon (see Lydgate, ed. Norton-Smith 1966: 119), but is nevertheless tender rather than formal in its expressions of sympathy for those members of the household and circle who will be deprived of Chaucer's hospitality and friendship. The prayers offered for his safe return are made with feeling:

> And for my part, I sey right as I thenk,
> I am pure sory and hevy in myn hert,
> More þan I expresse can wryte with inke (lines 71–3).

It is perhaps no coincidence that this poem, which is clearly rather personal in nature, survives in only one manuscript.

The difficulty of writing for certain patrons is evident in a number of poems addressed to Lydgate's major patron, Humfrey, Duke of Gloucester. Lydgate's pecuniary petition known as the *Letter to Gloucester* is both witty and direct and contains little flattery after the opening address to the 'myghty prynce' (line 1). Motivated by Duke Humfrey's overdue payments for *Fall of Princes*, it first depicts the narrator in mourning for his personified purse whose illness is described with humorous hyperbole. The purse has had a severe case of diar-

rhoea, fever and consumption – its 'guttys wer out shake' (line 7) and a laxa-
tive has only made matters worse. The images of sickness combine with nautical
images (depicting the narrator as a drifting ship) and then financial, mercantile
and alchemical imagery and punning: gold coinage is the light that is needed to
brighten the purse's darkness, and is a restorative 'cordial' (line 44) for the acute
indigence suffered by the narrator and his purse. The narrator rather pointedly
makes clear that payment in instalments does not represent complete remuneration, and often threatens business agreements. Here again, the poet explores the
relationship of poet and patron in terms of power and negotiation.

In other poems, Lydgate's attempts to please patrons only thinly disguise his
doubts about potential problems in their ambitions: the difficulty of balancing
the demands of patronage with the duty of the poet to offer constructive advice
is keenly felt (Straker 2006: 107). The poem *On Gloucester's Approaching Marriage*
(1422–3), for example, is superficially a celebration of the virtues of the Duke
and his bride-to-be, Jacqueline of Hainault, (technically still married to the Duke
of Brabant) and jubilantly anticipatory of the lands that 'we may atteyne' (line
54) through the match of the heiress and the Duke. However, this poem begins
unsettlingly with a reference to uncertainty and political misfortune (Henry V's
untimely death in 1422 was probably in Lydgate's mind), which must be guarded
against by good marriages and the pursuit of peace as a political goal. Lydgate's
mention of Henry V's marriage to Katherine of France as an example of a match
to resolve conflict underlines the sense of anxiety in the poem: ironically, any
positive effects of this union could be destroyed by Humfrey's marital plans.
Gloucester's marriage was politically unwise, putting Duke Humfrey and the
Duke of Bedford on contrary lines of foreign policy by threatening the Burgundian alliance that was crucial to English interests in France after Henry V's death.
Lydgate's praise of Humfrey's 'wisdame and prudence' (line 126) in the poem
may be read as a pointed reminder to the Duke of how carefully he should behave.
And Lydgate was prescient in his veiled caution here: the marriage lasted only a
few years, as his subsequent poem *A Complaint for My Lady of Gloucester*, written
on the departure of Jacqueline, reminds us.

Other occasional poems reveal Lydgate to be a more complex poet in his
attitudes to power and to advice-giving than conventional accounts of him as
'poet-propagandist' (Pearsall 1970: 169; contrast Straker 2006) for the Lancastrian
regime suggest. Lydgate's poems addressed to Henry VI, including those on his
coronation and entry in London in 1430–32, are revealing about Lydgate's view
of the public role of the poet as commentator and advisor to those in power.
At their simplest, these poems – *The Title and Pedigree of Henry VI* (1426) for
example, which was commissioned by the Duke of Bedford – seek to legitimise
the still relatively young Lancastrian dynasty, which had just been deprived of
an energetic and popular monarch, and found itself with a minor to succeed to
the crowns of England and France. The *Ballade to King Henry VI*, written to mark
Henry's coronation, is a *speculum principis* poem reminding the young Henry
VI to be pious, just but merciful, charitable, and of sound judgement. Henry is
instructed to take example from figures from history and literary traditions such
as the Nine Worthies, but also from his father, who should be 'þy myrrour and
þy guyde' (line 402). Paul Strohm has described Lydgate's approach in this poem

and others addressed to Henry as 'to soar over problems in high generalities' (Strohm 1998: 180). However, in the *Ballade*, Lydgate does not avoid reminding Henry of the pressing concerns of his realm, such as the spread of Lollardy. And, his recommendation that Henry 'Preferre þe pees, [and] eschuwe werre and debate' (line 126) reminds the reader that although the dead king, Henry V, may have been an exemplary knight, whose governance of England and conquests in France made him a successful and admired king (Watts 1996: 113), his death at war has left England vulnerable – with the poem's infant addressee as monarch. It is worth remembering David Lawton's persuasive thesis that the poets of the Lancastrian period frequently adopted a posture of predictable conventionality in order to give pertinent advice to their patrons (Lawton 1987).

The *Ballade* warns Henry to 'eschuwe flaterye and adulacioun' (line 141) and such advice would have been excellent preparation for him when he received the welcome of his people on his return to England. Lydgate's poem on Henry VI's entry to London in February 1432 (when Henry was about 10 years old and no longer formally under protectorate), after two years in France, describes the finely dressed dignitaries who greeted the king, and the fountains of wine, rows of laden fruit trees, and seven elaborate pageants displayed at locations around the city. Lydgate probably witnessed the event, though he also used a Latin letter by London's town clerk, John Carpenter, as a source (Nolan 2005: 234). The poem's account of London's elaborate festivities shows how they are intended to give advice as well as salutation to the king: the pageants show Henry being invested with the gifts of wisdom, piety and justice. The giving of these gifts emphasises his youth and the importance of his education if he is to be worthy of his office. So although the coronation *Ballade* and *Henry VI's Triumphal Entry into London* are in many ways conventional, celebratory and legitimising, they also emphasise for the king the high expectations of his devoted people for good rule and indicate the anxiety with which minority rule was greeted in this period. Indeed, the *Triumphal Entry* ends with an address and tribute not to the king but to London's mayor and people, a reminder that the king is fortunate to have such loyal subjects (Benson 2006: 154). This is a theme that Lydgate returns to in poems such as *The Debate of the Horse, Goose and Sheep* (late 1430s) with its injunction that every member of society from the highest to the most humble has a contribution to make to the community and that this must be recognised by the king in particular: 'Beeth war, ye princis, your sogettis to despise' (line 635).

Themes of legitimate kingship, good governance and social harmony dominate the seven surviving mummings or disguising written by Lydgate (Lydgate, ed. Sponsler 2010). The Christmas mummings presented at Eltham (in 1425 or 1428) and Windsor (1429) were performed before Henry VI, as was the comic disguising at Hertford Castle (Sponsler 2008: 22–3; Nolan 2005: 154–72). The Eltham and Windsor mummings express the wish that Henry's reign will be peaceful and prosperous and celebrate his status as King of England and France, that at Windsor placing a particular emphasis on the legitimacy of his claim to these titles. The performances for non-royal audiences are more ambitious than these addresses to Henry, and resonate with the language of advice to nobles and princes as if to remind the audience of its responsibilities at a time when the Lancastrian monarchy was not at its strongest. The Mayday 'balade' presented 'by a poursyvant' to the 'Shirreves of London' (*The Mumming at Bishopwood*) hopes for the emergence of an idealised order for society, which is firmly hierarchical and depends on the king's good rule:

> Of alle estates þere shal beo oone ymage,
> And princes first shal ocupye þe hede,
> And prudent iuges, to correcte outrages,
> Shal trespassours const[r]eynen vnder drede. (lines 50–3)

The spring setting for the 'balade', and the celebration of the passing of winter, allows Lydgate to use the language of change and renewal to offer subtle political critique, and to remind the estates of their shared responsibilities to support royal rule:

> Beo faythfull founde in al [vertu],
> Mayre, provost, shirreff, eche in his substaunce;
> And aldremen, whiche haue þe governaunce
> Over þe people by vertue may avayle,
> Þat noone oppression beo done to þe pourayle. (lines 59–63)

The Christmas *Mumming at London* was, according to John Shirley's rubric in Cambridge, Trinity College, MS R. 3.20, performed before the 'gret estates of þis lande', and is strongly advisory, taking as its theme the cultivation of virtues of Prudence, Justice, 'Fortitudo' (the courage to fight all manner of vice) and temperance, which each member of the audience should bring to his or her own 'housholde' (line 337). The other two mummings were commissioned by the Mercers of London and Goldsmiths of London (Candlemass 1430) in honour of the mayor, William Eastfield. They employ complicated imagery and allusion (Nolan 2006: 186–92) to articulate pride in London's prosperity, and again invoke advisory discourses to both flatter the mayor and remind him of his responsibilities to preserve the city's peaceful order through 'good gouuernaunce' (*Mumming for the Goldsmiths*, line 20).

Perhaps the most popular of Lydgate's poems with early audiences were not those that considered literary matters, addressed important audiences, or marked political events. Lydgate's short poems on personal morality, including *A Dietary* and *Stans Puer ad Mensam*, seem to have had the widest circulation of all his shorter works. However, although they may seem to be far removed from the political or occasional poems in subject and intended audience, they actually have much in common with Lydgate's public verse. The ubiquitous *Dietary*, based on a Latin text *Flos medicinae*, and in the tradition of the *Secretum Secretorum*, is a poem about self-restraint – governing the body and conduct. With its emphasis on ethical conduct, its remit is actually not far removed from that of the coronation poem to Henry VI. It advocates personal virtues such as moderation: like the bird in *The Churl and the Bird*, its narrator warns against hasty conduct. Positioning its audience as socially elite, it encourages charity and fairness to those less fortunate. Like Lydgate's meta-poetical works it too considers the value of truth and the danger of listening to flattery, slander and gossip. *Stans puer ad mensam* is very much in the same mould – a didactic text for 'yonge childer' (line 93), deriving from the *Disciplina clericalis* tradition, which also combines practical material on bodily conduct with that on the cultivation of virtues such as honesty: although Henry VI was Lydgate's most distinguished young reader, his tutelage extended far beyond the king. The poem even contains encouraging advice for parents who might be at the end of their tether:

> In childeris werre now myrthe, now debate,
> In her quarell is no greet vyolence;
> Now pley, now wepyng, selde in on estate;
> To her pleyntes yeve no gret credence. (lines 85–8)

These instructional works by Lydgate, though sometimes more remote from modern experience than the lines just quoted, nonetheless remind us how important a voice his was for late medieval readers. Indeed, Lydgate's short secular poems, public, didactic, or fashionably literary, deserve appreciation by those seeking a full understanding of fifteenth-century English poetry.

Works cited

Barr, Helen, *Socioliterary Practice in Late Medieval England* (Oxford, 2001)

Benson, C. David, 'Civic Lydgate: The Poet and London', in Scanlon and Simpson, eds, *John Lydgate*, pp. 147–68

Boffey, Julia, and A. S. G. Edwards, 'Literary Texts', in *The Cambridge History of the Book in Britain, Volume III: 1400–1557*, eds Lotte Hellinga and J. B. Trapp (Cambridge, 1999), pp. 555–75

Cartlidge, Neil, 'The Source of John Lydgate's *The Churl and the Bird*', *Notes and Queries*, n.s. 44 (1997), 22–4

Cooper, Lisa, and Andrea Denny-Brown, eds, *Lydgate Matters: Poetry and Material Culture in the Fifteenth Century* (New York, 2008)

Dillon, Janette, *The Cambridge Introduction to Early English Theatre* (Cambridge, 2006)

Ebin, Lois A., *Illuminator, Makar, Vates: Visions of Poetry in the Fifteenth Century* (Lincoln, NE, 1998)

Edwards, A. S. G., 'Lydgate's Use of Chaucer: Structure, Strategy, and Style', *Revista Canaria de Estudios Ingleses*, 10 (1985), 175–82

——, 'The *Speculum Guy de Warwick* and Lydgate's *Guy of Warwick*: The Non-Romance Middle English Tradition', in *Guy of Warwick: Icon and Ancestor*, eds Alison Wiggins and Rosalind Field (Cambridge, 2007), pp. 81–93

——, 'Lydgate in Scotland', *Nottingham Medieval Studies*, 54 (2010), 185–94

Gillespie, Alexandra, *Print Culture and the Medieval Author: Chaucer, Lydgate and their Books, 1473–1557* (Oxford, 2006)

Fifteenth-Century English Dream Visions: An Anthology, ed. Julia Boffey (Oxford, 2003)

Lawton, David, 'Dullness and the Fifteenth Century', *English Literary History*, 54 (1987), 761–99

Lydgate, John, *The Minor Poems of John Lydgate, Part II: Secular Poems*, ed. Henry Noble MacCracken, EETS, o. s. 192 (London, 1934)

——, *John Lydgate: Poems*, ed. John Norton-Smith (Oxford, 1966)

——, *Mummings and Entertainments*, ed. Claire Sponsler (Kalamazoo, MI, 2010)

Nolan, Maura, *John Lydgate and the Making of Public Culture* (Cambridge, 2005)

——, 'The Performance of the Literary: Lydgate's Mummings', in Scanlon and Simpson, eds, *John Lydgate*, pp. 169–206

Pearsall, Derek, *John Lydgate* (London, 1970)

——, *John Lydgate (1371–1449): A Bio-Bibliography* (Victoria, BC, 1997)

Renoir, Alain, *The Poetry of John Lydgate* (London, 1967)

Scanlon, Larry, and James Simpson, *John Lydgate: Poetry, Culture and Lancastrian England* (Notre Dame, IN, 2006)

Simpson, James, '"For al my body . . . weieth nat an unce": Empty Poets and Rhetorical Weight in Lydgate's *Churl and the Bird*', in Scanlon and Simpson, eds, *John Lydgate*, pp. 129–46

Spearing, A. C., *The Medieval Poet as Voyeur: Looking and Listening in Medieval Love Narrative* (Cambridge, 1993)

Sponsler, Claire, 'Lydgate and London's Public Culture', in Cooper and Denny-Brown, eds, *Lydgate Matters*, pp. 13–33

Straker, Scott-Morgan, 'Propaganda, Intentionality, and the Lancastrian Lydgate', in Scanlon and Simpson, eds, *John Lydgate*, pp. 98–128

Strohm, Paul, *England's Empty Throne: Usurpation and the Language of Legitimation, 1399–1422* (New Haven, CT, 1998)

Watts, John, *Henry VI and the Politics of Kingship* (Cambridge, 1996)

Wolfgang, Lenora D., '"Out of the Frenssh": Lydgate's Source of *The Churl and the Bird*', *English Language Notes*, 32 (1995), 10–19

8

John Capgrave and Osbern Bokenham: Verse Saints' Lives

SARAH JAMES

Until relatively recently, hagiography was not really considered an appropriate subject for serious scholarly attention. The pioneering nineteenth-century editing efforts of scholars such as Carl Horstmann were almost exclusively philolog-ical in their approach, with little sense that the saintly narratives themselves were worthy of literary or historical consideration (Horstmann 1878, 1881). The comments of the editor of Osbern Bokenham's *Legendys of Hooly Wummen*, working in the 1930s, might be taken as evidence of a much more widespread disregard for the genre:

> My treatment of such questions as Bokenham's sources, literary value, and so forth, is obviously only the briefest of sketches. Though I am much attached to Bokenham, I am not at all sure that he is worth extended study from these points of view. Further investigation of the sources might, however, be a useful and interesting exercise. (Bokenham, ed. Serjeantson 1938: vii)

As late as the 1990s, similar views could be found; M. C. Seymour, discussing Capgrave's hagiographical endeavours, refers casually to 'the general medioc-rity of the genre', with no suggestion that such a judgement might require exami-nation or justification (Seymour 1996: 21). Happily the world has changed, and scholars of hagiography no longer find themselves compelled to defend their field of research. The popularity of saints' lives among all medieval social strata proclaims their importance to the social, cultural and religious historian; the rela-tionship between saints' lives and other narrative genres is now more widely appreciated and explored; detailed studies are gradually bringing to light the extent to which these highly conventional narratives are in fact deeply responsive to changing social, historical and political contexts. We even have a *Companion to Middle English Hagiography*, a book that could hardly have been contemplated a few decades ago (see, for example, Gurevich 1988; Heffernan 1988; Vauchez 1997; for a succinct overview, the 'Introduction' to Salih, ed., 2006).

In the fifteenth century the genre was flourishing. New copies of earlier saints' lives continued to be produced, and new versions were created, indicative of a continued appetite for saintly narratives, whether individual lives or collections, in verse or in prose. Among the most prominent exponents of the genre were the East Anglian trio of John Capgrave, John Lydgate and Osbern Bokenham. The saints' lives of John Lydgate are discussed elsewhere in this volume, and therefore Capgrave and Bokenham will be my focus here.

John Capgrave (1393–1464) joined the Austin friars in his teens, was ordained priest in 1416 or 1417, and studied theology in London from 1417 to 1422. In 1422 he went on to Cambridge, taking his B.Th. in 1423 and his doctorate in 1425. Between 1427 and 1437 we know nothing of his movements, but he reappears in the records from the late 1430s, by which time he was probably at the Austin friary at Lynn, Norfolk. He became Prior Provincial of his order in 1453, and was re-elected for a further two years in 1455; he died at Lynn in 1464 (Capgrave, ed. Lucas 1983: xix–xxiii). Capgrave appears to have been a prolific author in both Latin and English; the twelve extant works bearing his name include biblical commentaries, a chronicle, the histories of famous men bearing the name Henry, and a guide to the antiquities of Rome, as well as four saints' lives in English: those of St Augustine and St Gilbert of Sempringham are in prose, and those of St Norbert and St Katherine, which are considered here, in verse. Earlier Capgrave scholarship, which focused almost exclusively on linguistic analysis and manuscript studies, has confirmed that some Capgrave manuscripts may be holographs, or else were produced roughly contemporaneously at the Austin friars' house at Lynn, and were carefully corrected (Colledge and Smetana 1972; Colledge 1974; Lucas 1981; Seymour 1986; 'Introduction' to Capgrave, ed. Lucas 1983).

The Life of St Norbert, completed in 1440 according to its envoy, is dedicated to John Wygenhale, Abbot of the Premonstratensian house at West Dereham in Norfolk, and relates the life of the order's founder. It is a substantial work running to 4,109 lines written in rhyme royal stanzas, and is a close translation of the Latin *Vita Sancti Norberti*, one of the earliest extant versions of the saint's *vita* (Capgrave, ed. Smetana 1977). Capgrave makes few changes to his Latin source beyond the addition of a prologue and envoy, and on a first reading his *Life* offers a rather uncomplicated picture of the saint as a man of God and worker of numerous miracles, glossing over any aspects of the saint's life that might contradict such a view. For example, the Latin *Vita*'s references to Norbert's early years focused on courtly life are entirely omitted, and replaced with a rather anodyne description of him as 'Mery in word, of hert and hand ful fre,/ Large for to ȝeue and to take aschamed' (lines 124–5). Yet precisely because Capgrave clings so closely to his source, the small changes he does introduce are worthy of attention. In some cases they suggest the desire to inject liveliness of description or characterisation into a narrative that can otherwise seem a little bland. So, for example, to an incident in which Norbert is visited by the devil (in the form of a bear) during an all-night vigil in the monastery church, Capgrave adds a vigorous denunciation of Satan by the saint:

> What abides þou, what wilt þou, cruel beest?
> Thi hokes, þi teeth haue now no powere
> To sette on me no daungere ne areest.
> It is but vanyte þat þou schewis me here.
> Thi rolled skyn, whech is no þing clere,
> Is but fantasie as þouȝ it were a rynde.
> Thi fyry throte I counte it but a wynde. (lines 2745–50)

The terrifying aspect of the bear-devil's claws and teeth are vividly portrayed, only to be dismissed as mere 'vanyte' or deception. His wrinkled skin, sarcastically described as 'no þing clere', is recognised as mere 'fantasie' or empty appearance and is likened to a mere 'rynde' or husk; his fiery breath is no more frightening than the 'wynde'. Over the course of a single stanza the devil has been systematically diminished from a figure inspiring awe and dread to a rather moth-eaten empty bearskin. Remaining unmoved by mere appearances, the saint then proceeds to remind the devil of his Fall, before dismissing him summarily:

> Thou þat were þe merke of God aboue;
> Thou þat were swech an aungel bryth!
> And for þou fleddist fro þat goodly loue
> Whech þou had, þe loue of God almyth,
> Now art þou dampned sekirly, as it is rith,
> To dwelle in [d]erknesse, as þou apperist here.
> Awey þou Sathan, awey þou raggid brere! (lines 2759–65)[1]

There is a colour in the language that is Capgrave's own, a capacity to convey lively visual images in speech that is familiar and colloquial. Lucifer the bright angel is reduced to an untidy bramble, admittedly equipped with thorns to ensnare the unwary, but too ubiquitous to be truly terrifying. Capgrave's literary style has received previous scholarly attention, often in the form of more or less disparaging comparisons with Chaucer, but he has rarely been praised for either vividness or humour (for example, Stouck 1982; for a more positive assessment see Winstead 1996). Yet here he demonstrates both, together with a keen awareness of the needs of his audience; the vivid and familiar style surely has wide appeal, but perhaps especially for those who are less theologically sophisticated, among whom we might number his Premonstratensian dedicatees, since the order was not particularly renowned for its learning (Fredeman 1975).

Among the other changes Capgrave makes to his source are a number that gesture beyond the text itself to the contemporary religious and political context. In one incident Norbert, having been elected bishop, is turned back from the gates of the city by a porter who is misled by his poor appearance into thinking he is a beggar. While the populace castigates the hapless porter for his error, Capgrave gives a conciliatory speech to Norbert:

> 'Be not aferd, myn owne brothire dere,
> Ne fle not for my sake, what euyr þou sayde.
> For I sey the treuly, þere is no man here
> Hey ne lowe, woman ne no mayde,
> þou3 þei avisement in here langage layde,
> Coude a gessed þe treuth so weel as ded þou.
> Thyn eyne be more clere, I telle the rit now,
>
> That callest me a begger þan her eyne were
> That chose me to worchep or to degree.' (lines 2969–77)

---

[1] Emendation of the original 'þerknesse'. While the *MED* does not record 'þerknesse' as a variant form for the noun, it does note the erroneous adjectival use of 'þerk': see *MED*, 'derk' (adj.) and 'derknes(se' (noun).

This reference to an ideal of holy poverty is reinforced a few lines later when Norbert discovers how seriously the Church's property has been diminished by previous bishops, who have distributed its goods among their own relations. Capgrave again elaborates upon the Latin source, providing Norbert with an impassioned speech in which he declares his intention of eradicating corruption:

> 'I wil,' he seith, 'send oute in al hasty wyse
> To euery man þat they hem may avyse.
>
> Thei falle not in þat sentens whech I wil proclame!
> That whosoeuyr hath ony possessioun
> Longyng to my cherch in Goddis name
> I wil now charge hem, and on my benysoun,
> That þei resyne hem withouten condicioun,
> And lete þe cherch haue his rith ageyn'. (lines 3030–7)

Scant as these references are, they invite us to look beyond Norbert's own historical circumstances to those of Capgrave himself, and to anxieties about nepotism, clerical possessions and the worldly nature of the established church, which were exercising the ecclesiastical hierarchy at this period.

Similar contemporary concerns have been more widely explored in relation to Capgrave's second verse life in English, *The Life of St Katherine of Alexandria*, which consists of 8,624 lines, again in rhyme royal, divided into a Prologue and five books. Unlike most earlier versions of St Katherine's legend, Capgrave's gives equal attention to the saint's life before and after conversion to Christianity, providing particularly extensive coverage of her childhood, education and early womanhood (Lewis 2000). This has encouraged scholars to utilise *St Katherine* as a means of scrutinising contemporary social and political contexts. Karen Winstead has been at the forefront of this development, exploring the saint's life both as a reflection of contemporary concerns regarding the effectiveness of Henry VI's kingship, and as an exposition of the disruptive effects of female learning on social and political order (Winstead 1991 and 1994). Certainly the Katherine whom Capgrave presents to his audience is a woman of strongly independent mind, whose commitment to scholarship demands a solitary form of living that is at odds with the needs of her country and people, and which places her in conflict with her noble advisors and her family. In the face of her continued refusal to marry, her lords attack both her learning and her gender:

> Thus weyled the lordes as þei sete be-deene,
> Cursyng hir maysteris, cursyng hir bookis alle:
> 'Allas,' thei seyde, 'that euere ony queene
> Thus shuld be comered [distracted]! oure wurshype is doun falle!
> God sende neuere reem a kyng that wereth a calle!
> We prey god þat he neuere woman make
> Soo grete a mayster as she is, for hir sake.' (p. 169: ii, 1478–84)

Throughout the Marriage Parliament and beyond, the disastrous effects of her failure to govern actively are pitilessly exposed, as her country is subject to unrest within and attack from without. Winstead suggests that Capgrave's emphasis on

Katherine's governmental incapacity is a reflection of his own pessimism about the current state of England (Winstead 1997).

One of the most distinctive features of Capgrave's *St Katherine* is the considerable space devoted to debates: well over two-fifths of the poem are taken up with reporting direct speech. Katherine argues first with 110 pagan philosophers, then with her nobles and mother at the Marriage Parliament, and then with the emperor Maxentius in Books 4 and 5, as well as with a further group of fifty pagan philosophers. The latter are drafted in by the emperor to assist him in his conflict with Katherine, but instead she converts them all to Christianity. The use of debate was fundamental to the scholastic method, of course, and its inclusion here may reflect something of Capgrave's own intellectual background (Grabmann 1909–11; Lucas 1997). There are, however, particular advantages to using direct speech in this way. First, the effect of allowing disputants to be heard in their own words is highly dramatic and engaging for the audience; no longer mere spectators, they become involved, empowered to judge the strength of claim and counter-claim. Furthermore, by presenting arguments through the speech of others, Capgrave is distancing himself from the views expressed. The narratorial distance thus introduced may be especially valuable when the issues under discussion are contentious, as for example when Katherine argues in Book IV against the use of images in worship.

> If thei be made, than arn þei creatures,
> And he that made hem, [he] is god allone.
> ley hem in water, alle youre mysty figures,
> ffor noȝt arn thei, neither þe stok ne the stoone. (iv, 1625–28)

The suggestion that these images are mere sticks and stones that should be cast into the waters might well have created a *frisson* among an audience conscious of contemporary controversies arising from Wycliffite iconomachy, particularly since the reference to images as 'stok' and 'stoone' appears elsewhere in a specifically Lollard context (for example, *Selections*, ed. Hudson 1978: 85, 87). The fact that it is Katherine, Christian saint and hence staunch upholder of orthodoxy, speaking at this point simply increases the tension of the moment. While the images to which she refers are, of course, pagan idols rather than Christian statues, the issues at stake throughout this debate are perhaps uncomfortably close to those raised by Lollardy in fifteenth-century England. In such a context, Capgrave's preference for direct speech over narratorial comment may be entirely understandable (James 2005).

As in *St Norbert*, in *St Katherine* Capgrave indulges in moments of vividly imagistic and colloquial language. When Maxentius offers to erect a statue of Katherine, to be venerated by the people, she is unimpressed. The statue, she says:

> [...] shal be insensible,
> Stonde liche a ston, and byrdes flye rounde aboute,
> As I suppose it shal be right possible
> That þei shal come somtyme a ful grete route,
> her on-clene dunge shul thei there putte oute
> And lete it falle right on the ymagis face. (v, 470–75)

It is impossible to read these lines without visualising first the 'ful grete route' of chattering birds fluttering around the statue, and then the inevitable scatological onslaught. Even the most disengaged and secular-minded listener would surely respond to the humour of this hypothetical event, while a more serious auditor might well be stimulated to appreciate so fitting a fate for an idolatrous image. We do not have a clear idea of the audience Capgrave had in mind for this work; unlike his other saints' lives, all of which have named or at least clearly speci-fied dedicatees, the *Life of St Katherine* was written 'that more openly it shalle/ Be knowe a-bovte of woman and of man' (Prologue, 45–6). This reference is tantalisingly vague, but the dramatic and expressive qualities of the language again suggest wide-ranging appeal. Derek Pearsall traces connections between this language and popular late-medieval verse romance, and suggests that this might gesture towards a relatively unsophisticated audience for the saint's life; however, he also concedes that Capgrave clearly envisages that at least some of his audience will be reading, rather than hearing, his text (Pearsall 1975; see also Fredeman 1980). The existence of a Gild of St Katherine at Lynn in the 1390s, open to both sexes, suggests one possible audience for this work, although it is unnecessary to be so specific; there is clear evidence of a substantial audience for pious literature in East Anglia in the fifteenth century, whether attached to gilds or not (Gibson 1989; Beadle 1991).

Osbern Bokenham was born in the same year as Capgrave, perhaps in Old Buckenham in Norfolk, or in Suffolk, and was also an Augustinian. He received his bachelor's degree at Cambridge one day after Capgrave, and from 1427, by which time he was at Clare Priory, Suffolk, he is referred to as *magister* in the records. He tells us that he travelled to Italy at least twice, and the latest mention of his name occurs in a will of 1463. Bokenham's writings include the *Mappula angliae*, a partial translation of Higden's *Polychronicon*, and probably at least two other works: a translation of Claudian, *De Consulatu Stilichonis*; and a dialogue recounting the genealogy of Joan of Acre (Delany 1998). However, he is prob-ably best known for a series of saints' lives generally known as *Legendys of Hooly Wummen*. This title was given to the texts by their first editor, Mary Serjeantson, and is taken from the *Prolocutorye in-to Marye Mawdelyns lyf*, in which the author summarises his hagiographical endeavours thus far as 'dyuers legendys, wych my rudnesse/ From latyn had turnyd in-to our language,/ Of hooly wummen' (lines 5038–40). One of the extant manuscripts contains a Prologue and the lives of SS Margaret, Anne, Christina, the eleven thousand virgins, Faith, Agnes, Dorothy, Mary Magdalene, Katherine, Cecilia, Agatha, Lucy and Elizabeth. A. S. G. Edwards suggests that, by focusing exclusively on female saints, it partic-ipates in a wider fifteenth-century trend for producing miscellanies in which gender 'forms a distinctive criterion in establishing content' (Edwards 2003: 131).

The conception of Bokenham's work is complicated by ongoing research on the Abbotsford manuscript (Horobin 2008). For Arundel 327, Edwards has argued convincingly that that the legend of St Margaret was devised by Bokenham as a free-standing piece, with no intention of producing others. He suggests that subsequent legends were produced piecemeal as patrons or occasion demanded, and may have circulated in booklet form, only later being drawn together into a single text by Thomas Burgh, a friar of Cambridge (Edwards 1994). Scholars remain divided on this issue: Paul Price (2001) concurs with Edwards' conclusions, while Carroll Hilles (2001) rejects them. Patronage is certainly central to the texts in this manuscript; several of the legends were written for named patrons, and perhaps somewhat unusually, these were in the main lay women. The name of Katherine Denston is associated with the legends of St Anne and St Katherine; Katherine Howard is also associated with the latter. John and Isabel Hunt are remembered at the end of St Dorothy, and Agatha Flegge is the dedicatee of St Agatha. Bokenham's two most distinguished patrons were Elizabeth de Vere, Countess of Oxford, for whom he wrote the life of St Elizabeth, and Isabel Bourchier, Countess of Eu, whose commission is the subject of the three-hundred line *Prolocutorye in-to Marye Mawdelyns lyf* mentioned above. In the *Prolocutorye* Bokenham provides a detailed account of the circumstances of the commission, describing the Twelfth Night festivities at the Countess' residence, and their discussions about saints' lives. It was on hearing that Bokenham was engaged in writing the life of St Elizabeth for Elizabeth de Vere that the Countess made her own request for a life of Mary Magdalene, perhaps motivated by a sense of pious competition. Sarah Salih suggests that hagiography in this context can be imagined as 'a very superior kind of consumer good, fittingly adorning the glamour of Lady Bourchier's Christmas party' (Salih 2006: 12). It also clearly serves other purposes, however; the existence of so many named dedicatees has provided fertile ground for scholars seeking to pursue a sociopolitical approach to Bokenham's work. Most of these patrons can reasonably be identified with the powerful Yorkist affinity in Suffolk, as Sheila Delany discusses in detail; thus she suggests that Bokenham's legendary might be read, at least in part, as Yorkist propaganda (Delany 1999). She develops this position more extensively in *Impolitic Bodies*, aligning the *Legendys* with the mid-fifteenth-century body politic, fragmented under Henry VI's ineffective rule and anxiously awaiting the reunification that would be possible under Richard, Duke of York (Delany 1998). Carroll Hilles also finds Yorkist sympathies in Bokenham's work, suggesting that the spiritual fecundity of his virgin martyrs parallels the physical fecundity of the Yorkist female line, in contrast to 'the impoverished Lancastrian dynasty' (Hilles 2001: 200). The *Prolocutorye in-to Marye Mawdelyns lyf* certainly bears such a reading, with its emphasis on the Countess' pedigree, being 'Doun conueyid by þe same pedegru/ That þe duk of york is come, for she/ Hys sustyr is in egal degre' (lines 5006–8).

The description of the Countess' commission goes beyond this, however, as Bokenham uses it as an opportunity to invite his audience to participate in the details of his own life and experience at this moment. The 'reuel', 'daunsyng' and 'fressh aray' he sees conjure up an image of an aristocratic household at play: a household in which he is clearly a privileged visitor. Although expressing doubts about his ability to fulfil the task satisfactorily, he agrees to the undertaking,

> Vp condycyoun þat she me wolde respyt
> Of hir ientyllnesse tyl I acomplysyd
> My pylgramage hade, wych promysyd
> I to seynt Iamys wyth hert entere
> Had to performe þe same yere,

þere to purchase thorgh penytence
Of myn oolde synnys newe indulgence. (lines 5090–6)

This addition is not strictly necessary, but its inclusion allows us to hear Bokenham's speaking voice, which is somewhat garrulous, perhaps a little pedantic
concerning details, and keen to ensure that we receive as much circumstantial
information as possible. Elsewhere he indulges a similar desire to regale his audience with personal anecdotal material. In the Prologue he describes his experiences of sheltering from heavy rain in Italy, which stimulated his desire to write a
life of St Margaret, accompanied by some wry observations on the honesty of the
locals and their tendency to 'begyle/ The wery pylgrymys' (lines 114–15). In the
Vita S. Margaretae, he asks permission to break off for a while and rest:

> For sykyr myn handys gynne to feynte,
> My wyt to dullyn, and myn eyne bleynte
> Shuld be, ner helpe of a spectacle;
> My penne also gynnyth make obstacle,
> And lyst no lengere on paper to renne. (lines 895–9)

Given these disadvantages, he requests a holiday until Michaelmas, and a few
lines later resumes his task, apparently refreshed by his short vacation. Such
authorial insertions give a particular flavour to Bokenham's work as he invites
his audience into his world to share the pains and pleasures of writing hagiography. It may be that these personal interventions are intended to inspire
belief and confidence in his readers and listeners; Ian Johnson has suggested
that 'attempted valorisation by alleged associated circumstances which strictly
in themselves prove little or nothing – authentication through specificity that
cannot be refuted – turns out to be a hallmark of Bokenham' (Johnson 1994: 110).
Alternatively, they may be a way to elicit sympathy; Bokenham seems at pains
to present himself not as a distant authorial figure in full control of his work and
his powers, but as a fallible individual with whom the audience can identify and
sympathetically share the trials of the writing process. Or perhaps they may point
to the distinctive realities of coterie textual production. The author, being known
to his audience, has no need to construct an impression of authorial distance,
and can instead rely upon a shared body of knowledge and experience through
which readers and listeners will respond to his work. If Bokenham really did
suffer from eyestrain and poor quality pens, the audience can sympathise with,
and vicariously participate in, his experience; alternatively, it is entirely possible
that he was known for his sharp eyesight and excellent writing equipment, in
which case such a moment becomes a delightful private joke to be enjoyed by
those 'in the know'.

Bokenham's negotiations with his audience reflect a wider concern with questions of *auctoritas*. In a careful examination of the prologues and other paratextual
matter in the *Legendys*, Ian Johnson suggests that Bokenham energetically displays
his commitment to the Aristotelian tradition of textual causation and appraisal,
and hence incidentally demonstrates the continued vitality and serviceability of
that tradition. But he also identifies what he describes as the writer's 'perpetu-
ally petitionary disposition', and suggests that far from regarding himself as an

auctor, or even a *rhetor*, Bokenham sees textual production as a form of prayer and a means of winning grace (Johnson 1994: 118). Such a stepping back from claims to *auctoritas* may stem in part from Bokenham's rather uneasy relationship with his poetic predecessors, evidenced by claims of poetic inadequacy such as that which opens his *Vita Sanctae Annae matris Sanctae Mariae*:

> If I hadde cunnyng and eloquens
> My conceytes craftely to dilate,
> Als whilom dede the fyrsh rethoryens,
> GOWERE, CHAUNCERE, & now LYTGATE,
> I wolde me besyn to translate
> Seynt anne lyf in-to oure langage.
> But sekyr I fere to gynne so late,
> Lest men wolde ascryuen it to dotage
> [...]
> Wherfore me thinkyth, & sothe it ys,
> Best were for me to leue makynge
> Of englysh... (lines 1401–8, 1417–19)

The pressure applied by his literary antecedents Gower, Chaucer and Lydgate, against whose works his own will suffer by comparison, leads Bokenham to contemplate abandoning his own poetic creation. However, there follow almost seven hundred lines on the very subject about which he claims he cannot write; thus it seems that the achievements of the illustrious threesome, however weighty, are not sufficient to prevent his continued 'makynge/ Of englysh'. Indeed Paul Price suggests that while there may be an element of Bloomian 'anxiety of influence' at play here, Bokenham in fact genuinely believes in the moral superiority of an unadorned style (Price 2001; Delany 1998 concurs). Such a claim seems to be substantiated elsewhere in the *Legendys*. Returning once more to the *Prolocutorye in-to Marye Mawdelyns lyf*, we find him refusing to invoke the aid of the Muses, instead turning to God for aid. He expresses his mistrust of the aureate poetic tradition,

> Not desyryng to haue swych eloquence
> As sum curyals han, ner swych asperence
> In vttryng of here subtyl conceytys,
> In wych oft tyme ful greth dysceyt is. (lines 5225–8)

Eloquence is dangerous, it seems, providing a vehicle for deception, which is inappropriate to the task in hand.

However, I wish to suggest that Chaucer, Gower and Lydgate are not the only poets who present both an artistic and a moral challenge to Bokenham; in the prologue to his version of the legend of St Katherine, he also seems to have his sights fixed on his contemporary, Capgrave. He cautions his audience not to expect extensive coverage of the saint's early life, referring those who wish to know about such things to Capgrave's version 'In balaadys rymyd ful craftyly' (line 6359). He continues:

> But for-as-mych as þat book is rare
> And straunge to gete, at myn estymacyoun,

Compendyously of al I wyl declare
No more but oonly þe passyoun,
Of kateryne Howard to gostly consolacyoun,
And to conforte eek of Denstoun kateryne,
If grace my wyt wyl illumyne.
O blysful Ihesu, sum beem lete shyne
Up-on me of heuenely influence,
That þis legende begunne I may termyne. (lines 6361–70)

It is not entirely fanciful to interpret this as restrained censure of Capgrave's excess in producing a life incorporating so much material, embellished with crafty rhymes, and in a book that is hard to obtain. Bokenham's own version, by contrast, is to be compendious, concerned only with the passion, and furthermore it will be produced with the assistance of a beam of 'heuenely influence', which, we are to infer, Capgrave's was not. It may be significant that while this prologue is in rhyme royal, the *Lyf of S. Kateryne* itself is in less 'crafty' rhyming couplets. In the manuscript as it is now arranged, this is the first legend that deviates from either rhyme royal or an eight-line stanza (the latter is the form for the Prologue and the *Vita Sanctae Christianae* only). Perhaps the length and elaboration of Capgrave's life stimulated a desire to produce a plainer text. Whether or not this is the case, the three following lives are also in rhyming couplets, with Bokenham reverting to the eight-line stanza for the *Lyf of S. Elyzabeth*.

The morality or otherwise of textual excess has a counterpart in the physical excess of both Bokenham's *Legendys* and Capgrave's *St Katherine*. Torture, mutilation and violent death are, of course, mainstays of the hagiographic genre, or at least of that part of it concerned with virgin martyrs (Ashton 2000). Delany conceives the *Legendys* as a somatised text concerned with the fragmentation and reconstruction of saintly body parts, and indeed her own reading re-enacts this; the heads, feet, faces, wombs, tongues, mouths, breasts, genitals and guts of these young women are itemised and subjected to her critical scrutiny before being reassembled in support of her argument for Bokenham's theological and political intentions (Delany 1998). Such a reading demands that the *Legendys* were conceived as a single collection, and thus is at odds with the model of conception proposed by Edwards. Yet both these models, the one insisting upon the wholeness of the text, the other upon its contingent and fragmentary nature, sit in fascinating relation to the saints' lives themselves, demanding that we think both about the text as body and about the body as text. Margaret Bridges, for example, considers Bokenham's practice as a translator in terms of the processes of 'excision, elision, and maltreatment/impairment', activities which, she suggests, are reflected in the physical translation of St Margaret's relics in his version of her legend (Bridges 2003: 277). Such a reading is challenging and exhilarating, but there is perhaps a danger in too readily associating the female martyr with subversion and the repressive power of authority. As Price astutely points out, the depiction of an intelligent, articulate and persuasive female saint may as easily be interpreted as an argument in favour of the status quo as otherwise. The reason is precisely that she is a saint, hence the site of miraculous occurrences that we cannot expect to replicate in 'reality' (Price 2001: 166).

As I noted at the start of this paper, serious study of late-medieval hagiography is still a relatively new phenomenon, and while a great deal of work has been done in a short period of time, there are many opportunities for further research. I shall restrict myself to the mention of four areas that seem particularly likely to yield interesting results. While much recent published research has focused on the lives produced by Capgrave, Bokenham and Lydgate, it seems clear to me that there is room to pursue further research on texts by lesser-known authors, such as the verse life of Becket by Laurentius Wade (Horstmann 1880), or indeed on texts for which we have no named author, nor any prospect of recovering one. Fertile as the mainstream ground is, there is an extensive hinterland, much of which remains almost untouched by scholarly notice. There is also much to be learned from further manuscript study, as Horobin's work on Bokenham suggests; while particular texts, such as those discussed in this chapter, have been well served, others have not yet enjoyed that careful consideration of their manuscript context that can be highly revealing. Edwards' examination of CUL, MS Add. 4122 exemplifies the fruitful possibilities of such work (Edwards 2003). Comparative studies of the lives of particular saints, or of collections, across different European vernaculars would certainly extend our knowledge significantly, and enable us to think both more broadly and more incisively about the ways in which saints' lives relate to particular social, political and historical contexts. Incidentally, such studies would also lend themselves to collaborative research projects, as would my final, perhaps rather ambitious, suggestion. Large-scale interdisciplinary projects bringing together literary scholars, cultural historians, archaeologists, art historians, and perhaps even psychologists and anthropologists, to study particular saints in all their cultural manifestations, would add significantly to our understanding of the place and function of saints in medieval spirituality. Lest such a suggestion be considered grandiose, I turn to Bokenham himself. His *Prolocutorye in-to Marye Mawdelyns lyf* clearly suggests that he considered the revels, dancing and elaborate attire of the party-goers to be important contextualisation of the narrative that was to follow; we could do worse than to take a lead from him.

Works cited

Ashton, Gail, *The Generation of Identity in Late Medieval Hagiography: Speaking the Saint* (London, 2000)

Aston, Margaret, *Lollards and Reformers: Images and Literacy in Late Medieval Religion* (London, 1984)

Ball, R. M., 'The Opponents of Bishop Pecok', *Journal of Ecclesiastical History*, 48 (1997), 230–62

Beadle, Richard, 'Prolegomena to a Literary Geography of Later Medieval Norfolk', in *Regionalism in Late Medieval Manuscripts and Texts*, ed. Felicity Riddy (Cambridge, 1991), pp. 89–108

Bernau, Anke, 'A Christian *Corpus*: Virginity, Violence, and Knowledge in the Life of St Katherine of Alexandria', in Jenkins and Lewis, eds, *St Katherine of Alexandria*, pp. 109–30

——, Ruth Evans and Sarah Salih, eds, *Medieval Virginities* (Cardiff, 2003)

Bokenham, Osbern, *Legendys of Hooly Wummen*, ed. Mary Serjeantson, EETS, o. s. 206 (London, 1938)

Bridges, Margaret, 'Uncertain Peregrinations of the Living and the Dead: Writing (Hagiography) as Translating (Relics) in Osbern Bokenham's Legend of St Margaret', in *Chaucer and the Challenges of Medievalism: Studies in Honor of H. A. Kelly*, eds Donka Minkova and Theresa Tinkle (Frankfurt, 2003), pp. 275–87

Capgrave, John, *The Life of St Katharine of Alexandria*, ed. Carl Hortsmann, EETS o. s. 100 (London, 1893)

——, *The Life of St Norbert*, ed. Cyril Lawrence Smetana, O.S.A. (Toronto, 1977)

——, *Abbreuiacion of Cronicles*, ed. Peter J. Lucas, EETS, o. s. 285 (Oxford, 1983)

——, *The Life of St Katherine*, ed. and trans. Karen A. Winstead (Kalamazoo, MI, 1999)

Chaste Passions: Medieval English Virgin Martyr Legends, ed. Karen A. Winstead (Ithaca, NY, 2000)

Colledge, Edmund, 'The Capgrave "Autographs"', *Transactions of the Cambridge Bibliographical Society*, 6 (1974), 137–48

——, and Cyril Smetana, 'Capgrave's *Life of St. Norbert*: Diction, Dialect and Spelling', *Mediaeval Studies*, 34 (1972), 422–34

Delany, Sheila, *Impolitic Bodies: Poetry, Saints, and Society in Fifteenth-Century England* (Oxford, 1998)

——, 'Matronage or Patronage? The Case of Osbern Bokenham's Women Patrons', *Florilegium*, 16 (1999), 97–105

Edwards, A. S. G., 'The Transmission and Audience of Osbern Bokenham's *Legendys of Hooly Wummen*', in *Late-Medieval Religious Texts and their Transmission: Essays in Honour of A. I. Doyle*, ed. A. J. Minnis (Cambridge, 1994), pp. 157–67

——, 'Fifteenth-Century English Collections of Female Saints' Lives', *Yearbook of English Studies*, 33 (2003), 131–41

Fredeman, Jane C., 'John Capgrave's First English Composition, *The Life of St Norbert*', *Bulletin of the John Rylands Library*, 57 (1975), 280–309

——, 'Style and Characterization in John Capgrave's *Life of St Katherine*', *Bulletin of the John Rylands Library*, 62, (1980), 346–87

Gibson, Gail McMurray, *The Theater of Devotion: East Anglian Drama and Society in the Late Middle Ages* (Chicago, IL, 1989)

Görlach, Manfred, *Studies in Middle English Saints' Legends* (Heidelberg, 1998)

Grabmann, Martin, *Die Geschichte der Scholastischen Methode*, 2 vols (Freiburg, 1909–11)

Gurevich, Aron, *Medieval Popular Culture: Problems of Belief and Perception*, trans. János M. Bak and Paul A. Hollingsworth (Cambridge, 1988)

Heffernan, Thomas J., *Sacred Biography: Saints and Their Biographers in the Middle Ages* (Oxford, 1988)

Hilles, Carroll, 'Gender and Politics in Osbern Bokenham's Legendary', *New Medieval Literatures*, 4 (2001), 189–212

Horobin, Simon, 'A Manuscript found in the Library of Abbotsford House and the Lost Legendary of Osbern Bokenham', *English Manscript Studies*, 1100–1700, 14 (2008), 130–62

Horstmann, Carl, ed., *Sammlung Altenglischer Legenden* (Heilbronn, 1878)

——, 'Thomas Beket, epische Legende, von Laurentius Wade (1497), nach der einzigen Hs. im Corp. Chr. Coll. Cambr. 298, p. 1 ff', *Englische Studien*, 3 (1880), 409–69

——, ed., *Altenglische Legenden: Neue Folge* (Heilbronn, 1881)

James, Sarah, '"Doctryne and studie": Female Learning and Religious Debate in Capgrave's *Life of St Katharine*', *Leeds Studies in English*, n.s. 36 (2005), 275–302

Jenkins, Jacqueline, and Katherine J. Lewis, *St Katherine of Alexandria: Texts and Contexts* (Turnhout, 2003)

Johnson, Ian, 'Tales of a True Translator: Medieval Literary Theory, Anecdote and Autobiography in Osbern Bokenham's *Legendys of Hooly Wummen*', in *The Medieval Translator: 4*, ed. Roger Ellis and Ruth Evans (Binghamton, NY, 1994), pp. 104–24

Kurvinen, Auvo, 'The Source of Capgrave's *Life of St Katharine of Alexandria*', *Neuphilologische Mitteilungen*, 61 (1960), 268–324

Lewis, Katherine J., *The Cult of St Katherine of Alexandria in Late Medieval England* (Cambridge, 2000)

——, 'Pilgrimage and the Cult of St Katherine in Late Medieval England', in Jenkins and Lewis, eds, *St Katherine of Alexandria*, pp. 37–52

Lucas, Peter J., 'John Capgrave and the *Nova legenda Anglie*: A Survey', *The Library*, 5th series, 25 (1970), 1–10

——, 'A Fifteenth-Century Copyist at Work under Authorial Scrutiny: An Incident from John Capgrave's Scriptorium', *Studies in Bibliography*, 34 (1981), 66–95

——, *From Author to Audience: John Capgrave and Medieval Publication* (Dublin, 1997)

McSheffrey, Shannon, *Gender and Heresy: Women and Men in Lollard Communities, 1420–1530* (Philadelphia, PA, 1995)

Mycoff, David, 'Two Sources of Osbern Bokenham's *Lyf of Marye Maudelyn*', *Notes and Queries*, n.s. 32 (1985), 310–12

Obermeier, Anita, 'Joachim's Infertility in the St Anne's Legend', in *Chaucer and the Challenges of Medievalism: Studies in Honor of H. A. Kelly*, eds Donka Minkova and Theresa Tinkle (Frankfurt, 2003), pp. 289–307

Pearsall, Derek, 'John Capgrave's *Life of St Katharine* and Popular Romance Style', *Medievalia et Humanistica*, n.s. 6 (1975), 121–37

Price, Paul, 'Trumping Chaucer: Osbern Bokenham's *Katherine*', *Chaucer Review*, 36 (2001), 158–83

Salih, Sarah, *Versions of Virginity in Late Medieval England* (Cambridge, 2001)

——, ed., *A Companion to Middle English Hagiography* (Cambridge, 2006)

Selections from English Wycliffite Writings, ed. Anne Hudson (Cambridge, 1978)

Seymour, M. C. 'The Manuscripts of John Capgrave's English Works', *Scriptorium*, 40 (1986), 248–55

——, *John Capgrave*, Authors of the Middle Ages, 11 (Aldershot, 1996)

Stanbury, Sarah, 'The Vivacity of Images: St Katherine, Knighton's Lollards, and the Breaking of Idols', in *Images, Idolatry, and Iconoclasm in Late Medieval England: Textuality and the Visual Image*, eds Jeremy Dimmick, James Simpson and Nicolette Zeeman (Oxford, 2002), pp. 131–50

Stouck, Mary–Ann, 'Chaucer and Capgrave's *Life of St Katherine*', *American Benedictine Review*, 33 (1982), 276–91

Tracy, Larissa, 'The Middle English *Life of Saint Dorothy* in Trinity College, Dublin MS 319: Origins, Parallels, and its Relationship to Osbern Bokenham's *Legendys of Hooly Wummen*', *Traditio*, 62 (2007), 259–84

Vauchez, André, *Sainthood in the Later Middle Ages*, trans. Jean Birrell (Cambridge, 1997)

de Voragine, Jacobus, *The Golden Legend: Readings on the Saints*, trans. William Granger Ryan, 2 vols (Princeton, NJ, 1993)

Winstead, Karen A., 'Piety, Politics, and Social Commitment in Capgrave's *Life of St Katherine*', *Medievalia et Humanistica*, n.s. 17 (1991), 59–80

——, 'Capgrave's Saint Katherine and the Perils of Gynecocracy', *Viator*, 25 (1994), 361–76

——, 'John Capgrave and the Chaucer Tradition', *Chaucer Review*, 30 (1996), 389–400

——, *Virgin Martyrs: Legends of Sainthood in Late Medieval England* (Ithaca, NY, 1997)

——, *John Capgrave's Fifteenth Century* (Philadelphia, 2007)

9

Peter Idley and George Ashby

JOHN SCATTERGOOD

'"Al that is writen is writen for our doctrine", and that is myn entente', writes Chaucer, quoting Romans 15: 4, and seeking to excuse himself for his 'trans-lacions and enditynges of worldly vanities' (*CT*, X. 1083). But even if this claim were generally true of the Middle Ages, it would also be possible to maintain that some writings are more obviously intended to transmit learning than others. Books of instructional or educational advice, which are the subject of this chapter, are designed to transmit the accumulated wisdom – both bookish and experien-tial – from one generation to the next. Characteristically, experienced spiritual advisors set out rules for novices; sophisticated political philosophers counsel kings and princes; fathers and mothers instruct their sons and daughters in suit-able comportment and behaviour.

The repetitive generality of advice manuals – the conventionality of their senti-ments and their heavy dependence on traditional sources, well-known stories, and exempla – have caused them to be held in low modern esteem: they have been called 'empty' books. Referring specifically to 'mirrors for princes' Judith Ferster explains why – though what she says could as easily apply to other, non-political, types of manuals. It is a view she proceeds to contest interestingly: 'they are often seen as compilations of platitudes, clichés, and ancient stories so general, so distant in time and place, and so inert that they have no bearing on political concerns contemporary with their writers and translators' (Ferster 1996: 2). But, most books of advice are individualised and reflect the conditions in which they were produced. And certainly, Peter Idley and George Ashby, who are the subjects of what follows, made their books sharp and relevant to their addressees by discussing, in the context of counsel, important contemporary social and political questions, on which they had opinions which, though often blandly expressed, were deeply held and to which they were committed.

They were particularly well qualified to intervene in these matters. Both were royal officials of some standing, not major makers of policy but people accus-tomed to operate close to where important decisions were made. Both were now what would be called civil servants and this was a category of society whose members were becoming increasingly likely to write. They were professional men who, in T. F. Tout's words, '[...] made their career and earned their living in the service of the state and went on with their work until death, promotion, pension or dismissal bought their official careers to an end'. In the early Middle Ages in England, he says, they were 'to a large extent clerks, that is, actual or potential ecclesiastics' (Tout 1929: 366–9; Kerby-Fulton and Justice 1997). But later, in the fourteenth and fifteenth centuries, '[...] the lay civil servant came increasingly to the fore, gradually making his way into posts hitherto regarded as the exclusive preserve of the clerk, so that the word clerk began to connote not ecclesiastic so much as writer' (Tout 1929: 369). They would be required to have a good knowledge of the three languages then in official use – Latin, French and English – the traditional formalities and precedents associated with their offices, and skill in reporting, letter-writing and accounting. Some knowledge of the workings of Parliament and the law were also necessary. According to Tout, 'the normal school of the civil servant was a sort of apprenticeship, either in the royal household or in some government office under a senior officer' (ibid.: 369) – as was apparently the case with Idley and Ashby. They were accustomed to receiving orders and instruction and, because they had some authority and responsibility for others, accustomed to giving orders and instruction too. As part of their day-to-day occupations, they listened and were listened to, they learned and they taught.

Both Idley and Ashby, who were contemporaries, had reference points in the precedents of earlier civil service poets – particularly Chaucer and Hoccleve – which, no doubt, gave them confidence that they were well informed and clever people in regard to contemporary issues of national and personal governance, and who had a legitimate voice, which might appropriately comment on contemporary issues and might, conceivably, influence policies and events.

'I was born in Kent', says Peter Idley in his *Instructions to his Son* (Idley, ed. D'Evelyn 1935: II, A. 1426), but most of his activities were located in Oxfordshire, where he possessed a manor in Drayton St Leonards and a tenement called Segrave Place in Dorchester and other property elsewhere (Idley, ed. D'Evelyn 1935: 1–35). He was a prosperous country squire and is associated with the important families of the area, particularly the Stonors to whom he may have been related by marriage. But, like some people from this area of fifteenth-century society, he was called, on occasion, to public office. In 1439 he was appointed 'bailiff for the honour of Wallingford and St Valery and the four and a half hundreds of Chiltern' (ibid.: 5), part of the duchy of Cornwall. At its centre was the town and imposing castle of Wallingford, a royal residence. Idley's duties consisted largely of collecting rents and keeping accounts: he had a superior, the Receiver, to whom he was accountable, and at least seven sub-bailiffs to assist him. He held this post until 1447. On 16 July 1453 he was appointed gentleman falconer and under-keeper of the royal mews and falcons. Whether Idley trained or flew the falcons cannot be determined: he had two underlings, Henry Kemp and the appropriately named Hankyn Faucon. Again this is likely to have been an administrative and accounting position. But he did not keep this job for long. On 8 March 1456 he was appointed for life as Controller of the King's Works throughout the kingdom. He worked alongside the clerk and supervisor – a position Chaucer had earlier held – each of whom had a deputy and subordinate clerks. The maintenance of royal palaces – the provision of materials and the organisation of labour – was a highly responsible job and Idley held it until 20 July 1461, when Edward IV had him replaced: it looks as though he was the victim of dynastic change when the Yorkists came to power. This was the last public appointment that he held: the rest of his life was probably spent largely on his Oxfordshire estates. Idley made his will on 12 November 1473 and died probably in early 1474. He was not buried in his local parish church but, in splendid fashion, in the nearby Dorchester Abbey: his grave was in the south chancel and was marked by a memorial brass, which in its original form showed Idley armed, except for helmet and gauntlets, flanked by his two wives, Elizabeth and Anne, and their children, five boys and five girls, together with the coats of arms of the families, the Idleys, the Draytons and (probably) the Cretings. A rhyme royal stanza in English commemorating them all appears beneath their feet. The brass is a very calculated and comprehensive family memorial, but perhaps also an oblique belated reference to the fact that in his lifetime Idley had written thousands of lines of poetry in this form.

Other than this, there is nothing in the records of Idley's busy and successful life that suggests he may have had literary ambitions, albeit modest ones. He says in his *Instructions to his Son* that the subject matter of the poem came 'som by experience and som by writynge' (II, A. 31), but most of it comes from earlier literary sources. When Idley wanted to write a book of advice to his son he turned to books that were directly and appropriately relevant – initially to the three treatises written by the Italian lawyer Albertanus da Brescia between 1238 and 1246 for his three sons. But though Idley is heavily dependent on Albertanus for the advice he gives, Idley uses it very much in his own way: he refers to the *De Amore et Dilectione Dei* in his Latin heading and uses Latin quotations and Latin headings to divide up his own work, but he jumps from text to text (Idley, ed. D'Evelyn: 36–44). The narrative framework of the story of Melibeus and Prudence, which had shaped the *Liber de Consolationis et Consilii* (which Chaucer had followed), Idley ignores and simply adopts much of the advice. He also intersperses this advice with other material – often from the Bible, Seneca, Cato's *Distichs*, traditional gnomic wisdom and proverbs. Characteristically, he will begin a stanza following Albertanus, but extrapolate from other texts. In a stanza justifying war in one's own defence he writes:

> Also for thy persone to make sauffgarde
> It is leeful to haue wapon in hande,
> Manly to fight and not to flee as a cowarde,
> Thyn enemys malice to withstande,
> Be stronge in herte, bow not as a wande,
> Or as a dormoyse þat al day slepeth:
> A good castell saueth he þat his body kepeth. (Idley: lines 862–68)

The sentiments informing the opening of this are from Albertanus, but the final line is ultimately from St Bernard, probably by way of *The Prick of Conscience*, where the reference is given: 'A gude castelle', he says, 'kepes he þat his body kepes in honeste' (Whiting 1968: C 427 and C 72). St Bernard twice says that this is a popular proverb and proverbs are very much to the point in lines 866–7: 'bow not as a wand' or its variants are common in Middle English (ibid.: W 30, W 34), and the following line is an unrecorded version of 'to sleep like a dormouse', earlier than the earliest versions cited in the standard collections (Tilley 1950: D 568).

Idley opens his treatise by reminding his son of the disparity of their ages: 'thi fadre in age is' but the son is 'yonge and somedele wylde' (I, 7). He is passing wisdom on to his son, he says, so that he should learn things in youth so that when he does not have his father to guide him he may be able to 'helpe thysilf and thy frendis alle' (line 34) by using what he has learnt: 'teche it forthe [...] ffor connyng enclosed is litell worthe' (lines 43–5). The wisdom that this book has to offer is essentially of a conformist moral kind, which takes for granted the hierarchical nature of late medieval society and the responsibilities and mores of the gentry class:

> ffirst God and thy kyng þou loue and drede
> Aboue all thyng þou this preserue. (lines 8–9)

Idley thinks in a prudential and cautionary way. The preservation of social cohesion and the avoidance of strife are high on his agenda: 'Peas aboue all thyng is beste' (line 188). Therefore, one should consider carefully what one says so as not to appear malicious or censorious and thus make enemies (lines 50–98), not be too hasty in making promises or taking vengeance (lines 225–38), readily take advice and counsel in all things (lines 239–490), be patient in adversity (lines 638–65), behave with kindness and mercy (lines 953–87), and be generous and charitable to the poor because 'Al that we geve [...] in this wretched vale' will be restored in 'the blis aboue' (lines 1037–8). At a more personal level, Idley advises his son to choose his company carefully and 'flee tauernes and felawshippe of women' (line 391), be true to one's friends and not trust strangers too readily (lines 931–52), reward one's useful councillors (lines 540–6) and good servants (lines 1288–95) and behave well and considerately towards one's wife (lines 1226–302). But implicit in all this is the concept of a society that is not only stratified but also static, built on a wish for stability and a contentment with one's estate:

> Desire no more þan may be hadde be kynde;
> Clymbe no hyer þan þou may reche belowe,
> ffor drede lest þou be ouerthrowe. (lines 843–5)

One should not be ostentatious in dress (lines 99–119) and be modest in expenditure (lines 197–220), take no pride in the possession of temporal goods (lines 666–707), and beware of the instability of fortune (lines 603–37) lest it lead to poverty and necessity, the worst of all fates:

> Nede of alle synnes is chieff modre and Queene;
> She dryueth a man to thefte and murdre alsoo;
> She dryueth a man to purge hem. (lines 708–10)

Need is harmful both socially, morally and personally, says the practical, wealthy gentry landowner, because 'who hath goodis temporall hath a noble frende' (line 684): they enable one to 'purchase blisse and voyde payn' (line 692).

Idley distinguishes Book II of his *Instructions to his Son* from what he had already written by saying that he had earlier spoken of 'certen thyngis in esspeciall' and now he was turning to what was more 'generall' (II, A. 1–2) – possibly meaning that what the second book contains is not so directly applicable to Thomas – but actually the second book is driven by a much more overtly religious agenda. Idley proposes to treat the ten commandments, the seven deadly sins, sacrilege, the seven sacraments, the twelve points of Christ and the 'xij gracis of Goddis gyfte' (line 20). An exposition of the Decalogue is fully covered with various exemplary stories, as is the section on the capital sins, though it ends with a promise of a story that is not told, and the same is true of the section on sacrilege. But the other topics are not treated. Idley evidently abandoned the work, possibly because of the death of Thomas, who is known to have predeceased his father. The text did, however, have a circulation outside the immediate family context: eleven manuscript copies have survived in various states of completeness (see Sullivan and *NIMEV* 1540).

Like the first book, Book II is heavily derivative: much of it is based on Robert Mannyng of Bourne's *Handlyng Synne*, which is itself a fourteenth-century translation of an earlier French penitential manual. Idley largely adopts the structure of Mannyng's treatise, but more than this, he uses (as he can because he is dealing with English) Mannyng's own words – though Mannyng wrote in short couplets and Idley in rhyme royal. Sometimes this is sporadic, but on occasions it is more comprehensive. In an uncompromising analysis of the mechanical poetic process involved, Charlotte D'Evelyn explains: 'Idley found that he could construct one rhyme royal stanza by the simple process of alternating the first two couplets *ab ab*, adding a fifth line of his own *b*, and ending with the third couplet unchanged *cc*' (Idley, ed. D'Evelyn 1935: 46, and for the examples that follow). In his account of the pot of manna (Exodus, 16: 32–6) Mannyng has the following:

> Yn þe potte was a floure,
> Whyte, and swete of al sauoure,
> Þat floure is kalled 'aungelis mete'
> Þat God ȝafe þe folke to ete
> Whan þey were yn wyldernes
> Forty wyntyr, yn hard stres. (ed. Furnivall: lines 4999–5004)

Idley's version of this is:

> In the pott was put a precious floure
> The floure was called Aungelis meete,
> White and swete and of al goode odoure,
> That God gaffe the people for to eete
> When they were in deserte and noght cowde gete;
> ffourty winter in right grete distresse
> they lieved right streite and harde in wildirnesse. (II, B. 1444–49)

Idley likewise plunders Lydgate's *Fall of Princes*: 'from it Idley has taken undisguisedly forty-six stanzas' (Idley, ed. D'Evelyn 1935: 49). Interestingly, some of these occur in the section of the Decalogue on theft, against which Idley speaks with characteristic moral vehemence: 'Allas! It is a foule name to be called a theif' (II, A. 2231). But he does steal, not only the ideas of previous writers but also their words. For him, literary appropriation clearly did not count as theft: *autres temps, autres moeurs.*

But despite his reliance on earlier sources, his conventionalism, his general espousal of the political and social status quo, and his generational cast of thinking, Idley does have things to say about the contingencies of his own society, its pressures and problems. He is especially sensitive to developments that might bear on his idea of a comfortable and stable existence for himself and his family.

These are many, but they are apparent usually in his nuancing of his sources. Albertanus, for example, has a single statement on the defence of one's country: *'pugna pro patria'* [fight for the fatherland]. Idley emphatically expands this, perhaps conscious, like a loyal Lancastrian servant, of the comparative weakness of English military positions in France or the threats to Henry VI from various quarters:

> Looke in the be founde noo necligence
> To stande with thy kynge in the Reawmes defence. (I, 858–9)

The patriotic duty to defend one's country is a traditional sentiment in advice manuals, and much of Idley's thought is traditional in the sense that he distrusts the modern. He adds his voice, for example, to the chorus of criticism that was made against the extravagance of contemporary dress: the 'galaunt' was a common figure of ridicule (Scattergood 1971: 339–47). Like others, Idley criticises short gowns for their impracticality and immodesty:

> They be cutted on the buttok even aboue the rompe.
> Euery good man truly suche shappe lothes;
> It maketh hym a body short as a stompe,
> And if they shull croke, knele othir crompe,
> To the middes of the backe the gowne woll not reche. (II, B. 44–8)

Yet these are worn by everyone, he complains, rich or poor, and this leads some to adopt the 'craft of a theif' in order to be able to pay for them (II, B. 55). But worst of all there is a blurring of social rank, which is all due to pride: it is hard to discern the difference between 'a tapester, a cookesse, or an hostellers wyffe/ ffro a gentilwoman' because they compete with each other as to who is 'freshest' in dress (II, B. 267–70). And it is the same with men: 'A man shall not now kenne a knaue from a knyght' because they dress in the same way. And here the hierarchical and class-based nature of Idley's thinking and that of his culture comes through. It would be more fitting, he explains, for 'eche man to kenne hymsilf and his better' and for clothes to vary according to rank:

> And as they be in ordre set of degree,
> Right so shall her clothyng and arraie be. (II, B. 69–70)

'In heuene and erthe an ordre must be accepte', says Idley, and unless there is a hierarchy 'somme to obeie and somme to gouerne aboue', all 'welthe, worship and love' will be destroyed (71–84). This was a major concern of the sumptuary legislation enacted in 1463 (Scattergood 1996: 240–57). But, equally, Idley knows that there is potential for social movement in his society, the possibility of prospering, and he is determined to make Thomas study the law, even threatening to disinherit him if he does not (ibid.: 223–5). He knows that the law is corrupt

– that it is lax (II, A. 2610–3), that lords promote servants who 'with the lawe [...] can wrastill and wrangle' for their masters' advantage (II, B. 1054), that executors make profits for themselves out of the maladministration of wills (II, B. 1632–6) and that perjury is prevalent in the law courts (II, A. 2708–13) – but, nevertheless, he intends his son for the profession, if he can behave morally within it because, 'To grete worshippe hath the lawe / Brought forth many a pouere man' (I. 141–2). It was a common route for the children of the gentry to follow.

Like Idley, George Ashby was a lifetime Lancastrian servant, who both prospered from his allegiance and suffered for it, a situation he ponders in *A Prisoner's Reflections*, written in the Fleet in 1463 (Ashby, ed. Bateson 1965: I, 337–8), where he had been 'a hoole yere and more' (line 30). He had made his career, he tells us, 'in the hyghest court that I coude fynd' (line 59), serving Humfrey, Duke of Gloucester, Henry VI and Margaret of Anjou, working for forty years as a clerk in the Signet Office, 'aswell beyond the see as on thys syde' (lines 64–5). And practically everything he says is borne out by the public records (Summers 2004: 142–4; Meyer-Lee 2007: 140–1; Scattergood 2004, II, 619–20). In 1437 he is mentioned as one of the four clerks of the Signet Office and in 1439 he was 'appointed by the king to go beyond the sea to Calais' (Scattergood 2004) with the secretary Thomas Beckington. He was rewarded for this work by annuities, such as that for £10 yearly for life in 1441, or by grants: he was made constable of Dinevor Castle in 1438 and appointed steward of Warwick in 1446, from which he would have taken the fees while paying for the work to be done by substitutes, though he may have maintained some contact with Warwick because he was MP for Warwick in 1459. In 1444 he was one of the embassy who brought Margaret of Anjou to England, and in 1446 the queen wrote to an unidentified lady in gratitude 'for service to George Ashby, Clerk of our Signet' (Scattergood 2004) – so he may have worked for her at that time. The affection she evidently had for him was matched by that of Henry VI who, in 1452, wrote to the abbot and convent of Glastonbury that they should admit him to their house and minister to him 'in consideration of the good and unpaid service with the queen on either side of the sea' (Scattergood 2004). Evidently, Ashby, like other medieval civil servants, sometimes found it difficult to get his wages paid on time. But this did not prevent him from acquiring the manor of Breakspeares in Harefield (Middlesex), along with some other land in that county, where he presumably had a family life with his wife Margaret and son John away from the court.

But it was almost certainly because he was a Lancastrian adherent that Ashby was imprisoned – part of the reprisals after the crushing Yorkist victory at Towton in 1461: he was imprisoned, he tells us, in the autumn, probably of that year, 'At the ende of somer, when wynter began / And trees, herbes and flowres dyd fade' (lines 1–2). All that Ashby says about his committal is that it was by a 'gret commaundment of a lord' (line 9), but on what grounds is not stated: nor, it appears, was Ashby ever brought to trial. In Cambridge, Trinity College, MS R. 3. 19, the unique copy of Ashby's poem is preceded by a Middle English version of Boccaccio's savage story of Guiscardo and Ghismonda, from *Decameron*, IV. 1, which involves wrongful imprisonment on the grounds of revenge, and it looks as though the compiler of the book wanted this juxtaposition, for Ashby constantly maintains that he was 'commytted geynst right and reason' (line 7) and 'wrongfully certeyn' (line 52; Scattergood 1996: 266–74).

Ashby's poem is a compelling mixture – the personal leading to the general. As has been seen, he is precise about who he is, about his experience, about where he is imprisoned, and about how long he has been there, but he says little about the experience of imprisonment. We do not know, either, what books – if any – Ashby had with him in the Fleet, but the movement of his poem, from his personal history to more general considerations, may be modelled on *The Consolation of Philosophy* I, Prose 4 or *The Testament of Love* I, vi–vii and x, where Boethius and Thomas Usk, both imprisoned public servants, respectively review their careers and talk about the political reasons for their imprisonment, before moving on to more general moral and philosophical considerations arising from their misfortunes. And it may have been from these sources – perhaps to hand, perhaps remembered – that Ashby got the theme that informs and shapes his poem, that imprisonment is best countered and addressed in terms of the virtue of patience or suffering. He may have read in Chaucer's translation of Boethius that 'at laste, it byhoveth the to suffren with evene wil in patience al that is doon inwith the floor of Fortune (that is to seyn, in this world) syn thou hast oonys put thy nekke under the yoke of hir' (Chaucer, *Boece* I, Prose 1, 91–5). Or he may have read, more politically, in Usk: 'What power hath ony man to lette another in living in virtue? For prisonment, or ony other disease, [if] he take it paciently, discomfiteth he nat, the tyrant over his soule no power may have' (Usk: II, xi, 53–6). At any event, like them, he sees himself as his own exemplum (Summers 2004: 150–5; Meyer-Lee 2007: 141–2). His poem will set out a 'lesson' (line 12), he says, it will furnish 'lore' (line 33):

> I thynke to wryte of trouble rehersall,
> How hyt may be takyn in pacyence. (lines 113–14)

Though he has no 'termes of eloquence' he feels he can say something so that 'euery man' (line 119) can be instructed. He presents himself, as Joanna Summers puts it, as 'an imprisoned public servant whose experiences are redeployed for the philosophical pedagogical benefit of his readers' (Summers 2004: 152).

The autobiographical mode chosen by Ashby is plain and direct: he does not use interlocutors, as Boethius and Usk had, nor does he use humour, irony or textual games such as can be found in other prison writings. But he does frame his thinking with reference to other, usually homiletic, writings. For him, patience and suffering were not inert virtues. They were traditionally regarded as sovereign remedies against the capital sin of anger, and Ashby alludes to this when he says that he cultivates them 'the better from tene me refreyne' (line 87). Ashby details his sufferings. He complains that he has been reviled with 'vnfyt-tyng langage/ as thaugh I were neyther wytty ne sage' (lines 74–5). Of his loss of property he instances 'takyng awey hors, money, and goodes/ pullyng myne houses downe and grete woodes' (lines 20–1). He has been left without 'a dyssh, neyther cup' (line 24) and complains of his 'pouert' (line 77) and 'unpayable det' (line 44). It looks as though his estates were plundered as soon as it was known that he was out of favour and not there to defend them – a fairly common occurrence in the fluctuating fortunes of the Wars of the Roses. About his physical suffering Ashby says little and that little is metaphorical: he has had to bear false imputations (line 27), and imprisonment without hope of release 'greveth myn hert heuyly and sore' (line 32). But there is nothing about torture or actual physical hardship: it looks as though his gaolers, at least, had some regard to his age. The enforced idleness of imprisonment also causes him, because, as his autobiography has established, he always worked busily, to fear that he may fall into the sin of sloth, to which idleness was traditionally the gateway. Ashby maintains, with reference to this concept, that patience and suffering are also means of standing against 'gostly sorow', by which he means *accidia* or *tristitia*. But writing is another means. In his *envoi* Ashby says he writes because he has nothing else to do, 'thus occupying me' (line 339). And this is all part of a general tendency in the poem: Ashby constantly extrapolates from patience to other virtues – 'temperaunce' (line 180), 'mekenes' (line 210), 'humilyte and soburnes' (line 302) – which are also important in the *envoi* to his poem.

Ashby ostensibly offers a traditional *envoi*: he opens it with the 'Goo forthe, lytyll boke' formula and his version does what is expected – recapitulates the purpose of the poem, expresses modesty and amenability 'my defaut to correct' (line 328) and seeking the 'favour, support and goodnesse' (line 331) of his readers. But, interestingly, this does not appear to refer simply to poetry. Ashby's wording here is important: the statement that 'I wyll nat kepe presumptuously / any errour or feynyd opinion' (lines 324–5) and his attribution of any offence that he may have committed to ill-advised ignorance and not to 'wylfulnesse' (lines 333–4) suggest that he is amenable to correction in political as well as literary terms, that he is not politically dangerous or intransigent. He presents himself as a thanklessly discarded old retainer and the hope of being in 'heuyn menyall / seruant' (lines 208–9) is consistent with this. This is an underling's poem, a dependent's poem, and Ashby no doubt felt justified in claiming that what had caused his fall from fortune was not attributable to anything he had done personally. His counsel here is for every man and the lesson of patience is for all classes who suffer 'greuance' as he lists them, 'kyng, Queene, Duke, Prynce and Emperoures / Erle, Baron, lord' and so on down the social scale ending with 'counseylours' (lines 260–6). But when he wrote these seemingly bland lines Ashby knew that the king and queen whom he had served, Henry VI and Margaret of Anjou, were fugitives in exile, and that he had been committed to prison in the autumn after a battle they had lost. In a subtle and penetrating reading of the autumnal opening of this poem, Robert Meyer-Lee writes: 'In just a few lines Ashby has [...] linked the decline of the natural world, the decline of the political world and located their intersection in his internal struggle to regain a sense of cosmic order' (Meyer-Lee 2007: 143). Ashby's misfortune is that of the Lancastrian dynasty. The abandoned servant suffers with his masters, but can still counsel them to the patience he adopts himself in the hope of better times.

A change of fortune for the Lancastrian dynasty and for their loyal servant George Ashby are assumed in the rest of his surviving and identifiable poetry, which consists of 'mirror for princes' advice written for Edward (1453–71), the son of Henry VI and Margaret of Anjou and heir to the throne. Mary Bateson distinguished two pieces, the *Active Policy of a Prince*, 918 lines of advice, both general and specific, and the *Dicta et Opiniones Diversorum Philosophorum*, 1,263 lines of discontinuous advice in English based on Latin texts that precede each stanza. As I have argued elsewhere, however, it seems to me that both texts are part of the same project of advising (Scattergood 1996: 167–76). Both texts occur uniquely in CUL, MS Mm. 4. 42: both are mentioned in a much-defaced Latin preface in which the poet names himself, speaks of his work at the Signet Office for Queen Margaret, of the intention of the work as being for the benefit of Prince Edward, of the division of the work into a contemplation of past, present and future, after which he mentions the 'edicta et opiniones diuersorum philoso-phorum' as if they were to be regarded as ancillary material, supporting and verifying the main thrust of the argument of the *Active Policy*, with which they are wholly consistent. The practice of using a Latin text to preface a stanza of English advice, characteristic of the procedure of the *Dicta*, also appears sporadi-cally in the *Active Policy* (see lines 331, 352, 653, 793, 821, 828 and 842), and the two texts are written continuously without a break in the manuscript.

It also seems highly likely that the *Active Policy* and the *Dicta* were probably begun at the same time as Ashby's animadversions on his imprisonment in 1463. In two consecutive stanzas (lines 527–40) he echoes two related acts of parlia-ment promulgated in that year (see *Rotuli Parliamentorum*, ed. Strachey, V: 501, 504). The acts begin in the traditional way, 'Prayen the Comens in this present Parlement' and go on, in the first instance, to ask for support for the indigenous cloth-making industry to prevent people from falling into 'ydelnes', and, in the second, to ask that sumptuary laws be enacted as in 'the days of youre moost noble Progenitours' because of the 'excessive and inordynat arayes' assumed by the populace. Ashby recommends to Prince Edward what Edward IV had already enacted, alluding unmistakably to these acts:

> Yif ye wol bring vp ayen clothe makyng,
> And kepe youre Comyns oute of ydelnesse (lines 527–8)

And assures him that if he did this he would receive 'many a blessyng'. He is also urged to forbid the 'pouer Comyns' 'excesse […] in their arraye' according to the 'statute of youre progenitours' (lines 534–40). Whether or not Ashby was still in prison at the time he wrote this is impossible to know, but, if he was, he certainly knew in detail what was going on in the political world outside.

It is important, it seems to me, to realise that Ashby's ideas are sometimes grounded in contemporary contingent actualities, because the way he presents his advice to Prince Edward suggests a rather different perspective. The phrase that Ashby uses of his texts in the manuscript preface is 'compilatus, extractus et anglicatus' [compiled, extracted and put into English] and it looks as though he regards himself less as an *auctor* and more as a *compilator*, one who gathers and repeats or reports the words of others (Minnis: 100–2, 194–200). And this is also very much how he presents himself and the poetic lineage to which he belongs in the *Active Policy*, which opens with the almost obligatory modesty formula and deference to 'Maisters Gower, Chaucer & Lydgate' (line 1), whom Ashby follows 'not as a master but as a prentise' (line 28) – the underling's stance again. To all these writers he does owe something, but throughout Ashby's writings – as a kind of absent presence – is his civil service predecessor Thomas Hoccleve: as James Simpson rightly puts it, Ashby's writing is 'saturated with Hocclevian echoes' (Simpson 2002: 225). Ashby complains in his opening to the *Active Policy* that he has 'not seien scripture/ of many bookes right sentenciall' and particularly that he has not had access to 'the gloses sure' (lines 50–2). What precisely he had in mind here is not clear, but it is known that he appropriated a stanza, now *Active Policy* 688–94, from *The Court of Sapience* (*Court*, ed. Harvey 1984: xxiii–xxiv), that the concluding stanza, lines 912–18, is based heavily on a stanza on temperance from an anonymous poem on the virtues required of a prince (Kekewich), that the Latin prefacing eight stanzas of the *Dicta* depend on material from the *Liber de dictis philosophorum antiquorum* (Bühler), and that lines 426–7 may be taken from Benedict Burgh's *Distichs of Cato* (but see Whiting 1968: S 559 for other versions of this proverb). It may be that evidence of other borrowings will emerge.

Much of the advice in the *Active Policy* and the *Dicta* is conventional and derivative, and stated at a high level of generality. There are moments, however, when it looks as though Ashby is thinking in more specific terms. The poem on Ashby's imprisonment was for 'euery man', but this sequence of advice is for one person, Prince Edward, and some of it is focused on his particular situation. Though Ashby refers to 'cronicles' (line 155), there are no narrative exempla in these texts that would suggest the long perspectives of history, but a narrow concentration on the problems of the Lancastrian dynasty, the civil wars and breaches of public order in disturbed times. The opening of the *Active Policy* not only establishes Ashby's poetic lineage, but, more importantly, the lineage of its addressee:

> youre highnesse Edwarde by name,
> Trewe sone & heire to the high maieste
> Of oure liege lorde / Kynge henry and dame
> Margarete, the Queene. (II, 92–5)

This is not simply a eulogistic compliment from poet to possible benefactor, but propaganda designed to establish Prince Edward's status as the heir to the throne of England and perhaps also to counter rumours of his illegitimacy, circulated at times by the Yorkists. Ashby's lessons from history seem to be from recent history. 'There hath be in late daies right grete change/ of high estates and grete diuision' (lines 169–70), he writes, thinking probably of the 'grete batellis dispiteous' (line 193), like Towton, of the civil wars. He refers also to the feuds between noble and gentry families, endemic at the time, sustained by private armies of indentured retainers: gentlemen, he says, should 'maynteine no people' nor 'false quarrels take thorough maintenance' (lines 549–52) – which Edward IV acted on in 1468 – but Ashby articulates all this in terms of general precepts. So too with the advice to 'suppresse youre false conspiratours' (line 381), 'subdewe al maner rebellyon' (line 388) and 'be ye ware of the reconsiled' (line 427), which last warning may refer to the public reconciliation between Henry VI and the Yorkists of 1458, which did not last long, or to the accord between Henry VI and Richard, Duke of York in 1460, which did not last long either. Ashby also stresses the need to make sure the commons 'be welthy/in richesse, goodes and prosperite' because they are more likely to be law-abiding (lines 499–505), which may have been prompted by a memory of Jack Cade's rebellion of 1450. But again, typically of the genre in which Ashby is writing, wisdom based on experiential knowledge is shrouded in generality. In this text the specific shimmers in and out of view. But underlying these seemingly self-evident precepts runs an insistent voice, which urges prudence and caution, a need for wariness about who one can trust and who is to be regarded with suspicion, and Ashby predictably makes a case for himself and others like him in this respect: he points out that he has 'fallen in decrepit age/ right nygh at mony yeres of foure score' (lines 64–5) and counsels the choosing of old and tried servants 'remembryng with whom thei haue been vpbrought' (line 473); and, no doubt remembering the 'unpaid service' he had performed, says bluntly 'paie youre men theire wages & dues' (line 296). He also recommends remuneration and support especially for 'suche as be makers' because these 'may exaltat youre name & werkes' (lines 613–4). The allusion here is to the ancient idea that writers 'bear up', to use Chaucer's phrase, the fame of great men by memorialising their deeds for posterity, though Ashby, typically, sees it as part of the transaction between royal master and civil servant.

'Fifteenth-century writing is to a great extent the literature of public servants, and these men were adroit survivors, men of letters and politically expert', David Lawton argues – and there is some truth in this, if only at the level of their aspirations (Lawton 1987: 788). Peter Idley's descendants, despite his careful will, fell into prolonged legal dissention and sometimes violence, over the ownership of his property (Idley, ed. D'Evelyn 1935: 31–5). In George Ashby's case, the recipient of all his good advice died at the battle of Tewkesbury in 1471, and with him died Lancastrian aspirations to regaining the throne of England until 1485. After his imprisonment it looks as though Ashby had no further role in public service, unless he joined his former masters in exile: he died in 1475, though once again in possession of his manor at Breakspeares. It would be easy to say that all this well-meant advice did not work, that it was rendered irrelevant by 'fortune' and the overwhelming contingencies of local and national politics. Perhaps so. But the intention of the authors of these essentially Boethian, conservative, earnest poems was to assemble and restate what they saw as the collective wisdom of the ages, insisting on certain continuities of right thinking and morally sound behaviour leading to social unity in contexts that they knew to be unstable and in which the centres of authority were uncertain. They recognised their dependent status, that their fates were largely in the hands of their more powerful masters, and accordingly attempted to use what influence they had through the civilised medium of persuasive words. That they failed to shape events is clear, but it would be wrong to say that they were not right to try.

Works cited

Ashby, George, *George Ashby's Poems*, ed. Mary Bateson, EETS, e. s. 76 (London, 1899; repr. 1965)

The Court of Sapience, ed. Ruth E. Harvey (Toronto, 1984)

Bühler, Curt F., 'The *Liber de Dictis Philosophorum Antiquorum* and Common Proverbs in George Ashby's Poems', *PMLA*, 65 (1950), 282–9

Ferster, Judith, *Fictions of Advice: The Literature and Politics of Counsel in Late Medieval England* (Philadelphia, PA, 1996)

Idley, Peter, *Peter Idley's Instructions to his Son*, ed. Charlotte D'Evelyn (Boston, 1935)

Kekewich, Margaret, 'George Ashby's *The Active Policy of a Prince*: An Additional Source', *Review of English Studies*, n.s. 41 (1990), 533–5

Kerby-Fulton, Kathryn, and Steven Justice, 'Langlandian Reading Circles and the Civil Service in London and Dublin, 1380–1427', *New Medieval Literatures*, 1 (1997), 59–83

Lawton, David, 'Dullness and the Fifteenth Century', *English Literary History*, 54 (1987), 761–99

Mannyng, Robert, *Handlyng Synne*, ed. F. J. Furnivall, EETS, o.s. 119, 123 (London, 1901–03)

Meyer-Lee, Robert J., *Poets and Power from Chaucer to Wyatt* (Cambridge, 2007)

Minnis, A. J., *Medieval Theory of Authorship: Scholastic Literary Attitudes in the Later Middle Ages* (London, 1984)

Rotuli Parliamentorum, ut et petitiones et placita in Parliamento : tempore Edwardi R. I. [Edwardi II., Edwardi III., Ricardi II., Henrici IV., V., VI., Edwardi IV., Ricardi III., Henrici VII., 1278–1503], [collected and arranged by R. Blyke, P. Morant, T. Astle and J. Topham; and edited by J. Strachey] (London, 1767–77)

Scattergood, V. J., *Politics and Poetry in the Fifteenth Century* (London, 1971)

——, *Reading the Past: Essays on Medieval and Renaissance Literature* (Dublin, 1996)

——, 'George Ashby', in *Oxford Dictionary of National Biography*, ed. H. C. G. Matthew and Brian Harrison, 60 Vols (Oxford, 2004), II, 619–20

Simpson, James, *Reform and Cultural Revolution* (Oxford, 2002)

Sullivan, Matthew, 'More Poetry by Peter Idley Transcribed from British Library MS Additional 57335'; *Neuphilologische Mittelungen*, 97 (1996), 29–55

Summers, Joanna, *Late-Medieval Prison Writing and the Politics of Autobiography* (Oxford, 2004)

Tilley, M. P., *A Dictionary of the Proverbs in England in the Sixteenth and Seventeenth Centuries* (Ann Arbor, MI, 1950)

Tout, T. F., 'Literature and Learning in the English Civil Service in the Fourteenth Century', *Speculum*, 4 (1929), 365–89

Usk, Thomas, *The Testament of Love*, in *Chaucerian and Other Pieces*, ed. W. W. Skeat (Oxford, 1897), pp. 1–145

Whiting, B. J., and H. W. Whiting, *Proverbs, Sentences and Proverbial Phrases from English Writings Mainly before 1500* (Cambridge, MA, 1968)

10

John Audelay and James Ryman

SUSANNA FEIN

John Audelay and James Ryman are linked in literary history by virtue of the circumstance that each has his name attached to a large fifteenth-century collection of religious lyrics. Collections ascribed to an author are quite rare for the period. Additionally, both Audelay's and Ryman's anthologies contain many carols, a fashionable form of lyric from the late fourteenth through the early sixteenth centuries. The two are therefore frequently paired as named authors with large corpuses of similar kind, each preserved primarily by means of a single manuscript: the Audelay manuscript (Bodl., MS Douce 302) and the Ryman manuscript (CUL, MS Ee.1.12). Each book is thought to have been made in the writer's lifetime in a religious house and in direct contact with him. Such commonalities separate Audelay and Ryman from other English writers who attracted anthologised treatments in the late Middle Ages, such as Minot, Gower, Chaucer, Lydgate, Hoccleve, Charles d'Orléans, and Bokenham (Edwards 2000); the earlier writer most like Audelay and Ryman in these shared ways is the Oxford Franciscan William Herebert (d.1333), whose holograph Latin sermons and English lyrics appear in BL, Add. MS 46919 (Herebert, ed. Reimer 1987). In the survival of English lyrics, the more usual circumstance is blank anonymity, with the making of a collection best explained as the action of a compiler who selected texts to suit the tastes or needs of specific readers. Anonymous lyrics do not allow us to define the shape of an individual poet's corpus, career or 'attitude' – a term I borrow from Rosemary Woolf: 'the value of these attributions lies not in the precise information that they convey but in the attitude that they express' (Woolf 1968: 379). To glean a sense of how individual men of the church were moved by liturgical, devotional or meditative practice to compose bodies of religious verse in English – wherein they represent a growing movement within orthodoxy to vernacularise sacred Latin prayer and hymn – the extant evidence resides disproportionately in the manuscripts of Audelay and Ryman.

Attribution has not, however, led to wide recognition of Audelay's or Ryman's merits by modern scholars. Each was edited in the late nineteenth or early twentieth century in the bare-bones, often obfuscating manner of much of the vast collective effort to put the Middle English corpus into print. For Audelay, the chief early editors were James Orchard Halliwell (1844), R. W. Chambers and F. Sidgwick (1910–11, carols only) and Ella Keats Whiting (1931). The Ryman manuscript was printed in a lengthy article by Julius Zupitza with German commentary added later (1892, 1894; Ryman's poems are here identified by Zupitza's numbers). The very fact of attribution caused these writers to be *excluded* from the most influential anthology of their type, Carleton Brown's *Religious Lyrics of the XVth Century* (1939: xviii). Eventually, their carols alone (26 items among Audelay's 87 overall, 121 among Ryman's 166) were skilfully edited but anthologised in a very disruptive fashion – arranged by theme rather than by authorial ascription or manuscript order (*Early English Carols*, ed. Greene 1977). Richard Leighton Greene's anthology has proven invaluable, but when it appeared, the definitions leading to Greene's selections and omissions were controversial. Brown, for example, questioned Greene's omission of the Ryman manuscript's *The False Fox* (Brown 1937: 125). The situation has improved recently for Audelay, his full manuscript (poetry and prose) having been newly edited (Audelay, ed. Fein 2009) and given fresh appraisal by means of a collection of new essays (Fein 2009a, containing: Bennett, Boffey, Driver, Easting, Fein 2009b and 2009c, Green, Hirsh, Meyer-Lee, Pearsall, Pickering, Powell, Stanley), and a spate of articles (Stanley 1996, 1997; Green 2001; Simpson 2004; Fein 2003, 2011a, 2011b, 2012; see also Machan 1994: 103–6; Matsuda 1997: 167–73; Citrome 2006: 84–110; Wheatley 2010: 212–19). For Ryman the editorial situation remains dismal, his noncarols left in oblivion by omission (see *Early English Carols*, ed. Greene 1977: xci, c–ci), and only a few modern scholars paying him – and generally only his carols – heed (Gneuss 1968: 216–20; Jeffrey 1984; Reichl, 2003, 2005; Edwards 2010, 531–3).

Medieval English literary studies of the present day are broadly receptive to the possibilities of what may be discovered by studying lyrics in their manuscript conditions and arrangements. There is also a growing regard for the historical knowledge to be gleaned by showing respect for the rhythms and routines, the daily sameness, of medieval religion as practised in a religious house, or even a devout secular household, which might yet bring to flower idiosyncratic sorts of poetry – Latin-inflected, inspired by hymn, antiphon and liturgy – in the vernacular. Perhaps the sheer volume of each writer's literary remains has worked against him, but, as the new work on Audelay may be demonstrating, a magnitude of evidence can be a rich resource for working out strains of thought foreign to modern sensibilities and yet evoking a lyricism for its time and place. The few anthologists who have included an individual poem or two from Audelay or Ryman have been able to capitalise on the modern preference for singularity, isolating poems that are especially striking:

> Ladé, help! Jhesu, mercé!
> Timor mortis conturbat me.
>
> Dred of deth, sorow of syn,
> Trobils my hert ful grevysly:
> My soule hit nyth with my lust then –
> Passio Christi conforta me.
>
> Fore blyndness is a hevé thyng,
> And to be def therwith only,
> To lese my lyght and my heryng –
> Passio Christi conforta me.
>
> (Audelay, in *Medieval English Lyrics*, ed. Davies 1963: 170)

O dredeful deth, come, make an ende!
Come unto me and do thy cure!
Thy payne no tunge can comprehende,
That I fele, wooful creature.
O lorde, how longe shall it endure?
Whenne shall I goo this worlde fro,
Out of this bitter payne and woo?

Full harde it is for to departe,
And harde it is this payne to abyde.
O good lorde that in heven art,
Thou be my helpe, comfort, and guyde,
Both nyght and day and every tyde,
And take my soule into thy blis,
Wherof the joye shall nevir mys.

(Ryman, no. 95; in *A Selection*, ed. Gray 1975: 94–5)

Woolf singles out Audelay's poem as the 'most personal and moving' of English death lyrics (Woolf 1968: 387), and Gray highlights Ryman's poignant address to death by selecting it to end a sequence of eleven otherwise anonymous lyrics on 'Last Things'. Like Brown, though, most anthologists bypass Audelay and Ryman altogether; the few exceptions tend to include just one poet or the other, and just one or two poems (for example, *Medieval English*, ed. Kaiser 1958; *A Selection*, ed. Greene 1962; *Oxford Book*, ed. Sisam and Sisam 1970; *English Lyrics*, ed. Silverstein 1971; *English Spirituality*, ed. Jeffrey 2000; *Medieval Lyric*, ed. Hirsh 2005).

Life records for these poets, who lived at different ends of the century, are scant outside the bare clues contained in the relatively prodigious corpuses attributed to them. For Audelay, the crucial book is MS Douce 302, dated 1426 in a Latin colophon closing the first section of the book: 'This book was composed by John Audelay, chaplain, who was blind and deaf in his affliction, to the honour of our Lord Jesus Christ and to serve as a model for others in the monastery of Haughmond, in the year 1426 A.D.' (fol. 22vb; my translation). For Ryman, virtually all evidence of his activity exists in MS Ee.1.12, where, as in Audelay's book, an internal Latin colophon records a name and date: 'Here ends the book of hymns and songs, which Brother James Ryman of the order of Friars Minor composed to the praise of omnipotent God and his most holy mother Mary and all the holy saints in the year of our Lord 1492' (fol. 80r; my translation). Beyond the 167 poems in this manuscript (164 ascribed to Ryman), two more Ryman carols – readily recognisable by style and burden – survive in the Bradshaw fragment (CUL, Add. MS 7350 [Box 2]), a bifolium similar yet not identical to MS Ee.1.12 in size and hand, and of paper instead of vellum (Robbins 1966; Croft 1981). Supplementing the manuscripts and fragment with a handful of clues from other records, we may with some confidence sketch outlines of both men's professional lives within a circumscribed span of years.

John Audelay was a secular chaplain of the West Midlands; his patron was Richard Lestrange of Knockin, member of parliament and marcher lord, who led a life of small distinction outside his part in a violent brawl in a church in London on Easter 1417. By association, Audelay was complicit in this scandal. He is named in the court record and may have taken part in the sentence of public penance imposed on Lestrange and his wife (Bennett 1982, 2009a). This intriguing life record is often taken to suggest an earnest personal motive behind the penitential force of Audelay's verse, but such a reading warrants caution. The record does yield insight, however, into Audelay's occupation as chaplain to a noble whose name also arises in the book. Audelay probably spent the greater part of his career in active service to Lestrange, dwelling in Knockin Castle (a little west of Shrewsbury) and travelling regularly in the lord's retinue, as in 1417. Later, at the time of the colophon, Audelay was sick, suffering failed eyesight and hearing (to what degree we do not know), and residing at Haughmond Abbey as priest for a Lestrange family chantry newly established there. Haughmond, an Augustinian house, is presumably where Audelay oversaw production of MS Douce 302. Copied by two scribes – one inscribing texts, the other making corrections and adding titles and decorations – the anthology contains programmes of devotion, verse sermons and paraliturgical aids, that is, works likely to have been created in Audelay's capacity as spiritual advisor to Lestrange and associates. Piecing this basic outline together with Audelay's numerous autobiographical statements and signatures suggests that the poet remained of the secular clergy, that is, he likely did not take vows as a monk.

The records for James Ryman begin fifty years later and set him in a different region of England. Whereas Audelay hailed from the West Midlands, in a place near the Welsh border, Ryman was a Kentish man whose religious career, to judge from the slim records, was fixed in Canterbury, where he belonged to the Franciscan convent. The register of Thomas Bourgchier, archbishop of Canterbury (1454–86), records that Ryman served as acolyte in Christ Church Canterbury on 30 March 1476 and as subdeacon there on 21 September 1476 (Bourgchier, ed. du Boulay 1957; Reichl 2003). The colophon dates the Ryman manuscript in 1492, so the sixteen years from 1476 to 1492 set the parameters of Ryman's known career in Canterbury, presumably always as a Franciscan friar. The book itself is the product of three scribes, one of whom is thought to be Ryman himself, providing a compelling analogy to Audelay's book: a verse anthology with authorial oversight in its production. At the end of the Middle Ages, the Franciscan community in Canterbury is said to have covered eighteen acres, including where the structure still known as Greyfriars straddles the River Stour. This site must be where Ryman lived and the manuscript was produced. As friar, Ryman would have been free to move about the city and region and to compose material suitable for worship in churches, perhaps even the cathedral. The Bourgchier records of his service at Christ Church suggest the ways in which Ryman interacted with community worship, as do the contents of the Ryman manuscript, although it remains unknown how the hymns and carols found there were actually used.

Audelay and Ryman each authored many carols, a lyric category defined by the presence of a burden, an external refrain sung at the start and between every verse (*Early English Carols*, ed. Greene 1977; Reichl 2005). Carols by both may have enjoyed some degree of circulation. Six of Audelay's appear in other manuscripts, and his versions are generally the oldest to survive. For these, the degree to which he acted as original author or adapter is a matter of dispute. Audelay set his carols in an original sequence, so even when he borrowed and adapted, he exercised an authorial function. His manuscript passed into minstrel ownership before landing in another Augustinian house in Leicestershire, so its carols were perhaps circulated for a time directly from MS Douce 302. In the case of Ryman, some evidence exists that his carols had a life beyond MS Ee.1.12 and the Franciscan friary of Canterbury. The Bradshaw fragment indicates that another manuscript was begun contemporaneously in much the same manner as MS Ee.1.12, ending up somehow at a college in Cambridge. It acquired only two poems (carols not found in MS Ee.1.12) before being abandoned (Croft 1981: 13). Sometime later the bifolium was extracted and used by two new hands to record two ribald parodies, one pointedly about a 'frier of order gray' and a nun. Wittily macaronic, it delivers 'a sophisticated human reaction to the unremitting piety of Ryman and his kind' (ibid.: 2). The fragment reveals that Ryman's poems were known outside of MS Ee.1.12, and also that Ryman's reputation was wide enough to provoke parody. Another possible instance of Ryman's piety being slandered comes from a curious snippet in a Kentish manuscript, Dublin, Trinity College, MS 490, which reads: 'let eure Ryman take hyede how he doht leue/ and not to ssyne hym sselff to geue/ ffor Sant Paule sayht let not ssyne Rayne [reign]/ In yowre mortale body lest ye ssolde a [...] [Romans 6:12]' (Scattergood 2006: 274). Why Ryman, whose known verse *never* wavers in its 'unremitting piety', should be warned not to sin is a mystery. It is of course possible that the writer's finger wags at a different Ryman.

Pairing Audelay with Ryman as named purveyors of the Middle English carol thus makes good sense. Yet scholars should also be mindful that neither composed solely in carol form, nor did they share the same moment in history. To gauge each poet's attitude, one wants a full sense of their oeuvres, seeing contrasts as well as commonalities. As men of high religious sensibility, Audelay and Ryman both treated a secular theme that tellingly encapsulates the ecclesiastical-political temperament of their pious century: both wrote in praise of England's King Henry VI. In essence, as Lancastrian poets, Audelay and Ryman bookend that king's troubled reign, each imbuing it with optimistic nationalism fed by orthodox fervour. As Rossell Hope Robbins notes, 'Two of the prolific writers of religious lyrics may be counted political by virtue of a single poem each: Audelay, by his recollection of Henry V [...] written about 1429; and James Ryman, by a comparable poem on Henry VI [...] a retrospective review composed in 1492, thirty years after the deposition' (*Historical Poems*, ed. Robbins 1975: 1386). Audelay's carol calls for prayers to aid and preserve the young King Henry, celebrating with romantic nostalgia his father's victory over France and his courtship of the French Katherine. This long carol invokes the popular linkage of Henry V's military prowess with tennis, whereby the king's mastery of the game comes jokingly to signify his skill at volleys in war. Here Audelay gives the clearest proof found anywhere that the etymological root for *tennis* is the French word for 'hold' (Gillmeister 1997: 116–17):

> Then was he wyse in wars withalle,
> And taght Franchemen to plai at the balle –
> With *tenés*, 'hold!', he ferd [frightened] ham halle! –
> To castelles and setis [cities] thi floyn away.
>
> (*Audelay*, ed. Fein 2009: 108)

Written between 1426 and 1432, Audelay's carol earnestly petitions heaven's Prince to guard England and its vulnerable king (eight years old in 1429), the burden: 'A, perles Pryns, to thee we pray,/ Save our kyng both nyght and day!'

Composing much later, Ryman supports a posthumous campaign to celebrate Henry VI as a saint, promoted by Henry VII, benefactor of the Franciscans in Canterbury. Beginning 'O good Herry, the sixte by name,/ Bothe of Inglond, ye & of Fraunce', Ryman's poem rehearses royalist sentiments quite similar to Audelay's, seen now at the other end of history (and without mentioning Henry's madness or loss of throne) (no. 96; *Historical Poems*, ed. Robbins: 199–201). Unlike Audelay's carol, Ryman's is a hymn, its eight stanzas set in rhyme royal with a refrain, 'Wherefore in blisse the king of grace/ Hath graunted the a Ioyefull place' ($ababbCC_4$). It lauds a saintly king, long deceased, celebrating his miracles at Windsor. Left unnoticed in discussions of Ryman is how often he presents his poems as units of metrically uniform, verbally modulated verse sequences. The piece in honour of Henry VI is the last element of such a sequence (nos. 89–96), to which *O Dredeful Deth* (quoted above) belongs. Its items share the same rhyme royal metre and begin in petitionary address: 'O man vnkyende', 'O my dere sonne', 'O woofull hert', 'O cruell deth', 'O prince of pese and kyng of grace', 'O dredeful deth', and 'O good Herry'. (No. 93 addresses Ryman's Franciscan brothers, but without 'O': 'Beholde, how good and iocunde it is/ Brothers to dwell in vnite'.)

Secular themes are rare in each poet's corpus, and when there are also stylistic anomalies, attributions have sometimes come to be doubted. Authoritative establishment of the corpus remains an issue for both. Concerning Audelay, some old questions are now being re-examined and new answers emerging because we understand more clearly how Audelay shifts and mixes his authorial function: sometimes as original creator, sometimes as translator or adapter of Latin materials made English, sometimes as direct borrower, as with a prose extract from Rolle, into which he nonetheless interpolates his own verses (Fein 1994). Whatever his source, Audelay remains ever-attentive to matters of compilation, each section of his book exhibiting a sequential order into which elements meaningfully fit. In terms of disputed authorship, the most controversial items in Audelay's book are two gems near the end composed in dense long-line alliterative stanzas: *Paternoster* and *Three Dead Kings*. Their aesthetic polish has been thought to lie beyond Audelay's reach, yet recent work disputes this view, showing how they suit the poet in vocabulary, style, and import (Stanley 2009; cf. Putter). To the book as a whole they bring solemn closure: the Lord's Prayer intoned before presentation of an austere moral sign (mirror of the reader's own mortality), which Audelay himself amplifies with an exemplum of his own dying in the book's autobiographical last poem, 'Deeff, sick, blynd, as he lay' (*Audelay's Conclusion*; see Fein 2002, 2009c).

A problem of attribution for a work less pious than its environment exists for *The False Fox* (no. 111), a jolly lyric preserved solely in the Ryman manuscript (*Secular Lyrics*, ed. Robbins 1955: 44–5; see also Reichl 2003: 206–9). The poem's metre in eighteen stanzas – two four-stress lines with a rollicking two-line refrain – can be seen in the first stanza:

The false fox came vnto our croft,
And so our gese ful fast he sought.
With how fox, how; with hey fox, hey!
Come no more vnto our howse to bere our gese aweye!

The False Fox seems a musical invitation to dance boisterously. The incessant theft of fowl by the *faux* fox (a sly, bilingual pun) constructs a primitive folk narrative, as housewife in smock and farmer with flail chase after the cunning beast. Its falseness notwithstanding, the enemy warrants a measure of admiration, the outsmarted man wryly remarking, 'This fals fox lyveth a mery lyfe!' In the Ryman manuscript *The False Fox* is the first item copied *after* the colophon ('Here *ends* the book of hymns and songs, which Brother James Ryman […] composed'). Setting it outside Ryman's canon seems therefore a right assessment, one readily conceded by the compiler, but it misses a broader point made by its inclusion (perhaps by Ryman, its likely transmitter): the comedy of fox and geese functions as marginalia in this cathedral of holy song. The fox grabbing a goose by the neck is an iconic type among medieval misericords (droll carvings on the undersides of choir seats) found in English churches, appearing, for example, in the cathedrals of Wells, Peterborough, Beverley, Ripon and Hereford. In the fox-goose misericord of Manchester Cathedral an upset housewife springs from her house to give chase. Seventeenth-century copies of thirteenth-century misericords at Canterbury Cathedral include the fox-goose theme. Setting secular worldliness at the margins of a holy life and a holy edifice of hymnody is what *The False Fox* represents in the Ryman manuscript. It also conveys a bemused, insiders' parody of false friars and preachers – a standard medieval reading of the sign. In St George's Chapel at Windsor Castle, a fifteenth-century misericord depicts a fox in priest's garb preaching to a flock of geese, a theme common in the decorated margins of contemporary psalters. So, too, does the poem's devilish, Reynardian, heretical fox preach false doctrine and merrily mimic how true priests elicit heartfelt confessions: he 'shrove our gese there in the flore', 'assoyled our gese both grete & small', and 'made [the goose] to sey "wheccumquek"'.

For the preponderance of texts in each manuscript, however, attribution is not in question. Consequently, the main challenge they pose is simply to be understood. What meanings did these complicated, idiosyncratic books hold for their authors? Who were their intended audiences? How do they represent their specific time and place? And what distinguishes these religious writers among their contemporaries and other poets? For Audelay, the emerging profile is of a chaplain who instructs his readers as he provides them with instruments of worship and prayer. The book is filled with couplets of guidance in Audelay's characteristic idiom, telling a reader what to pray, how to string texts together to practise a devotion, and where to sprinkle in Aves and Paternosters to acquire an indulgence. Audelay uses a few Middle English sources, but he is closest to Latin ones. A model for his project in vernacular religion may have been the Vernon manuscript, constructed a few decades earlier in the West Midlands (Fein 2011a). In general, Audelay's use of Latin in MS Douce 302 is limited to incipits, explicits, a few poems styled with Latin stanza headings, and an occasional macaronic composition. Latin prayers calling for congregational participation are sometimes situated near devotions designed for private use, suggesting the parali-turgical function of programmes devised for laypersons. A Passion sequence opens in Latin, borrowing a standard meditative prayer from books of hours, but soon turns to English, translated by Audelay; midway in this sequence, Audelay suspends devout contemplations to explain the efficacy of the Mass (Fein 2012).

Analysis of the generic structuring of texts in the Audelay manuscript provides more insight upon the poet's attitude. Audelay's book has four well-defined sections: (1) a compendium of religious verse called *The Counsel of Conscience* (*CC*); (2) a set of salutations to Mary and four female saints; (3) the twenty-five carols; (4) a multipart meditation on dying and the world's vanity. Scholars are still working out the meanings embedded in the selection and sequencing of individual items of each section, but all sections tend to move towards thoughts of death and the beatific vision (illustrated in a drawing at the end of section 3), an intensely imagined spiritual 'sight' for this blind poet (Fein 2011b). Moreover, in sequencing items within sections, Audelay shows a concern for endings, his mind habitually linking the close of his book (or its sections) with the outcome of a human life (Fein 2003). The Latin heading for the final stanza of Audelay's last poem reads (in translation): 'Whose end is good, is himself entirely good. The book is finished. Praise and glory be to Christ' (fol. 34rb). Here, in *Audelay's Conclusion*, the poet converts the whole manuscript into a figure for the divine 'bok of lyfe in hevun blys' wherein God inscribes saved souls.

For the purpose of allowing direct comparison to Ryman, I will focus here on the chaplain's sequence of twenty-five carols, discussed as five groups of five. Audelay's is a controlled collection, arranged by topic and number, with twenty-five likely to be a symbolic number. The twenty-fifth and last carol honours St Francis, blessed in his capacity to experience the five wounds with stigmata and wont to divide his food into five parts before he consumed it. The number five thus memorialises Christ's wounds and passion. A sense of meaningful number runs through Audelay's verse. In *CC*, poems are devoted to the Seven Bleedings, Seven Hours and Seven Words on the Cross. Similar numerical basics launch the carol sequence: Ten Commandments, Seven Deadly Sins, Seven Works of Mercy, Five Wits, Seven Gifts of the Holy Ghost. Each of these five inaugural carols has four lines with a tag and two-line burden ($abab_4C_2CC_4$), a formula used by Audelay in nine carols. The next five carols exhibit a new metrical uniformity: three monorhyming lines plus one that rhymes with the two-line burden ($aaa_4b_2BB_4$), Audelay's most typical carol metre. Used eleven times, this stanza type occurs in Audelay's two longest carols, those honouring St Winifred and Henry VI, and he tweaks it in two more by making the fourth line a refrain ($aaa_4B_2BB_4$), as in the macaronic *Dread of Death Carol* (quoted above) and *Nativity Carol*, sixth in the sequence:

> Welcum be ye, Steven and Jone,
> Welcum, childern everechone,
> Wellcum, Thomas marter, alle on –
>   Welcum, Yole, forever and ay!
>   Welcum, Yole, in good aray,
>   In worchip of the holeday! (Audelay, ed. Fein 2009: 180–1)

The next four carols flow from this welcome, honouring (as named) St Stephen, St John, the Holy Innocents and St Thomas, whose feasts occur on December 26, 27, 28 and 29 respectively. Thus do the first ten carols display metrical and topical unity in groups of five: first, lessons of doctrine; then, a celebration of saints and the Christmas season.

The third group of carols lauds virtuous manhood as set forth by Jesus' childhood (his circumcision, the visit of the Magi), by Henry V and Henry VI (father and son), by Audelay's own childhood innocence, and by the 'four estates' – Audelay's original topic for the middle, thirteenth carol. Socially conservative in outlook ('Hit is the best, erelé and late,/ Uche mon kepe his oun estate'), Audelay warns that men ought to avoid perversions ('obisons') of their estates: (1) a priest must not be bold, but rather meek, loving, and charitable; (2) a friar must not be proud, but rather love holiness, prayer, penance, and poverty; (3) an old man must not be lecherous, but rather loyal in wedlock; (4) a knight must not be cowardly, but rather fight with a manly, righteous spirit. Thus, in this middle subset of carols, the worldly virtues of men and boys succeed Audelay's praise of male saints, old and young. To underscore that sequential message, Audelay in the fourth group lauds the virtues inspired by holy women: Mary's mother St Anne, Mary as Jesse's tree, Mary's Joys, Mary as the flower of all women, and Audelay's own celibacy for Mary's love. In the last group, Audelay exhorts the necessary virtues of secular women – that maids stay virgins and wives stay chaste – before he ends on sublime themes: love of God, fear of death, and honour to St Francis, who lived an exemplary life in love of God, and died an exemplary death. Though not a friar, Audelay reserves space to praise fraternal piety, both in his estates carol (centre of the sequence) and in his Francis carol (last of the sequence), which venerates the originator of religious song.

Audelay's carol sequence, varied in topic while also logical in exposition, differs substantially from Ryman's mode of carol composition. While every Audelay carol conveys a distinct message, Ryman's topics are few and (for him) inexhaustible, with whole stanzas frequently reworked and recycled. A survey of topics in Greene's anthology displays the friar's narrow range: To the Virgin (38 carols), To the Trinity (17), Of the Nativity (14), Of the Annunciation (14), To/ Of Christ (13), Of the Epiphany (4), Of the Shepherds (4), Christ to Sinful Man (3), Dialogue of Virgin and Child (2), The Sorrowing Mary (2). Topics that attract a single carol tend to be offshoots of these preoccupations: Mary the Rose, The Magnificat, Farewell to Advent, The Prophecies Fulfilled, and The Mystery of the Incarnation. Another topic, The Trouble with Joseph (no. 88), seems at first glance rather bold for Ryman, opening 'Iosephe wolde haue fled fro that mayde'. Joseph's trouble rapidly becomes, however, another pretext for devout Marian praise: 'But to abyde he was affrayde/ In here so good and pure presence'. In Ryman's Christian aesthetic, praise for Mary, Christ, and the Trinity has no end or limit. As John Stevens remarks, Ryman 'never did anything by halves' (1979: 52).

There remain four Ryman carols, curiosities amid such conformity, which lean in the direction of Audelay's moral didacticism: Let Us Amend (no. 49; see Jeffrey 1975: 255–7) and a cluster – Against Love of Riches, Of the Vanity of Riches, and Of the Eucharist (nos. 54–6) – that rests at the heart of the Ryman anthology. Like the placement of *The False Fox* at the end, this cluster may be part of an overall

Gothic design. To understand how this is possible requires a review of the scribal makeup of the Ryman manuscript. Three hands contributed to MS Ee.1.12. Scribe A, who wrote some fragments on the opening leaves and some wordless musical notation on fol. 81r, is of little importance to the Ryman corpus except to show how the book was regarded as a songbook. On fols 11r–80r, Scribe C inscribed the core of the Ryman oeuvre: nos. 1–110 and colophon. The same scribe copied *The False Fox* on fols 80v–81r. Scribe B augmented the Ryman corpus by inscribing 38 poems (nos. 112–49) on fols 81v–104v. He also added verse on a new gathering inserted near the beginning of the book (fols 3r–10v): variant stanzas that go with other poems and 14 full poems (nos. 152–65). Deducting *The False Fox*, the remaining 164 items are generally accepted as Ryman's work. Ryman himself is thought to be either Scribe B or Scribe C. Greene supports the case for C (*Early English Carols*, ed. Greene 1977: 321), but outnumbering him are Zupitza, Helmut Gneuss and Karl Reichl (2003), who think B is more likely the poet. Activity on fol. 3r may show Scribe B writing down stanzas as reminders to himself; other moments demonstrate the friar working out alternate translations of specific Latin hymns. The Ryman manuscript presents an opportunity to observe a medieval poet's working methods.

In this regard, Scribe C's labour might itself be considered a complete 'book', for it seems to have been initially planned that way. Thus, it may be intentional that the cluster of moral carols, nos. 54–6, forms the numerical centre of the original 110 (55, reminiscent of Audelay's love of five), turning from the riches of the world, which lead to death and dust – 'Alle worldly welth passed me fro:/ *Nunc in puluere dormio*' (no. 55, called by Woolf 'the most distinctively meditative' of Middle English death lyrics [387]) – to the everlasting life offered in the Eucharist – 'Ete ye this brede, ete ye this brede/ And ete it so, ye be not dede' (no. 56).

Looking beyond the relatively small number of subjects treated by Ryman, a neglected feature of his verse is his balance of Latin to English. Ryman is commonly thought to compose 'learned' carols in macaronics, and this is true to some extent: far more than Audelay, Ryman aureates his style with internal Latin patterns. But the sheer volume of what he wrote solely in English, sixty-three poems, has been scarcely acknowledged. At the core of Ryman's vast poetic labour rests an active allegiance to delivering songs of worship in the vernacular.

Finally, to raise another kind of analysis that Ryman's oeuvre currently lacks: the friar frequently composes, like Audelay, by sequence. Evidence for this method is ubiquitous, existing in the book's arrangement of carols and noncarols (as in the rhyme royal group closing with *O Good Herry*). Ryman constructs fluid links among sets of poems by modulating phrases that occur in rhymes, at stanza beginnings, and/or in final lines of successive poems. An intriguing specimen is a set marked by the initial and repeating phrase 'Shall I?' (nos. 62–7). Matched metrically ($a_4b_3a_4b_3$), these six English lyrics all start with a question asked innocently by Christ of his mother. For example, the first poem begins:

> '*Shalle I*, that heuen and erth did make,
> Dere, moder, *shall I* soo?
> *Shall I* die for mannes sake
> And suffre payne and woo?'

The lyric keeps pressing Christ's questions without receiving a response, reverberating with 'Shall I?' until Christ's voice softly shifts to declaratives: '*I shall* be iuged vnto dethe', 'To a pilloure *I shall* be bounde', 'Than *I shall* bere my crosse, i-wys', 'Thanne *I shall* ryse on the iij.^de day'. The succeeding lyric continues the phrase 'Shall I?' as an anaphora that commences every stanza, with Mary still not responding. Now every *b*-rhyme-pair is *soo/woo*, forming an internal refrain that musically plays off the 'Shall I?' questions. The third lyric, opening with a slight variant of the stanza quoted above, allows Mary to answer Christ now in alternating stanzas. Mother and son maintain the *b*-rhyme, expanding it to five words: *soo, woo, also, foo* and *froo*, while the verb *shall* glides into *will*, so that Christ can declare 'it is my faders *wille*' and 'to blis I *wille* go'. The three subsequent lyrics continue in this vein, building emotion by repetition, incremental addition, and occasional internal rhymes, creating drama by simple dialogue made gradually more complex and aureate. Ryman here uses language consciously to deepen devotion and reinforce doctrine. To a modern reader, the repetitive simplicity of this verse may seem underdeveloped and monotonous, but we lack knowledge of the setting in which it was enacted, perhaps by a choir, or two choirs singing in turn, with repetitions incrementally building to reverently sublime uplift. The notion that Ryman was a 'closet' hymnist, writing merely for himself, needs to be tested against evidence that real Latin hymns and musical sequences define the metrical forms of his verse (Stevens 1979: 48–52; see also Stevens 1981; *Mediaeval Carols*, ed. Stevens 1970; *Early English Carols*, ed. Greene 1977: lxxxi–cxvii). As Reichl comments, 'The melodies extant give us a glimpse of what the poems as songs might have been like, but their fragmentary state also makes us painfully aware of the incompleteness of our knowledge of so much of Middle English lyric' (2003: 221).

   Most of all, in future work on these poets, we must come to better understand Audelay and Ryman each in his own time: Audelay, properly perceived, as the contemporary of Hoccleve, Lydgate, Mirk, Love and Kempe; and Ryman as situated much later, in the world of Caxton, Malory, Skelton, Henryson and Dunbar. Thus may we hear in Ryman's Franciscan address to 'good Fraunces, of oure knyghthood' (no. 143; see Jeffrey 1975: 249–50) some of the same nostalgia for a noble brotherhood that dwells in Malory's reminiscence of worshipful knighthood. And when the 'Shall I?' poems begin to burst with internal rhyme, we may catch a faint whiff of Skeltonics: 'My faders wille I must fulfille:/ Moder, sith it is so,/ For man so ylle it is but skille/ To suffre payne and woo' (no. 67). Elsewhere, as a good Franciscan, Ryman recalls the blindness of St Francis, whose infirmities signified Christ's love: 'Whome Criste hath fixte, that louer true,/ Hert, hande and foote transfourmed new/ [...] Dumb, blynde, and lame' (no. 69; for Ryman's other lyrics on Francis, all noncarols, see nos. 93, 109, 142, 143). St Francis' exemplary blindness was commonly regarded a sign of his bodily closeness to Christ (Wells 2010; Gray 1972: 21–5; Ó Clabaigh 2006: 154). In celebrating this holy infirmity of the founder, Brother Ryman plausibly discloses why it is that an old, blind chaplain from Shropshire would himself have wanted some fifty years earlier to honour St Francis, model of devout song *and* of inward sight.

Works cited

Audelay, John, *The Poems of John Audelay: A Specimen of the Shropshire Dialect in the Fifteenth Century*, ed. James Orchard Halliwell (London, 1844)

——, 'Fifteenth-Century Carols by John Audelay', eds R. W. Chambers and F. Sidgwick, *Modern Language Review*, 5 (1910), 473–91; 6 (1911), 68–84

——, *The Poems of John Audelay*, ed. Ella Keats Whiting, EETS, o. s. 184 (London, 1931)

——, *John the Blind Audelay, Poems and Carols (Oxford, Bodleian Library MS Douce 302)*, ed. Susanna Fein (Kalamazoo, MI, 2009)

Bennett, Michael J., 'John Audley: Some New Evidence on his Life and Work', *Chaucer Review*, 16 (1982), 344–55

——, 'John Audelay: Life Records and Heaven's Ladder', in Fein, ed., 2009a, pp. 30–53

Boffey, Julia, 'Audelay's Carol Collection', in Fein, ed., 2009a, pp. 218–30

Bourgchier, Thomas, *Registrum Thome Bourgchier, Cantuariensis Archiepiscopi A.D. 1454–1486*, ed. F. R. H. du Boulay, The Canterbury and York Society 54 (Oxford, 1957)

Brown, Carleton, Review of *The Early English Carols*, ed. Richard Leighton Greene, *Modern Language Notes*, 52 (1937), 125–9

Citrome, Jeremy J., *The Surgeon in Medieval English Literature* (New York, 2006)

Croft, P. J., 'The "Friar of Order Gray" and the Nun', *Review of English Studies*, n.s. 32 (1981), 1–16

Driver, Martha W., 'John Audelay and the Bridgettines', in Fein, ed., 2009a, pp. 191–217

The Early English Carols, ed. Richard Leighton Greene, 2nd edn (Oxford, 1977).

Easting, Robert, '"Choose yourselves whither to go": John Audelay's *Vision of Saint Paul*', in Fein, ed., 2009a, pp. 170–90

Edwards, A. S. G., 'Fifteenth-Century Middle English Verse Author Collections', in *The English Medieval Book: Studies in Memory of Jeremy Griffiths*, eds A. S. G. Edwards, Vincent Gillespie and Ralph Hanna (London, 2000), pp. 101–12

——, 'Poetic Language in the Fifteenth Century', in *A Companion to Medieval Poetry*, ed. Corinne Saunders (Oxford, 2010), pp. 520–37

English Lyrics before 1500, ed. Theodore Silverstein (York, 1971)

English Spirituality in the Age of Wyclif, ed. David L. Jeffrey (Vancouver, 2000)

Fein, Susanna Greer, 'A Thirteen-Line Alliterative Stanza on the Abuse of Prayer from the Audelay MS', *Medium Ævum*, 63 (1994), 61–74

——, 'Life and Death, Reader and Page: Mirrors of Mortality in English Manuscripts', *Mosaic*, 35 (2002), 69–94

——, 'Good Ends in the Audelay Manuscript', *Yearbook of English Studies*, 33 (2003), 97–119

——, ed., 2009a. *My Wyl and My Wrytyng: Essays on John the Blind Audelay* (Kalamazoo, MI, 2009)

——, 2009b. 'John Audelay and His Book: Critical Overview and Major Issues', in Fein, ed., 2009a, pp. 3–29

——, 2009c. 'Death and the Colophon in the Audelay Manuscript', in Fein, ed., 2009a, pp. 294–305

——, 2011a. 'Example to the *Soulehele*: John Audelay, the Vernon Manuscript, and the Defense of Orthodoxy', *Chaucer Review*, 46 (2011), 182–202

——, 2011b. 'Mary to Veronica: John Audelay's Sequence of Salutations to God-Bearing Women', *Speculum*, 86 (2011), 964–1009

——, 'Devotions for a Noble Household: The Long Passion in Audelay's *Counsel of Conscience*', in *After Arundel: Religious Writing in Fifteenth Century England*, eds Vincent Gillespie and Kantik Ghosh (Turnhout, 2012), pp. 325–42

Gillmeister, Heiner, *Tennis: A Cultural History* (London, 1997)

Gneuss, Helmut, *Hymnar und Hymnen im englischen Mittelalter* (Tübingen, 1968)

Gray, Douglas, *Themes and Images in the Medieval English Religious Lyric* (London, 1972)

Green, Richard Firth, 'Marcolf the Fool and Blind John Audelay', in *Speaking Images: Essays in Honor of V. A. Kolve*, eds Robert F. Yeager and Charlotte C. Morse (Asheville, NC, 2001), pp. 559–76

——, 'Langland and Audelay', in Fein, ed., 2009a, pp. 153–69

Herebert, William, *The Works of William Herebert, OFM*, ed. Stephen R. Reimer (Toronto, 1987)

Hirsh, John C., '"Wo and werres ... rest and pese": John Audelay's Politics of Peace', in Fein, ed., 2009a, pp. 230–48

Historical Poems of the XIVth and XVth Centuries, ed. Rossell Hope Robbins (New York, 1959)

Jeffrey, David L., *The Early English Lyric and Franciscan Spirituality* (Lincoln, NE, 1975)

——, 'James Ryman and the Fifteenth-Century Carol', in *Fifteenth-Century Studies: Recent Essays*, ed. R. F. Yeager (Hamden, CT, 1984), pp. 303–20

Machan, Tim William, *Textual Criticism and Middle English Texts* (Charlottesville, VA, 1994)

Matsuda, Takami, *Death and Purgatory in Middle English Didactic Poetry* (Cambridge, 1997)

Mediæval Carols, ed. John E. Stevens, Musica Britannica, 4, 2nd edn (London 1970)

Medieval English: An Old English and Middle English Anthology, ed. Rolf Kaiser, 3rd edn (Berlin, 1958)

Medieval English Lyrics: A Critical Anthology, ed. R. T. Davies (London, 1963)

Medieval Lyric: Middle English Lyrics, Ballads, and Carols, ed. John C. Hirsh (Oxford, 2005)

Meyer-Lee, Robert J., 'The Vatic Penitent: John Audelay's Self-Representation', in Fein, ed., 2009a, pp. 54–85

Ó Clabaigh, Colmán, 'The Other Christ: The Cult of St Francis of Assisi in Late Medieval Ireland', in *Art and Devotion in Late Medieval Ireland*, eds Rachel Moss, Colmán Ó Clabaigh, and Salvador Ryan (Dublin, 2006), pp. 142–62

The Oxford Book of Medieval English Verse, eds Celia and Kenneth Sisam (Oxford, 1970)

Pearsall, Derek, 'Audelay's *Marcolf and Solomon* and the Langlandian Tradition', in Fein, ed., 2009a, pp. 138–52

Pickering, Oliver, 'The Make-Up of John Audelay's *Counsel of Conscience*', in Fein, ed., 2009a, pp. 112–37

Powell, Susan, 'John Audelay and John Mirk: Comparisons and Contrasts', in Fein, ed., 2009a, pp. 86–111

Putter, Ad, 'The Language and Metre of *Pater Noster* and *Three Dead Kings*', *Review of English Studies*, 55 (2004), 498–526

Reichl, Karl, 'James Ryman's Lyrics and the Ryman Manuscript: A Reappraisal', in *Bookmarks from the Past: Studies in Early English Language and Literature in Honour of Helmut Gneuss*, eds Lucia Kornexl and Ursula Lenker (Frankfurt am Main, 2003), pp. 195–227

——, 'The Middle English Carol', in *A Companion to the Middle English Lyric*, ed. Thomas G. Duncan (Cambridge, 2005), pp. 150–70

Religious Lyrics of the XVth Century, ed. Carleton Brown (Oxford, 1939)

Robbins, Rossell Hope, 'The Bradshaw Carols', *PMLA*, 81 (1966), 308–10

——, 'Poems Dealing with Contemporary Conditions', in *A Manual of the Writings in Middle English 1050–1500, Volume 5*, gen. ed. Albert E. Hartung (New Haven, CT, 1975), pp. 1385–1536

Scattergood, John, 'Two Unrecorded Poems from Dublin, Trinity College Library MS 490', in his *Manuscripts and Ghosts: Essays on the Transmission of Medieval and Early Renaissance Literature* (Dublin, 2006), pp. 269–77 (repr. from *Review of English Studies*, n.s. 38 (1987), 44–9)

Secular Lyrics of the XIVth and XVth Centuries, ed. Rossell Hope Robbins, 2nd edn (Oxford, 1955)

A Selection of English Carols, ed. Richard Leighton Greene (Oxford, 1962)

A Selection of Religious Lyrics, ed. Douglas Gray (Oxford, 1975)

Simpson, James, 'Saving Satire after Arundel's *Constitutions*: John Audelay's "Marcol and Solomon"', in *Text and Controversy from Wyclif to Bale: Essays in Honour of Anne Hudson*, eds Helen Barr and Ann M. Hutchison (Turnhout, 2004), pp. 387–404

Stanley, Eric Gerald, '*The True Counsel of Conscience*, or *The Ladder of Heaven*: In Defence of John Audelay's Unlyrical Lyrics', in *Expedition nach der Wahrheit: Poems, Essays, and Papers in Honour of Theo Stemmler*, eds Stefan Horlacher and Marion Islinger (Heidelberg, 1996), pp. 131–59

——, 'The Verse Forms of Jon the Blynde Awdelay', in *The Long Fifteenth Century: Essays for Douglas Gray*, eds Helen Cooper and Sally Mapstone (Oxford, 1997), pp. 99–121

——, 'The Alliterative *Three Dead Kings* in John Audelay's MS Douce 302', in Fein, ed., 2009a, pp. 249–93

Stevens, John, *Music and Poetry in the Early Tudor Court*, 2nd edn (Cambridge, 1979)

——, '*Angelus ad virginem*: The History of a Medieval Song', in *Medieval Studies for J. A. W. Bennett*, ed. P. L. Heyworth (Oxford, 1981), pp. 297–328

Wells, Scott, 'The Exemplary Blindness of Francis of Assisi', in *Disability in the Middle Ages: Reconsiderations and Reverberations*, ed. Joshua R. Eyler (New York, 2010), pp. 67–80

Wheatley, Edward, *Stumbling Blocks before the Blind: Medieval Constructions of a Disability* (Ann Arbor, MI, 2010)

Woolf, Rosemary, *The English Religious Lyric in the Middle Ages* (Oxford, 1968)

Zupitza, Julius, ed., 'Die Gedichte des Franziskaners Jakob Ryman', *Archiv für das Studium der neueren Sprachen und Literaturen*, 89 (1892), 167–338

——, ed., 'Anmerkungen zu Jakob Rymans Gedichten. II Tiel', *Archiv für das Studium der neueren Sprachen und Literaturen*, 93 (1894), 369–98

PART III

THEMES AND GENRES

11

Fifteenth-Century Chaucerian Visions

AD PUTTER

This chapter is devoted to a group of Chaucerian visions: *The Flower and the Leaf, The Assembly of Ladies, La Belle Dame sans Mercy* and *The Isle of Ladies*. 'Chaucerian' has been a common epithet for these poems in modern scholarship ever since Skeat edited all of them except *The Isle of Ladies* in his collection *Chaucerian and Other Pieces* (1897). The association of these poems (and others) with Chaucer, however, goes back much further, to scribal attributions in medieval manuscripts and to Chaucer's earliest printers, who naturally had an interest in presenting as wide a corpus as possible (see Robbins 1973; Forni 2001b).

Although today the earliest surviving witness for *The Flower and the Leaf* is an early edition of Chaucer's works by Thomas Speght (1598, *STC* 5077), the poem once existed in Longleat, MS 258, as we know from the original table of contents of this manuscript (Hammond 1905). Unfortunately, the quire containing the poem was removed from the manuscript at an early date. Written in the Chaucerian rhyme royal stanza, the poem is a fine example of a courtly poem reflecting the leisured aristocratic life. One popular variation on the aristocratic 'Game of Love' (Stevens 1961: 152–202) was for courtiers to divide themselves in May-time into two camps, the order of the Flower (those looking for love or new lovers) and that of the Leaf (those who were not). The title of our poem evidently alludes to that game.

The poem begins, significantly, on a May morning when the lady speaker lies awake, unable to sleep without knowing why. The situation recalls Chaucer's *The Book of the Duchess*, which also features an insomniac narrator; the parallels continue when, at the break of dawn, the lady wanders into a pleasant grove:

> In which were okes great, streight as a line,
> Under which the grasse so fresh of hew
> Was newly sprong; and an eight foot or nine
> Every tree well fro his fellow grew,
> With braunches brode, lade with leves new.
>
> (*Floure*, ed. Pearsall 1980: lines 29–33)

This draws on *The Book of the Duchess* (lines 416–426), but two interesting changes are made to the source, both of which serve the argument that Leaf is superior to Flower. First, the lady, unlike Chaucer, *really* does not know why she cannot sleep. Her mind is at rest (line 21), and she does not fall asleep, unlike Chaucer, who suffers from a mysterious illness about which he is not at liberty to speak.

This illness, from which the lady, as follower of the Leaf, is naturally immune, is love-sickness. The second peculiarity of *The Flower and the Leaf* is its garden. It has been argued that the garden is described in 'stereotyped phrases' and represents an 'earthly paradise offering sunlight, trees, a flowery meadow, rich fragrances [etc.]' (McMillan 1982: 34), but in fact the garden has no flowers. Their absence becomes conspicuous as the lady progresses into a secluded arbour:

> And at the last a path of litle breade
> I found, that greatly had not used be,
> For it forgrowen was with grasse and weede. (lines 43–5)

Because the untrodden path, promising privileged access to a world normally hidden from view, is a common motif in visions (*Floure*, ed. Pearsall 1980: n. to lines 43–6), this again looks unoriginal, but compare these lines with the poet's probable source – '[I] folwed [...] Doun by a floury grene wente/ Ful thikke of gras, ful softe and swete/ With floures fele, faire under fete,/ And litel used' (*The Book of the Duchess*, lines 398–404) – and the difference is clear: the poet has de-flowered the *locus amœnus*. Thus the 'rich field' is covered with 'corn and grass' (lines 73–5), and the 'savour soote' comes not from roses, but from the laurel (lines 110–2) and the eglantine (lines 79–84), better known as the sweet-briar on account of the sweet scent of its *leaves*. When flowers are finally mentioned, they are the 'blosomes' (line 88) of a stunted medlar tree, and a dainty bird is eating them:

> Therin a goldfinch leaping pretile
> Fro bough to bough, and as him list he eet,
> Here and there, of buds and floures sweete. (lines 89–91)

The passage convinces as a piece of naturalistic observation, but the poet is already preparing her moral (flowers are transitory) and establishing the contrast between the gaudy goldfinch and the reclusive bird that 'answers' (line 100) its song: the nightingale, which does not flit about (cf. line 489) but sits 'all the day' (line 435) under the leaves of the laurel. The implication is that followers of the Leaf are steadfast and modest creatures. The natural world is delicately pressed into allegorical service.

Sheltered by the laurel tree, the lady observes a little drama involving two companies, each governed by a lady. First to appear (the order, too, has allegorical meaning) is a busy group of ladies, dressed in white, and wearing chaplets of laurel, woodbine and *agnus castus* ['chaste lamb']. Associated with them is a group of knights in similar garb, followed by nine knights each with a royal herald and a large group of lesser knights. After an orderly joust (lines 286–7), the men join the ladies, and hand-in-hand they go 'unto a faire laurel' with such abundant foliage that a hundred people could shelter underneath it without 'grevance/ Of raine ne haile' (lines 311–2). Leaves, in other words, are very useful things.

Later that day, a second cohort of knights and ladies arrive, wearing chaplets of flowers and dressed in green. Instead of jousting, the knights dance with the ladies until, 'aboute noone' (a time when humans were traditionally vulnerable to the dangers of idleness: Friedman 1966), the sweltering sun and the wind destroy all flowers 'Save suche as succoured were among the leves' (line 365). Shortly afterwards the company themselves run for cover, for the heat of the sun is followed by a sharp shower of hail and rain, and all are soaked to the skin. The lady in charge of the company of the Leaf comes to their rescue, inviting them to join them under the shelter of the laurel tree, where all ills are soon mended. At the end of the day, the two companies ride off, joined by the birds: the nightingale flies to the sovereign lady of the Leaf, the goldfinch to the lady of the Flower.

As the narrator leaves the secluded arbour from which she has witnessed these events, she encounters a follower of the Leaf who expounds their allegorical significance. The company of the Leaf consists of chaste or faithful ladies and loyal knights; their leader is Diana (goddess of chastity), which is why they wear white and favour *agnus castus*. The laurel signifies triumph in battle and perseverance; its leaves are not withered by the sun and so signify lasting value. The nine knights were the Nine Worthies and the jousting knights included knights of Arthur's Round Table, Charlemagne's paladins, and Knights of the Garter. In short, all celebrities of yore sided with the Leaf. Flowers, however, wither, and so fit the company in green (headed by Flora) who 'are such that loved idlenes/ And not delite of no busines' (lines 536–7). The rest of the allegory follows, though the two lady narrators in the poem are both much too tactful to spell it out: the followers of the Flower are *not* steadfast and loyal, and the extremes of heat and cold they endure are a fitting punishment for them, since their passions also blow hot and cold. They wear green because green symbolised inconstancy (cf. Chaucer, *Against Women Unconstant*, line 21: 'In stede of blew, thus may ye were al grene'). The poet's reticence avoids indelicacy and also preserves the integrity of the story at the literal level.

In any case, the moralising in the poem should not be taken too seriously, since it is expended on the frivolous question of whether we should this year pledge allegiance to the Flower or the Leaf: 'and which woll ye honour/ Tell me, I pray, this yeere, the Leafe or the Flour?' (line 574). The question reminds us of the game of the Flower and the Leaf that provided the occasion for the poem. The game evidently involved pleading, tongue-in-cheek, the moral superiority of one or other side. For example, in two ballades advocating the Flower, Eustache Deschamps writes that flowers bear fruit, that leaves fade and fall, that leaves are the 'servants' of the flower, protecting it from wind and rain (Deschamps: ballades 764 and 765). In another ballade (767) he redeploys these same tropes to extol instead the virtues of the leaf: flowers emerge from leaves, so leaves are their 'mothers', they are destroyed by sun and wind, from which leaves, shield us, etc. Although *The Flower and the Leaf*, unlike Deschamps, presents only one side of the argument, its poet could no doubt have used a remarkable gift for allegory and moralisation just as effectively in support of the Flower.

Long associated with *The Flower and the Leaf*, *The Assembly of Ladies* was once assumed to be by the same lady poet. This is most unlikely. Pearsall (*Floure* 1980: 64–6) gives a substantial list of differences, to which I would add that the nature of allegory in the *Assembly* is the opposite of that in *The Flower and the Leaf*. In the latter an abstract, quasi-moral argument is exemplified *in concreto* in the natural world of birds and trees; in the *Assembly*, by contrast, the poet's inner thought is externalised in the shape of a personification allegory involving a quest to the court of Lady *Loiaulté* (meaning 'loyalty' but also 'fairness', 'equity'), who hears the complaints of aggrieved ladies. The allegorical setting is not a natural habitat but a pseudo-world peopled with household officials who personify the qualities (for example, Largesse, Remembrance, Discretion) you need to possess and receive if your complaint is to succeed.

Critics have not responded well to this allegorical mode. 'Allegory', Bennett wrote, 'has laid a heavy hand on the *Assembly*; and in place of the charming groups which gathered about Flora and Diana [in *The Flower and the Leaf*], we are confronted with such stock characters as Perseveraunce, the usher; Countenance, the porter; Largesse, the steward; Remembrance, the chamberlain; and many others who are servants to the Lady Loyalty, dwelling at Pleasant Regard' (Bennett 1947: 135). By 'stock characters' Bennett means that their personalities are predictable, but, of course, predictable is what personified abstractions should be. Since the logic that circumscribes their behaviour is linguistic rather than psychological, they must live up to their names.

Perseverance in the *Assembly* illustrates the art of personification allegory beautifully. Like everyone else in the vision – with the significant exception of the narrator herself – Perseverance wears a 'word' (motto) embroidered on her clothes, in her case the motto *Bien loialment*. Her mission is to invite the narrator to Loyalty's court to present her petition, but unfortunately she cannot stay to explain the matter:

> '[…] Farewele, now have I don.'
> 'Abide', quod I, 'ye may nat go so soone.'
>
> 'Whi so?' quod she, 'and I have fer to go
> To yeve warnyng in many dyvers place
> To your felawes and so to other moo,
> And wele ye wote I have but litel space.'
> (*Assembly* in *Floure*, ed. Pearsall 1990: lines 139–44)

How was the narrator to 'wote' (know) that Perseverance is in a hurry? The answer is that she is Perseverance, and so must 'persevere' in the etymological sense of that word (*perseverare* = 'to continue steadfastly', 'to go on or proceed steadily'). After the ladies have arrived at Loyalty's castle and wait for their cases to be heard, she is sent for again, and asks the ladies to persevere while she has a word with the chamberlain (lines 390–1). So off she goes once more, always doing her name justice: 'Thus she parted and come agayne anon' (line 421). When the ladies are in danger of being crowded out by the many other lady petitioners, Perseverance 'perseveres' and leads her friends though the crowds. But before we know it she is off again (line 441), only to reappear as the woman who prepares the way for Lady Loyalty. Her last role in the poem is to insist to the authorities that her friends' bills should be read first, since they were the first to arrive. The moral is that if you want to get anywhere at court you need perseverance. Of course that is also true in the real-life situation that the allegory encodes: unsatisfactory love relationships (and most of the complaints presented to Lady Loyalty are about that) require perseverance. In that sense the ladies, who all wear blue – for *they* have stayed loyal – know all about perseverance: in allegorical terms, she and they are 'old acquaintances' (lines 376, 402).

In self-reflexive allegory of this kind, questions of what office and what motto you give to each personification are obviously interesting. Perseverance is usher. An usher had to escort people in hall and chamber, and that suits Perseverance perfectly, for she can be always be on the move, yet continue 'steadfast' in her dedication – *bien loialment* as her motto says. Countenance has also found her calling as the castle porter, though Pearsall obscures the point by glossing 'Countenance' as 'self-control'. In fact 'countenance' here has the older sense 'demeanour or manner towards others as expressing good ... will' (*OED*, II.7) or 'good manners', as it is glossed by Boffey in *Fifteenth-Century English Dream Visions*. Again this is a virtue you need in order to succeed at court (and in love), as Perseverance implies – 'Of hir were goode to have som aqueyntaunce;/ She can telle how ye shal yow beste avaunce' (lines 179–80). It is also what you want from a porter, who needs to be charming to visitors. When Countenance welcomes the Dreamer we have no business complaining that she is a 'stock character':

> With wordis feyre she sayde ful gentily:
> 'Ye ben welcome, iwis [...]
> Now than,' quod she, 'I pray yow hertily,
> Take my chambre as for a while to rest
> To yowre felawes bien comen, I hold it for the best' (lines 282–7)

Miss Countenance must do her name's bidding by being gracious to strangers and charming them into thinking that sitting in a waiting room is 'resting' in her chamber.

The *Assembly* is also self-conscious about the relationship between the frame and the allegorical dream vision itself. In fact, the poem has a double frame. It opens ominously with an autumn setting, with the lady and her friends amusing themselves by walking in a garden maze. But they are not alone: a group of knights and squires are also in the garden, and one of them asks the lady what she is doing. To this she gives an unexpectedly bleak reply, 'To walke aboute the mase, in certeynte,/ As a woman that nothyng rought' (lines 17–18), before embarking on a 'tale' (line 21) to explain her feelings. This 'tale', too, has a frame. Not long ago, the lady recounts, she was walking in this same maze with five ladies and four gentlewomen. She had managed to penetrate further into the maze than her companions and had found a flowery garden, where she waited for the others to catch up. Pondering on past events, she fell asleep. Then the allegorical vision begins.

The relationship between this double frame and the vision is suggestive. The four other ladies and four gentlewomen who walk about the maze (no men are present) are transported with her to the dream world, which is also exclusively female (lines 147–52). In the frame the lady is ahead of her companions, as she is in the dream, where she is the first to arrive at Loyalty's castle, though in true dream-like fashion she worries that she might be the last to arrive (lines 215–16), and that her fellows have gone ahead and left her behind (lines 245–6). When she in fact arrives before them her anxiety persists: she now worries that her friends will never turn up (lines 299–301), that time is running out (lines 418–20), and so on. Like the frame, the vision raises more questions than it answers. Lady Loyalty hears the ladies' petitions and accepts their legitimacy, but the final judgement and remedy are postponed indefinitely. This open-endedness is typical both of dreams and of allegorical visions involving Courts of Love (such as *Les accusations contre la Belle Dame sans Mercy* [see Chartier, ed. McRae], and Jean de Werchin's *Songe de la barge*, ed. Grenier-Winther), but also reflects the psychological situation that generates the allegory. The 'I' of the poem has been badly treated by a man; she has complained to *Loiauté* who is on her side (for Fairness is fair) but brings no remedy (for Life is not).

The allegorical story thus animates the lady's thoughts before she fell asleep, when 'Remembrynge of many dyvers cace/ Of tyme past, musyng with sighes depe,/ I set me downe and ther fil in slepe' (lines 75–7). As we have seen from the Prologue to *The Book of the Duchess*, the 'Game of Love' in this period demanded absolute secrecy, and so the lady neither identifies herself by name or motto, nor specifies the precise nature of her grievance (cf. Boffey). The frame merely alludes to 'dyvers cace' and, although the allegorical fiction teases us with the prospect of full disclosure when the bills are to be read out in public, none of them gives anything away. For example, the lady's own petition, supposedly plain-speaking, begins:

> What shuld I more desire, as seme ye –
> And ye knewe al aforne it for certeyne
> I wote ye wold; and for to tell yow pleyne,
> Without hir help that hath al thing in cure
> I can nat thynk that it may long endure. (lines 696–700)

What exactly is the 'it' that 'you' might have known all along? Is 'you' the person to who the bill is notionally addressed (Loyalty), the knight to whom the tale is addressed, or the addressee in real life? And who is the 'she' who is in charge of everything? Is she the lady of the house, Venus or Mary (Stephens 1973: 139), or a real-life lady who has the power to save or destroy this relationship? The 'dyvers cace' of the Prologue are 'explained' in a way that leaves us none the wiser. This poet has a secret and is determined to keep it.

The continuities between the 'real' waking world and the dream world not only suggest a psychological reality behind the allegorical fiction but also push the story of the frame itself towards allegory. It is no coincidence that the garden where the Dreamer has space to reflect on her life is full of flowers named after reflections: 'Ne m'oublie-mies [forget-me-nots] and sovenez [remember-mes] also, / The poore penses [pansies, from French *pensée* = thought] ne were nat dislodged there' (lines 61–2). Similarly, the 'maze' in the two frames becomes symbolic of the lady's state of mind (Stephens 1973: 133). The connection is firmly established when the lady wakes up 'al amased' in an epilogue that closes the gap between the frame and the dream, the real world and the fictional one:

> Al sodainly the water sprang anone
> In my visage and therwithal I woke.
> 'Wher am I now?', thought I, 'al this is goon',
> Al amased; and up I gan to looke.
> With that anon I went and made this booke. (lines 736–40)

The water that awakens the Dreamer has presumably splashed from the streams in the garden where she fell asleep (lines 67–70). The vision leaves her 'amased' and she writes it down in 'this booke', which is at once the book inside the fiction and the manuscript that medieval readers would have had in their hands.

La Belle Dame sans Mercy, extant in seven manuscripts, is usually attributed to Sir Richard Roos (c.1410–82), but since the attribution is based on a single manuscript, and since there is more than one Richard Roos who could have written the poem (Gray 2008: 351), it would be hazardous to read the poem through the prism of Sir Richard's eventful life as soldier and diplomat (but see Seaton 1961). The title will be familiar from a poem by John Keats, who borrowed the title of his *Belle Dame sans Mercy* from the medieval poem, though little else besides. The Middle English *Belle Dame* is in turn a translation of a brilliant poem by Alain Chartier (1395–1430) who is remembered in the prologue as 'maister Alyn [...] of remembraunce (worthy to be remembered: Symons glosses 'to be recorded' in *Chaucerian Dream Visions*, but cf. 853)/ Chief secretary with the kyng of Fraunce' (lines 10–11).

Chartier tells us how, shortly after the death of his lady, his friends dragged him off to a party. There his attention is drawn by a man in black who is obviously desperately in love. The melancholy narrator, who recognises himself in this fellow sufferer, withdraws at the first opportunity, and in a secluded garden he overhears a debate between the lover and his lady, who shows him no sympathy. Since the lover's pleas fall on deaf ears, his last words are addressed not to her, but to God, whom he reproaches for failing to create pity in his lady. The lady adds a devastating final rejoinder:

> Mon cuer ne moy ne vous feïsmes
> Onc riens dont plaindre vous doiez.
> Riens ne vous nuyst fors vous meïsmes:
> De vous mesmes juges soiez.
> Une foiz pour toutes croiez
> Que vous demourez escondit.
> De tant redire m'ennuyez
> Car je vous en ay assez dit.

> [Neither my heart not I have done anything to you that gives you reason to complain. The only thing that harms you is yourself: therefore be your own judge. Once and for all, try to understand that you have been refused without respite. You annoy me with your repetitions, for I have already said enough to you.]
>
> (Chartier, ed. and trans. McRae: lines 761–8)

This stanza allows us to see Roos the translator at his best. Using the same stanza form (the *huitain*), he unobtrusively converts the French octosyllables into English pentameters:

> Myn hert, ner I, have doon you noo forfet
> By whiche ye shuld complain in any kinde.
> Ther hurtith you nothing but your owne conceyt;
> Be jugge yourself, for so ye shal it finde.
> Ons for always lete this synke in youre mynde –
> That the desire shal never rejoysed be.

Ye noye me sore in wasting al this winde,
For I have said inought, as semeth me.
                    (*Chaucerian Dream Visions*, ed. Symons: lines 789–96)

Chartier's poem took Europe by storm (Cayley and Kinch 2008). Accused of impugning the honour of ladies and love in general, Chartier was 'banished' from the *Cour Amoureuse*, which convened at the French royal court to consider the rights and wrongs of courtly love and to enjoy love poetry. Various continuations and denunciations of the poem followed, including Chartier's self-defence (*L'excusation*). Roos probably knew about this furore, and his English translation enabled English readers to join the *querelle* that had gripped fashionable France (Kinch 2006).

How to explain the impact of the poem? The idea of a lady refusing to reciprocate the affections of a knight was not novel. What *is* new is Chartier's portrayal of a *dame* who feels harassed by the importunity of *amour courtois* and treats her suitor as indulging in sentimental tropes that cannot be taken seriously. The above-cited passage illustrates the resulting communicative deadlock. *L'amant* says it is pointless to plead with her any longer, and so directs his final words to God; she replies by saying he should stop complaining to *her*, as if his 'complaining to God' were only a figure of speech. Similarly, when he says he will die unless she relents, she dismisses the idea as a literary trope: no one has ever really died of love. The cumulative effect of these skirmishes is to raise fundamental issues about courtly love: is its discourse in earnest (as the lover insists) or is to be put in inverted commas (as *la dame* argues)? Faced by radical scepticism, the lover is finally driven to assert his sincerity not in language (which proves inadequate) but in deeds: he does not answer the lady's final retort because, when he said he now had only God to complain to, he meant it; and he finally dies of heartbreak because he meant that, too. Or rather – for Chartier does not quite settle the argument in *l'amant's* favour (Cayley 2006: 109–17) – the narrator tells us he has *heard* that the lover has died.

Roos adequately conveys the tenor of Chartier's poem, but, although he can be a very good translator (as we have seen), the English poem is inferior to the original. Chartier's allegorical vignettes particularly suffer in translation. For example, 'La Mort m'a tollu ma maistresse/ Et me laisse seul, langoureux,/ En la conduite de Tristesse' (lines 6–8) is feebly translated as: 'The deth hath take my lady and maistres/ And left me soul, thus discomfit and mate,/ Sore languishing and in wey of distresse' (lines 34–6). French *conduite* could mean 'way', as Roos has it, but surely not in 'En la conduite de Tristesse' ('under Sadness's escort'), where Sadness is poignantly imagined as a travel guide. As well as blunting Chartier's poetic edge, Roos occasionally misconstrues the French original. Thus he confuses grammatical subject and object at line 265 (cf. Chartier: line 237), mistakes a concessive ('Soit d'escripre' [Be it to write], line 15) for an imperative ('Lete it be writen', line 43), and writes feeble lines as a result. The opinion that Roos is 'polished and fluent' (Gray: 351) errs on the side of generosity.

In Chartier the 'I' who rides out and reports the dialogue between the *amant* and the *dame* is *l'acteur*, i.e. Chartier himself. To clarify his non-identity with this 'I', Roos framed his translation with a prologue and epilogue (each in four rhyme royal stanzas) where he says he was tasked with translating Chartier 'as part of my penaunce' (line 9) and develops a witty modesty *topos*. Dreading his task because of his 'unconnyng and [...] gret simplesse' (line 17), he woke up one morning and went for a walk:

> Tylle I came to a lusty grene valy
> Full of floures, to se gret plesaunce.
> And so bolded [...]
> Thus I began, if it please you to here. (lines 24–8)

In the epilogue, he asks his readers to forgive the 'boldnesse' of his 'litel boke': readers must remember that without boldness no book would ever see the light of day (lines 838–9). They may also remember that the translator lacked boldness until his morning walk, which 'bolded' him to begin his translation. We have 'the lusty grene valy, full of floures' to thank (or blame) for Roos' poem.

The Isle of Ladies, probably another fifteenth-century composition, although surviving only in two sixteenth-century manuscript booklets (Forni 2001b), is an exuberantly emotive dream vision about the pains and joys of love. The wild oscillation between grief and bliss, and the necessary co-existence of the two, are the essence of the story; they are also meant to authenticate the seriousness of the poet's condition: he is in love, and love is 'a wofull blisse/ A lusti fievere, a wounde softe' (Gower, *Confessio Amantis*, 5.5993–4, ed. Macaulay 1899–1902: III: 110). It also leads to disturbed dreams. In his discussion of dreams in *The House of Fame*, Chaucer contrasts reliable visions (which come from outside) to dreams that come from our own troubled imaginations: to the former category belong pure visions worked by 'spirites' (intelligences like angels or demons) (*The House of Fame*, line 41); to the latter, the dreams of lovers 'That hopen over-muche or dreden,/ That purely her impressiouns/ Causeth hem avisiouns' (lines 38–40). The scene with which *The Isle of Ladies* opens – a lover lying awake on a night in May thinking about his lady – promises a dream of the second type, but the poet also suggests the possibility that some 'good spirit' may have been at work:

> Wherfore is yet my full beleve
> That some good spirite, that eve,
> By maner of some cureux port
> Bare me where I saw payne and sport.
> > (*The Floure and the Leafe, The Assembly of Ladies, The Isle of Ladies,*
> > ed. Pearsall 1990: lines 27–30)

The Dreamer's location, in a hunting lodge 'beside a well in a foreste' (line 19, cf. line 191), lends weight to this suggestion, for wells were thought to be places where spirits dwelled. The poet's dream is thus ambiguously poised between the disturbed sleep of the lover and the spiritual vision. When the Dreamer wakes up, this ambiguity is kept in play as he reflects that his lady has the power to turn the substance of his dream into 'cognisaunse, and cognisaunce to very preve' (lines 2193–4). Whether the dream was vacuous or prophetic depends on the lady's response.

In this poem, strictly speaking, there are two dreams, both transporting us from 'plesaunce' to 'paine' (line 34) and back again. At the start of the first dream, the Dreamer finds himself as the only man on an Isle of Ladies. The ladies are troubled by his presence and politely ask him to leave. The Dreamer's initial joy (lines 142–7) now gives way to apprehension (lines 257–64), but great joy (line 452) is restored when the queen returns from one of her regular expeditions to fetch three apples that give eternal youth, health and wish-fulfilment. On this occasion, she almost died when a prince tried to abduct her. Fortunately, a lady came to her rescue and revived her with an apple. Repenting of his rashness, the prince has sailed back with the queen and the lady, who turns out to be the Dreamer's love.

We now have two pairs of lovers, the prince and the queen, and the Dreamer and his lady, and their stories are deftly intertwined. Their fates converge when the queen decides that it would be best if the prince, too, left the Isle. On hearing this, the prince faints and almost dies. The resulting scene is an endearing tribute to Chaucer's *Troilus*. It includes a lady trying to rouse the prince from his swoon ('Awacke, for schame! / What will ye do? Is this good game?', lines 545–6, cf. *TC* 3.1126–7); the queen herself worrying that her reputation would suffer if he died ('Yf he dye here, lost is my name. / How shall I pleye this perilous game?' (lines 561–2; cf. *TC* 2.459–62); the prince, restored to his senses, unable to say anything apart from '"Mercy" twies' (line 588), just like Troilus (cf. *TC* 3.98). Unlike Criseyde, however, the lady does not change her mind until a *deus ex machina* arrives: the God of Love invades and easily conquers the realm, since the ladies' customary defences – armour of 'goode language' and shots of 'fayre wordes' (lines 739–41) – are useless against his naval forces. Cupid, who is patently on the side of men in this poem, commands the queen and the lady to accept their suitors.

When the lady leaves the Isle in a boat to return home, 'for wiche leve wepte many a wyght' (line 1136), the Dreamer plunges into the sea, is hauled on board, and gains the lady's confidence. 'Plesaunce' seems finally to have won the day when the company arrive 'with joyeux chere and hartes light' (line 1298) on the lady's native shore, but the poet keeps the pendulum moving by interrupting the Dreamer's sleep just as that point:

> With whiche landinge tho I woke,
> And found my chaumbre full of smoke,
> My chekes eke, unto the eares,
> And all my body weate of teares;
> And all so feble and in suche wise
> I was, that unnethe might I rise,
> So fare traveled [much troubled / far travelled] and so feynte.
>
> (lines 1301–7)

Our emotions are not allowed to rest happily. Nor are we allowed to forget the question raised by the prologue: what kind of dream is this? Are the Dreamer's tears due to his copious crying inside the vision or to smoke irritation? Is he 'traveled' because his imagination is overwrought, or is he physically exhausted from the sea journey in the dream? 'So fare traveled' neatly covers both possibilities.

The second dream is, if anything, frothier than the first, and its emotional ups and downs are even more extreme. For while the first dream gives us several near-deaths, in the second the prince and the queen really do die – only to be miraculously restored to life. The drama is precipitated by another sea journey: the prince has to leave the Isle of Ladies to set affairs in his home country in order, but the queen sets a strict deadline for his return. These sea journeys are narrative conveniences – as the poet readily admits. The prince's boat is 'a manes thowght': 'Yt nedethe nether mast ne rother [...] Hit sayled by thowght and by plesaunce' (lines 1377–84). When he finally returns to the Isle of Ladies, he has no difficulty fitting his 60,000 followers into his 'littull barge' (line 1374), for it is subject to the poet's omnipotence of thought and will take as many passengers as he likes (lines 1565–6). However, 'pleasaunce' turns to pain when the prince discovers the queen has died because he has broken her deadline; and in despair he kills himself. The corpses are taken to an abbey where they are miraculously brought back to life.

This triumph over death itself sets the tone for the joyful climax. If the art of poetry consists 'of intensifying emotions by assembling the scattered objects that naturally arouse them' (Santayana 1900: 263), this poet does an excellent job by setting his drama in a vividly imagined world of sound and colour. His world of death is one of sensory deprivation – the survivors wear only black clothes (line 1776); the corpses are brought to 'an abbye of nonnes wiche were blacke' (line 1799, i.e. Benedictines), where the only sound is the murmur of liturgical prayer, 'Witheowt note, ful softely' (line 1809). This deadened world is suddenly invaded by birds 'All fulle of collors straunge and cointe' (line 1828) that sing 'songes in armonye' (line 1832) and bring a 'flowerles' plant that bursts into blossom and produces life-restoring seed (lines 1871–3). Soon afterwards, the birdsong is echoed by the 'newe joyeux accordes' (line 2156) of humans as they celebrate the recovery and marriage of the prince and the queen. Since this couple have throughout the story acted as surrogates for the Dreamer and his lady, it stands to reason that the latter, too, exchange marriage vows. The dance music at the feast before the marriage night is so rousing that the Dreamer wakes up and finds he has actually leapt from his bed 'weninge to be at the feast' (line 2169). Bereft of the 'plesaunce' of his dream, he wakes up to 'pain', and gloom descends once more. When the poet looks up all he can see is an old wall painting, 'Of horsemen, hawkes, and houndes, / And hurte deare full of woundes / Some lyke bytton, some hurtte with shott' (lines 2173–5), that reflects back to him not only his own suffering but, worse, the emptiness of his dream. All that remains is the hope that the poet's lady will deliver him from volatility by turning the happiness of the dream into a permanent reality.

As my discussions of these poems will have suggested, none of them is 'Chaucerian' in the sense that it is like Chaucer. This is true also of other visions (such as *The Castle of Love*, in *Chaucerian Apocrypha*, ed. Forni, and John Clanvowe's *Book of Cupid*, in *Chaucerian Dream Visions*, ed. Symons) which found their way into the Chaucer canon. But the admiration shown by early readers for these Chauceriana – especially for *The Flower and the Leaf*, 'generally regarded as the best of Chaucer's allegories' (*Floure*, ed. Pearsall 1980: 1) – was not just based on Chaucer's reputation but also on their intrinsic merits. The Chaucerian apocrypha are worth reading; and I hope this chapter has given some idea of the qualities that make them so.

Works cited

Bennett, H. S., *Chaucer and the Fifteenth Century* (Oxford, 1947)

Boffey, Julia, '"Forto compleyne she had gret desire": The Grievances Expressed in Two Fifteenth-Century Dream-Visions', in *Nation, Court and Culture: New Essays on Fifteenth-Century English Poetry*, ed. Helen Cooney (Dublin, 2001), pp. 116–28

Cayley, Emma, *Debate and Dialogue: Alain Chartier in his Cultural Context* (Oxford, 2006)

——, and Ashby Kinch, eds, *Chartier in Europe* (Cambridge, 2008)

Chartier, Alain, *The Quarrel of the Belle Dame sans Mercy*, ed. and trans. by Joan E. McRae (New York, 2004)

Chaucerian and Other Pieces, ed. W. W. Skeat (Oxford, 1897)

The Chaucerian Apocrypha: A Selection, ed. Kathleen Forni (Kalamazoo, MI, 2005)

Chaucerian Dream Visions and Complaints, ed. Dana M. Symons (Kalamazoo, MI, 2004)

Deschamps, Eustache, *Oeuvres complètes*, eds Marquis Queux de Saint-Hilaire and G. Raynaud, 11 vols (Paris, 1878–1903)

Fifteenth-Century English Dream Visions, ed. Julia Boffey (Oxford, 2003)

The Floure and the Leafe and The Assembly of Ladies, ed. Derek Pearsall (Manchester, 1962; repr. 1980)

The Floure and the Leafe, The Assemblie of Ladies, The Isle of Ladies, ed. Derek Pearsall (Kalamazoo, MI, 1990)

Friedman, J. B., 'Eurydice, Heurodis, and the Noon-Day Demon', *Speculum*, 41 (1966), 22–9

Forni, Kathleen, 2001a. '"Chaucer's Dreame": A Bibliographer's Nightmare', *Huntington Library Quarterly*, 64 (2001), 139–50

——, 2001b. *The Chaucerian Apocrypha: A Counterfeit Canon* (Gainesville, FL, 2001)

Gower, John, *The Complete Works of John Gower*, ed. G. C. Macaulay, 4 vols (Oxford, 1899–1902)

Gray, Douglas, *Later Medieval English Literature* (Oxford, 2008)

Hammond, Eleanor P., 'MS Longleat 258: A Chaucerian Codex', *Modern Language Notes*, 20 (1905), 77–9

Jean de Werchin, *Le Songe de la barge*, ed. Joan Grenier-Winther (Montreal, 2006)

Kinch, Ashby, 'A Naked Roos: Translation and Subjection in the Middle English *La Belle Dame Sans Mercy*', *Journal of English and Germanic Philology*, 105 (2006), 415–45

McMillan, Ann, '"Fayre Sisters Al": *The Flower and the Leaf* and *The Assembly of Ladies*', *Tulsa Studies in Women's Literature*, 1 (1982), 27–42

Robbins, Rossell Hope, 'The Chaucerian Apocrypha', in *A Manual of the Writ-*

ings in Middle English, 1050–1500, Volume 4, gen. ed. J. B. Severs and Albert E. Hartung (New Haven, CT, 1973), pp. 1061–101, and 1285–306

Santayana, George, *Poetry and Religion* (New York, 1900)

Seaton, Ethel, *Sir Richard Roos, c. 1410–1482: Lancastrian Poet* (London, 1961)

Stephens, John, 'The Questioning of Love in the *Assembly of Ladies*', *Review of English Studies*, n.s. 24 (1973), 129–40

Stevens, John, *Music and Poetry in the Early Tudor Court* (London, 1961, repr. 1979)

12

Historical and Political Verse

ALFRED HIATT

Historical and political writing are related – at times identical – concepts, but ones that have enjoyed different trajectories in medieval and post-medieval literatures. While strong traditions of historiography were inherited from classical antiquity and refined and altered in various ways during the Middle Ages, the category of 'political writing' is largely a modern scholarly invention. Evidently, medieval political writing existed, as did a sense of the political, but it is not clear that it was recognised by medieval authors or readers as a distinct literary genre. (There is, for example, no equivalent to the term 'historia' to describe a work of political commentary or theory). In considering fifteenth-century historical and political verse, then, we are confronted with certain asymmetries. Historical verse comprises a sprawling, diverse corpus extending generically across many different forms of writing, and in its temporal scope from creation to the present. Political verse is at once more focused on contemporary or near-contemporary matters, but also, in many of its articulations, deeply interested in exemplarity – in searching out, that is, political matters from the historical record for the purposes of edifying the present. Given the somewhat diffuse and overlapping nature of both concepts, a rigid demarcation of their boundaries seems counterproductive. Instead, in this chapter, I will pay particular attention to moments at which historical and political verse intersected: to the intrusion of political commentary into historical narrative, to political verse as a form of contemporary history, and to history as a source of authority for political writing.

At the beginning of the fifteenth century, writers wishing to compose historical or political verse had a number of genres at their disposal. The most obvious of these was the chronicle, a genre that allowed historical narrative to be conjoined with political advice and commentary. However, it is possible to see elements of historical and political writing in several other verse genres, none of which should be viewed as clearly defined for medieval authors and readers. Perhaps the most obvious of these at the turn of the century would have been the genre of satire in the tradition of *Piers Plowman*, in which, through the dextrous use of allegory, the ills of the polity could be distilled and criticised (*Piers Plowman Tradition*, ed. Barr 1993). Closely related to Langlandian satire was complaint: usually written in the first person, complaints articulated a range of grievances, from the amatory to the financial, but with the potential to make implicit or explicit criticism of government (Robbins 1975: 1403–12, 1416–22; Scase 2007; Matthews 2010: esp. 108–34). Another genre to emerge with some force in English writing in the late fourteenth and early fifteenth centuries was that of advice to princes. A form of literature with strong Latin pedigree, and with the attraction of direct address to a powerful reader, the genre had major exponents in John Gower and Thomas Hoccleve (Gower, ed. Macaulay 1900–01; Hoccleve, ed. Blyth 1999; see also Scanlon 1994; Perkins 2001). 'Advice to princes' poems made heavy use of historical examples to enable the poet to counsel his sovereign from a position of moral and intellectual authority, in ways that mark their affinity to the *de casibus*, or 'Fall of Princes' tradition. The latter – typified by Boccaccio's *De casibus virorum illustrium*, and in Middle English writing by Geoffrey Chaucer's the 'Monk's Tale' and John Lydgate's *Fall of Princes* – emphasises the historically contingent nature of all power through its susceptibility to Fortune. This mode of writing demanded the force of the example from history while conveying a message to contemporary power. Finally, a great deal of historical and some political writing took place within the über-genre of romance. Romance narratives are habitually set in the past, and very often focused on renowned historical personages, including Alexander, Arthur (and his knights), Aeneas, and even the emperor Octavian, as well as the matter of classical epic, such as the fall of Troy or the siege of Thebes. Such romance poems had the capacity to cast an oblique light on contemporary political circumstances and events, and to articulate ideal standards of political behaviour.

All of these genres were present and accessible by the end of the fifteenth century. However, as the following discussion will suggest, the significant constitutional turmoil of the century contributed, if not to the construction of new genres, then to an increase in the number of occasional poems. Particularly notable was the rise of an antagonistic literature, in which prominent individuals became targets for intense criticism. In general, the trend seems to have been towards shorter, more pointed texts, with counsel transmuting into the concept of 'policy', and the verse chronicle, by 1500, looking increasingly unfashionable. Given that prose chronicles, by contrast, continued to flourish well into the sixteenth century, it is worth giving some consideration to the question of why historical and political texts were composed in verse at all.

Around the middle of the fifteenth century John Hardyng, ex-soldier and erstwhile faithful retainer of the northern magnates Henry Percy, Earl of Northumberland, and Sir Robert Umfraville, began to compose a chronicle of British history in rhyme royal. He started with the first inhabitation of the island by the Greek princess Albina and her sisters and concluded, some 2,700 stanzas later, in the reign of Henry VI of England. Hardyng was, that is to say, very much writing in the tradition of historiography decisively established by Geoffrey of Monmouth's *Historia Regum Britanniae*, and thereafter consolidated by the chronicles of Wace, Layamon, Robert of Gloucester, and by the anonymous (multi-authored) Middle English *Brut*. *Castleford's Chronicle*, a northern English verse 'Boke of Brut' tentatively and perhaps incorrectly dated to the fourteenth century (it survives in a single, fifteenth-century manuscript), shows notable similarities with Hardyng's history: beginning with Albina, it too contains a disproportionately large Arthurian section, and an interest in Anglo-Scottish relations (*Castleford's Chronicle*, ed. Eckhardt). The appeal of such history is undoubtedly its scope: the grand narrative of the island connects first foundation with present-day reality, encompassing the Trojan War, Julius Caesar, Arthur, Alfred, William the Conqueror, giants, incubi, saints and Saxons in its sweep.

The logic at work in the *Brut* tradition is fundamentally genealogical, as shown in the unique manuscript of the first version of Hardyng's *Chronicle* by a fine illuminated pedigree that demonstrates Edward III's claim to the French throne (BL, MS Lansdowne 204, fol. 196r). More than other examples of the *Brut* tradition, Hardyng's history was written with the explicit motive of demonstrating the legal right of the English Crown to sovereignty over Wales and Scotland, which together would re-establish the unity sundered by the initial division of the island between the three sons of Brutus. Along with his chronicle, Hardyng constructed a series of forged documents, in which kings of Scotland appeared to acknowledge English overlordship. These he submitted to Henry VI in 1440 and 1457 (Hiatt 2004: 102–35). The *Chronicle*, also submitted to Henry in 1457, contextualises the forgeries, citing them as evidence of the historical narrative it presents and recording Hardyng's delivery of them to the English Crown. At the time of his death around 1465 Hardyng was putting the finishing touches on a significantly revised version of the *Chronicle* dedicated to the new Yorkist monarch, Edward IV. This second version of the *Chronicle* survives in twelve manuscripts and three fragments (Edwards 1987: 75–84), suggesting a reasonably extensive dissemination amongst Edward's supporters, and the utility of the genre in asserting Yorkist legitimacy.

However, there is more to Hardyng's *Chronicle* – and to the *Brut* tradition as a whole – than the dynastic and national, as important as these elements are in explaining the popularity of this form of historical writing. For the lengthy sequence of kings provides precisely the kind of material from which counsel and commentary can be drawn. A striking example is an apostrophe inserted by Hardyng in the midst of a series of pre-Roman British kings, in which he laments the breakdown of government as a result of civil war. In part an imitation of Geoffrey's criticism of internal discord at the corresponding point in his narrative, Hardyng's complaint crucially identifies lawlessness as the condition for the injurious rise of upstart 'trespassers' on the royal sovereignty:

> What is a kyng withouten lawe or pese
> With in his Reame suffyciently conserued?
> The porest of his Reame may so increse
> By iniury and force to bene preserued,
> Tyll he his kynge with strenght haue so ouer terned
> And sette hym selff in riall mageste,
> Iff that it be in suche a Iuparte
>
> O ye prynces and lordes of hye estate,
> Kepe well the lawe and pese with gouernance
> Lesse your sugette3 you foule and deprecyate
> Whiche bene as able with wrongfull ordenaunce,
> To regne as ye and haue als grete pussaunce
> If pese and lawe be layde and unyte
> The floures ere lefte of all your souereynte.

(BL MS Lansdowne 204, fol. 26r)

Ostensibly conservative in their insistence on hierarchy and social order as the prerequisites of peace, these lines nevertheless contain the troubling admission that 'the poorest of the Realm' are 'as able' as high-end princes and lords to govern. True, the arrivistes can only rise to such heights through violence and the suspension of law, but that in itself bespeaks the repressive force of such apparently neutral concepts as law and governance. The second version of Hardyng's *Chronicle* contains a significant revision to these lines, a jolt of contemporary history to add potency to the counsel:

> What is a kyng withoutyn lawe and peace,
> Within his realme sufficiently conserued?
> The porest of his Reame maye encrease
> By iniury and force of menne preserued,
> Till he his kyng with strength haue ouerthrowed,
> And sette hym self in royall maieste,
> As tratour Cade made such a juperte
>
> O ye, my lorde of Yorke, and veraie heire
> Of Englande, so this matter [well] impresse
> Deipe in your breste, lette it synke softe and feire,
> And suche defautes sette you aye to represse:
> At [the] begynnyng lette your high noblenes
> The trespassoures to chastes, and restreine,
> And lette theim not lawe ne peace disobeine.
>
> O ye lordes that [been in] high estate,
> Kepe well the lawe and peace with gouernaunce,
> Lesse your subiettis you hurte and depreciate
> Whiche been as able, with wrongfull ordynaunce,
> To reigne as ye, and haue als greate puisaunce:
> For lawe and iustices in lordes vnpreserued
> Causeth many of theim to bee ouerthrowed. (Hardyng 1812: 59)

Hardyng has inserted an entirely new stanza addressed to his 'lord of York' (probably an indication that these lines were written with Richard, Duke of York in mind, and not revised after his death and Edward's seizure of the throne), refiguring his earlier complaint in specifically Yorkist terms to discourage compassion in dealing with the new regime's enemies. At the same time, he introduces a pointed reference to the uprising led by Jack Cade in 1450, as an example of precisely the sort of a-hierarchical disturbance that erupts in the absence of law's restraining hand (Peverley 2008). Cade's rebellion, which saw the murder and execution of several magnates including Lord Saye, Sir Humphrey Stafford and the sheriff of Kent, becomes the result of poor governance. Hardyng's allusion to Cade operates in the mirror for princes tradition, with a line drawn from pre-Roman Britain direct to the mid-fifteenth century. Such alterations to the second version of the *Chronicle* demonstrate amply the genre's flexibility: its capacity to serve two masters with its presentation of lines of descent and earnest exhortations on how to rule. By the same token, of course, the Lancastrian and Yorkist versions of the work reveal some of the continuities of outlook and rhetoric between even the bitterest of rival claimants to the throne.

One of the biggest growth areas of fifteenth-century verse appears to have been in poems that commemorated events – royal entries, coronations, battles, sieges, deaths of great men and the occasional woman – often from the recent past, and often with a decided slant. This type of verse was by no means new: in the fourteenth century the poet Laurence Minot, perhaps the best exponent of the genre, composed a series of poems on notable events, particularly battles and sieges, in the reign of Edward III (Robbins 1975: 1412–6; Matthews 2010: 135–55). Such poems act both as a historical record of a particular event, and as a political tool or, less instrumentally, as a means of making broader arguments relating to matters of state. The relationship between event poetry of this kind and historical writing of the *Brut* tradition is interestingly illustrated by John Page's 'Siege of Rouen', a poem that describes Henry V's protracted siege of the Norman town during 1419, in 1,314 lines of rhyming couplets. Page's poem survives in full only in two manuscripts, but it was incorporated into at least ten surviving manuscripts of the Middle English prose *Brut*. Curiously, compilers of one version of the *Brut* seem to have begun to copy the poem out in prose, before giving up and retaining the verse format for the remainder of the poem (Drukker 2005; Robbins 1975: 1422–30 lists ballads and poems in prose chronicles).

Henry V's successful campaign in France generated several adulatory poems, including the 'Agincourt carol' ('Owre kynge went forth to Normandy', in *Historical Poems*, ed. Robbins 1959: 91–2), and an account of the entire expedition into France in sixty-seven eight-line stanzas (*Chronicle*, ed. Nicholas 1827: 216–33; Scattergood 1971: 47–58). The 'Siege of Rouen' ostensibly celebrates the monarch's martial prowess with the same verve. Page claimed to have been personally present at the siege, and it may have been this eye-witness status that particularly recommended him to continuators of the *Brut* chronicle, as well as the parallels that the poet rather grandiosely draws with the historical sieges of Troy and Jerusalem. The poem establishes a dialogue between two spaces: the English camp outside the walls, boasting tents warm in mid-winter and a sparkling array of heraldry, and the increasingly desperate city within, where before too long inhabitants find themselves looking hungrily on the urban rat population (not to mention its horses, dogs, cats and, eventually, dead fellow citizens), and weighing up their newfound market value: 'A horssë-hedde at halfe a pound,/ A dogge for þe same mony round' (Page, ed. Huscher 1927: lines 475–6). Such depictions may carry an all-too-genuine thrill of historical authenticity, but they also owe much to Page's literary models, including perhaps Minot's poem on Edward III's siege of Calais, where similar culinary destitution befalls the besieged: 'oure horses, that were faire and fat,/ er etin vp ilkone bidene;/ haue we nowther conig ne cat,/ that thai ne er etin, and hundes kene' (in *Historical Poems*, ed. Robbins 1959: 34–7: lines 73–6). Meanwhile, from Henry's position of strength outside the city he emerges as a pious if unbending assailant, tightening the screws on the wretched Rouennois more in sorrow than anger. Page also draws attention to a third space, one located in between city and king: a huge ditch dug by the English. Into this liminal area the town sends its weak – women, children and old men – in the belief that they might find a new life beyond the city walls; the English refuse to let them pass, and they are left to die of the cold in the ditch, when, as Page points out, the warmth of a house would have saved them. Genuine detail or pathos? Criticism of French or English intransigence? The poem naturally loads the dice in favour of Henry, but Page's celebration of militarism and rightful sovereignty (the citizens of Rouen are clearly in the wrong in refusing to submit to the English Crown) carries the seeds for their critique. That said, the poem works hard to assert the validity of Henry's rule, based not only on his legal claim to Rouen, but also on the exemplary governance he immediately establishes once he gains possession of the city. The culmination of the 'Siege of Rouen' is Henry's entrance to the city, in which his lack of pride and concern for the starving citizens emerge as the poem's moral core, the violence of the siege apparently ameliorated by his establishment of sovereign rule.

The reverse perspective – that of English as besieged, not besiegers – emerges from the energetic poem on the siege of Calais of July 1436, one of several ballads produced in the build-up to, and aftermath of, this event (Doig 1995: 79–106, esp. 98–106). The poem celebrates the English defence of the city against the combined Flemish and French forces led by the Duke of Burgundy. Various English aristocrats are singled out, including the Earl of Morton and 'my lord Camoys' (that is, Roger, Lord Camoys), as well as a defiant Irish archer, and Goby, the water-bailiff's particularly aggressive dog. Humfrey, Duke of Gloucester, enjoys a ride-on part at the end of the poem as the Protector of Calais who reaches the city after the siege has been lifted, but decides to pursue the besiegers into Burgundian territory ('Bycaus they bod not ther,/ In Flanders he soght hem fer and ner', 'On the Siege of Calais. 1436', in *Political Poems*, ed. Wright 1861: II, 151–6; *Historical Poems*, ed. Robbins 1959: 78–83). The successful defiance of the siege is given particular piquancy by the treachery of Burgundy, whose switch of allegiance in 1435 to the French side had jeopardised the English position in France. Whereas Page's 'Siege of Rouen' presented the virtues of the king as an effective military leader and just ruler, poems such as the 'Siege of Calais' celebrate aristocratic prowess, to the extent that they may be the products of noble households. This possibility adds a level of complexity to what sometimes seem rather straightforward texts: while event poems tend to presuppose a partisan audience, there may be ways in which they write history from the perspective of a particular faction, and so present a version of events at odds with the interests and perhaps the memories of other factions.

Inter-factional conflict, of course, became a pressing concern of the mid-fifteenth century, as Henry V's gains in France rapidly disappeared, and court rivalries broke into open warfare. Allegory seems to have offered a particularly attractive way of dramatising (and perhaps sanitising) the violence of military conflict. Here, too, earlier literature had established important models: texts such as Book 1 of Gower's *Vox Clamantis* notably described the Rising of 1381 in terms of animal imagery, while Minot's 'Siege of Calais' styles Edward III as a boar. The poem 'On the Battle of Northampton' (1460) (in Robbins 1975) deploys twenty eight-line stanzas to recount this key Yorkist victory as an extended hunt allegory: 'The berward [Edward, Earl of March] and the bere [Warwick] thei did the dogges [Lancastrian lords Shrewsbury, Beaumont, Egremont] chace,/ And put theyme to flight, to gret confucioun'. The hunt [Henry VI] is brought to London, where an eagle [Salisbury] hovers and seizes four fish, leading to the conclusion: 'Now god, that madest both nyght and day,/ Bryng home the mayster of this game,/ The duke of yorke, for hym we pray,/ That noble prynce, Richard be name.' So urgently contemporary is the poem that it now appears frozen at the moment of emergent Yorkist victory, anxious but not certain of Richard's fate. A year later, and a Yorkist carol on the Battle of Towton seems to try to sprinkle some disinfectant religious imagery over the death toll. The heavy animal allegory is still present ('The wild kat fro norhampton with hur brode nose'), but the refrain ('blessid be þe tyme þat euer god sprad þat floure') and providential tone ('Upon a shrof tuesday on a grene leede,/ Be-twix Sandricche and saynt Albons, many man gan blede') work to solemnise and conclude violent conflict (Robbins 1975: 1516–36 for prophecy poems with animal imagery; Scattergood 1971: 190–1, for the poem's southern bias).

Poems on the deaths and the demises of kings and other notable figures similarly run the gamut from invective to praise. In the second category stand texts as far removed in time as Hoccleve's balade on Henry V's translation of the corpse of Richard II to Westminster ('Where-as that this land wont was for to be'), and an anonymous poem on the death of Edward IV in 1483 ('Wher is this Prynce that conquered his right', in *Historical Poems*, ed. Robbins 1959: 106–8 and 111–13). In the latter, ten stanzas of rhyme royal strike a suitably plangent note: 'Wher is he nowe, that man of noble men [...] O noble Edward, wher art thowe be-come [...] Art thowe agoo, and was here yestirday?/ All men of Englond ar bound for the to pray' (ibid.: 111, lines 15, 22, 27–8). Similarly laudatory is the epitaph for Humfrey, Duke of Gloucester ('Souerayne Immortal, everlastyng god'), which forms an interesting companion piece to 'Thorow-owt a palys as I gan passe', or 'The Lament of the Duchess of Gloucester', in which Humfrey's wife, Eleanor Cobham, reflects on her fall as a result of allegations of sorcery (ibid.: 176–83). The poem is a complaint, falling somewhere between the *Heroides* and *de casibus* traditions: Eleanor bids farewell to 'wordly joy and worthyness', citing in particular fine clothes, minstrels, and 'fayer places on Temmys syde', and contrasting this prosperity with her current state of humiliation and penance (Davenport 2001: 129–52, esp. 143–4). Each of the seventeen stanzas concludes with the refrain: 'Alle women may be ware by me'.

At the opposite end of the spectrum are a number of poems that loudly celebrate first the arrest and then the death of the controversial Duke of Suffolk, William de la Pole, in 1450. Suffolk had emerged as the most powerful magnate in the kingdom in the second half of the 1440s, a position consolidated by the death of Humfrey, Duke of Gloucester, in 1447. But he was deeply unpopular: blamed for territorial losses in France, and allegedly plotting to place his son on the throne, in February 1450 Suffolk was impeached by Parliament. The 'Arrest of the Duke of Suffolk' consists of thirty lines of exuberant allegory, in which the crimes of the 'fox' (Suffolk) are rehearsed and his 'driving to hole' proclaimed. The poem uses the abusive nickname 'Jack Napes' (i.e. ape) to describe Suffolk, a reference to de la Pole's heraldry. The 'Arrest' by and large adheres to the standard modes of medieval political criticism in targeting the counsellor and not the king, but in its conclusion it comes daringly close to transgression: 'God saue þe kyng, and god forbede/ þat he suche apes any mo fede./ And of þe perille that may be-fall/ Be ware, dukes, erles, and barons alle' (*Historical Poems*, ed. Robbins 1959: 186–7, lines 26–30).

Suffolk's murder at sea in May 1450, ambushed while heading into exile in the Low Countries, generated a vigorous satire, the longer version of which consists of 116 lines of macaronic verse, in which the poet adopts a voice of heavy irony, mimicking the liturgy to implicate Suffolk's erstwhile allies in his fate. Indeed the poem consists primarily of a list of prominent churchmen and aristocrats, each of whom is given a Latin tag: 'dominus custodit, thus seyth the bisshope of Rouchestre./ leuaui oculos meos, seyth frere stanbery [...] And all trew comyns ther to be bolde/ to sey 'requiescant in pace,'/ for all the fals traytors that engelond hath sold,/ And for Iake napis sowlle, placebo & dirige' (*Political, Religious, and Love Poems*, ed. Furnivall 1866: lines 21–2, 113–6 for the longer version printed from London, MS Lambeth Palace 306; *Historical Poems*, ed. Robbins 1959: 187–9, for the short version). Although it is tempting to assume a wide and popular audience for such poems, the manuscript evidence (only two surviving copies), use of (admittedly usually easily recognisable) Latin, and veiled allusions might indicate a relatively limited circulation within a literate, politically engaged, audience (Scattergood 1971: 167–68).

In vernacular usage the term 'policie' seems to have gained increasing currency in the course of the fifteenth century, to the extent that on her entry to London in 1501 Katharine of Aragon was confronted by a personified 'Pollici', who commended the young princess to 'thencreas/ Of thise two thynges, vertu and noblesse' (*Receyt*, ed. Kipling 1990: 17). Initially denoting the art of (good) government, 'policie' developed a sense of practical and even cunning efficacy (*MED*, s.v. *policie*; see Strohm 2005: esp. 125–7), something akin to modern 'strategy', while 'politik' (or 'politique') is attested as both a noun meaning the State, or the condition of a country, and as an adjective implying, at least in the thought of Sir John Fortescue, a realm in which the will of the sovereign might be constrained by law ('good pollitique and restfull governaunce', Fortescue, ed. Plummer 1926). Several poems in English were written in the name of policy during this period. In many ways a continuation of the advice tradition, at least two of these poems, the anonymous *Libel of English Policy* and George Ashby's *Active Policy of a Prince*, seem to shift in subtle ways the nature of counsel in striving towards a more corporate conception of governance.

The *Libel* appears from internal evidence to have been written after the siege of Calais in July 1436, but before the death of Emperor Sigismund ('whyche yet regneth') in 1437. Its survival in at least seventeen manuscripts, and in several recensions, indicates a fairly lively contemporary circulation (Robbins 1975: 1507–9; *Libelle*, ed. Warner 1926: xlvii; Meale 1995: 226–7). The *Libel* seems to operate with at least two audiences in mind. The evidence of an envoy to the poem suggests that it was initially presented to influential courtiers, including Walter, Lord Hungerford (who is said in one version to have read the poem 'alle over in a nyghte') and subsequently to lords of the Privy Council, including a 'gret prelate', possibly Cardinal Beaufort (*Political Poems*, ed. Wright 1861: II, 157, n. 1, for Beaufort; *Libelle*, ed. Warner 1926: xii, for Bishop John Stafford; Holmes 1961, for the influence of Gloucester; Meale 1995: 211, for Henry Chichele). At the same time, the poem's rather rugged verse (stanzaic prologue and epilogue, otherwise couplets) and forthright assertion of mercantile interests suggest a larger audience, perhaps located primarily in London (Meale 1995: 216–26).

The argument of the poem is that it is in the national commercial interests of the English Crown to retain military control over the sea – and in particular, over the English Channel. It proceeds by an examination of the commodities of neighbouring regions (Spain, Portugal, Brittany, Brabant and Zeeland, Flanders, Prussia and Lithuania ('Esterlynges'), Scotland and Ireland), and major European exporters and traders, from Venice to Iceland. The poem concludes with a call for unity, envisaging England as a city, with the sea for its wall, 'kepte by Goddes sonde' (1097):

> And thus shulde everi lande one with another
> Entrecomon as brother wyth his brother,
> And life togedre werreles in unite,
> Wythoute rancoure, in very charite.
>
> (*Libelle*, ed. Warner 1926: lines 1100–3)

This pacific conclusion jars with the heavily xenophobic invective of earlier passages, in which Flemings in particular are singled out for caricature, noted for their cowardice (their shameful exit from Calais is reprised, with more praise for Gloucester) and their prolific feats of urination (Robbins 1975: 1429 for anti-Fleming invective). Such invective colours a range of anxieties about the threats to English sovereignty and finance.

   The author of the *Libel* is, for one thing, deeply troubled by the sharp practices of foreign merchants: he urges restrictions on their movement and length of stay within England (as English merchants are allegedly restrained when abroad). He is also particularly exercised by the danger of hostile encirclement if Ireland and Wales were to form an alliance with England's enemies. At the same time the *Libel* stresses the importance of the English for international trade:

> But they of Holonde at Caleyse byene oure felles
> And oure wolles that Englysshe men hem selles,
> And the chefare that Englysshe men do byene
> In the martis, that no man may denyene,
> Is not made in Brabane that cuntre.
> It commeth frome oute of Henaulde, not be the see
> But all by londe by carris and frome Fraunce,
> Burgoyne, Coleyn, Camerete [Cambrai], in substaunce.
> Therfore at martis yf there be a resteryente,
> Men seyne pleynly, that liste no fables peynte,
> Yf Englysshe men be wythdrawene awey,
> Is grete rebuke and losse to here affraye,
> As thoughe wee sent into the londe of Fraunce
> Tenne thousande peple, men of gode puissaunce,
> To werre unto her hynderynge multiphary;
> So bene oure Englysshe marchauntes necessary.
>
> (*Libelle*, ed. Warner 1926: lines 546–61)

As these lines suggest, the *Libel* is driven by a sense of grievance, but equally by a need to sketch a system of trade that connects different European states and which, for all the poem's moments of bellicosity, ultimately depends on peace and political order. The register of commerce – 'chefare', 'martis', 'affraye'

– marks out the poem's insistent mercantilism, set within an historical consciousness in which the chief virtue is naval prowess. Towards the end of the *Libel*, three
exemplary English kings are identified, all notable for their mastery of the sea
and for their advance of national interests: Edgar, Edward III and Henry V. These
monarchs pursued 'true' or 'pure' policy ('pollicie') in that they kept control of
the seas. Peace, unity and prosperity, then, are to come as the fruits of militarism
– but, it might be inferred, a military policy that seeks maritime control of the
British archipelago, and a firm hand on Calais, rather than extensive territorial
expansion into mainland Europe.

Initially the 'policy' advocated in George Ashby's *Active Policy of a Prince*
(probably c.1463, written for the son of Henry VI: Edward, Prince of Wales)
seems about as intellectually adventurous as Polonius' advice to his son: 'A peny
spent bi wise prouision/ Auailith two in time seasonable' (Ashby, ed. Bateson
1899: lines 492–3). But viewed in light of the events of the 1450s and '60s it starts
to take on a sharper, even astringent tone. Ashby, former clerk of the signet to
Henry VI and Queen Margaret, gives advice pointedly based on the mistakes
of that monarch's reign – never let a temporal lord be a treasurer; don't make
too many lords, 'Make knyghtes, squiers and gentilmen riche,/ And the pore
Comyns also welthy,/ But to youre richesse make neuer man liche' (ibid.: lines
639–41). There is cogent financial and economic policy. And there are nuanced
reflections on war and justice. Ashby counsels against war undertaken out of
rashness or avarice, 'Or of fantesie or of symplenesse', and concludes with one
of his best couplets: 'For werre may be lightly commensed,/ Doubt is how it
shal be recompensed (ibid.: lines 679–80). These lines seem to mark an increased
thoughtfulness about the financial and moral consequences of war, presumably
born of the traumas of the Anglo-French and Anglo-Scottish conflicts, along with
the civil war of the 1450s. Similarly Ashby urges the importance of mercy, irre-
spective 'Of what maner bloode [the offender] be discended', at the same time
as advising swift suppression of any 'subuercion/ Of the Realme' (ibid.: lines
779–92). This is Hocclevian advice to princes, for sure, but the genre now bears
the bruises of recent conflict far more openly than it did in the early Lancastrian
years (see Meyer-Lee 2004, for Ashby as 'heir of Hoccleve'). Above all, we see
here the consolidation of 'polleci'.

Is this 'policy' different from the principles and codes advocated by Gower
and Hoccleve, or for that matter from the significant number of poems from
the period that advocate good governance, 'unity', 'one assent', 'good estate' –
poems that subscribe, in other words, to the ideal of a king governing firmly but
not tyrannically, upholding the law with the assent of the lords, commons and
clergy? What seems subtly different about Ashby's advice to the prince – apart
from its historical position as a fleeting and doomed gasp of Lancastrianism – is
that its 'policy' is something that may be expressed by the prince, but may in fact
emanate from a counsellor. The monarch's internalisation and representation of
policy remains paramount: the sovereign will as the ultimate source of secular
power has not been effaced. However, unlike counsel, policy implies a mode
of behaviour or set of attitudes subject to debate and agreement, rather than a
personal exchange between counsellor and sovereign. It also, as in the case of
the *Libel*, allows an address to an audience other than the monarch – an audience

whose agreement, support and active promotion of policy may be required for its success. Policy, that is, invokes and accepts the notion of government as a collective activity, in a way that a constitution founded on the royal will can never easily admit. This development of 'policy', it could be argued, is a response to the long-running crisis of rule occasioned by the reign of Henry VI. In the absence of a strong or coherent sovereign will, a subtle redefinition of power relations took place, in which advice to the king came to seem increasingly fraught or suspect, and in which as a consequence a different 'language of statecraft' began to emerge, one in which policy could govern the king, and not the other way around (cf. Strohm 2005; Watts 1996).

Since the public function of poetry is now much diminished by comparison with the fifteenth century, it seems worthwhile to consider why verse carried such an appeal for the authors of historical and political literature at the end of the Middle Ages. The answers to this question are not, perhaps, particularly obvious, especially given the lack of explicit explanations of the choice of literary form in fifteenth-century writing. One explanation advanced reasonably frequently by modern critics – at least for certain kinds of political verse – is the desire on the part of an author to reach a broader audience and to carry more popular appeal. An English poem, so it seems, would have been accessible to more people in fifteenth-century England than a Latin prose treatise. It does seem likely that at least some of the texts anthologised in medieval manuscripts such as the early fifteenth-century Oxford, Bodl., MS Digby 102, or BL, Cotton Roll ii.23, a Yorkist collection of anti-Suffolk texts, circulated in urban settings, possibly as songs. Such an explanation can only in some cases, however, cover the decision to write in verse, rather than prose. And it should be pointed out that verse frequently circulated alongside prose: Cotton Roll ii.23, for example, mingles poems and prophecy with documents and notes on contemporary events, while London, MS Lambeth Palace 306 contains poems, lyrics and romances but also the proclamation of Kentish Rebels, and the Yorkist *Short English Chronicle*. Of more weight in the decision to choose verse in the case of large-scale histories was probably its status in comparison with prose. John Page clearly states that he initially composed his 'Siege of Rouen' 'alle in raffe and not in ryme', but that when he had 'lyffe and space' he rendered it in verse (Page, ed. Huscher). Why? Page seems to have felt that he enhanced the status of his account of the siege – its value as a text – by turning it into a poem. Similarly, in choosing rhyme royal for his *Chronicle*, John Hardyng seems to have been motivated by a sense that this was the most fitting literary form for a history explicitly dedicated to a king. He could, of course, have found prose models, such as the prose *Brut* or Geoffrey of Monmouth, or less ornate verse, such as *Castleford's Chronicle*'s four-stress couplets. But the care taken in the preparation of the surviving manuscript of the first chronicle, probably presented to Henry VI, indicates Hardyng's interest in the material form of his text, and the importance of its status as a work of art, one studded with Chaucerian and Lydgatean borrowings (Edwards 1977; Edwards 1984). Verse, in other words, may have been the literary form best suited for a commoner seeking to address a monarch.

Above all, though, poetry enabled the deployment of a range of literary models to a greater extent than prose. Page, for example, surely wished to elevate the subject matter of his work through analogy with models such as the *Siege of Jerusalem*. Ashby certainly had in mind the advice to princes tradition in composing his *Active Policy*; indeed, one appeal of the genre was presumably the continuities it established with earlier Lancastrian poetry. The heavy use of allegory by the authors of event poems suggests at least one attraction of that genre, and one point of contact with fourteenth-century literature. Verse may also have offered opportunities for generic mixing in ways that prose did not. The *Libel* moves rather dizzyingly from complaint to invective to advice poem; inept or not, such transitions allow the poem to function within more than one register. Finally, the attraction of verse must have lain in no small part in its potency. Poetry allowed authors to impress and persuade, to commemorate and excoriate, to lament and to declaim in ways more flexible, and often more compelling, than prose.

Works cited

Ashby, George, *Active Policy of a Prince*, in *George Ashby's Poems*, ed. Mary Bateson, EETS, e. s. 76 (London, 1899), pp. 12–41

Castleford's Chronicle; or The Boke of the Brut, ed. Caroline D. Eckhardt, 2 vols, EETS, o. s. 305, 306 (Oxford, 1996)

A Chronicle of London from 1089 to 1483, eds Nicholas H. Nicholas and E. Tyrell (London, 1827)

Davenport, Tony, 'Fifteenth-Century Complaints and Duke Humphrey's Wives', in *Nation, Court and Culture: New Essays on Fifteenth-Century English Poetry*, ed. Helen Cooney (Dublin, 2001), pp. 129–52

Doig, James A., 'Propaganda, Public Opinion and the Siege of Calais in 1436', in *Crown, Government and People in the Fifteenth Century*, ed. Rowena E. Archer (Stroud, 1995), pp. 79–106

Drukker, Tamar S., 'An Eye-Witness Account or Literary Historicism?: John Page's *Siege of Rouen*', *Leeds Studies in English*, n. s. 36 (2005), 251–73

Edwards, A. S. G., 'The Influence of Lydgate's *Fall of Princes* c. 1440–1559: A Survey', *Mediaeval Studies*, 39 (1977), 424–39

——, 'Hardyng's *Chronicle* and *Troilus and Criseyde*', *Notes and Queries*, 229 (1984), 156

——, 'The Manuscripts and Texts of the Second Version of John Hardyng's *Chronicle*', in *England in the Fifteenth Century: Proceedings of the 1986 Harlaxton Symposium*, ed. Daniel Williams (Woodbridge, 1987), pp. 75–84

Fortescue, Sir John, *The Governance of England*, ed. Charles Plummer (London, 1926)

Gower, John, *Confessio Amantis*, in *The English Works of John Gower*, ed. G. C. Macaulay, 2 vols (London, 1900–01)

Hardyng, John, *The Chronicle of Iohn Hardyng*, ed. Henry Ellis (London, 1812)

Hiatt, Alfred, *The Making of Medieval Forgeries: False Documents in Fifteenth-Century England* (London, 2004)

Historical Poems of the XIVth and XVth Centuries, ed. Rossell Hope Robbins (New York, 1959)

Hoccleve, Thomas, *The Regiment of Princes*, ed. Charles Blyth (Kalamazoo, MI, 1999)

Holmes, G. A., 'The "Libel of English Policy"', *EHR*, 76 (1961), 193–216

The Libelle of Englyshe Polycye: A Poem on the Use of Sea-Power 1436, ed. Sir George Warner (Oxford, 1926)

Matthews, David, *Writing to the King: Nation, Kingship, and Literature in England, 1250–1350* (Cambridge, 2010)

Meale, Carol M., '*The Libelle of Englyshe Polycye* and Mercantile Literary Culture in Late-Medieval London', in *London and Europe in the Later Middle Ages*, eds Julia Boffey and Pamela King (London, 1995), pp. 181–227

Meyer-Lee, Robert J., 'Laureates and Beggars in Fifteenth-Century English Poetry: The Case of George Ashby', *Speculum*, 79 (2004), 688–726

Page, John, *John Page's Siege of Rouen*, ed. Herbert Huscher (Leipzig, 1927)

Perkins, Nicholas, *Hoccleve's 'Regiment of Princes': Counsel and Constraint* (Cambridge, 2001)

Peverley, Sarah L., 'Political Consciousness and the Literary Mind in Late Medieval England: Men "Brought up of nought" in Vale, Hardyng, *Mankind*, and Malory', *Studies in Philology*, 105 (2008), 1–29

The Piers Plowman Tradition: A Critical Edition of Pierce the Ploughman's Crede, Richard the Redeless, Mum and the Sothsegger, and the Crowned King, ed. Helen Barr (London, 1993)

Political Poems and Songs Relating to English History, ed. Thomas Wright, 2 vols (London, 1861)

Political, Religious, and Love Poems, ed. F. J. Furnivall, EETS, o. s. 15 (London, 1866)

The Receyt of the Ladie Kateryne, ed. Gordon Kipling, EETS, e. s. 296 (Oxford, 1990)

Robbins, Rossell Hope, 'Poems Dealing with Contemporary Conditions', in *A Manual of the Writings in Middle English 1050–1500, Volume 5*, gen. ed. Albert E. Hartung (New Haven, CT, 1975), pp. 1385–1536

Scanlon, Larry, *Narrative, Authority, and Power: The Medieval Exemplum and the Chaucerian Tradition* (Cambridge, 1994)

Scase, Wendy, *Literature and Complaint in England, 1272–1553* (Oxford, 2007)

Scattergood, V. J., *Politics and Poetry in the Fifteenth Century* (London, 1971)

Strohm, Paul, *Politique: Languages of Statecraft between Chaucer and Shakespeare* (Notre Dame, IN, 2005)

Watts, John, *Henry VI and the Politics of Kingship* (Cambridge, 1996)

13

Classical and Humanist Translations

DANIEL WAKELIN

yf thow fle ydelnes . Cupide hath no myght   *Ouidius* de remedio
hs bow lyeth broken . his fyre hath no lyght.   amoris
                             (Robbins 1959: 560, n. 6; *NIMEV* 1430)[1]

There is no known English translation of Ovid's verse before some excerpts from his *Ars amandi* were printed as a textbook in Latin translation, *The flores of Ouide de arte amandi*, in 1513 (*STC* 18934). But on the back of a songbook of music and carols (Bodl. MS Arch. Selden. B. 26, fol. 33v) some fifteenth-century person wrote this couplet translating two lines from Ovid's *Remedia amoris* (lines 139–40). It is a teasing fragment to add to a small but intriguing set of fifteenth-century translations from Latin – whether the classical Latin of authors such as Ovid or the fine Latin of their humanist imitators – into English verse.

These verse translators comment on their purposes only fleetingly. But one illuminating comment comes at the end of the translation by Gilbert Banester (d.1487) of a story from Boccaccio's *Il Decamerone* (*NIMEV* 4082). Like many fifteenth-century poets he addresses his little book, echoing Chaucer in *Troilus and Criseyde* (V.1786–99), but amid the conventions he describes his project precisely:

> Prey all tho, theras thou comyst in audiens,
> To haue piete on thy symple translacione,
> Oute off prose by myne vnkonnyng directioune
> Made in balade [...]
> Besekyng all the maisters of this science
> Me holde excused, for goode ys myne entencion,
> Thogh I florysh nat with metyr and cadence,
> Off rethoryk and poetry makyng mencioune;
> Such clerkly werkys passith my discrecion.
>   (Banester, ed. Wright 1937: 36, lines 612–21)

First, Banester comments explicitly on his use of 'translacione': he is open about his use of a source. And he is open too about a change that he makes while translating, reworking it 'Oute of prose' and into 'balade' (eight-line stanzas, *ababbcbc*). This recognition of his reworking into verse is strengthened by his

---

[1]   HEH, MS HM 28175, fol. 40v, has a similar couplet in a Book of Hours: 'O cupid I graunt thy might is much for sure thou loveth thy dart to shent at such'.

conventional apology for ineptitude in 'metyr and cadence'. He comments explicitly here, then, on something that defines the works discussed in this chapter: the decision to translate, even from prose, into verse. Were these works solely essays in the craftsmanship of poetry, or academic exercises designed to please 'maisters' of 'science'? Mastery of such arts is prominent in these literary experiments but it is not, ultimately, all that Banester and others achieve.

Yet the decision to turn 'prose' into 'balade' or 'metyr and cadence' is worth considering, for it is a decision that did not need to be taken. After all, other writers were willing and able to translate classical and humanist Latin into prose. At the start of the fifteenth century there is a prose translation of Vegetius's *Epitoma rei militaris* in 1408, which seems the tail-end of the interest in prose translation fostered by Sir Thomas Berkeley from the 1380s on (Hanna 1989; Nall 2012: 16–17). Later in the century, there is a prose translation of Aeneas Sylvius Piccolomini's letter on the origins of heraldry, from some milieu connected with veterans of the French wars (London, College of Arms, MS Arundel 26 (=Arundel 63), fols 41r–51v and MS L. 5 *bis*, fols 24r–26r; Bodl. MS Ashmole 764, fols 1r–8r, and MS Douce 271, fols 63v–64v). During the second half of the fifteenth century there were other prose translations of classical and humanist sources, which did recognise their classical or classicising credentials: William Caxton (1415x24–1492) printed in one volume in 1481 (*STC* 5293) a translation of Cicero's *De senectute*, a treatise 'on old age', in a translation probably by William Worcester (1415–1480x85); a translation of Cicero's *De amicitia*, 'on friendship', by William Worcester or by John Tiptoft, Earl of Worcester (1427–70); a translation of Buonaccorso da Montemagno's *Controversia de vera nobilitate*, a pair of speeches from fifteenth-century Florence about the nature of true nobility, probably by Tiptoft (Wakelin 2007: 153–9, 168–73). Caxton mentioned in 1491, but did not print, the fascinating translation by John Skelton (c.1460–1529) of Diodorus Siculus' *Bibliotheca historica*, which preserves the prose of his source (Griffiths 2006: 38–55), and Skelton's lost translation of Cicero's letters to friends (in Caxton, ed. Blake 1973: no. 36a, 92). Caxton made translations of French prose adaptations of Ovid's *Metamorphoses* and Virgil's *Aeneid*, which have been seen to reflect humanist interests despite their avoidance of the original classical source (Kuskin 2008: 243–57; Caxton, ed. Rumrich 2011: xi, xiv–xv); and there were in the 1480s single-line excerpts from the plays of Terence in a bilingual phrasebook or set of *Vulgaria* by the schoolmaster John Anwykyll (d.1487) of Oxford (Wakelin 2007: 134–40). There also survives a translation of Sallust's *Bellum Catilinae*, which is undated but in handwriting that could perhaps be late fifteenth century (CUL, MS Nn.3.6). Overall, there was a small but solid tradition of prose translation from classical and humanist works by the late fifteenth century. The presence of this prose tradition suggests that translators did not need to choose verse. So why did Banester and others do so?

Writing in verse makes sense when the source is itself versified, like that couplet based on Ovid's poem. For example, in 1445 most likely Osbern Bokenham (1392/3–c.1464), a friar of Clare Priory in Suffolk, translated an excerpt of Claudian's *De consulatu Stilichonis*, a panegyric in honour of the fourth-century Roman consul Stilicho, and framed it with praise of Richard, Duke of York (1411–60), a nobleman powerful in Bokenham's locality (Edwards 2001). Bokenham turned it into a form of verse deeply experimental for this period (as is noted below). But beyond *De consulatu Stilichonis* the other translations into verse were made from sources in prose. Why make this curious effort? There is something slightly excessive, or supplementary to requirements, in doing so. Such efforts suggest that the primary purpose of these translations was not, as we might expect it commonsensically to be, the mere imparting of ideas or information from a foreign language; rather, such efforts suggest that the primary purpose might be engagement with literary forms or Banester's 'rethoryk and poetry'. As it happens, one of the prose translations explains why one might be interested in poetry: Caxton's version of a French adaptation of Ovid's *Metamorphoses* explains, following its source, that with 'metres' and 'poetiques' the ancients 'conceyued' more ideas than they could by other means; they 'encoraged' people into 'feruour' and 'esprysid' or inspired them to fight; and 'in style poetiqe' they could speak 'congruly' or fittingly in worship (Caxton, ed. Rumrich 2011: 41.20, 43.2–3, 43.10–11, 43.18). Even this prose translation, then, conceded that metrical form and poetic style could get things done: they could not only impart information but could stir people to think afresh, inspire or move, and suit occasions better. For example, at the end of the century, Tiptoft's prose version of Buonaccorso's work was versified in the interlude *Fulgens and Lucres* by Henry Medwall. The ideas of Buonaccorso's work were already available in English, and in print too, but the verse drama offers those ideas more persuasively, tests them sceptically and fits them to performance in a grand household.

Other translations also add something to the mere content of the source by altering the form and style in poetry. The content is often oddly needless. So as well as the prose version of Vegetius's *Epitoma* in 1408, in 1460 somebody, tentatively identified as John Neele (Wakelin 2004: 264–6), made a second English translation of Vegetius's prose *Epitoma rei militaris*, entitled *Knyghthode and Bataile*, now into rhyme royal English verse, dedicated in its earliest redaction to Henry VI at the close of his reign. It was closely modelled on the style and manuscript presentation of another verse translation of a utilitarian work of classical Latin prose: the version of Palladius' agricultural treatise *De re rustica* as *On Husbondrie*, dedicated to Henry VI's uncle, Humfrey, Duke of Gloucester, between 1439 and 1443 (below). Humfrey, too, received between 1431 and 1438, from John Lydgate (c.1370–1449), a monk of Bury St Edmunds in Suffolk, a translation of a French version of Giovanni Boccaccio's Latin prose *De casibus virorum illustrium* as the poem *Fall of Princes*. This poem also included, embedded within it, snippets of classical Latin works, or perhaps of their French versions (Witlieb), and a translation of the humanist Coluccio Salutati's *Declamatio Lucretiae*, the story of a virtuous heroine (noted below). After Lydgate completed 'fall of pryncys' around 1438, another poet referred to it thus (*Die mittelenglische Umdichtung*, ed. Schleich 1924: 17–18) in his translation from another work of Boccaccio, *De mulieribus claris*, about famous women. This translation is anonymous and can only be located by its dialect, to East Anglia, and dated by its handwriting, to the mid-fifteenth century (Cowen 2000). By the 1470s or 1480s someone translated an extract and maybe more, now lost, (Wakelin 2011) of Francesco Petrarca's Latin prose dialogue, *Secretum*, into rhyming couplets; the translator is anonymous but the work survives in a manuscript probably from the school of the Benedictine monastery at Winchester Cathedral (Wilson 1981, intro.: 9–10, 13–16). In another milieu connected to educating the young, and around the same time that Banester translated the story of Guiscardo and Ghismonda, another poet made a second translation of that story (noted below). This duplication exemplifies the interest in retrying and reconsidering the classical and humanist sources that get translated, just as Medwall rethinks Tiptoft's source. It seems likely that some of these poets were unaware that there were already translations available, but others knew previous translations but decided to forge the form or ideas of the works anew.

The earliest of these fifteenth-century verse translations might hold the key to this shift from prose to verse. It is a rendering of Boethius' *De consolatione Philosophiae* (*NIMEV* 1597). Anagrammatic acrostics, some of them surviving only in a printed edition of 1525 (*STC* 3200), reveal that this poem was composed by John Walton and was dedicated to Elizabeth Berkeley, daughter of Thomas Berkeley who commissioned the prose version of Vegetius' *Epitoma* (Walton 1927: xliii–xliv; Hanna 1989: 899–902; Johnson 1996: 19–21; Donaghey et al. 1999: 399, 405–7). What is suggestive is that this translation was not wholly a shift from prose to verse: Boethius' work was already a *prosimetrum*, which offered within itself a sort of 'translation' or transferring of the prosy philosophical debate of some chapters (the *prosae*) into emotional or imaginative responses in the subsequent chapters in an ingenious variety of verse-forms (the *metra*). These verse transformations might well give an English poet the idea of virtuosic versifying. And Walton was transforming something wholly in prose into verse; for Geoffrey Chaucer had, in the 1380s, already translated Boethius' work and had rendered it all, *prosae* and *metra* alike, into prose; Walton's translation is based on Chaucer's English as well as the Latin (Walton 1927: li–lix). One copy of Chaucer's translation probably circulated in the Beauchamp household, into which Walton's dedicatee married (Hanna 1989: 902). Although we might consider the purpose of translation to be making the content accessible, the existence of a prior prose version makes Walton's choice of verse look like an attempt to surpass his predecessor or to explore the artistry of the verse-form. Indeed, he admits in his prologue that 'diuerse men':

> [...] wondir subtillye
> In metir sum *and* sum in prose pleyne,
> This book translated haue suffyshauntlye
> Into Englisshe tonge, word for word, wel neye.
> (Walton 1927: st. 4, lines 2–5)

So if other translations were sufficient, then another was needless. Yet Walton betrays a rationale for the diversity in translations when he notes the excellence of these versions in their own right: their wonderful subtlety. Indeed, in the printed copy derived from a likely presentation manuscript, this preface differs from that in other manuscripts as it describes how the other translators worked not 'wondir subtillye' but 'craftely' (ibid.: st. 4, line 2, textual note).[2] It may be

---

2   But it should be noted that this other version also does *not* say that they have done so 'suffyshauntlye' (Walton 1927: st. 4, line 4, textual note).

that their *craft* is the thing that he rivals, because he next notes their crafting into different forms, metre or prose. The possibly belittling description of the prose as 'pleyne' might be prompted merely by the need to rhyme 'i-seyne' (ibid.: st. 4, line 1), yet prose is contrasted with 'metir' quite deliberately in that chiasmic line, and the descriptive adjective 'pleyne' is bound to 'prose' by alliteration. The shift from prose to verse sounds considered.

Then, in Walton's other expressions of humility, he stresses his interest in poetic craft, just as Banester later would. Indeed, in the printed edition likely close to the presentation copy, Walton not only speaks in general of his poor 'abilite' but apologises specifically:

> Yf hyt be not with craft of eloquence
> Depaynted so as other bokes be. (ibid.: xlv; cf. st. 1, lines 5–6)

It is painting, a standard metaphor for rhetorical elaboration, which he strives to offer: we might wonder whether it was specifically an exercise in 'eloquence' that his patroness requested, a sort of rhetorical challenge of overgoing Chaucer's prose. Indeed, although Walton next says that he will translate the 'sentence' or sententious content as 'trewe' or 'als neigh as may be broght', he will only translate closely, he adds, 'Where lawe of metir is noght resistent' or, in the other version, where metre 'wyl therto consente' (ibid.: st. 3, lines 3–4, and textual note). He seems to grant the metre power over the content like a patroness over a poet: an astonishing admission that for him metrical accomplishment takes precedence.

It may be that the challenge of reconciling complex metaphysical content with an intricate verse-form proves too much for Walton. After rendering books I to III of *De consolatione Philosophiae* into ballade stanzas rhyming *ababbcbc*, he renders books IV and V into rhyme royal, that is, into seven-line stanzas rhyming *ababbcc*. He does not explain why he changes his stanzas, but is rhyme royal less testing in requiring only three rhymes for the *b* lines? Walton does not state as much outright, but what he does say, where the shift occurs, is that he fears that he is 'fer fro craft of eloquence' (ibid.: st. 582, line 3):

> This wote I well, my wittes be vnmete
> The sentence for to saue in metre trewe. (ibid.: st. 576, line 3–4)

He echoes his concerns with the 'craft of eloquence' in his prologue and echoes his worry there about balancing the 'sentence' with poetic craftsmanship – and now he states that it is the metre and not the sentence that he will keep 'trewe'. He did: his metrical accomplishment is great in this poem: his verse is often tidily decasyllabic and, as English decasyllables tend to be, often like iambic pentameter. To take as a sample the story of the poet Orpheus in book III, metre 12: in seventy-two lines (ibid.: st. 565–73) the text, as printed by the modern editor, is faulty in the number of syllables in only ten lines.[3] Several of those insufficiencies occur from omitting the first unstressed syllable – a 'headless' line typical of

---

[3] To count syllables, I followed the rules established for the verse of Walton's contemporary, Thomas Hoccleve (Hoccleve 1999: xxix–xxxi).

fifteenth-century versification; others can be removed by using variant wording, which the textual apparatus records in the early printed edition more closely related to the presentation manuscript (ibid.: st. 565, line 8; st. 570, line 8; st. 572, line 4). This reasonable metrical precision is typical too of the other rhyme royal translations in *On Husbondrie* and *Knyghthode and Bataile*. For whatever reasons, these translators were quite good metrists in English, as though they had paid attention not only to the content but to the verse-form.

Yet though Walton's translation showed what could be done in verse, it sits apart from the other translations in date and in its expressed attitude to antiquity. While Walton experiments in poetic craft, he is nervous about 'þese olde poysees derk' and the 'false goddes names' of pagan antiquity (ibid.: st. 6, lines 2, 6). The English word *poesy* at this time referred to fictional content rather than verse-form (*MED*, s.v. *poesie*, n., 1.a). As the fifteenth century developed, this fear of antiquity was replaced by zealous interest in it. The expression of this interest was known as the *studia humanitatis*, which we tend to render now as *humanism* but which might be more helpfully rendered as the 'study of the humanities'. For, with reference to this period, *humanism* denotes the study of classical and neo-classical Latin and Greek: their language, literature, philosophy, politics and history. In this sense, any translation from the classics or from a work imitating the classics might be encouraged by the *studia humanitatis* (Wakelin 2007: esp. 6–9).

For example, in the anonymous translation of Boccaccio's *De mulieribus claris* from East Anglia after 1438 (*NIMEV* 2642), the poet defines his craft in keenly classical terms. First, he puts his prologue between verses in Latin that were copied, in the sole manuscript, in handwriting modelled on that used by Italian humanists (Cowen 2000: 129; see also Cowen 2011). Then, although he like other poets protests that he is not fit to drink from Helicon's well (*Die mittelenglische Umdichtung*, ed. Schleich 1924: 46–7), he is elsewhere bullish about aping the ancients. If we envy his work, he tells us, then he'll console himself by remembering that 'Ovyde, Virgyle, Tully and Terence,/ Which be prencys of Latyn eloquence' had detractors 'bakbytynge' their 'poesys' (ibid.: 36–41). These lines are not translated from Boccaccio's prologue, which is only the source from the tenth stanza onwards (ibid.: line 64; Boccaccio: 9, pref.1), but the hope of emulating antiquity is as confident as Boccaccio's. Indeed, later the English translation adds to Boccaccio's prologue another classical detail, from Sallust's *Bellum Catilinae* (*Die mittelenglische Umdichtung*, ed. Schleich 1924: 6, lines 83–4; Boccaccio: 9, pref.2). Unlike Walton, this poet is happy comparing his work to the *poesy* of antiquity, and so are the other translators of the mid and later fifteenth century.

Among the people who nurtured humanist studies of antiquity, one of the most renowned was a patron, Humfrey, Duke of Gloucester (1390–1447), uncle of Henry VI (Petrina). After Walton's poem, the next two verse translations announce their dedication to Humfrey. Lydgate in his poem *Fall of Princes* (1431–38) tells us that the poem was commissioned by Humfrey, who likes 'To studie in bookis off antiquite' (Lydgate 1924, 1927: I.396, and in general I.372–448); and Humfrey's interest in the *studia humanitatis* is spelled out vividly in the translation of Palladius' agricultural treatise *On Husbondrie* (*NIMEV* 654). This was composed between 1439 and 1443 by a poet who remains anonymous, despite a couple of still unproven ascriptions (MacCracken 1913: 398–400; Howlett 1977: 249–50). The poem is suited to Humfrey, the patron of Latin scholarship, by being modelled so closely on Latin, both in the precision of its translation and in its Latinate style, which is often highlighted by glosses in what seems to be the presentation manuscript for Humfrey (Wakelin 2007: 45–8). For example, merely in the prologue and the epilogues to each book (in total 312 lines) the poet uses numerous words for the first or possibly only recorded time in English (according to *MED* and *OED*): *accite, adversant, aspire, celsitude, economy, florify, fuke, honorify, immune, intern, invident, mismetrify, outrace, preconize, provect, quad-rivial, rade, redivive, refluent* and maybe *fertility* and *protect*. Despite appearing in lines not translated from Latin, this inventive vocabulary is mostly Latin-derived and reflects reverence for that language. That reverence could be fostered by the aureate diction associated with the monk Lydgate's poetry or the related quirky wordplay and soundplay in fifteenth-century monastic Latin, known as the quest for *florida verborum venustas* ('the florid beauty of words': Rundle 2005: 72–3). After all, the prologue to *On Husbondrie* lists among Humfrey's erudite friends John Whethamstede, the learned abbot of St Albans (*Middle-English Translation of Palladius*, ed. Liddell 1986: prol. 102), whose monastery cultivated both Lydgate's poetry and florid Latin (Rundle 2005: 72–3). Yet Whethamstede dabbled in humanist studies too, and alongside him among the associates of Humfrey *On Husbondrie* also lists the Italian humanist scholars Pietro del Monte, Tito Livio Frulovisi and Antonio Beccaria (*Middle-English Translation of Palladius*, ed. Liddell 1986: prol. 102–3). This poem's style might support Duke Humfrey's claims to regal magnificence, just as might his employment of humanists such as Beccaria using a fashionable neoclassical Latin.

Yet the poet of *On Husbondrie* tells us little explicitly about his experiments in diction. Like Banester or Walton, he tells us mostly of his efforts to 'metur muse out of this prosis blake' (ibid.: II.486): it sounds as though the pages of Palladius' work look 'blake' with long inky lines reaching to the margins, as prose lines do; the poet hopes to 'muse' fancifully, creatively, those lines into verse. And though he describes Humfrey's humanist milieu, what he explicitly seeks from Humfrey himself is correction of the verse: he begs Humfrey 'Of my balade away to rade errour' in his 'incorrectid versis' which are 'mys metrified' (ibid.: prol. 6–7, I.1198–9). His worry paid off, for the metre stands up to close examination in its extreme regularity (Hammond 1925: 148).

This interest in versifying prose was transmitted to a poet who had evidently read *On Husbondrie* – often assumed to be the same person, but on shaky ground (Wakelin 2004: 261) – and then turned the prose of another practical treatise, Vegetius' *Epitoma rei militaris*, into the rhyme royal of *Knyghthode and Bataile* (*NIMEV* 3185). He speaks of his readers getting military advice but also taking pleasure in his verse:

> For their pleasaunce, out of this prosis storne
> The resonaunce of metris wolde I borne.
> As myghti herte in ryngynge herneysinge,
> So gentil wit wil in good metris springe.
> (*Knyghthode and Bataile*, ed. Dyboski and Arend 1936: lines 631–4)

Just as knights delight in weapons clanging on harnesses, so men of 'gentil wit' get pleasure from metre.

But the greatest metrical experiment among these translations is not in rhyme royal but in unrhymed verse. This is in an excerpt from Claudian's *De consulatu Stilichonis*, a poem in praise of the Roman consul Stilicho, translated at Clare in Suffolk in 1445 (*NIMEV* 1526). Claudian's poem is in Latin hexameters, with metrical feet measured by 'length' of syllables and unrhymed. Perhaps because he is tackling something already in metre, the translator of this cannot please his patron by musing prose into verse; he must try something even newer. He seems to imitate the hexameters by using unrhymed English verse in lines much longer than those of rhyme royal:

> The lernyd man may here þe speke .' of þingis þat be passyd
> Of ripe thyngis which sounde sadly .' though techist men right aged
> Thaventorous knyȝte by thyn reporte .' is warnyd of his perellys
> Thou strowist such saltcornys amonge þi spechis .' as amphion is founde vnlike
> To the in talkyng Aonias also .' which crafte of musys studyed
> And orpheus harpe which trees made trace .' in truthe þi tunge excellith.
> (Flügel, ed.: lines 185–90)

To English ears used to rhyming decasyllables, great length and an absence of rhyme might be enough to evoke classical Latin verse: yet the evocation is inexact, for the English lines do not follow syllable quantity, but stress, nor six feet, but seven. (I have underlined the stressed syllables.) Syllable quantity and six stressed feet were later used by other imitators of hexameters, such as Richard Stanyhurst and Arthur Hugh Clough. But this poet's frequent alliteration might evoke the alliterative tradition in English poetry. Lines like these with seven stresses would have a great future ahead of them for rendering classical verse, in Golding's version of Ovid's *Metamorphoses* and Chapman's of Homer's *Iliad*. Though it is unlikely to have influenced those later experiments, this version of *De consulatu Stilichonis* could reflect a similar sense of how to make English metre sound stately.

Such stately modes of speaking were one of the most important things these translations offered: a chance for English princes and dukes to imitate the 'prencys of Latyn eloquence', as *De mulieribus claris* called them. After all, the (above-quoted) lines from *De consulatu Stilichonis* not only praise Stilicho in fine style – and implicitly praise Richard of York thus; they also praise the consul and duke for themselves speaking in fine style. Stilicho, and by implication Richard, excels the poet Orpheus in his 'tunge' and skills of the 'musys'. And good speaking is a matter of substance, for the consul must counsel people about history and warfare seriously ('sadly'). Indeed, one of the princes of eloquence to whom he is compared is Amphion, who not only excels on the lyre but who with his music – a sister art for poetry – gets cities built. This myth from Ovid's *Metamorphoses* was well known in fifteenth-century England, as Lydgate and others used it to praise eloquence as the building-block of a good society (Lydgate, ed. Bergen 1924, 1927: VI.3487–500; Wakelin 2010a: 565–6). The fine metre and verbal inventiveness of these translations, then, might not be merely aesthetic 'pleasaunce', as for the knights reading *Knyghthode and Bataile*, but might be imagined to have some social or political force. The patrons who were seen to receive these transla- tions – Elizabeth Berkeley, Humfrey, Duke of Gloucester, Richard, Duke of York, Henry VI – might be thought thereby to harness that force. A. S. G. Edwards (2001: 277) has wondered whether there is any significance in the fact that two of the most powerful noblemen in England in the 1440s were both recipients of classical translations – *On Husbondrie* for Humfrey, *De consulatu Stilichonis* for Richard. The significance might be this loose but important one: that by receiving such works they seem to be mastering the eloquence needed to shape society and politics.

Other translations might be worth considering as other expressions of a similar mastery. For example, the cleric Benedict Burgh (d.c.1483) translated Cato's moralising verses, turning each couplet of Cato's *Disticha* into seven or fourteen lines of rhyme royal (*NIMEV* 894, 3955). Caxton reports that Burgh composed this translation 'in balade ryal' in order to teach Latin to William Bourchier (Caxton, ed. Blake 1973: no. 15.a.5–7). Whether his report is right or not, it captures the contemporary sense that a young nobleman – the nephew of Richard, Duke of York – might be glad to be reported mastering Latin through a translation in this fine, indeed 'ryal', form of verse. The writers' poetic control becomes a model for their patrons' political control.

Yet these poems also deliver more straightforward political comment. That of *De consulatu Stilichonis* is obvious and has been explicated elsewhere (Watts 1990; Edwards 2001: 273–5; Wakelin 2007: 75–8). And *On Husbondrie* and *Knyghthode and Bataile* show their dedicatees mastering not only, as *On Husbondrie* puts it, 'gram*er*', exemplified by the Latinity of the translation, but also 'ethic,/ Politic, monastic yconomye' and numerous other arts (*Middle-English Translation of Palla- dius*, ed. Liddell 1986: prol. 77–9). For instance, agriculture might signal 'rural retreat' from politics (Edwards 2003: 74–6) but might also like military skill signal one's expertise in governance, as authorities from Cicero's *De senectute* to Giles of Rome or Aegidio Romano's *De regimine principum* averred. In content as well as style, then, these translations could seem like tools of political mastery.

However, there are other voices in these poems – akin to the 'further voices' found in the poetry of Virgil and the 'other Virgil' of a pessimistic sort found in some fifteenth- and sixteenth-century classicism (Lyne 1987: 2; Kallendorf 2007: esp. 75). The other voices in fifteenth-century English humanist poems are rueful, doubtful, and sometimes thereby critical of people in political power. The critical tone is heard in the earliest poetry translated from humanist sources, notably the 'Clerk's Tale' in Chaucer's *Canterbury Tales* of the late-fourteenth century. In this work, Chaucer adapts a French version of Petrarch's Latin version of a story from Boccaccio's Italian *Il Decamerone*; he tells of a wife, patient Griselda, who is cruelly treated by her husband but remains loyal to him. As David Wallace has shown, Petrarch's Latin version seems to endorse the absolutism of the lordly husband over his wife; he finds some likeness between tyrannical absolutism, the oppression of women, and the humanists' mastery of a fine Latin style. But Chaucer adapts the story and demurs from its ideology, allowing criticism of the tyrannical husband and of the pompous humanist Petrarch (Wallace 1997: 261–93).

Fifteenth-century poets followed Chaucer in turning to the works of Italian humanists for other stories of women grievously wronged by men in power, and these humanist sources nurtured their pity for the women and critique of such men. The first such example is the story of Lucretia, who was raped by Tarquin, one of the last kings of Rome, whose punishment led to the establishment of a republic in Rome. In Lydgate's poem *Fall of Princes* (*NIMEV* 1168) he tells us that Humfrey, Duke of Gloucester, directed him to incorporate a translation of 'Collucyus' or Coluccio Salutati's *Declamatio Lucretiae*, of which Humfrey owned a copy (Lydgate, ed. Bergen, 1924, 1927: II.1006–15; Wakelin 2007: 34–5; Mortimer 2005: 69–72; Sammut 1980: 111–2). Salutati's work is a pair of speeches by Lucretia and her husband, which serve to comment on politics and virtue; Salutati wrote at a time when the republic in Florence was in peril. Lydgate translates Salutati's work very closely in about 110 of 315 lines (Lydgate, ed. Bergen, 1924, 1927: II.1016–330) and elsewhere closely paraphrases it. The closeness is marked in one manuscript of Lydgate's poem, which has tiny excerpts from Salutati's Latin in the margins, continuing the tendency in a few other copies to mark Lydgate's classical sources too (Wakelin 2007: 41; Wakelin 2010b: 439 n. 31), whether as accidental traces of his rough drafts or as deliberate invitations to note the poem's scholarliness. For one of the things that seems to matter to Humfrey is the use of this particular source. After all, as with Walton's revoicing of Boethius, revoicing Salutati does not purvey any new information, for Chaucer had already told the story of Lucretia, so that, as Lydgate concedes, there's no need to 'rehersyn' it again (Lydgate, ed. Bergen, 1924, 1927: II.974–980). Moreover, *Fall of Princes* itself repeats the story of Lucretia elsewhere and there Lydgate apologises for having 'Rehersed' it before (ibid.: III.981–83). Lucretia there even gets to speak in her own voice again (ibid.: III.1009–1148) so it is not even Salutati's ventriloquism of female complaint that is novel. But the needless repetition alerts us to some pressing concern with female complaint and the lessons it offers. Through such complaint, Lydgate, like Medwall in *Fulgens and Lucres*, imports Florentine orations and some Florentine civic humanist sentiment, as Lucretia criticises the cruel power of princes. The critique of cruel power is also influenced by Chaucerian models, and the rhyme royal of *Fall of Princes* at this point might recall the capricious wickedness of men in the 'Clerk's Tale'. Some combination of English poetry's plangency – which Maura Nolan (2004) has linked to Ovidian influences – and humanist political critique occurs in turning Florentine oratory into English verse.

Some of the stories in the English version of Boccaccio's *De mulieribus claris* work similarly. And this interest in the sufferings of women before powerful men, and in the lessons that it offers, is most evident in two other translations of a story by Boccaccio: the story of Guiscardo and Ghismonda from *Il Decamerone*. Ghismonda promises her father, King Tancred, that she will live chaste but then sleeps with her lover, the humbler-born Guiscardo; Tancred imprisons and kills Guiscardo, sending his heart to the defiant Ghismonda, who then kills herself. The story was first translated into rhyme royal by Banester, a composer, lay clerk of Edward IV's chapel and master of the king's choristers (Williamson 2000: 239–43). Banester claims to have written his version at the 'mocioune' of 'Iohn Raynere', who sounds like an Italian musician 'Raynerio' who visited the chapel of Edward IV around 1472 (Banester, ed. Wright 1937: lines 624–5; Firth Green

1978). One manuscript of Banester's translation was owned by a family with links to Edward IV's wife's and daughter's households (Boffey and Meale 1991: 158–9, 164–5). Curiously, someone then composed a second version (*NIMEV* 3258), evidently knowing Banester's and in places weaving into his anonymous version parts of Banester's, including seventeen of the final nineteen stanzas borrowed almost word-for-word (Banester, ed. Wright 1937: xxxvii–xliii; ibid., lines 932–1050; cf. anon. in Banester, ed. Wright: 476–97, 512–609). This reworking suggests once more the needlessness of these verse translations and, instead, some experiment in rewriting. For example, the anonymous second version of the story experiments with increased rhetorical decoration. Typically, in one short section there is an *occupatio* (anon. in Banester, ed. Wright: lines 78–84), a conventional opposition of joy and sorrow (anon.: lines 85–92) and some pathetic fallacy about the seasons (anon.: lines 92–108), all to cover a transition that Banester makes in just one line (Banester, ed. Wright 1937: 81). This second version also drops in eight references to classical deities, whereas Banester only uses one (ibid.: lines 138–9; anon. in Banster, ed. Wright: lines 62, 92, 95, 208, 271, 331, 334, 536). An interest in such deities as poetic decorations is evident in the manuscript in which this second version survives, for it also contains a poem about the pagan pantheon, *The Assembly of the Gods*, and a wonderful list offering an 'Interpretacion' of their names 'as poetys wryte' (Fletcher, intro.: fols 67v–97r, and see the marginal note on fol. 15r; *Assembly*, ed. Chance: lines 27–8). The second version of Guiscardo and Ghismonda's story, then, might seem an exercise in poetic style and pseudo-classicism.

Yet from their blend of Italian humanist sources and Chaucerian plangent form, these two poems offer some surprising and thought-provoking content. In theory these translations could be done from the French version of *Il Decamerone*, which was owned by Humfrey, Duke of Gloucester, and by Edward IV, in whose chapel Banester worked (Bozzolo 1973: 157–62; Sammut 1980: 121). But in their selection of just this one story from *Il Decamerone* and in their details of wording, the English versions seem closer to *Fabula Tancredi*, a Latin translation of just this story by Leonardo Bruni, a Florentine republican humanist. This Latin redaction circulated in England in manuscripts and imported printed books. One sign of English humanist interest in wronged women comes from a manuscript owned by Robert Sherborn (c.1454–1536), which contains the Latin story of Guiscardo and Ghismonda as well as that of patient Griselda, source of the 'Clerk's Tale', and a tale of a wronged woman and her lover by Aeneas Sylvius Piccolomini. Sherborn also likely commissioned a painting of classical female heroines (Boffey 2001: 287–90; de la Mare and Gillam 1988: 95–6). This humanist interest might not be solely sympathetic to wronged women, critical of men: Sherborn's book also includes Boccaccio's antifeminist *Corbaccio*, in a Latin translation given to Duke Humfrey by Antonio Beccaria. Beccaria claimed that this work was meant not to stir up hostility to women but to show the wit of Boccaccio (Sammut 1980: 164); yet the work is briskly sexist, and Sherborn's marginalia pick out, as if approvingly, comments on the wickedness of women some forty-three times over only ten pages (Bodl., MS lat. misc. d. 34, fols 18r–23v). Not all humanist interest in women allowed them a voice of complaint or critique, then. But the choice of Bruni's *Fabula Tancredi* therefore looks more thoughtful or original by contrast, and as they turn it into English verse Banester and the second translator seem to echo the plangency and dissenting tone of Chaucerian poetry. Not just humanism but a specifically vernacular humanism is the clearest context for these poems: Banester's version circulates in one manuscript with the 'Clerk's Tale' and with Dido's story from *The Legend of Good Women*; it circulates in another with what was probably the whole of *The Legend of Good Women*, presented as though part of Chaucer's 'legend of ladyse' – stories of classical heroines who suffered (Boffey and Meale 1991: 144–5, 165; Boffey 2001: 289). The blend of Florentine and English tradition helps these two versions of Guiscardo and Ghismonda's story to develop their critical approach to male tyranny.

In particular, the speeches by the mistreated daughter, Ghismonda, offer criticism of lordly and fatherly injustice or rigour. In Bruni's Latin version she is given long speeches (printed in Banester, ed. Wright 1937: lines 115–21) in which she is tearful but turns her sorrow into confident and clear-sighted criticism: as Banester puts it: 'hyr wo was but lytill espyed' and she spoke instead 'with corage right pacient' and 'Stedfast chere' (ibid.: lines 333–5). Her criticisms get extended in the second anonymous version. For example, in both English versions Ghismonda unexpectedly defends the way that younger generations can differ in their sexual ethics from older generations and requests a sort of pragmatism about youthful sexual experiment (ibid.: lines 354–64; anon. in Banester, ed. Wright: lines 638–85, 708–14). Banester takes these comments on board and rehearses them in his own closing 'lesson' to readers (Banester, ed. Wright 1937: 575–88). This is a striking thing for someone who taught young choristers, and had four daughters, to admit in the fifteenth century; and it is an astonishing understanding of love and sex to find in fifteenth-century poetry, which tends to oscillate between fatalism about Cupid's arrows and moralism about Venus' temptations. Moreover, when the daughter in question is a princess, these domestic subtleties become topics of public import. So Ghismonda too launches a defence of her choice of lover, Guiscardo, who is humble in rank but, she insists, noble in virtues. The anonymous, second translation extends this defence of nobility by virtue even further, alluding to the idea that when Adam delved and Eve span, 'That tyme was no dyfference betwyxt gentylman and page' (ibid.: lines 372–82; anon. in Banester, ed. Wright: lines 715–77; Wright: 124, 127–30). It would be tempting to link this greater egalitarianism with a London 'middle class' mercantile milieu, for this is where the only manuscript of this second version circulated, but this second English version is simply a fuller and more precise – in parts word-for-word – translation of Bruni's Latin, which itself develops hints in Boccaccio's Italian. Then the poem offers further criticism of princely folly (anon. in Banester, ed. Wright: lines 465–83) in a style evocative of the envoys in Lydgate's *Fall of Princes*. As when Lydgate translated Salutati's account of Lucretia there, so these poets, translating Bruni's account of Ghismonda, are led by their humanist sources not only into formal experiment but into fresh ideas about princely behaviour.

Despite Banester's comments on his 'clerkly' experiment in verse-form (quoted above), despite the obvious stylistic exuberance of the other translators, and despite the use of translation for acquiring and displaying mastery, these verse translations sometimes offer something besides formal experiment and claims to political power. They offer voices of regret, critique, or differing perspective.

This could be demonstrated with the other translations here too – say, in the ideas of good governance that emerge in *De consulatu Stilichonis* and *Knyghthode and Bataile* or in the ideas of female achievement, and not merely female suffering, found in the version of Boccaccio's *De mulieribus claris*. Diverse other concerns emerge in the translation of Petrarch's *Secretum* into English couplets (Wakelin 2011) or in the numerous translations from classical and humanist Latin into prose too. These verse translations deserve to be more closely read and more widely enjoyed for their brilliant experiments balancing humanist scholarship with English poetic forms and for their interesting political balance of mastery and critique.

Works cited

The Assembly of Gods, ed. Jane Chance (Kalamazoo, MI, 1999)

Banester, Gilbert, et al., *Early English Versions of the Tales of Guiscardo and Ghismonda and Titus and Gisippus from the Decameron*, ed. Herbert G. Wright, EETS, o.s. 205 (London, 1937)

Boffey, Julia, '"Twenty thousand more": Some Fifteenth- and Sixteenth-Century Responses to *The Legend of Good Women*', in *Middle English Poetry: Texts and Traditions: Essays in Honour of Derek Pearsall*, ed. A. J. Minnis (York, 2001), pp. 279–97

——, and Carol Meale, 'Selecting the Text: Rawlinson C. 86 and some other Books for London Readers', in *Regionalism in Late Medieval Manuscripts and Texts*, ed. Felicity Riddy (Cambridge, 1991), pp. 143–69

Bozzolo, Carla, *Manuscrits des traductions françaises d'oeuvres de Boccace: XVe siècle*, Medioevo e Umanesimo, 15 (Padua, 1973)

Caxton, William, *Caxton's Own Prose*, ed. N. F. Blake (London, 1973)

——, *The Middle English Text of 'Caxton's Ovid', Book I*, ed. Diana Rumrich, Middle English Texts, 43 (Heidelberg, 2011)

Cowen, Janet, 'An English Reading of Boccaccio: A Selective Middle English Version of Boccaccio's *De mulieribus claris* in British Library MS Additional 10304', in *New Perspectives on Middle English Texts: A Festschrift for R. A. Waldron*, eds Susan Powell and Jeremy J. Smith (Cambridge, 2000), pp. 129–40

——, 'The Name Elizabeth Darcy in British Library MS Harley 1766 and British Library MS Additional 10304', *Notes and Queries*, n.s. 58 (2011), 214–6

[De la Mare, Albina C., and Stanley Gillam], *Duke Humfrey's Library and the Divinity School, 1488–1988* (Oxford, 1988)

Donaghey, Brian, Irma Taavitsainen, and Erik Miller, 'Walton's Boethius: From Manuscript to Print', *English Studies*, 80 (1999), 398–407

Edwards, A. S. G., 'The Middle English Translation of Claudian's *De Consulatu Stilichonis*', in *Middle English Poetry: Texts and Traditions: Essays in Honour of Derek Pearsall*, ed. A. J. Minnis (York, 2001), pp. 267–78

——, 'Duke Humfrey's Middle English Palladius', in *The Lancastrian Court: Proceedings of the 2001 Harlaxton Symposium*, ed. Jenny Stratford (Donington, 2003), pp. 68–77

Firth Green, Richard, 'The Date of Gilbert Banester's Translation of the Tale of
  Guiscardo and Ghismonda', *Notes and Queries*, 223 (1978), 299–300
Fletcher, Bradford Y., intro., *Manuscript Trinity R. 3. 19: A Facsimile* (Norman, OK,
  1987)
Flügel, Ewald, ed., 'Eine Mittelenglische Claudian-Übersetzung (1445)', *Anglia*,
  28 (1905), 255–99, 421–38
Griffiths, Jane, *John Skelton and Poetic Authority: Defining the Liberty to Speak*
  (Oxford, 2006)
Hammond, Eleanor Prescott, 'The Nine-Syllabled Pentameter Line in Some Post-
  Chaucerian Manuscripts', *Modern Philology*, 23 (1925), 129–52
Hanna III, Ralph, 'Sir Thomas Berkeley and his Patronage', *Speculum*, 64 (1989),
  878–916
Hoccleve, Thomas, *Thomas Hoccleve's Complaint and Dialogue*, ed. J. A. Burrow,
  EETS, o. s. 313 (Oxford, 1999)
Howlett, D. R., 'The Date and Authorship of the Middle English Verse Transla-
  tion of Palladius' *De Re Rustica*', *Medium Aevum*. 46 (1977), 245–52
Johnson, Ian, 'New Evidence for the Authorship of Walton's Boethius', *Notes and
  Queries*, 241 (1996), 19–21
Kallendorf, Craig, *The Other Virgil: Pessimistic Readings of the 'Aeneid' in Early
  Modern Culture* (Oxford, 2007)
*Knyghthode and Bataile. A XVth Century Verse Paraphrase of Flavius Vegetius
  Renatus' Treatise 'De re militari'*, eds R. Dyboski and Z. M. Arend, EETS, o. s.
  221 (London, 1936)
Kuskin, William, *Symbolic Caxton: Literary Culture and Print Capitalism* (Notre
  Dame, IN, 2008)
Lydgate, John, *Lydgate's Fall of Princes*, ed. Henry Bergen, 4 vols EETS, e. s. 121–24
  (London, 1924, 1927)
Lyne, R. O. A. M., *Further Voices in Vergil's Aeneid* (Oxford, 1987)
MacCracken, Henry Noble, 'Vegetius in English: Notes on the Early Transla-
  tions', in *Anniversary Papers by Colleagues and Pupils of George Lyman Kittredge*,
  eds F. N. Robinson, W. A. Neilson and E. S. Sheldon (Boston, MA, 1913), pp.
  389–403
The Middle-English Translation of Palladius De Re Rustica, ed. Mark Liddell (Berlin,
  1986)
Mortimer, Nigel, *John Lydgate's 'Fall of Princes': Narrative Tragedy in its Literary and
  Political Contexts* (Oxford, 2005)
Nall, Catherine, *Reading and War in Fifteenth-Century England* (Cambridge, 2012)
Nolan, Maura. '"Now wo, now gladnesse": Ovidianism in the *Fall of Princes*',
  English Literary History, 71 (2004), 531–58.
Petrina, Alessandra, *Cutural Politics in Fifteenth-Century England: The Case of
  Hunphrey, Duke of Gloucester* (Leiden, 2004)
Robbins, Rossell Hope, 'Middle English Carols as Processional Hymns', *Studies
  in Philology*, 56 (1959), 559–82
Rundle, David, 'Humanist Eloquence among the Barbarians in Fifteenth-Century
  England', in *Britannia Latina: Latin in the Culture of Great Britain from the Middle
  Ages to the Twentieth Century*, eds Charles Burnett and Nicholas Mann, Warburg
  Institute Colloquia, 8 (London, 2005), pp. 68–85

Salutati, Coluccio, *Editi e inediti Latini dal Ms. 53 della Biblioteca Comunale di Todi*, ed. Enrico Menestò, Res Tudertinæ, 12 (Todi, 1971)

Sammut, Alfonso, *Unfredo duca di Gloucester e gli umanisti italiani*, Medioevo e Umanesimo, 40 (Padua, 1980)

Schleich, Gustav, ed., *Die mittelenglische Umdichtung von Boccaccios De claris mulieribus nebst der lateinischen Vorlage* (Leipzig, 1924)

Wakelin, Daniel, 'The Occasion, Author and Readers of *Knyghthode and Bataile*', *Medium Aevum*, 73 (2004), 260–72

——, 'Scholarly Scribes and the Creation of *Knyghthode and Bataile*', *English Manuscript Studies*, 12 (2005), 26–45

——, *Humanism, Reading and English Literature, 1430–1530* (Oxford, 2007)

——, 2010a. 'Hoccleve and Lydgate', in *A Companion to Medieval Poetry*, ed. Corinne Saunders (London, 2010), pp. 557–74

——, 2010b. 'Instructing Readers in Fifteenth-Century Poetic Manuscripts', *Huntington Library Quarterly*, 73 (2010), 433–52

——, 'Religion, Humanism and Humanity: Chaundler's Dialogues and the Winchester *Secretum*', in *After Arundel: Religious Writing in Fifteenth Century England*, eds Vincent Gillespie and Kantik Ghosh (Turnhout, 2011), pp. 225–44

Wallace, David, *Chaucerian Polity: Absolutist Lineages and Associational Forms in England and Italy* (Stanford, CA, 1997)

Walton, John, *The Consolation of Philosophy*, ed. Mark Science, EETS, o. s. 170 (London, 1927)

Watts, John, '*De Consulatu Stiliconis*: Texts and Politics in the Reign of Henry VI', *Journal of Medieval History*, 16 (1990), 251–66

Williamson, Magnus, 'Royal Image-Making and Textual Interplay in Gilbert Banaster's *O Maria et Elizabeth*', *Early Music History*, 19 (2000), 237–78

Wilson, Edward, intro., *The Winchester Anthology: A Facsimile of British Library Additional Manuscript 60577* (Cambridge, 1981)

Witlieb, Bernard, '*Ovide Moralisé* as a Source for *Fall of Princes*', *Notes and Queries*, n.s. 57 (2010), 480–4

14

Romance

ANDREW KING

Romance, as a literary mode, is frequently characterised by its resistance to narrative closure – a resistance fuelled, as in any Charles Dickens novel, by multiple and multiplying incidents and characters, frequently spanning generations as well as continents (Parker 1974: 1 and *passim*). That picture of generation, movement and the crossing of new boundaries fits well with the history of verse romance texts themselves in fifteenth-century England. As more and more romance texts are sent forth, like young aspirant adventurers, by their makers or foster-parents – 'Go, litel bok, go' (*TC*, V.1786) – and as older textual 'warriors' continue to find new armour in which to fight their battles, romance texts seem to venture forth with the inexhaustible strength and generative capabilities of the romance heroes themselves. Romance, in the hands of fifteenth-century readers, authors and redactors, is as prolific and procreative as the worlds that it depicts.

If previous accounts of fifteenth-century verse romance have tended to denigrate its achievements in comparison to Ricardian literature (Wallace 1999: xii), then a corrective defence needs to be mounted first of all in relation to the multitude, variety and later influence of verse romance writing in the fifteenth century. The focus of this chapter must be on romance in verse, though the strong development of prose romance in the latter part of the century is not a self-contained act: the success of Caxton's romances inevitably owed something to the century's insatiable appetite for romance narratives of all kinds. But even focusing on romance in verse in the fifteenth century does not confine us to a homogeneous group of texts. The redaction and revision of older romances flourished alongside the composition of newer, authorially more ambitious forms, with inevitable exchanges between the two. The overall picture is one of plenitude, growth and the ineluctable genesis of new forms and hybrids (Cooper 2004: 3–7). Furthermore, this sense of the quantitative as well as the qualitative impact of romance in that century is a fundamental part in a larger and vital project: exploring the negotiations and continuities that bind together, particularly in the English tradition, the traditionally segregated periods of medieval and Renaissance, or early modern. The awkwardness and implausibility of that imposed division have been exposed in recent important work by scholars such as Helen Cooper, James Simpson, Cathy Shrank, Greg Walker, Brian Cummings and others (King 2000; Cooper 2004; Cummings and Simpson 2010). Romance, as the most widely read or encountered form of narrative (up to the present day), is a crucial element in understanding how the fifteenth century is a period of continuity, translation and transformation.

Just as medieval romance is a fundamental part of early modern English collective memory, embedded in books such as *The Faerie Queene* or indeed the Percy Folio MS, so too fifteenth-century verse romance cannot be understood merely in terms of what is newly conceived, composed or translated into English for the first time within that century. What needs emphasis from the outset is that the fifteenth century is the period that transmits, extends and, to some extent, transforms the earlier native verse romance tradition, originating in the thirteenth and fourteenth centuries. Derek Pearsall aptly notes:

> This is the first point to stress about the fifteenth century, that it is the great age of fourteenth-century romance, not because it instils in us a proper gratitude to fifteenth-century scribes, but because the way a work is read and used contributes significantly to its place in literary history, and because the work of copying is, with these poems, often a work of re-composition.
>
> (Pearsall 1976: 58)

A significant majority of Middle English romances from these earlier centuries survive in fifteenth-century copies, sometimes exclusively (Bennett 1947: 167–8; Edwards and Pearsall 1989: 257). The sense in which fourteenth-century romance is also very much part of fifteenth-century romance activity is evident when considering how an early manuscript such as the Auchinleck MS (Edinburgh, National Library of Scotland, Advocates' MS 19. 2. 1, c.1330) could still appeal to readers 150 years later and beyond – as marginal annotations by the book's many users, from the fourteenth century through to the seventeenth century, attest (Pearsall and Cunningham 1977: xv–xvi). Out of its some fifteen romances, ten also survive in later manuscript versions and, in some cases, printed editions. The fact that these texts were sometimes reworked and lightly modernised in their language in the century following Auchinleck indicates not so much the antiquity that might have struck a fifteenth-century reader encountering this earlier manuscript, but rather that these texts were still valued for their currency and their role as part of a living literary culture.

The strength of interest in earlier native verse romances throughout the fifteenth century is attested in the evidence of various contexts of reading, redaction and collecting that we can still recover in some detail. Robert Thornton, a fifteenth-century member of the Yorkshire gentry, was the creator of two extant manuscript anthologies (Lincoln Cathedral, MS 91 and BL, Add. MS 31042) that contain a number of romances, as well as other forms of writing (Brewer and Owen 1975; Guddat-Figge 1976: 135–42, 161–4; Thompson 1983, 1991; Boffey and Thompson 1989). These books are likely to have satisfied personal and familial needs for entertainment as well as religious instruction. Amongst the generic variety offered by the manuscripts, romance is prominent. The Lincoln Thornton manuscript of c.1430–50 brought into the literary culture of the fifteenth century earlier romances such as *Sir Perceval of Galles* (early fourteenth century), *Octavian* (mid-fourteenth century), *Sir Isumbras* (early fourteenth century) and *Sir Eglamour of Artois* (mid-fourteenth century). The overall ten romance texts in this manuscript anthology appear roughly grouped together at the start of the book. The anthology also demonstrates strong interest in religious narratives and texts, such as saints' lives, prayers, texts of Christian instruction, and several works

by Richard Rolle. The book indicates a degree of awareness of generic boundaries – some of the romance texts are titled as 'romances' in the manuscript – but
equally the anthology as a whole embodies the sense that these romances can
be accommodated together with religious texts as acceptable family reading (cf.
the still more developed family anthology, Bodl., MS Ashmole 61, as discussed
by Blanchfield 1991 and 1996). Any reader encountering the romances in Lincoln
Thornton, in the context of the book's religious items, was implicitly invited to
explore that accommodation. The older romances, far from seeming antiquated,
offered engrossing entertainment whilst chiming with texts of didactic value and
demonstrating their (dread word) relevance.

The work of Henry Lovelich, a London skinner, affords a glimpse of new and
different contexts for the reception of romance's narrative structures and ideals.
Lovelich offers new translations into English of old French texts, *The History of
the Holy Grail* (c.1420) and *Merlin* (c.1425), taking these texts from courtly and
gentrified contexts and relocating them in the mercantile and guild worlds of the
city (Ackerman 1952). Lovelich's verse translations were directed towards the
Company of Skinners (Cooper 1999: 692), and it is interesting to speculate how
the ideal of chivalric fraternity embodied in the Arthurian narratives would resonate with a London guild's or company's sense of its corporate identity. *Merlin*,
in particular, has passages that must have had a powerful appeal to a London
mercantile audience, such as the expression of the commons' support for the new
King Arthur, in the teeth of the barons' and other kings' opposition:

> whanne that þe communes Syen Arthewr fo fyhte,
> Fulfaste they cryden anon þere ryhte,
> So that the cry there ros al abowte,
> and to Arthewr they comen, with-owten dowte,
> and seyden to Arthewr there as blyve:
> 'we scholen the helpen, whyles we han lyve;
> For liven and deyen we scholen with the here
> and thin ryht to Sosteyne al in fere'.
>   (Lovelich, ed. Kock 1904–32: lines 8489–96)

Other passages, such as Arthur's later welcoming of the now reconciled kings
into London (lines 9273–5), and the great feasting in the Tower and throughout
the city, inevitably carried particular resonances for their initial London audiences. Unlike much of Malory's later prose *Morte D'Arthur*, Lovelich's verse
translations tend to be slavish. But that failure to tweak the text into explicit
dialogue with its London contexts could highlight the lack of any need to do so:
skinners, amongst other London readers, were sufficiently equipped to feel the
draw of a world of fraternal bonding, strict rules of corporate identity, and coded
patterns of behaviour. Certainly a play of approximately 150 years later, Thomas
Dekker's *A Shoemaker's Holiday*, in which London cordwainers are styled as 'true
Trojans' and 'Brave shoemakers, all gentlemen of the Gentle Craft' (Dekker, ed.
Palmer 1975: I.iv.113 and II.iii.45–6) suggests that the perceived correspondence
between London mercantile and chivalric life still had currency.

It is salutary to keep constantly in mind how earlier romances such as *Bevis
of Hampton*, *Guy of Warwick*, and others maintained their appeal throughout

the fifteenth century, adapting themselves to new contexts of readership and innovative perceptions of romance's recreational and didactic value. The clear presence of the alliterative *Morte Arthure* in Malory's 'Tale of King Arthur and the Emperor Lucius' seems to offer us a sense of the indelible presence of verse romance and its ability to transform itself into new forms (Malory, ed. Vinaver 1990: i, 181–247). And if the alliterative text is rather more hidden in Caxton's more prosaic (in all senses) edition of the *Morte D'Arthur*, then its stronger emergence in the text of the Winchester manuscript (BL, Add. MS 59678) suggests the power that the alliterative original could still wield. In this context of the development of prose romance alongside the ongoing presence of verse romance, both old and new, a crucial question to ask is what did it mean to write romance *in verse* in the fifteenth century – newly composed works as well as redactions of older romances? The influence of Chaucer's legacy may be part of the answer, but the longevity and ongoing vitality of earlier verse romances throughout the fifteenth century is another dimension to it.

Two romances with earlier origins continued to exert pervasive influence on fifteenth-century verse romance: *Guy of Warwick* and *Sir Bevis of Hampton*. These narratives provide exemplary demonstrations of the ongoing existence and vitality of earlier romances throughout the fifteenth century, transformed into substantially new versions in this century. Both texts are based on Anglo-Norman originals that possibly functioned as dynastic, foundation narratives for great families. Both romances have, especially in the earliest surviving English redactions in the Auchinleck MS, a particular focus on English placenames and collective understanding, often in the context of Christian identity (Cooper 1999: 704–5; King 2000: 59–69). *Bevis* in particular offers a narrative that embodies the ingredients of the quintessential English medieval romance for the fifteenth century and beyond: the displaced youth. *Bevis* is not the original form of this story (we have it in *Horn* and *Havelok*, and indeed in the adolescent Jesus in *Cursor Mundi*), and this important narrative of the displaced youth recurs often throughout the fourteenth and fifteenth century. Furthermore, it is employed by Spenser in Book I of *The Faerie Queene* in the figure of Redcrosse, with a particularly ingenious Protestant adaptation of the narrative to fit the Calvinist paradigm for salvation (King 2008: 184–7). Between the earliest versions of *Bevis* and Spenser's new realisation of the narrative lie fifteenth-century acts of copying, redaction and reading. Jennifer Fellows notes that the changes evolving in *Bevis* 'go beyond the lexical and stylistic to manifest varying attitudes towards the story and varying conceptions as to its meaning' (Fellows 2008: 80). One of the most interesting elements in later medieval versions of works such as *Bevis* is the development of larger and more detailed accounts found of Bevis' battles with Saracen foes (Fellows 2008: 89). Although Bevis' Christian identity, signalled through the narrator's emphasis on baptism in relation to both Josian and Ascopard, is an intrinsic element in the narrative from the outset, this aspect is intensified in later redactions, a sign that the text is current rather than fossilised for its latest readers. The fall of Constantinople in 1453 sent shockwaves throughout Europe and incited the literature of crusade (Cooper 1999: 698). In this context, it is hardly surprising that another older verse romance, *Richard Coeur de Lion* (like *Bevis* and *Guy*, also in the Auchinleck MS), continued to be copied in the fifteenth century, and was printed in the following one (*STC* 21007–8). That text's focus on the Third Crusade found a new application to readers in the second half of the fifteenth century. Cambridge, Gonville and Caius MS 175/96 (c.1450–75) has *Richard* with *Bevis*, *Sir Isumbras* (also intensely anti-Saracen) and the quasi hagiographical *Athelston* (Guddat-Figge 1976: 82–3). The evidence is persuasive that the late medieval experience of reading a text like *Bevis*, *Guy*, or indeed *Richard Coeur de Lion*, was not so much an encounter with an old 'classic' as a process full of contemporary resonances and a minimal or carefully controlled sense of the archaic. Indeed, the story of the displaced heir struggling to assert his identity and regain his patrimony, present in *Bevis* and in a number of other key earlier romances still circulating in the fifteenth century, must have had a particularly striking, if shifting, function in the context of the century's dynastic feuds (Cooper 1999: 694).

Bevis is an essential part of the cultural memory of the fifteenth century, but it is equally part of that century's ongoing engagement with current narratives and their contemporary resonances. The same point could be made for the equally prolific *Guy of Warwick*, which also extends its creative influence beyond the fifteenth century and into *The Faerie Queene* (Cooper 2007). Even though *Guy* and *Bevis* are both parodied in *Sir Thopas* (see *CT*, VII. 897–902), Chaucer's satire did not sound the death-knell for older verse romances in the fifteenth century. A work as brilliant and stimulating as *Sir Thopas* could only add to a literary culture, however paradoxical that influence. Later, Spenser would outdo *Sir Thopas'* irony in his own highly ironic response, drawing on it to put Thopas' dream of an elf queen at the heart of *The Faerie Queene*, and drawing also upon the native romances that *Sir Thopas* mocks (King 2000: 10–11), thus demonstrating that readers could enjoy Chaucer's satire whilst also retaining affection for its target. The same century (the fifteenth) that saw the building of Chaucer's authority, based in part on texts such as *Sir Thopas* and 'Chaucers Wordes Unto Adam, His Owne Scriveyn' (Lerer 1993), also saw the continued copying and dissemination of the romance texts that Chaucer's authority seems to repudiate as part of the process of its own definition.

Chaucer's poetry made an impact of another kind on the writing of fifteenth-century verse romance. Alongside and at no point entirely distinct from the continuing life of texts such as *Guy* and *Bevis*, the fifteenth century witnessed the development of a new kind of romance writing in verse clearly influenced by Chaucer (in particular, by the polish and control of *Troilus*), and thus different in several ways from the ongoing traditions of the older romances. One striking feature of some of these 'post-Chaucerian' romances is their production by named authors. Unlike an anonymous work such as *Bevis*, available to scribes or redactors who might adjust the text in various ways (Fellows 1991: 7; Pearsall 1994: 31), post-Chaucerian texts such as John Lydgate's *Troy Book*, John Metham's *Amoryus and Cleopes*, and others are the work of named authors. More than that, these authors locate their own fictionalised personae in their writings, often in the context of praising Chaucer or certainly in a manner that imitates the Chaucerian narrator. Metham and Lydgate both project themselves into their works, imitating Chaucer's 'Go, litel bok' (*Amoryus*, in Metham ed. Craig 1916: lines 2117–9; Lydgate, ed. Bergen 1906–35: *Lenvoye*, lines 92–9) as well as both referring

to Chaucer as their 'mayster' (*Amoryus*, 2189; *Troy Book*, V. 3521). Similarly, they
both perform the humility topos – at once a Chaucerian imitation and perhaps
something genuinely felt when writing in the context of Chaucer's reputation.
Even a romance for which we do not have an author's name, *Partonope of Blois*,
presents a strongly Chaucerian fictionalised narrative persona throughout: the
one who is unlucky and unlikely in love (*Partonope*, ed. Bödtker 1912: lines 2310–
4). Chaucer's instructions to readers to take responsibility for their selection of
tales in the *Canterbury Tales* (*CT*, I. 3176–81) is recalled by *Partonope*'s narrator:

> Where-fore y Sey yow sykerly:
> In thys boke shalle ye fynde wrytte
> Both goode *and* euelle. I do yow to wytte:
> The goode taketh, the euelle leve,
> For all goode moste well preve. (*Partonope*, ed. Bödtker 1912: 59–63)

Chaucer's voice is transformed in this work in much the same way that earlier
versions of *Guy* or *Bevis* develop into new states in the fifteenth century. And the
same point could be made for the very late fifteenth-century *Partenay*, which is in
'Chaucerian' rhyme royal stanzas.

In aspiring to Chaucerian eloquence, this group of romances coincidentally
respond to Chaucerian anxiety regarding textual stability in a predominantly
manuscript and dialectal culture (*TC*, V. 1793–9). Of course, the use of the rhyme
royal stanza in some of these romances not only imitates Chaucer, but it also
produces a text of stanzaic intricacy that discourages the sort of 'deliberative
and constructive' reworkings (Fellows 1991: 7) that any scribe could bring to a
text such as *Bevis*. In rhyme royal, a dialectal or arcane rhyme word unpalatable
to a scribe could require the changing of one or two other rhyme words, with
concomitant redrafting of much if not all of the stanza. Metham's first stanza,
in a slight variation of rhyme royal, is a relatively accomplished imitation of the
first stanza of *Troilus* (I. 1–7), and it bristles before any scribe, like a threatened
hedgehog, with a sense of its own intactness:

> The chauns of loue and eke *th*e peyn of Amory*us*, *th*e knyg[h]t,
>   For Cleopes sake, and eke how bothe in fer*e*
> Louyd and aftyr deyd, my purpose ys to endyght.
> And now, O goddes, I *th*e beseche off ku*n*nyng, *tha*t Lanyfyca hyght!
>   Help me to adornne *th*er chauns in sqwyche man*er*e
> So *tha*t, qwer*e th*is matere dotht yt reqwyr*e*,
> Bothe *th*er louys I may co*m*pleyne to lou*er*rys dysyr*e*.
>   (Metham, ed. Craig 1916: lines 1–7)

Formal complexity and assuredness of tone also suggests the text's suitability for
a socially more elevated class of reader. Metham's poem, for instance, is dedicated to Sir Miles and Lady Stapleton, well-connected Norfolk gentry (ibid.:
viii–ix). And such a readership is usefully in a position to offer the text and its
author support, patronage, and further connections to a privileged readership.
With deliberate Chaucerian irony, the narrative voice in many of these ambitious,
new fifteenth-century romances deprecates its own putative shortcomings even
as it aspires in its linguistic eloquence to draw the sort of reader – sophisticated,

courtly, and very likely socially well placed – who will nourish further the poet's efforts. Even as the narrator of *Partonope* laments his limited linguistic ability, he subtly asserts ownership of the text as well as invoking royal protection:

> For y am comawndyt of my souereyne
> Thys story to drawe fulle *and* playne,
> Be-cawse yt was ful vnkowthe *and* lytel knowe,
> Frome frenche ynne-to yngelysche, that bet*er* nowe
> Hyt my3th be to euer-y wy3the.
> There-fore y do alle my my3the
> To saue my autor ynne sucche wyse
> As he that mater luste devyse,
> Where he makyth ynne grete compleynte
> In frenche so fayre thatt yt to paynte
> In Engelysche tun*n*gge y saye for me
> My wyttys alle to dullet bee.
>
> (*Partonope*, ed. Bödtker 1912: lines 2335–46)

The presentation of himself as merely translator, and a dull one at that, is disingenuous. Its subtle evocation of the amanuensis narrator of *The General Prologue*, who is comparably restrained by his duty to 'reherce as ny as evere he kan / Everich a word' (*CT*, I. 732–3) told to him, implicitly advances this new narrator as a follower of Chaucer. And his comment in the context of this passage that he was 'comawndyt of my souereyne/ Thys story to drawe fulle *and* playne' (*Partonope*, ed. Bödtker 1912: lines 2335–6) links royal authority with his own authority as a writer. Similarly, Lydgate's *Troy Book* aspires to the sort of controlled language and expression, also under royal aegis, that implicitly both defies the potential violation of scribes and addresses itself to a sophisticated and empowered readership. If Lydgate only offers rhyme royal for the relatively brief 'Lenvoye' and not the whole voluminous poem (in couplets), its function here is nevertheless clear. Employing the 'Go, litel bok' motif (Lydgate, ed. Bergen 1906–35: 'Lenvoye', line 92), Lydgate urges his book to seek a place not with classical authors (as in *Troilus*) but rather under the king's protection: 'put þe in þe grace/ Of hym þat is most of excellence' (ibid., lines 92–3). The tactic may seem self-effacing in relation to Lydgate's authorial role, and yet the possibility for irony is strong: the book, after all, is under the *king's* protection. The development of the Chaucerian narrator, alongside Chaucerian verbal and formal polish, has enabled a situation where Lydgate can seem to be self-deprecating in Chaucer's shadow, whilst paradoxically advancing the claims of the worth of his poetry at the highest social and artistic levels.

Lydgate's *Troy Book* is in many ways the great verse romance of the fifteenth century, and Metham praises Lydgate (*Amoryus*, in Metham, ed. Craig 1916: line 2192) in the same breath as acknowledging Chaucer as his master. This praise deserves serious consideration, since Lydgate's alignment of his masterpiece with Chaucer's work is arguably more subtle than has been generally recognised. It is one thing to have a number of clearly signalled alignments of his book with Chaucer's, such as an imitation of the opening sentence of *The General Prologue*:

> Whan þat þe soote stormis of Aprille,
> Vn-to þe rote ful lawe gan distille
> His lusty licour, with many holsom schour,
> To reise þe vertu vp in-to þe flour;
> And Phebus was ascendyng in his spere,
> And on þe brest smote his bemys clere
> Of þe Ram, ful colerik at al,
> Halvynge in ver þe equinnoccial;
> Whan May kalendis entre in for-sothe,
> And Zephirus, ful agreable and smoþe,
> Þe tendre braunchis enspireþ & doþe springe.
>   (Lydgate, ed. Bergen 1906–35: I. 3907–17)

One can imagine Lydgate extracting from Chaucer's famous opening sentence a list of crucial words – 'soote', 'Aprille', 'rote', 'licour', 'vertu', 'flour', 'Ram', 'Zephirus', 'tendre', 'enspireþ' – and then crafting his own variation on this. But Lydgate's imitation is more thoughtful and self-aware than one might at first think. Chaucer's *Troilus* was encouraged by its author to 'go', and Lydgate's *Troy Book* seems to be the offspring resulting from that book's fertile wanderings. However, the works alluded to frequently in Lydgate's epic include not just Chaucer's own 'Troy Book', but also, and equally, *The General Prologue* (see Lydgate, ed. Bergen: Prol 126–46; I. 623–44; I. 1222; I. 1316). Famously, Lydgate joins the Canterbury pilgrims and his master Chaucer in his *Siege of Thebes*, which is framed as one of the *Canterbury Tales*. Similarly, if more obliquely, *Troy Book* also appears, in its recurring thread of allusion to Chaucer's story-collection, to become part of the *Canterbury Tales*. Chaucer's story of English pilgrimage not just through places but through storytelling and generic variety – though a kind of House of Fame experience – is sufficiently capacious and incomplete to take on Lydgate's vast narrative.

Just as Spenser hopes to surpass Ariosto, there seems to be the embodiment of that aspiration at the heart of *Troy Book*, entailed in the very qualities that make it less attractive than Chaucer's *Troilus* to the majority of today's readers: its encyclopaedic completeness, its learning, and its careful presentation of its Latin authority, Guido delle Colonne's *Historia destructionis Troiae*. Lydgate's work is not just complete, but replete – a storehouse of narrative interest and information. The work derives a particular sense of its importance from its function to instruct the prince in good kingship and mirror political events at the highest level. This is a possibility that has been implicit in Middle English romance, such as *Havelok* (Staines 1976), from the start, but it is now much stronger, especially given that English has become by the fifteenth century the language of king and court. *Troy Book* is dedicated to Prince Henry, the future Henry V, and it is offered as a mirror in which Henry can fashion himself, particularly in relation to the chivalric idea of Hector:

> Þe first of birþe, so as bokis telle,
> Was worþi Ector, of kny3thod spring & welle,
> Flour of manhood, of strengþe per[e]les,
> Sadde & discret & prudent neuere-þe-les,
> Crop & rote, grounde of chiualrie,

Of cher demvre, and of curtesye
He was example – þer-to of sobirnes
A verray merour, & for his gentilnes
In his tyme þe most[e] renomed.

(Lydgate, ed. Bergen 1906–35: II. 4802–9)

The text concludes with the hope that England and France will be reconciled and peaceful during Henry's rule (V. 3411–42). The comparison with Greece and Troy is implicit, and Henry, in his 'new Troy', must achieve both a military and diplomatic victory that eluded even Hector. Of course, the ease with which fifteenth-century romance could mirror contemporary and recent politics was aided by the fact that some historical works were still written in verse and borrowed from the descriptive techniques and narrative structuring of romance (Cooper 1999: 707–13). John Hardyng's verse *Chronicle* (1457), for example, is strongly tinged with the qualities of romance, not least in the work's extended interest in Arthur.

Having identified as a related cluster these large, authorially ambitious and generally erudite post-Chaucerian romances, it is salutary to recall that this new tradition was not entirely separate from the older, anonymous verse romances that continued to be copied and revised throughout the fifteenth century; the boundary was porous. An interesting hybrid case is *The Wars of Alexander*, from the first half of the fifteenth century. In some ways, this text is not Chaucerian at all: Chaucer's Parson would surely dismiss it as 'rum, ram, ruf, by lettre' (*CT*, X. 43). However, it matches the ambition of post-*Troilus* texts, such as Lydgate's *Troy Book* or the *Laud Troy Book*, in its length, relative polish and its learnedness, derived from the late twelfth- or early thirteenth-century version of *Historia de preliis Alexandri Magni*. Like a number of these newer fifteenth-century romances, it focuses on a classical theme and is 'epic' in its scale and sense of grandeur. However, as an alliterative work, the *Wars of Alexander* is at the same time profoundly traditional and native. And other new verse romances emerging in the very late fourteenth and early fifteenth centuries, such as *Ipomedon* and *Generydes*, also present the sense of a hybrid, caught between 'old' and 'new'. These two romances cohere with Lydgate's text and other late medieval romances in their intensified interest in chivalry and courtly behaviour; yet they still resonate with the older story-types, instantly familiar to anyone brought up on a diet of *Bevis*, *Octavian*, or *Sir Tryamour*. Ipomedon adopts the role of the 'Fair Unknown', in the almost Quixotic sense that he seems to have been spending too much time reading a text like *Lybeaus Desconus* or studying the character Florent in *Octavian*. *Generydes* is similarly focused on courtly manners, offering readers a guide to correct behaviour in worlds beyond their reach (*Generydes*, ed. Wright 1873, 1878: stanzaic version, lines 3305–18). However, despite this modish element, *Generydes* also offers a summation of the narrative ingredients of the earlier popular verse romances: in particular, the story of the displaced youth. The same narrative patterns – disunited families, exiled heirs, slandered women – that dominated verse romance in the fourteenth century (in texts that continued to be copied and adapted throughout the fifteenth century, such as *Sir Degare*, *Octavian*, and *Sir Eglamour of Artois*) are here too in the 'new' courtly romances of the fifteenth century, if decked out in finer raiment. Indeed, some of these romances that seem to be generated in part by Chaucer's achievement, such as *Partenope* and *Amoryus*, are insatiable in their appetite for the terrain of *Sir Thopas*, including encounters with fairy mistresses, giants, dragons and magical adventures. Ironically, *Sir Thopas* had not led to a rejection of the narrative stuff of older romances. Rather, Chaucer's parody continued to provoke throughout the fifteenth century varieties of 'Thopas redivivus'. It is as if those taking pleasure in both Chaucer and romance simply did not take on board the full implications of the satire, but rather sought to give more polished versions of the same.

Throughout the fifteenth century, romance narratives continued to escape their originators' control or putative purpose. Older romances were recopied, redacted and given new contexts. The writing of Chaucer, among others, stimulated a new kind of ambitious text. The catalogue of romance heroes in *Sir Thopas* – 'Of Horn child and Ypotys,/ Of Beves and sir Gy,/ Of sir Lybeux' (*CT*, VII. 898–900) – appears again in the early fifteenth-century *Laud Troy Book* with additions that Chaucer's enthusiastic narrator would surely have sanctioned, had he not felt his audience getting restless:

> Off Bevis, Gy, and of Gauwayn,
> Off kyng Richard, & of Owayn [...]
> Off Hauelok, Horne, & of Wade [...]
> Here dedis ben in remembraunce
> In many faire Romaunce.
> (*Laud Troy Book*, ed. Wülfing 1902, 1904: lines 15–26)

The emerging dominance of prose in the fifteenth century, particularly in relation to romance and in the context of the printed book and new styles of readership, has been variously discussed (Keiser 1984). Caxton's romances echo some of the newer verse romances in aiming at a gentrified readership, or else the aspirant reader who sought to acquire from the text their courtly manners. Given the similarity here, it is interesting to ask in what sense newly composed verse romance is different from prose romance in the fifteenth century. As prose grew to greater prominence in the later fifteenth century, what did it mean to write or read romance in verse? It is perhaps unwise to put too much pressure on this question, but the answer seems to lead back to Chaucer, whose authority and works reached prominence partly because of the expansion of textual production and literacy in the fifteenth century (Pearsall 1977: 223–4). Fifteenth-century 'Chaucer', if not Chaucer himself, is a crucial figure in the development of an authorial tradition focused on poetry. Lydgate and others acknowledged him as their poetic master, even as they helped to create that tradition and their place within it. To imitate Chaucer, then, was first and foremost a *formal* imitation (verse), before a generic one (romance). Romance writers interested in Chaucer had to be poets first and romance writers second. As Seth Lerer notes, to write poetry in the fifteenth century meant a conscious effort to be 'Chaucerian' (Lerer 1993: 11). The fact that such 'Chaucerian' romance writers could also recall, consciously or not, the older verse romances that continued to circulate and flourish testifies to romance's capacity to enthral and endure.

Works cited

Ackerman, Robert W., 'Henry Lovelich's *Merlin*', *PMLA*, 67 (1952), 473–84

Bennett, H. S.,'The Production and Dissemination of Vernacular Manuscripts in the Fifteenth Century', *The Library*, 5th series, 1 (1947), 167–78

Blanchfield, Lynne S., 'The Romances in MS Ashmole 61: An Idiosyncratic Scribe', in *Romance in Medieval England*, ed. Maldwyn Mills, Jennifer Fellows, and Carol M. Meale (Cambridge, 1991), pp. 65–87

——, 'Rate Revisited: The Compilation of the Narrative Works in MS Ashmole 61', in *Romance Reading on the Book: Essays on Medieval Narrative Presented to Maldwyn Mills*, ed. Jennifer Fellows et al. (Cardiff, 1996), pp. 208–22

Boffey, Julia, and John J. Thompson, 'Anthologies and Miscellanies: Production and Choice of Texts', in *Book Production and Publishing in Britain, 1375–1475*, eds Jeremy Griffiths and Derek Pearsall (Cambridge, 1989), pp. 279–315

Brewer, D. S., and A. E. B. Owen, intro., *The Thornton Manuscript (Lincoln Cathedral MS 91)* (London, 1975)

Cooper, Helen, 'Romance after 1400', in *The Cambridge History of Medieval English Literature*, ed. David Wallace (Cambridge, 1999), pp. 690–719

——, *The English Romance in Time: Transforming Motifs from Geoffrey of Monmouth to the Death of Shakespeare* (Oxford, 2004)

——, 'Guy as Early Modern English Hero', in *Guy of Warwick: Icon and Ancestor*, eds Alison Wiggins and Rosalind Field (Cambridge, 2007), pp. 185–99

Dekker, Thomas, *The Shoemaker's Holiday*, ed. D. J. Palmer (London, 1975)

Edwards, A. S. G., and Derek Pearsall, 'The Manuscripts of the Major English Poetic Texts', in *Book Production and Publishing in Britain, 1375–1475*, eds Jeremy Griffiths and Derek Pearsall (Cambridge, 1989), pp. 257–78

Sir Eglamour of Artois, ed. Francis E. Richardson, EETS, o. s. 256 (London, 1965)

Fellows, Jennifer, 'Editing Middle English Romance', in *Romance in Medieval England*, eds Maldwyn Mills, Jennifer Fellows and Carol M. Meale (Cambridge, 1991), pp. 5–16

——, 'The Middle English and Renaissance *Bevis*: A Textual Survey', in *Sir Bevis of Hampton in Literary Tradition*, eds Jennifer Fellows and Ivana Djordjević (Cambridge, 2008), pp. 80–113

Generydes: A Romance in Seven-Line Stanzas, ed. W. Aldis Wright, EETS, o. s. 55, 70 (London, 1873, 1878)

Guddat-Figge, Gisela, *Catalogue of Manuscripts Containing Middle English Romances* (Munich, 1976)

Hardyng, John, *The Chronicle of John Hardyng [...] Together with the Continuation by Richard Grafton*, ed. Henry Ellis (London, 1812)

Ipomedon in drei Englischen Bearbeitungen, ed. Eugen Kölbing (Breslau, 1889)

Keiser, George R, 'The Romances', in *Middle English Prose: A Critical Guide to Major Authors and Genres*, ed. A. S. G. Edwards (New Brunswick, NJ, 1984), pp. 271–86

King, Andrew, *'The Faerie Queene' and Middle English Romance: The Matter of Just Memory* (Oxford, 2000)

——, '*Sir Bevis of Hampton*: Renaissance Influence and Reception', in *Sir Bevis of Hampton in Literary Tradition*, eds Jennifer Fellows and Ivana Djordjević (Cambridge, 2008), pp. 176–91

The Laud Troy Book, ed. J. Ernst Wülfing, 2 vols, EETS, o. s. 121, 122 (London, 1902, 1904)

Lerer, Seth, *Chaucer and his Readers: Imagining the Author in Late-Medieval England* (Princeton, NJ, 1993)

Lovelich, Henry, *Henry Lovelich's Merlin*, ed. E. A. Kock, 3 vols, EETS, e. s. 93, 112, o. s. 185 (London, 1904, 1913, 1932)

Lydgate, John, *Lydgate's Troy Book*, ed. Henry Bergen, 4 vols, EETS, e. s. 97, 103, 106, 126 (London, 1906, 1908, 1910, 1935)

Malory, Sir Thomas, *The Works of Sir Thomas Malory*, ed. Eugène Vinaver, rev. P. J. C. Field, 3 vols (Oxford, 1990)

Metham, John, *The Works of John Metham, Including 'The Romance of Amoryus and Cleopes'*, ed. Hardin Craig, EETS, o. s. 132 (London, 1916)

Parker, Patricia, *Inescapable Romance: Studies in the Poetics of a Mode* (Princeton, NJ, 1974)

Partonope of Blois, ed. A. Trampe Bödtker, EETS, e. s. 109 (London, 1912)

Pearsall, Derek, 'The English Romance in the Fifteenth Century', *Essays and Studies*, n. s. 29 (1976), 56–83

——, *Old English and Middle English Poetry*, Routledge History of English Poetry, 1 (London, 1977)

——, 'The Uses of Manuscripts: Late Medieval English', *Harvard Library Bulletin*, n.s. 4 (1994), 30–6

——, and I. C. Cunningham, intro., *The Auchinleck Manuscript: National Library of Scotland Advocates' MS 19.2.1* (London, 1977)

The Romance of Guy of Warwick: The Second or 15th-Century Version, ed. Julius Zupitza, 2 vols, EETS, e. s. 25, 26 (London, 1875, 1876)

The Romance of Sir Beues of Hamtoun, ed. Eugen Kölbing, 3 vols, EETS, e. s. 46, 48, 65 (London, 1885, 1886, 1894)

Severs, J. Burke, ed., *A Manual of the Writings in Middle English, 1050–1500, Volume 1: Romances* (New Haven, CT, 1968)

Staines, David, '*Havelok the Dane*: A Thirteenth-Century Handbook for Princes', *Speculum*, 51 (1976), 602–23

Thompson, John J., 'The Compiler in Action: Robert Thornton and the "Thornton Romances" in Lincoln Cathedral MS 91', in *Manuscripts and Readers in Fifteenth-Century England: The Literary Implications of Manuscript Study*, ed. Derek Pearsall (Cambridge, 1983), pp. 113–24

——, 'Collecting Middle English Romances and Some Related Book-Production Activities in the Later Middle Ages', in *Romance in Medieval England*, eds Maldwyn Mills, Jennifer Fellows and Carol Meale (Cambridge, 1991), pp. 17–38.

Wallace, David, 'General Preface', in *The Cambridge History of Medieval English Literature*, ed. David Wallace (Cambridge: Cambridge University Press, 1999), pp. xi–xxiii.

The Wars of Alexander, eds Hoyt N. Duggan and Thorlac Turville-Petre, EETS, s. s. 10 (Oxford, 1989)

15

Scientific and Encyclopaedic Verse

ANKE TIMMERMANN

The fifteenth century witnessed two significant developments in the communication of information. The invention of print towards the end of the century may be the more prominent of the two. But a sudden, persistent and energetic demand for vernacular scientific texts, particularly in verse form, was no less significant. Indeed, this thirst for scientific information defined and changed the role of the written word in fifteenth-century England.

The genre of scientific and encyclopaedic poetry is more emblematic of the fifteenth century than prose texts or non-scientific verse in many respects. This is partly due to its various connections with classical literature. Thanks to the humanistic interest in classical works by Lucretius and Pliny, Manilius and pseudo-Aristotle, verse was considered a perfect medium for education and the transmission of knowledge, including scientific lore of supposedly ancient origin.[1] The ensuing translation and imitation of classical texts typically took place in monasteries, around the development of university curricula, in royal courts and other centres of learning. With its natural emphasis on the sciences this scholarly, linguistic and exegetic engagement with classical literature had produced a vernacular scientific vocabulary from the fourteenth century onwards. The fifteenth-century translation of Gilbertus Anglicus' pharmaceutical treatises is a prime example for the transposition of technical medical terms into Middle English prose (*Healing and Society*, ed. Getz 1991). Versified versions appear in compendia such as Longleat House, MS 174; this contains Gower's *Confessio Amantis* as well as Middle English medical verse (Harris 2001).[2] Fifteenth-century readers' knowledge of science may have resembled that of their grandfathers in content, but the number of texts accessible to them and the nature of their reading had changed. The fifteenth century produced roughly six times more texts than the fourteenth century, a much higher proportion of vernacular texts and an unanticipated number of scientific poems (Jones 1994: 100–1). Science now spoke not just the language of the man outside the university, but also in a rhythmic, melodious voice.

---

[1] For a comprehensive history of didactic poetry see Schuler and Fitch (1983). Haye provides a study of European *Lehrdichtung* in Latin, including scientific poetry.

[2] For a discussion of the Middle English translation of medical prose texts in this context see Voigts 1984, esp. 315–16.

Scientific poetry in late medieval and early modern England was closely connected with royal sponsorship. Humfrey, Duke of Gloucester, was the most prominent and influential patron of the arts and sciences in England in the first half of the fifteenth century. He counted John Lydgate, the author of the *Fall of Princes*, among his poets. Another, unnamed poet created an elaborate English verse tract counting 6,613 lines, entitled *On Husbondrie*, for Humfrey; it was based on Palladius' agricultural treatise *De re rustica* (*NIMEV* 654; *Palladius*, ed. Lodge 1873-9). Its Latinate style, rhyme royal verse form, and general humanistic air were considered particularly appropriate for this purpose. At the other end of the social scale, audiences for pragmatic poems included medical practitioners, craftsmen and newly literate readers who sought out vernacular scientific texts as a source of practical information. Scientific poetry, in particular, helped them to access and understand texts, and to carry knowledge from book to laboratory, workshop, kitchen and sickbed.

The world of knowledge preserved in Middle English scientific poetry is rather more inclusive than a modern concept of science and its objects would imply. For the purposes of this chapter the terms 'science' and 'scientific' are shorthand references for any branch of natural philosophy and its practical applications. This chapter focuses particularly on poetic works relating to alchemy, to medicine and botany, to astronomy, astrology and cosmology, as well as to encyclopaedic poetry, an extensive digest of various branches of scientific knowledge. Topics not discussed here (for pragmatic reasons) include technical poetry, for example: on masonry; culinary recipes and household books; grammatical rules and other items related to academic education and the *artes* proper.[3]

Alchemy was the most popular topic for scientific poetry in England in the fifteenth century and, therefore, deserves special attention. England brought forth two alchemist poets whose names and works have dominated the modern history of fifteenth-century alchemy: Thomas Norton and George Ripley. Norton (c.1433–1513/14) was born into a well-established family in Bristol. Not much is known about his life, and his biography has been rewritten and revised several times (Norton, ed. Reidy 1975: xxxvii–lii). Norton appears to have held several official positions in city and county councils as well as at court, including a post as advisor to Edward IV. He wrote the *Ordinal of Alchemy*, the only text attributed to him, in the final quarter of the fifteenth century. It explains the alchemist's work in no less than 3,102 lines plus preface, in the obscure metaphorical language common to alchemical works of the time (*NIMEV* 3772; Norton, ed. Reidy 1975; and Ashmole 1652: 1–106). Since its composition, the *Ordinal* has fascinated its readers in England and abroad: nearly forty manuscript witnesses survive from its vivid contemporary reception; the famous German physician, alchemist and

---

[3] On scientific manuscripts in the fifteenth century, see e.g. Voigts 1989 and 1990. For the evolution of categories of historical science in relatively recent secondary literature compare Voigts 1989 with Keiser 1998, Voigts and Kurtz 2000. Luckily the scholarly awareness of scientific verse in English manuscripts has increased significantly in recent years. Pioneering research and the provision of research tools were undertaken by the above-mentioned and Singer 1928-31; Schuler, and *Alchemical Poetry*, ed. Schuler; Mooney 1981; Keiser 2003 and 2005. Kahn 2010 and 2011, and Tavormina 2010, are examples of recent work on alchemical and medical verse.

writer of allegorical *alchemica* Michael Maier created a line-by-line translation of the *Ordinal* into Latin in 1618; a German verse version from the Latin version followed in 1625 (Maier 1618; *Chymischer Tractat Thomae Nortoni* 1625). A single substantial poem thus ensured Thomas Norton's role as a figurehead for English alchemy in the fifteenth century.

George Ripley (c.1415–c.1490), some years Norton's senior, is a similarly historically elusive figure whose poetic oeuvre superseded his persona in time. We do know that Ripley was a canon regular of Bridlington priory in Yorkshire and travelled to Louvain (Flanders) and Italy to study with masters of the arts and alchemy. He preserved his laboratory experiences in his rather large body of alchemical poetry, mostly an adaptation of Latin sources using alchemical principles commonly attributed to the thirteenth-century philosopher and doctor Ramon Lull. *The Compound of Alchemy*, also known as *The Twelve Gates*, details a dozen steps, or procedures, towards the production of the philosophers' stone (*NIMEV* 595; Ashmole 1652: 107–93; Ripley, ed. Linden 2001; see also Rampling 2010, where the history of Ripley biographies is detailed on 126, fn. 2). The success of Ripley's work is evident from the late fifteenth and early sixteenth centuries onwards, when pseudo-Ripleian works and poems in his style dominated alchemical compendia. Some appeared on beautifully illuminated alchemical scrolls erroneously known as the 'Ripley Scrolls' until today (see, for example, the description of the Edinburgh witness in McCullum 1996). *Terra Terrae Philosophicae*, a Latin prose translation of the anonymous fifteenth-century poem *Verses upon the Elixir*, was another work spuriously attributed to Ripley. The prose medium, Latin language, and unquestioned, consistent ascription show that in the audience's minds, the iconic Middle English alchemical poet George Ripley had long joined the ranks of the very authorities he emulated.

It is interesting to note here that Middle English alchemical poetry has been neglected, at times even scorned by modern scholarship, because its literary merits pale before the poems of Chaucer, Gower and their fifteenth-century peers. In his monumental *A History of Magic and Experimental Science* (1924–58) Lynn Thorndike recognised alchemical poetry as a genre, but dismissed the work of George Ripley as 'very stupid and tiresome reading' (Thorndike: IV, 352). Also, a child of the early to mid-twentieth century, the history of alchemy initially focused on biographical history and substantial poems. Beyond Norton and Ripley, however, the fifteenth-century English tradition of alchemical poetry was largely an anonymous one, at times studded with spurious or changing attributions to ancient and contemporary authorities. As *Gebrauchstexte* proper most alchemical poems did not require a fixed named author to lend authority to their contents. These anonyma contain much information about the circulation of alchemical knowledge in manuscripts. A recently identified corpus of Middle English *alchemica* will illustrate this point.

The poem *Verses upon the Elixir*, an anonymous recipe for the philosophers' stone, survives in at least four fifteenth-century copies and a further forty-nine copies dating from the sixteenth and early seventeenth centuries (*NIMEV* 3249, and 2712.5; Ashmole 1652: 269–74, there attributed to the historically elusive 'Pearce the Black Monk'). Rather than being transmitted and circulated in isolation, the poem shows connections both textual and contextual with at least twenty other alchemical poems. Four fifteenth-century manuscripts (Bodl., MS Ashmole 759; BL, MSS Sloane 1091 and 3447, and BL, MS Harley 2407) form the nucleus of this corpus, which is formed by the following poems and their variants: the 'Exposition' (*NIMEV* 2666; Ashmole 1652: 428–30) and 'Wind and Water' (*NIMEV* 3257; Ashmole: 431), which frequently follow the *Verses* as if to form part of the poem; 'The Bost of Mercury' (*NIMEV* 1276 and 3271), 'Mystery of Alchemists' (*NIMEV* 4017; Ashmole: 380–8), 'Liber Patris Sapientiae' (*NIMEV* 1150; Ashmole: 194–209), 'Richard Carpenter's Work' (*NIMEV* 1555, 2656 and 3255; Ashmole: 275–7 and 377–8); 'The Short Work' (*NIMEV* 3721; Ashmole: 393–6), and poems that also appear on the above-mentioned 'Ripley Scrolls': 'In the sea' (*NIMEV* 1561.7; Ashmole: 376–7) 'On the ground' (*NIMEV* 2688; Ashmole: 378–9), 'I shall you tell' (*NIMEV* 1364; Ashmole: 375–6) and 'Trinity' (*NIMEV* 1558.5; Ashmole: 211). Readers' and copyists' vivid reception of these poems, their annotations and alterations almost mimic the experimentation of an alchemist in the laboratory on a linguistic level. Similar forms of the communication and circulation of knowledge can be observed throughout the body of fifteenth-century scientific poetry.

Alchemy may have been so much more prone to versification than, for example, medicine due to its essentially practical, applied character. On one hand, recipes lend themselves to versification for mnemonic purposes. Using a recipe from memory is easier when important information about ingredients and methods can be remembered in pairs of rhymes. On the other hand, readers' intense engagement with the language of alchemy, as in the above-mentioned active reception of the corpus around the *Verses upon the Elixir*, prompted the employment of verse. It was believed that only a worthy alchemist would be able to understand a recipe and discover the secrets of nature behind alchemy's obscure, metaphorical terminology and expression. The emerging vernacular tradition in the fifteenth century further forced copyists and readers to interpret alchemical terminology derived from the Arabic, Greek and Latin in Middle English terms.[4] Here, rhyme words ensured that unfamiliar terms had a phonetic point of reference and that a copyist's attention would be drawn to important information, which was often placed towards the end of lines. In this sense poetry offered a serviceable structure for *alchemica* while they slowly made the transition into the vernacular.

Vernacular alchemical poetry throughout continental Europe pales before the sheer bulk, variety and consistency of Middle English *alchemica*. German alchemical verse, for instance, favoured not practical recipes or extensive explanations but mostly comprised received knowledge about alchemy in useful phrases and pithy maxims, so-called gnomic texts. The illustrated poem *Sol und Luna* makes for a particularly colourful and noteworthy exception in the German tradition, and an indirect addition to the corpus of English *alchemica* (Telle 1980). The German text was modelled on the *Rosarium philosophorum* (published as part two of *De alchimia* in 1550), a florilegium or collection of 'dicta' in Latin, which enjoyed much popularity across medieval Europe in the fifteenth century.

---

4   Pereira 1999 discusses the use of the vernacular in alchemical texts of the late Middle Ages.

Running to ninety-seven lines, this vernacularisation survives (with and without images) in the staggering number of nearly one hundred witnesses and editions in manuscript and print. Its transposition into English prose and verse in the first couple of centuries after its composition documents the English appetite for fifteenth-century alchemical poetry even after the century closed.

The thriving manuscript production and reception of Middle English alchemical poetry in particular continued well into the seventeenth century without a concurrent representation in print. By the time some alchemical poems appeared in printed volumes the genre had almost become a matter of history.[5] Elias Ashmole's *Theatrum Chemicum Britannicum*, a compendium of alchemical verse published in 1652 as an homage to the English language, marks the beginning of the afterlife of alchemical poetry (Kahn 2010: 255–6; Ashmole 1652). Many of the items edited by Ashmole in a conservative fashion, albeit with adjusted spelling, date from the fifteenth century: Ripley and Norton are represented, as well as Chaucer's 'Canon's Yeoman's Tale' and several anonyma well known to readers of the manuscript sources. Ashmole's bibliophile (rather than purely linguistic) interest in alchemy, astronomy and the boundaries of medieval science also inspired his manuscript collection, now kept at the Bodleian Library in Oxford, where his notes on the compilation of his *Theatrum*, and thus his knowledge of fifteenth-century verse, fill several volumes (Bodl., MSS Ashmole 971, 972). The *Theatrum Chemicum Britannicum* therefore occupies a place between the sources for and scholarship on the history of alchemy.

Medicine was by far the most popular topic for scientific texts in fifteenth-century England, and indeed throughout Europe. But manuscripts relating to the human body, its illnesses, and the work of the medical practitioner only occasionally included verse (Jones 1994: 101; Keiser 2003: 301; see also Robbins 1970). Conversely, medical themes appeared in literary works and verse written by poets without a professional interest in natural philosophy. Chaucer's oeuvre, the *Romaunt de la Rose*, and Lydgate's *Dietary* are prime examples. The last of these is an eighty-line verse regimen. Its style is indistinguishable from scientific poems by lesser or unknown authors:

> ffor helth of body couer fro cold þi hede
> Etc non raw mete take gode hede þer to
> Drynke holsom drynke fede þe on lyȝht brede
> And with Apytyte ryse fro þi mete also
>   (Lydgate, ed. MacCracken: 763; *NIMEV* 824 and 1418)

The *Dietary* could, and did, sit comfortably beside scientific poems in fifteenth-century manuscripts, especially medical ones. With more than fifty surviving manuscript witnesses in total, the *Dietary* turned out to be Lydgate's most popular work by far, even if his more elaborate non-scientific works are better known today.

Lydgate's pithy *Doctryne for Pestilence*, a work of three eight-line stanzas, which was often copied together with the *Dietary*, is only one of many plague tracts

---

5   The first Latin collection of *alchemica* is Zetzner 1602–51.

from the period (*NIMEV* 4112 edited in Bühler 1934: 52). Another verse plague treatise, running to 117 lines and surviving in a sole fifteenth-century manuscript, was based on a fourteenth-century treatise by John of Burgundy (*NIMEV* 1190; BL, MS Egerton 1624; Bowers 1956).[6] Given the recurring, frightening bouts of plague across Europe at the time, the *Doctryne*'s incipit, 'Who will be whole and keep him from sickness', almost sounds like a rhetorical question. Other popular verse texts on the maintenance or restoration of health comprise verse phlebotomies detailing the places of and favourable times for bloodletting in accordance with the stars and the signs of the zodiac, and verse regimen discussing man's diet, hygiene and other healthy or harmful habits (for verse phlebotomies see for example *NIMEV* 3848; Keiser 1998: Nos 288–9). Poems on veterinary medicine, gynaecology and the mechanical procedures of surgery were much rarer than those on uroscopy (*Urines and Humors in Verse and Prose* is *NIMEV* 1109.5 and 1201.3. See also Tavormina 2010).[7]

The most epitomical of fifteenth-century poems are recipes, which fit practical instructions into the smallest possible poetic format. Hundreds of Middle English pragmatic medical, alchemical and culinary recipes survive; *secreta* such as instructions for mixing inks or making vessels for use in a laboratory or kitchen, and indeed alchemical recipes, were closely related to this recipe literature. The following headache remedy provides a stylistically typical example:

> A medicyn I hawe in mynde
> For hedwerk to telle, as I fynde:
> Take eysyl and pulyole ryale
> And camomylle, and sethe with-all;
> And with þe jous anoynte þin noethryl wel
> And make a playster of þe to þer del,
> And do it in o good gret clowte
> And wynde þin heed þer-with abowte;
> As sone as it be leyd þeron,
> All þe heedwerk away xal gon.
>   (Stockholm, Royal library MS X. 90, as cited in Holthausen 1896:
>   79, B, lines 1436–45)

Apart from providing ingredients for medical recipes (here pennyroyal and camomile), botany or herbal lore also held a place of its own in fifteenth-century verse. Long texts dedicated to plants and their properties were often inspired by Macer's herbal and its medieval derivates. The *De viribus herbarum*, originally a Latin medical or herbal poem of 2,269 hexameter lines, was written by the French physician Odo of Meung-sur-Loire under the pseudonym Macer (alluding to the Roman poet Aemilius Macer, first century BC) in or before the eleventh century. It had been translated into German prose in the thirteenth century and a little

---

[6] For the long-term reception of John of Burgundy's plague treatise across Europe see Matheson 2005.

[7] *A Latin Technical Phlebotomy*, ed. Voigts and McVaugh 1984: 19–24 provides a useful overview of the role of verse in Middle English medical manuscripts. I have not found any fifteenth-century poems specifically on surgery or obstetrics. A rare verse veterinary charm is *NIMEV* 2903.

later into English prose and verse (Magdunensis 1477). Although variations on a theme, many of the texts imitating Macer continued to be copied throughout the period. The verse *Tretys of Diverse Herbis*, for instance, survives in at least twenty-one copies from the fifteenth century onwards (*NIMEV* 2026.5 and 2627, also 417.8, 1496.3 and 3754; an edition can be found in Holthausen 1896: 307–30; *NIMEV* 3578 provides a verse introduction to the *Tretys*). Its five hundred couplets explain the properties of twenty-four herbs and provide advice on good times for planting, harvesting and medicinal uses. Further, the Dominican friar and botanist Henry Daniel's work was adapted in two verse treatises on rosemary. Daniel's text predates yet had a strong influence on herbal teachings in the fifteenth century, perhaps thanks to the fact that rosemary had been introduced to England relatively recently (*NIMEV* 3754; see also Keiser 2005). On the whole, herbal poetry adds to the otherwise sparse Middle English body of verse texts related to medicine.

Like alchemical volumes, medical manuscripts preserve a context for well-known poems and historically obscure recipes beyond any evidence of their owners, writers and origins.[8] The fifteenth-century medical doctor Thomas Fayreford's *Practica* provides a striking example for the ease with which scientific poetry was incorporated in medical commonplace books (now BL, MS Harley 2558; see Jones 1994: 103–6).[9] Indeed, scientific commonplace books, their format and method of recording information are as iconic a product of the fifteenth century as Middle English scientific verse (Jones 1999: 436–7). As Fayreford details in the case study of a patient, he based his knowledge about the medicinal properties of betony on Macer's *De viribus herbarum*. The copy in Fayreford's commonplace book also supplies a Middle English list of plant-name equivalents. Here the vernacular reception of a Latin text from the early high Middle Ages, originally written in reverence of a classical poet, serves as an authorisation of a fifteenth-century doctor's medical practice.[10]

Two of Fayreford's influential contemporaries in particular contributed further to the collections of scientific prose and verse now found in Oxford and Cambridge college libraries. Gilbert Kymer, Chancellor of the University of Oxford, had a keen interest in medicine and alchemy. Roger Marchall, medical doctor at Cambridge, approached medicine through study of the stars (Jones 1999: 437–8). Fayreford, Kymer and Marchall's activities, positions in society, and connections to universities and other centres of learning are emblematic of the environs in which scientific poetry of all ages and origins thrived in the fifteenth century, in Middle English translation, reception and application.

Poems on astronomy, astrology and cosmology occupied scholars and medical practitioners as much as laymen and women who sought guidance for their

---

[8] For medical and alchemical verse in commonplace books, as evidence of medical practitioners' approaches to remedies and alchemy, see Timmermann 2008 (a case study on a series of sixteenth-century medical notebooks).

[9] Haye 1997 discusses individual fifteenth-century manuscripts containing Latin scientific verse from all over Europe, esp. 79, 100f, 311ff, 345ff.

[10] On the linguistic aspects of the vernacularisation of medicine, particularly the Middle English context, see Taavitsainen and Pahta 1998.

everyday lives. Fifteenth-century lay people would have been inclined to consult astronomical-astrological poems that they could interpret and use without any specialised training or knowledge. Middle English prognostications, almanacs, lunaries and other calendrical computations, although sometimes extensive, had the advantage that they were intended to be read in stages, as the passage of the stars and passages of text applied to different months of the year or signs of the zodiac. The *Storia Luna*, an anonymous English verse lunary written around the year 1400, consists of 123 six-line stanzas with a strong biblical thread running through them (*NIMEV* 1171, 3342 and 4264; Farnham 1923: 73–82; Taavitsainen 1987). It was sufficiently popular to serve as a basis for a prose paraphrase as well as for several further prose lunaries. A more concise contemporary poem of similar subject matter dedicates just one quatrain to each month of the year. It survives in just a single manuscript witness (*NIMEV* 1253; the first stanza (on aquarius) is published in *Secular Lyrics*, ed. Robbins 1955: 251). Other copies may have fallen victim to the discarding of ephemera, which also affected so many almanacs from this period. It should finally be noted that most Middle English poems on the stars and their influence that circulated in the fifteenth century date from earlier periods (Keiser 1998: 3611–6324). While it is therefore difficult to gauge the impact of individual astronomical or astrological poems in the fifteenth century, surviving manuscripts certainly provide evidence of the ubiquitous appearance of verse in calendars, almanacs and other documents with a natural expiration date.

The most miscellaneous and comprehensive of verse texts, encyclopaedic poems, are comparatively more substantial in every respect. Encyclopaedic poems may discuss anything from royal morals to dietary advice, often run over several thousand lines, enjoy a long life in manuscript copies throughout the centuries, and are frequently modelled on or even translated from a classical original. Notably the translation would often include a transposition of a prose original into verse, which made previously privileged knowledge accessible to a new group of readers. *Sidrak and Bokkus*, a poem composed in the thirteenth century and rather popular with fifteenth-century audiences (*NIMEV* 772 and 2147; *Sidrak and Bokkus*, ed. Burton 1998–9 is a Middle English verse translation of an Old French prose text, a fictional dialogue between a Christian philosopher and a heathen king. The latter's inquisitiveness, which runs to up to 415 questions in total, mirrors the thoughts of the text's intended audience. Its question-and-answer format was traditionally used in university disputations and related to scholarly works; in the poem it provides a structure for an otherwise only loosely organised cluster of questions. Notably this was first published in print in England around 1530 (*STC* 3186).

Another encyclopaedic poem, John Lydgate's version of the pseudo-Aristotelian *Secreta Secretorum*, inspired several fifteenth-century English verse incarnations (*NIMEV* 935; Renoir and Benson 1980: no. 166; Lydgate, ed. Steele 1894; Ashmole 1652: 397–403; Telle 1994). Originally a Latin adaptation of an Arabic work of the tenth century, the *Secreta Secretorum* covered topics as diverse as ethics, hygiene, politics, justice, astrology, alchemy, physiognomy and plants, which clearly appealed to fifteenth-century English audiences as much as to the original ones. Lydgate's *Secrees of old philosoffres* adopts a rhyme royal structure to translate the Latinate characteristics of its classical forerunner into a classic style for the fifteenth century.

Finally, the Scottish poet Sir Gilbert Hay, born at the very beginning of the fifteenth century and best known for his *Buik of King Alexander the Conqueror* (see Martin 2006), is probably the translator of a physiological section of the *Secreta Secretorum*. The result, *The Scots Buke of Phisnomy*, shows connections with a substantial regimen section from the *Buik of King Alexander* (Mapstone 1994): apparently Hay extracted medical sections from classical encyclopaedic poetry and elaborated upon it with rhetorical wit. The ideal man is described thus:

> Thik braid hoches, with filletis stark *and* sture,
> Great brandis, *and* weill made at measour,
> With gudlie fassion, baythe of fute *and* hand,
> And weill breistit, of visage well-farand,
> In hair als dosk, yallow, blak or broun,
> In midlin way of compositioun,
> With guidlie chei, well favored in visage,
> Myngit *with* reid *and* guid messurage,
> Broun, blak, or gray the roundall of the ey,
> Cleir voceit and haill, þat is a man for the.
> (NLS, MS Adv. 34.3.12, pp. 16–7; Mapstone 1994: 42)

Here the *Secreta Secretorum* offers a template for a fifteenth-century poet's personal observations. Significantly, Hay's version places Scotland on the map of scientific and encyclopaedic poetry, and Scots dialects into the periphery of linguistic questions about the development of a Middle English scientific terminology (see also Bawcutt and Williams 2006). An investigation of the connections between vernacular languages and encyclopaedic poetry in particular would reveal much about national attitudes towards scientific knowledge.

The range of subjects covered in scientific poetry is not identical to that of scientific prose. Middle English texts about disciplines without practical application, such as pure mathematics and music, do not employ verse. Magic, a subject now firmly associated with the canon of late medieval natural philosophy, presents a particular conundrum: charms, regularly used by medical practitioners to cure patients, certainly have a discernible rhythmic quality; occasionally they show linguistic parallel constructions reminiscent of blank verse. Even the term 'charm' may refer to either prose or verse, either written down or performed orally, in the fifteenth century (Skemer 2006: 17; see also Smallwood 2004). But not many medical charms in Middle English verse survive in written form, and those that are extant and can be identified as having medical relevance do not show consistent quality of text and rhyme. Admittedly all pragmatic vernacular scientific poems often just comprise a handful of couplets utilising serviceable standard rhymes and a metre that bow to the poem's content whenever necessary. Phrases added to fill out metre and rhyme seem generic rather than meaningful in nature, as in the following poem on the calculation of Easter dates:

> In merche, after þe fyrst C,
> Loke the prime wher-euer he be

The 3d sonday, full I-wysse,
Ester day trewly yt ys.
& yf þe prime on þe sonday be,
rekyne þat sonday for one of þe thre.

> (CUL, MS Ff 6.8, fol. 3v; *Secular Lyrics*,
> ed. Robbins 1955: 63; *NIMEV* 1502)

Yet the following fifteenth-century charm for sprained wrists or ankles emphasises parallel structures to the point of being formulaic, a quality that would come to carry when the charm was performed in multiple repetitions, almost like an incantation:

> Oure lorde Ihesu criste
> ouere a den roode
> And his foole sloode
> And ovre lorde Criste aboode
> And layde lithe to lithe
> And flesshe to flesshe
> And bone to bone
> And com hym to boote
> I praye Criste Ihesu so this moote

> (HEH, MS HM 64, fol. 145ra; *NIMEV* 2723.33)

Overall, charms form part of the intertextual and cultural influences on the core body of scientific poetry in the fifteenth century, as do a variety of rhymed texts used in other crafts and sciences omitted from this chapter. Generally, the picture presented by Middle English scientific poetry is as varied and intriguing as its underlying scientific disciplines imply.

The advent of print towards the end of the fifteenth century did not affect scientific poetry and its dissemination. Much of the Middle English scientific poetry in particular was simply too practical, ordinary or ephemeral to be printed together with a corpus of works intended to preserve a legacy of human knowledge. Scientific poems that were published at the time were overwhelmingly Latin compositions by continental Europeans (for example, in medicine Grünpeck and two *Regimen*, 1477–83 and 1480; for herbal lore Magdunensis, and for astronomy Dati, the last an Italian exception). As a medium primarily circulated in manuscript form, scientific verse therefore offers a direct glimpse into the production of scientific knowledge at a time when language, media and the sciences were changing. Indeed, a comprehensive investigation of the fifteenth century through the eyes of scientific poets and their audiences may just be a task appropriate for the twenty-first century.

Works cited

Alchemical Poetry 1575–1700: From Previously Unpublished Manuscripts, ed. Robert M. Schuler (New York, 1995)

Ashmole, Elias, *Theatrum Chemicum Britannicum* (London, 1652)

Bawcutt, Priscilla J., and Janet Hadley Williams, eds, *A Companion to Medieval Scottish Poetry* (Cambridge, 2006)

Bowers, R. H., 'A Middle English Mnemonic Plague Tract', *Southern Folklore Quarterly*, 20 (1956), 118–25

Bühler, Curt, 'Lydgate's Rules of Health in MS Lansdowne 699', *Medium Aevum*, 3 (1934), 51–6

Chymischer Tractat Thomae Nortoni eines Engelländers, Crede Mihi seu Ordinale genandt (Frankfurt, 1625)

Dati, Leonardo or Gregorio, *La Sfera* (Florence, 1472)

De alchimia opuscula complura veterum philosophorum, Volume 2: Rosarium philosophorum. Secunda pars alchimiae de lapide philosophico vero modo praeparando (Frankfurt, 1550)

Farnham, Willard, 'The Dayes of the Mone', *Studies in Philology*, 20 (1923), 70–82

Grünpeck, Joseph, *De pestilentiali scorra, sive Mala de Franzos, originem remediaque ejusdem continens* (Leipzig, 1496)

Harris, Kate, 'The Longleat House Extracted Manuscript of Gower's *Confessio Amantis*', in *Middle English Poetry: Texts and Traditions: Essays in Honour of Derek Pearsall*, ed. A. J. Minnis (York, 2001), pp. 77–90

Haye, Thomas, *Das lateinische Lehrgedicht im Mittelalter* (Leiden, 1997)

Healing and Society in Medieval England: A Middle English Translation of the Pharmaceutical Writings of Gilbertus Anglicus, ed. Faye Getz (Madison, WI, 1991)

The History of Kyng Boccus, [and] Sydracke, ed. John Twyne (London, [1530?])

Holthausen, Ferdinand, 'Medicinische Gedichte aus einer Stockholmer Handschrift', *Anglia*, 18 (1896), 293–331

Jones, Peter Murray, 'Information and Science', in *Fifteenth-Century Attitudes: Perceptions of Society in Late Medieval England*, ed. Rosemary Horrox (Cambridge, 1994), pp. 97–111

——, 'Medicine and Science', in *The Cambridge History of the Book in Britain, Vol. 3: 1400–1557*, eds Lotte Hellinga and J. B. Trapp (Cambridge, 1999), pp. 433–48

Kahn, Didier, 'Alchemical Poetry in Medieval and Early Modern Europe: A Preliminary Survey and Synthesis, Part I: Preliminary Survey', *Ambix*, 57 (2010), 249–74

——, 'Alchemical Poetry in Medieval and Early Modern Europe: A Preliminary Survey and Synthesis, Part II: Synthesis', *Ambix*, 58 (2011), 62–77

Keiser, George R., ed., *A Manual of Writings in Middle English, 1050–1500, Volume 10: Works of Science and Information*, gen. ed. Albert E. Hartung (New Haven, CT, 1998)

——, 'Verse Introductions to Middle English Medical Treatises', *English Studies*, 84 (2003), 301–17

——, 'A Middle English Rosemary Treatise in Verse and Prose', *American Notes and Queries*, 18 (2005), 7–17

Lydgate, John, *Lydgate and Burgh's Secrees of old philosoffres*, ed. Robert Steele, EETS, e. s. 66 (London, 1894)

Lydgate, John, *The Minor Poems of John Lydgate,. Part II:. Secular Poems*, ed. Henry Noble MacCracken, EETS, o. s., 192. (London, 1934)

Magdunensis, Odo, *De viribus herbarum* (Naples, 1477)

Maier, Michael, *Tripus Aureus* (Frankfurt, 1618)

Mapstone, Sally, 'The *Scots Buke of Phisnomy* and Sir Gilbert Hay', in *The Renaissance in Scotland: Studies in Literature, Religion, History, and Culture*, eds A. A. MacDonald, Michael Lynch and Ian B. Cowan (Leiden, 1994), pp. 1–44

Martin, Joanna, '"Of Wisdome and of Guide Governance": Sir Gilbert Hay and *The Buik of King Alexander the Conqueror*', in Bawcutt and Williams, eds, *A Companion*, pp. 75–88

Matheson, L. M., '"Médecin sans frontières?": The European Dissemination of John of Burgundy's Plague Treatise', *American Notes and Queries*, 18 (2005), 17–28

McCullum, R. I., 'The Ripley Scroll of the Royal College of Physicians of Edinburgh', *Vesalius*, 2 (1996), 39–49

Mooney, Linne R., 'Practical Didactic Works in Middle English' (unpublished PhD Thesis, University of Toronto, 1981)

Norton, Thomas, *Thomas Norton's Ordinal of Alchemy*, ed. John Reidy, EETS, o. s. 272 (London, 1975)

Palladius on husbondrie, ed. Barton Lodge, EETS, o. s. 52 (London, 1873, 1879)

Pereira, Michela, 'Alchemy and the Use of Vernacular Languages in the Late Middle Ages', *Speculum*, 74 (1999), 336–56

Rampling, Jennifer, 'The Catalogue of the Ripley Corpus: Alchemical Writings Attributed to George Ripley (d. *ca.* 1490)', *Ambix*, 57 (2010), 125–201

Regimen sanitatis Salernitanum (Louvain, 1477–83)

Regimen sanitatis cum expositione magistri Arnaldi de Villanova Cathellano noviter impressus (Venice, 1480)

Renoir, Alain, and C. David Benson, eds, *A Manual of Writings in Middle English, Volume 6: John Lydgate*, gen. ed. Albert E. Hartung (New Haven, CT, 1980)

Ripley, George, *George Ripley's Compound of Alchymy (1591)*, ed. Stanton J. Linden (Aldershot, 2001)

Robbins, Rossell Hope, 'Medical Manuscripts in Middle English', *Speculum*, 45 (1970), 393–415

Schuler, Robert M., *English Magical and Scientific Poems to 1700: An Annotated Bibliography* (New York, 1979)

——, and John G. Fitch, 'Theory and Context of the Didactic Poem: Some Classical, Mediaeval, and later Continuities', *Florilegium*, 5 (1983), 1–43

Secular Lyrics of the XIVth and XVth Centuries, ed. Rossell Hope Robbins, 2nd edn (Oxford, 1955)

Sidrak and Bokkus, ed. Tom L. Burton, 2 vols, EETS, o. s. 311, 312 (Oxford, 1998, 1999)

Singer, Dorothea Waley, *Catalogue of Latin and Vernacular Alchemical Manuscripts in Great Britain and Ireland Dating from before the Sixteenth Century*, 3 vols (Brussels, 1928–31)

Skemer, Don, *Binding Words: Textual Amulets in the Middle Ages* (Philadelphia, PA, 2006)

Smallwood, T. M., 'The Transmission of Charms in English, Medieval and Modern', in *Charms and Charming in Europe*, ed. Jonathan Roper (Basingstoke, Hampshire, 2004)

Taavitsainen, Irma, 'Storia Lune and its Paraphrase in Prose: Two Versions of a Middle English Lunary', in *Neophilologica Fennica*, ed. Leena Kahlas Tarkka, Mémoirs de la Société Néophilologique de Helsinki, 45 (Helsinki, 1987), pp. 521–55

——, and Paivi Pahta, 'Vernacularisation of Medical Writing in English: A Corpus-Based Study of Scholasticism', *Early Science and Medicine*, 3 (1998), 157–85

Tavormina, M. Teresa, 'Three Middle English Verse Uroscopies', *English Studies*, 91 (2010), 591–622

Telle, Joachim, *Sol und Luna: Literatur- und alchemiegeschichtliche Studien zu einem altdeutschen Bildgedicht*, Schriften zur Wissenschaftsgeschichte, 2 (Hürtgenwald, 1980)

——, 'Aristoteles an Alexander über den philosophischen Stein: Die alchemischen Lehren des pseudo-aristotelischen *Secretum secretorum* in einer deutschen Versübersetzung des 15. Jahrhunderts', in *Licht der Natur: Medizin in Fachliteratur und Dichtung*, ed. Josef Domes and others (Baden-Baden, 1994)

Thorndike, Lynn, *A History of Magic and Experimental Science*, 8 vols (New York, 1924–58)

Timmermann, Anke, 'Doctor's Order: An Early Modern Doctor's Alchemical Notebooks', *Early Science and Medicine*, 13 (2008), 25–52

Voigts, Linda Ehrsam, 'Medical Prose', in *Middle English Prose: A Critical Guide to Major Authors and Genres*, ed. A. S. G. Edwards (Brunswick, NJ, 1984), pp. 315–35

——, 'Scientific and Medical Books', in *Book Production and Publishing in Britain 1375–1475*, eds Jeremy Griffiths and Derek Pearsall (Cambridge, 1989), 345–402

——, 'The *Sloane Group*: Related Scientific and Medical Manuscripts from the Fifteenth Century in the Sloane Collection', *British Library Journal*, 16 (1990), 26–57

——, and Patricia Deery Kurtz, *Scientific and Medical Writings in Old and Middle English: An Electronic Reference* (Ann Arbor, MI, 2000)

——, and Michael R. McVaugh, *A Latin Technical Phlebotomy and its Middle English Translation* (Philadelphia, PA, 1984)

Zetzner, Lazarus, *Theatrum Chemicum*, 6 vols (Ursel and Strassburg, 1602–51)

16

Popular Verse Tales

JULIA BOFFEY

From most vantage points the fifteenth century in England must appear to be the age of the long poem, more often than not responding somehow to Chaucer, whether directly or through the influential oeuvres of his most prolific imitators. A number of these long poems were evidently widely read, and thus 'popular' in the sense that they were widely transmitted and had substantial reputations: works of this kind by Lydgate, Hoccleve, Hardyng and Walton survive in some numbers, as other chapters in this book make clear. But it is probably fair to assume that readers with the means to acquire copies of such works, and the time to spend appreciating them, were from comparatively limited social strata. What do we know of verse with a more widespread appeal, whose circulation crossed social boundaries in the ways that have come to be associated with what is properly 'popular'? (for some definitions, see Davis 1992; Putter and Gilbert 2000: 1–38).

Verse of this kind was clearly in circulation in the fifteenth century, supplying a number of devotional, instructive, social, diverting and other needs. It is, however, frustratingly hard to gain much sense of its nature, or any accurate understanding of the scale and patterns of its circulation, since one of the features most likely to have determined its popularity – shortness – must also have ensured its exiguous survival. Short works are much more quickly lost than long ones, and many popular works, in both prose and verse, must simply have perished. Some of this material, particularly the lyrics, carols and ballads which are the shortest of all its manifestations, may in the first place have had a predominantly oral circulation of a kind that left few material remains (O'Donoghue 2005; Reichl 1985). Other varieties of it may have been committed to written form only in ephemeral copies, on fragile loose sheets and bifolia, or in single gatherings or small booklets. The material considered in this chapter – a clutch of some thirty comic and pious verse tales with a predominantly fifteenth-century circulation – is thus likely to be the tip of a much larger, now lost iceberg.[1]

---

[1] Editions of the tales discussed here, if not in the list of Works cited, can be located from *NIMEV* and *STC* numbers; references to editions and bibliography are also available in Cooke 1993 (who includes Scottish verse tales not discussed here). Useful anthologies are *Ten Fifteenth-Century Comic Poems*, ed. Furrow 1985; *Middle English Verse Romances*, ed. Sands 1966; *Middle English Metrical Romances*, ed. French and Hale 1930. For ballads, see Green 1997 and Gray 2008: 392–405.

As will become apparent, the popular verse tale of this date is a genre with notably porous boundaries, allowing for overlap with romance, prophecy, saint's life, miracle and other narrative forms (Cooke 1993 discusses definitions and the relationship between tale collections and independent tales). Mostly just a few hundred lines long, and in forms dominated by varieties of tail-rhyme and couplet, the content and flavour of these works is best suggested by some representative examples. The attractions of *The Tale of the Basin* (*NIMEV* 2658), for instance, are announced immediately in its opening stanza: readers are promised the 'gle and [...] game' that arise from 'talys and trifulles [...] and oþer mery spellis' (*Ten Fifteenth-Century Comic Poems*, ed. Furrow 1985: 45, lines 1–5). It is a farce about the trick contrived by a parson to expose the activities of his brother's bossy wife and her lover, Sir John the priest. The trick revolves around a 'priue experiment' performed by the parson on the wife's chamber pot, to which Sir John's hands, and those of several others – the wife, the wife's 'wench', the priest's clerk and a carter – become serially stuck, as he capers helplessly to the church (the joke is enhanced by the fact that several of those stuck to the pot are naked). Once the charm has been undone by the parson, the priest leaves in shame, and the wife is duly chastened.

The activities of libidinous wives and lecherous clerks and priests feature in a number of these tales; there is overlap here with the subgenre of the gossips' poem best represented by *The Ten Wives Tales* (*NIMEV* 1852). But anti-feminist stereotypes are upturned in some comic stories, like *The Wright's Chaste Wife* (*NIMEV* 252), *The Lady Prioress* (*NIMEV* 2441) and *How a Merchant Did his Wife Betray* (*NIMEV* *2602.3/1897). As demonstrated most abundantly by the (mostly prose) miracles of the Virgin with which these comic and pious tales often circulated (see Cooke 1993: 3177–3258), misogyny is by no means a routine feature of popular tales. Even the pious tale of *The Adulterous Falmouth Squire* (*NIMEV* 2052), a warning against the perils of breaking 'spowsode', targets husbands rather than wives with its grisly account of the vision granted to the son of a Falmouth adulterer: the young man's father burns in hell, suspended 'by the membrys', and torn apart by fiends, while his virtuous brother (the young man's uncle) enjoys the pleasures of heaven. As well as the striking warning of this vision, the poem offers sound practical advice:

> Man, yf thou wist whate it were
> To take a-noþer manes wyffe,
> Thou wolde rather suffer here
> To be quycke slayne with a knyffe;
> For yf thou take a-noþer manes wyffe,
> A wrong aire thou moste nedis gett. (Kölbing 1884: lines 134–9)

Although all eight surviving copies of *The Adulterous Falmouth Squire* are fifteenth century (possibly in one case early sixteenth century), the 'Ensampill' it relates is located in the early fourteenth century, 'In Falmowthe [...] Thirty winter be-for the dethe' (Kölbing 1884: lines 152–3; that is, thirty years before the Black Death). Whatever its veracity, the tale may well have existed in some form before 1400. A characteristic of popular tales of this kind is that their written origins are often hard to date with any precision, and it is likely that a number of those in circulation in the fifteenth century were already of some antiquity. The collection of tales in octosyllabic verse known as *The Seven Sages* (*NIMEV* 3187), *exempla* with a widespread European currency, survives in different versions in manuscripts dating from the fourteenth right through to the early sixteenth centuries, as well as in two early printed editions (*STC* 21297–8). It is not uncommon to find stray tales from much earlier collections in fifteenth-century manuscript anthologies. The pious collection that is now Leeds, Brotherton Library, MS 501, includes (along with the *The Prick of Conscience* and other texts) a group of Marian tales from the older *South English Legendary*; while the extremely varied assortment of materials in NLW, MS Brogynton II.1 (formerly Porkington 10) incorporates a Miracle of the Virgin (*NIMEV* 1641) from the earlier *Northern Homily Cycle*. Even without affiliations to larger collections, some individual works had long lives. *How a Merchant Did his Wife Betray*, which survives complete in two fifteenth-century manuscript witnesses and in fragmentary form in a further one, is a close relative of a verse tale that first appears in the mid-fourteenth-century Auchinleck manuscript (Edinburgh, NLS Advocates' 19. 2. 1) as *A penni worthe of witte* (*NIMEV* *2602.3; both versions are edited by Kölbing). In some cases fifteenth-century origins are simply imputed to works that survive only in later witnesses: *The Smyth and his Dame, Dane Hew Munk of Leicestre* and *How the Plowman Learned his Paternoster*, for example, survive only in sixteenth-century printed editions (*STC* 22653.5–53.9, 13257, 20034); *The Felon Sew* and *John the Reeve* (*NIMEV* 989) only in late transcriptions (*John the Reeve* in the Percy Folio, BL, Add. MS 27879, along with a number of popular romances).

Circulating in fairly informal ways over long periods of time, like the popular romances with which they often kept company, popular verse tales readily invited various kinds of revision and *remaniement*. The fabliau-like tale of *The Friar and the Boy* (*NIMEV* 977), also known as *Jack and his Stepdame*, survives in its fifteenth-century and later witnesses in two versions. One describes young Jack's comic triumph over his stepmother, a friar, and his father with the aid of three magic gifts; the other (represented largely by post-medieval copies, but also present in one fifteenth-century witness) adds various forms of a coda in which Jack's triumph is confirmed in a court-scene that turns to chaos as the litigious friar and stepmother are helplessly forced to dance to the sound of his magic pipe (see *Ten Fifteenth-Century Comic Poems*, ed. Furrow 1985: 67–153, especially 137–53). Among pious tales, the thrillingly gruesome and long-lived *Trentalle sancti Gregorii* (*NIMEV* 83, 1653, 3184), which recounts the salvation of the soul of Pope Gregory's sinful mother, survives in three significantly different versions, with further variation even within individual textual traditions (see Kaufmann 1889).

The forms of *remaniement* identifiable range from variations in verse form to changes of narrator and varieties of expansion and compression. While both versions of *The Friar and the Boy* are in six-line stanzas, the different versions of the *Trentalle sancti Gregorii* are in couplets (versions A and B) and in quatrains (version C), with some variation in the narrating voice. *The Child of Bristowe* (*NIMEV* 1157), in twelve-line stanzas, is almost twice as long as its close relative *The Merchant and his son* (*NIMEV* 1909), in long couplets. The different versions of *The Lady Who Buried the Host* (*NIMEV* 622) and *The Tale of an Incestuous Daughter*

(*NIMEV* 1107 and 1762) retain the same rhyme schemes (eight- and six-line stanzas respectively), but are characterised by differences in phrasing and, in the case of *The Tale of an Incestuous Daughter*, by variations in the moralising framework. Typically, variation between versions is especially marked in the ways in which these popular poems bring themselves to a close. This feature is also no doubt related to the impulses that brought into being independent extensions to some of the texts considered here. The burlesque *Turnament of Tottenham* (*NIMEV* 2615), for example, is accompanied in one of its two witnesses by *The Feest of Tottenham* (*NIMEV* 2354), a form of sequel to the *Turnament* in which Tottenham is not named but the protagonists of the *Turnament* reappear. *The Adulterous Falmouth Squire* in some way became linked to, if it did not directly spawn, *The Lament of the Soul of Sir William Basterdfeld* (*NIMEV* 172), a warning spoken from purgatory by the one-time *bon viveur* Sir William: 'I my3ht not fast, I wold not praye, […] I droffe eu*er* forth from dey to dey, […] It is me gyue*n*, for*e* myne hyre,/ Eu*er* to bryne in þe pytte of helle' (in *Political, Religious and Love Poems*, ed. Furnivall 1903: lines 64–71). In one manuscript the *Lament* prefaces *The Adulterous Falmouth Squire*, although its circulation was otherwise independent.

The fossilised reminders of oral circulation present in many popular tales (as also in popular romances) underline this propensity for variation. Many of these works begin with a request for attention from a listening audience:

> Lysteneþ, lordyngys, y yow pray,
> How a merchand dyd hys wife betray
> Bothe be day and be nyght,
> Yf ye wyll herken aright!
>   (*How a Merchant Did his Wife Betray*; Kölbing 1884: lines 1–4)

> God that died for vs all
> And drank both eysell and gall
> Bring vs oute of bale,
> And graunt theym good liff and long
> That woll listyn to my song
> And tend to my tale.   (*Jack and his Stepdame*, in *Ten Fifteenth-Century Comic Poems*, ed. Furrow 1985: 95, lines 1–6)

Frequently, regardless of the piety of their content, the tales end with a prayer:

> God, that ys of grete renowne
> Saue all the gode folke of pys towne!
> Jesu, as thou art heuyn kynge,
> To the blys of heuyn owre soules brynge.
>   (*How a Merchant Did his Wife Betray*; Kölbing 1884: lines 269–72)

> That Lorde yow kepe, frendes all,
> That drake both eysill and gall,
> Holy God in His empere. Amen.
>   (*Jack and his Stepdame*, in *Ten Fifteenth-Century Comic Poems*, ed. Furrow 1985: 138, lines RQ 10–2)

More often than not, these tales are anonymous. Those named individuals who feature as the supposed authors or speakers of some of them are usually obvious fictions. *The Lament of the Soul of Sir William Basterdfeld* is attached to a speaker whose name seems likely to be a generic one related to his lifetime of fornication, while the narrator of *The Cokwolds' Dance* (*NIMEV* 219), is an Arthurian lord with the apt but clearly invented name of Sir Corneus (his name has become an alternative title for the tale). The author of *The Felon Sew*, which survives only in late transcriptions of a copy said to have been made in 1565 by Ralph Rokeby, was reputedly someone acquainted with Rokeby's grandfather. Of the other works considered here, only *The Wright's Chaste Wife* is attributed to a named author: an unidentified 'Adam of Cobsam' (in *Political, Religious and Love Poems*, ed. Furnivall, line 620), who, if he even existed, seems hardly likely to have been someone concerned to exert authorial rights.

The geographical spread of these works, in terms of both their field of reference and their circulation, is striking. Miracles of the Virgin constitute a special case, their often distant settings no doubt reflecting the wide European circulation of this body of material. The French setting of *How the Plowman Learned his Paternoster*, a tale that sees simple faith triumph over clerical learning, may again derive from its relationship to European analogues (it survives only in a printed edition, from 1510, and may have been a translation of a French original). But although some other English verse tales may reflect tale types in wider European circulation, most give the impression of having roots in English localities. Some, like *The Adulterous Falmouth Squire*, *The Turnament* and *The Feest of Tottenham*, the pious tale of *The Child of Bristowe*, and *Dane Hew Munk of Leicester*, explicitly proclaim connections with particular English places (to these might be added the so-called 'Battle of Brackonwet', from Nottinghamshire, *NIMEV* 3435; see Turville-Petre 1983: 137–8). Others have more vaguely specified but still plausibly recognisable settings: the action of *The King and the Hermit* (*NIMEV* 1764), one of several surviving king-and-outlaw stories, takes place in Sherwood Forest; that of *John the Reeve*, in the same genre, somewhere close enough to Windsor for the hero to make the journey there from his home to be rewarded by Edward Longshanks. The Rokeby connections of *The Felon Sew* connect its actions to the area around Richmond, in North Yorkshire. The backdrop to the fabliau-like *Prologue to the Tale of Beryn* (*NIMEV* 3926), a farce involving Chaucer's pilgrims, and the sorry outcome of the Pardoner's overnight designs on a tapster named Kitt, is Canterbury: the work perhaps functioned as some kind of advertisement for ecclesiastical celebrations in the city (see Brown 1991), just as a verse Miracle of the Virgin, *The Foundation of the Chapel at Walsingham* (*NIMEV* 2664.5), was used in a late fifteenth-century printed edition for publicity purposes (*STC* 25001). For works circulating in such variant and long-lived forms as most of these popular tales, dialectal features can be only approximate guides to localising origins or reconstructing patterns of transmission. *The Prologue to the Tale of Beryn* is unusual in that the southeast Midlands and southern England forms that have been observed in the language of the single surviving witness seem to corroborate what has been conjectured about its composition in Canterbury (a colophon at the end of the *Tale of Beryn*, not necessarily by the same author as the *Prologue*, attributes it to a 'filius ecclesie Thome'). *The Turnament* and *Feest of Tottenham*, in contrast, appear to have been composed in northern England dialects, at some distance from the location of their action; as is true of one of the versions of *The Child of Bristowe* (northern, again).

The variety of manuscripts in which these works were copied confirms a widespread geographical circulation. Their survival has depended on their inclusion in larger mixed anthologies of the kind that became increasingly common during the course of the fifteenth century: manuscripts made of paper, copied either by one individual or by a group of scribes associated with one community (a household, perhaps); destined for a mixed readership, including both men and women, possibly children too, whose tastes would favour a mixture of diversion and instruction. Bodl., MS Ashmole 61, a collection of material copied by a scribe who signed his name as 'Rate', includes *The Adulterous Falmouth Squire* (together with *The Lament of William Basterdfeld*), *King Edward and the Hermit* and *The Cokwolds' Dance*, alongside a number of popular romances, verse saints' lives and miracles, pious works such as *The Northern Passion*, and instructive poems such as *How the Wise Man Taught his Son*, *How the Goodwife Taught her daughter*, and Lydgate's *Dietary*. The dialectal forms point to a scribe from northeast Leicestershire – and suggestions that Rate may have been a Leicester guildsman and merchant, compiling material for household use in a volume whose tall, narrow, 'account book' format reflected his professional preoccupations, are persuasive (see Blanchfield 1991 and 1996; *Codex Ashmole 61*, ed. Shuffelton 2008).

Rate's manuscript has some works in common with a late fifteenth-century collection probably compiled somewhere on the borders of east Derbyshire and west Nottinghamshire, now Edinburgh, NLS, MS Advocates 19. 3. 1. Copied in large part by a single scribe, who names himself as Heege, this collection includes *The Hunting of the Hare* and 'The Battle of Brackonwet', with a version of *Trentalle sancti Gregorii*, alongside romances, saints' lives, pious and instructive works, and some nonsense verse. Like Rate's manuscript, this has the air of a compilation designed to cater for household needs. What seems a special focus on educating the young has prompted the suggestion that Heege may have been 'not the head of a family but [...] a professional educator, a schoolmaster or tutor in a provincial gentry household' (Hardman 2006: 41).

Some of the manuscript witnesses to the tales considered here are frustratingly bare of evidence concerning their earliest readers. CUL, MS Ff. 2. 38, dominated by romances and works of religious instruction, and with some contents in common with the books of Heege and Rate, contains *The Adulterous Falmouth Squire*, *How a Merchant Did his Wife Betray* and *The Merchant and his Son*. Although the scribe's origins may have been in Leicestershire (McSparran and Robinson 1979, intro.: xviii, note 15), he did not record his name, and there are no other indications of the manuscript's provenance or early use. Aberystwyth, NLW, MS Brogynton II. 1 (formerly Porkington 10), a substantial anthology compiled by many different scribes, contains much the same mixture of contents as these other household collections, but nothing is known of its earliest owners beyond their likely residence somewhere in the northwest Midlands near the border with Wales (Boffey and Thompson 1989: 294). Although it has been argued that CUL, MS Ff. 5. 48 is likely to have been a 'clerical miscellany' rather than a collection for household use (Ohlgren 2007: 29–51), the contents of this collection do not differ markedly from the Heege and Rate collections, or from CUL MS Ff. 2. 38. Along with the earliest Robin Hood poem (*Robin Hood and the Monk, NIMEV* 1534), the popular prophecy associated with the name of *Thomas of Erceldoune* (*NIMEV* 365), and a wealth of other works in prose and verse, it contains a notable collection of verse tales: *King Edward and the Shepherd, The Tale of the Basin, The Turnament* and *The Feest of Tottenham, The Adulterous Falmouth Squire, The Lady Who Buried the Host* and *The Tale of an Incestuous Daughter*.

The contents of these collections from the east and northwest Midlands are reflected in scattered witnesses from other parts of the country, in particular CUL, MS Ee. 4. 35, with East Anglian connections, containing *The Adulterous Falmouth Squire, The Lady Who Buried the Host, The Friar and the Boy*, as well as *Robin Hood and the Potter* and *The King and the Barker* (*NIMEV* 4168). And some are also duplicated in compilations made in late fifteenth- and early sixteenth-century London: anthologies for urban readers, whose tastes incorporated pious and comic verse tales alongside the other favourite popular genres of saints' lives and romances. Both Oxford, Balliol College, MS 354, made by the London grocer Richard Hill, and the more studiedly literary anthology that is now Bodl., MS Rawlinson C. 86 include *The Friar and the Boy*, while Lambeth Palace, MS 306 has *The Wright's Chaste Wife* and *The Adulterous Falmouth Squire* (Boffey and Meale 1991; Lay 2008). The obvious appetite for these works among London readers may have been influential on their gradual transmission into print, marketed as small books by early London printers such as Wynkyn de Worde, or still later sixteenth-century ones. De Worde printed *The Friar and the Boy* (*STC* 14522), *King Edward and the Shepherd* (*STC* 7502.5, ?1508), *The Smith that Forged him a New Dame* (*STC* 22653.5, c.1505), and *How the Plowman Learned his Paternoster* (*STC* 20034, ?1510). A printed edition of *Dan Hew Munk of Leicester* (*STC* 13257) survives from 1560, and an edition of *The Turnament of Tottenham*, rather misleadingly entitled 'A briefe description of the towne of Tottenham', from 1631 (*STC* 19925). The longevity of some of these works, once in the hands of printers, mirrors that of popular romances, ballads and Robin Hood poems.

The attractions of short verse-tales for readers, possibly also for the listening audiences who may have existed in fifteenth-century household or other communal contexts, are plain. Their narrative lines are pacy and gripping, involving varieties of suspense leading to comic dénouement and/or satis-fyingly just punishment for wrongdoing (*Dane Hew Munk of Leicester*, a black comedy involving the corpse of a lustful young monk, is rich in both). They sometimes feature grisly or mildly titillating visions, and occasional magical interventions of other kinds (young Jack's magic pipe in *The Friar and the Boy*; a magical drinking horn in *The Cokwolds' Dance*). Comic bodily functions supply some of the humour, as do riotous overturnings of activities that would normally follow prescribed forms. The knightly feast at the centre of *The Cokwolds' Dance* turns into a celebration of cuckolds; *The Turnament of Tottenham* stages a ludicrous rustic contest for the hand of a village girl; *The Hunting of the Hare* (*NIMEV* 64; see Green 2005) and *The Felon Sew* describe hunts that go energetically and comi-cally wrong. There is plenty here for those eager to explore the role of the carni-valesque in popular culture (Meale 2001). Although the individuals depicted in popular stories are occasionally from the knightly or gentle classes, their casts are more usually people from the middle levels of urban or rural society – merchants

and their families, reeves and potters, smiths, yeomen, plowmen, and the ubiquitous friars – with preoccupations that predictably match their ways of life (*The
Smyth and his Dame*, for example, concerns a proud blacksmith who hammers
his wife completely out of shape). A number of these stories, particularly the
pious ones, raise the interestingly dangerous matters of adultery, incest, domestic
abuse, sibling rivalry and, even, insufficient faith (*The Lady Who Buried the Host*
stages a miracle that restores the faith of a woman in 'dyspere'). Typically, their
narrative development hinges on family relationships of different kinds, and on
means of restoring harmony between husbands and wives, or siblings, or parents
and children.

Studies of these forms of popular narrative have explored their structures,
their European analogues, and their different manifestations in Middle English
prose and verse. Certain tale types are indeed readily distinguishable, from
burlesque hunts and tournaments (*The Hunting of the Hare*, *The Turnament* and
Feest of Tottenham, 'The Battle of Brackonwet') to king-and-commoner stories
(*King Edward and the Shepherd*, *John the Reeve*, *King Edward and the Hermit*, *The
Hermit and the Outlaw*, NIMEV 260, on which see Green 2004). Their relationships
and generic affiliations can constitute rewarding areas of study. More recently,
popular tales have featured in discussions of popular piety and popular culture
in the Middle Ages, and as affording illuminating insights into medieval attitudes towards social fabric, family and emotion (for example, see Hahn 2000;
Hutjens 2009). One particular approach has been to situate analysis of popular
tales in discussion of the larger manuscript contexts in which they have been
preserved. Prominent in these larger contexts are seen to be themes of family life,
the passion and the afterlife, courtesy, property and religious duty (*Codex Ashmole
61*, ed. Shuffelton 2008); also parody and paradox, adventure and nurture, sainthood and womanhood, and piety and penitence (Hardman 2006).

Although there is a generally consistent flavour to the manuscripts in which
popular tales were copied, one that suggests a secular readership for whom
matters of family reputation and inheritance, material as well as spiritual profit,
would have been important, it would be wrong to suggest that the tales' circulation was in any way narrowly circumscribed. In some collocations, popular verse
tales sit alongside works of more artfully literary kinds. In the London collection
that is now Bodl., MS Rawlinson C 86, for example, *The Friar and the Boy* occurs
in a section of the manuscript that also includes the 'Clerk's Tale', the 'Prioress's
Tale', an English prose condensation of parts of Ranulph Higden's *Polychronicon*,
an English verse translation of Boccaccio's tale of *Guiscardo and Ghismonda*, and
a number of short poems, some anonymous and others by Lydgate (Boffey and
Meale 1991: 144–8). The former Delamere manuscript of the *Canterbury Tales*,
now Tokyo, Takamiya 32, also contains *The Adulterous Falmouth Squire* (here with
the slightly upmarket title 'Here begynniht a tale of the dignite of Wedlock'),
together with extracts from Gower's *Confessio Amantis*, some pious verse items,
and the romance of *Partonope*. In the light of the taste evident in this compilation
for romance, a genre sometimes so close to that of the popular tale, it interesting
to see the popular romance *Gamelyn* brought into the text of the *Canterbury Tales*
here to fill the gap at the end of the unfinished 'Cook's Tale' (Manly and Rickert
1940: 108–16).

These collocations suggest that what we might now want to define as a sepa-rate genre of the 'popular' verse tale did not necessarily have such a distinctive flavour for its medieval readers. Although it may be tempting to imagine that these popular stories, with their creaky verse-forms and stereotypical charac-ters, might for sophisticated readers have constituted material for derision, it is worth remembering that in many contexts a tale was simply a tale. Chaucer, after all, knew popular romances well enough to work with them in *Sir Thopas*; and Hoccleve produced his own version of a popular tale in *The Monk who Clad the Virgin by Singing Ave Maria* (*NIMEV* 4122: its opening line, 'Ther was whilom [...] In France a ryche man and a worthy', sounding like the start of any number of the tales discussed above). Some of the works considered here (particularly *the Prologue to the Tale of Beryn*, and burlesques such as *The Turnament of Tottenham*) are in fact quite self-conscious narratives, displaying relatively informed aware-ness of the workings of particular genres. What remains most striking about these stories, perhaps, is the widespread appeal suggested by their longevity. Although miracles and many pious narratives were to be submerged by the tide of religious reform in England in the early sixteenth century, a number of comic or broadly moral verse tales clearly enjoyed a circulation that lasted for some hundreds of years.

Works cited

Blanchfield, Lynne S. 'The Romances in MS Ashmole 61: An Idiosyncratic Scribe', in *Romance in Medieval England*, eds Maldwyn Mills, Jennifer Fellows and Carol M. Meale (Cambridge, 1991), pp. 65–87

——, 'Rate Revisited: The Compilation of the Narrative Works in MS Ashmole 61', in *Romance Reading on the Book*, eds Jennifer Fellows et al. (Cardiff, 1996), pp. 208–20

Boffey, Julia, and John J. Thompson, 'Anthologies and Miscellanies: Production and Choice of Texts', in *Book Production and Publishing in Britain, 1375–1475*, eds Jeremy Griffiths and Derek Pearsall (Cambridge, 1989), pp. 279–315

——, and Carol M. Meale, 'Selecting the Text: Rawlinson C. 86 and Some Other Books for London Readers', in *Regionalism in Late Medieval Manuscripts and Texts*, ed. Felicity Riddy (Cambridge, 1991), pp. 143–69

Brown, Peter, 'Journey's End: The Prologue to *The Tale of Beryn*', in *Chaucer and Fifteenth-Century Poetry*, eds Julia Boffey and Janet Cowen (London, 1991), pp. 143–74

Codex Ashmole 61: A Compilation of Popular Middle English Verse, ed. George Shuffelton (Kalamazoo, MI, 2008)

Cooke, Thomas D., with Peter Whiteford and Nancy Mohr McKinley, 'Tales', in *A Manual of the Writings in Middle English 1050–1500, Volume 9*, gen. ed. Albert E. Hartung (New Haven, CT, 1993), pp. 3138–3328 and 3472–3570

Davis, Natalie Zemon, 'Toward Mixtures and Margins', *American Historical Review*, 97 (1992), 1409–16

Duncan, Thomas G., ed., *A Companion to the Middle English Lyric* (Cambridge, 2005)

Gray, Douglas, *Later Medieval English Literature* (Oxford, 2008)

Green, Richard Firth, 'The Ballad and the Middle Ages', in *The Long Fifteenth Century: Essays for Douglas Gray*, eds Helen Cooper and Sally Mapstone (Oxford, 1997), pp. 163–84

——, '*The Hermit and the Outlaw*: An Edition', in *Interstices: Studies in Middle English and Anglo-Latin Texts in Honour of A. G. Rigg*, eds Richard Firth Green and Linne R. Mooney (Toronto, 2004), pp. 137–66

——, '*The Hunting of the Hare*: An Edition, in *Studies in Late Medieval and Early Renaissance Texts in Honour of John Scattergood*, eds Anne Marie D'Arcy and Alan Fletcher (Dublin, 2005), pp. 129–45

Hahn, Thomas, 'Playing with Transgression: Robin Hood and Popular Culture', in *Robin Hood in Popular Culture: Violence, Transgression and Justice*, ed. Thomas Hahn (Cambridge, 2000), pp. 1–11

Hardman, Philippa, intro., *The Heege Manuscript: a facsimile of National Library of Scotland MS Advocates 19.3.1*. Leeds Texts and Monographs, n. s. 16 (Leeds, 2006).

Hutjens, Linda, 'The Disguised King in Early English Ballads', in *Literature and Popular Culture in Early Modern England*, eds Matthew Dimmock and Andrew Hadfield (Farnham, 2009), pp. 75–89

Kaufmann, A., ed., *Trentalle Sancti Gregorii, eine mittelenglische Legenden in zwei Texten*, Erlanger Beiträge, 3 (Erlangen, 1889)

Kölbing, E., 'Kleine Publicationen aus der Auchinleck-hs', *Englische Studien*, 7 (1884), 101–25

Lay, Christopher, '"A brief collection of matters of Chronicles": Notes by John Stow in Lambeth Palace Library MS 306', *English Manuscript Studies*, 14 (2008), 207–18

Manly, John M., and Edith Rickert, *The Text of The Canterbury Tales*, 8 vols (Chicago, IL, 1940)

McSparran, F., and P. R. Robinson, intro., *Cambridge University Library MS Ff. 2. 38* (London, 1979)

Meale, Carol M., 'Romance and its Anti-Type? *The Turnament of Totenham*, the Carnivalesque, and Popular Culture', in *Middle English Poetry: Texts and Traditions: Essays in Honour of Derek Pearsall*, ed. A. J. Minnis (York, 2001), pp. 103–27

Middle English Metrical Romances, eds Walter Hoyt French and Charles Brockway Hale (New York, 1930)

Middle English Verse Romances, ed. Donald B. Sands (New York, 1966)

O'Donoghue, Bernard, '"Cuius Contrarium": Middle English Popular Lyrics', in Duncan, ed., *A Companion*, pp. 210–26

Ohlgren, Thomas H., *Robin Hood: The Early Poems, 1465–1560: Texts, Contexts and Ideology* (Cranbury, NJ, 2007)

Political, Religious and Love Poems, ed. F. J. Furnivall, rev. edn, EETS, o. s. 15 (London, 1903)

Putter, Ad, and Jane Gilbert, eds *The Spirit of Medieval English Popular Romance* (Harlow, 2000)

Reichl, Karl, 'The Middle English Carol', in Duncan, ed., *A Companion*, pp. 150–70

Ten Fifteenth-Century Comic Poems, ed. Melissa M. Furrow (New York, 1985)

Turville-Petre, Thorlac, 'Some Medieval English Manuscripts in the North-East Midlands', in *Manuscripts and Readers in Fifteenth-Century England: The Literary Implications of Manuscript Study*, ed. Derek Pearsall (Cambridge, 1983), pp. 125–41

The Wright's Chaste Wife, ed. F. J. Furnivall, rev. edn, EETS, o. s. 12 (London, 1869)

17

Beyond the Fifteenth Century

A. S. G. EDWARDS

The Great Chronicle of London, written in the fifteenth and early sixteenth centuries, contains a number of poems in addition to its main prose narrative. One of these was composed as an attack on John Grimaldi, a crony of Henry VII's much loathed ministers, Richard Empson and Edmund Dudley, both executed in 1510. The poem includes the following passage:

> O most cursid Caytyff, what shuld I of the wryte
> Or telle the particulers, of thy cursid lyffe
> I trow if Skelton, or Cornysh wold endyte
> Or mastyr moor, they myght not Inglysh Ryffe
> Nor yit Chawcers, if he were now in lyffe
> Cowde not in metyr, half thy shame spelle. (Edwards, ed., 1981: 46–7)

These lines offer a version of the medieval inexpressibility topos: not even the several poets named here, 'Skelton', 'Cornysh', 'mastyr moor' and 'Chawcer' could adequately express in their verse the revulsion felt at Grimaldi's rapacity.

The conjunction of those names is worth some consideration. Geoffrey Chaucer still provides a touchstone of poetic excellence more than a century after his death. But the *Great Chronicle* also invokes a different range of reference, one that does not look to the past, but to the work of contemporary poets: John Skelton (c.1460–1529), William Cornish (d.1525) and Thomas More (1478–1535) were all at the beginning of their literary careers when this passage was composed. It is, in this respect, one without precedent. For the first time in the sixteenth century, contemporary poets are seen as points of literary reference comparable with those figures of undisputed past greatness. The passage as a whole signals a sense of literary value in which past and present poets are seen as equivalent in their significance as touchstones of poetic worth.

The bulk of the poetry composed in the fifteenth century had been created under the shadow of Chaucer. The historical significance of his achievement as a writer of English verse was recognised early and widely; the terms of that praise frequently acknowledge his foundational position in that tradition. To his name were often added those of his contemporary, John Gower (c.1330–1408) and his most influential heir, John Lydgate (c.1370–1449). This trio, frequently conjoined, became a fixed reference point for later poets who routinely invoked their names (see further Spurgeon 1925: I, for numerous examples).

The distinctive qualities of this literary tradition are extensively articulated in the early sixteenth century by Stephen Hawes (b.c.1474 – d. before 1529). In his *Pastime of Pleasure* (1509; STC 12948), as he apostrophises his own work:

> Remembre the[e] of the trace and daunce   1315
> Of poetes olde with all thy purueyaunce.
>
> As morall gower whose sentencyous dewe
> Adowne reflayreth with fayre golden beames
> And after Chaucers all abrode doth shewe
> Our vyces to clense his depured stremes   1320
> Kyndlyng our hertes with the fyry leames
> Of morall vertue as is probable
> [...]
> And after hym my mayster Lydgate   1338
> The monke of Bury dyde hym well apply
> Bothe to contryue and eke to translate
> And of vertue euer in especially.
>   (Hawes, ed. Mead 1928: lines 1315–22, 1338–41)

Emphasis falls on the ethical qualities of that literary past: 'morall' (lines 1317, 1322), 'vertue' (lines 1322, 1341), 'sentencyous' (line 1317). For Hawes, such qualities retained their exemplary appeal and are reflected in his own lengthy verse allegory. That the qualities of the poetic past remained, to at least some degree, those valued by a poet a century or so later, may suggest both the durability of literary tradition and some of the limits of Hawes's own poetic.

But by the early sixteenth century there were indications that the shadow of the literary past was slowly shortening. To the passage in the *Great Chronicle* quoted above, can be added the testimony of Henry Bradshaw (d.1513), a monk of St Werburgh's, Cheshire. In his posthumously printed saints' lives, he also sets his own verse in relation to past and present poets. This is from his *Life of St Werburge of Chester* (1513; STC 2506):

> To all auncient poetes litell boke submytte the
> Whilom flouryng in eloquence facundious
> And to all other which present nowe be
> Fyrste to maister Chaucer and Ludgate sentencious
> Also to preignaunt Barkley nowe beyng religious
> To inuentiue Skelton and poet laureate. (Edwards, ed., 1981: 47)

Chaucer's name is again conjoined with Lydgate's, while to Skelton's is added that of another contemporary poet, Alexander Barclay (c.1484–1552). The living poets are given distinctive qualities: Barclay is 'preignaunt', while Skelton is 'inuentiue'. Chaucer, Lydgate, Barclay and Skelton reappear in Bradshaw's *Life of St Radegunde* (c.1521; STC 3507), where Chaucer and Skelton are both hailed as 'fathers of eloquence' (Edwards, ed., 1981: 48). The qualities of the verse of the past and that of the present share both parallels and distinctive differences. They point to a sense of literary values that, like the passage in the *Great Chronicle*, balances an awareness of tradition against a sense of the contemporary. This quickening sense of the new, manifested in two works written close in time in places as far apart as London and Cheshire, is particularly striking. Something was clearly felt to be in the air.

Such novelty lay in part in new cultural factors. The names invoked in the *Great Chronicle* – Skelton, Cornish and More – were all part of a new generation of writers associated with the creation of forms of court culture. They included other poets such as Hawes and Thomas Wyatt (c.1503–42), and Henry Howard, Earl of Surrey (1516/17–47), all of whom were directly associated with the circles of Henry VII and/or Henry VIII; other poets such as Barclay, William Peeris (fl. 1520), William Forrest (fl. 1530–75), William Walter (fl. c.1525–33) and William Neville (1497–c.1545), were connected with prominent royal, noble or clerical households.

Such forms of court culture shaped literary activity in various ways. At the most obvious level, poetry was a form of social diversion, linked to both drama and music (Henry VIII was himself an accomplished poet and musician). Some of the verse produced during the first half of the sixteenth century was clearly coterie verse of various kinds created within royal or noble environments designed to provide entertainment, often with musical accompaniment (Stevens 1961 still provides a valuable introduction).

Such environments raise questions about the contexts for the production and circulation of verse in this period and about its subject matter. For a number of these courtly poets, manuscript was the primary means of transmission for their works. Thomas Wyatt and Henry Howard, Earl of Surrey are the most obvious examples of this tendency. They were members of the social elite for whom they primarily wrote; the texture of the relationship between author, work and audience in such contexts is extremely difficult to define. At a very general level, a manuscript culture of this kind allows the possibility of a close, direct relationship between text and audience, as we see in such courtly manuscripts of the time as the so-called 'Devonshire' manuscript, BL, Additional MS 17492 (on which see especially Heale 1995). It has been argued that for such court poets, manuscript was the preferred literary medium because it could be targeted to a precise audience, whether collective or individual. Such targeting was not available through the emergent medium of print (to which I will turn shortly). Indeed, the relationship between manuscript composition and circulation has been seen as an active resistance to the so-called 'stigma of print' because of the elite nature of the courtly audience (see Saunders 1951). But it seems doubtful that the failure to seek print publication was necessarily anything more than a matter of circumstance. Both Wyatt and Surrey died untimely and their deaths make it impossible to establish what relationship with print culture either poet might have finally contemplated, had they lived.

But in the earlier sixteenth century such relationships were most likely shaped by factors that had less to do with class than the sense that any particular poet might have had of their appropriateness for his compositions – and any printer's sense of their marketability. The nature of their compositions, mainly comprising short poems, some written for particular occasions or circles, scarcely lent itself to print circulation during their lifetimes, while their oeuvres were still in the process of creation. In the environments in which they composed, they clearly had a sense of a coterie audience or audiences, which could be effectively reached by the forms of personalised production that a manuscript culture afforded. In such manuscript environments the social elements, those that affect tone and relationship, are hard to recover, but were clearly highly significant. And the relationship that is established is not just with an audience: for example, one poem survives in different forms in manuscript copies ascribed to both Wyatt and Surrey. It is possible that each poet wrote a different version of it (see Edwards 2012). One short poem by Surrey has come down in multiple versions, a fact that may suggest it was adapted for different audiences, and that some of these adaptations were possibly not by Surrey (see Edwards 2005). The fluidity of manuscript circulation created complex issues of transmission.

The relationships that seem to have existed between manuscript and print culture in the early sixteenth century resist easy categorisation (see Edwards 2011). By the early sixteenth century English verse had begun to circulate in the new form of print, introduced by William Caxton into England around 1476. The verse Caxton printed was entirely medieval. Once again, Hawes points to this in his *Pastime of Pleasure* when he links his praise of the figures from the literary past (quoted above) to the present forms in which their works survive. He points to the fact that Chaucer's works 'in printed bokes dothe remayne in fame' (line 1337). He is clearly referring to the various printed editions of Chaucer's works produced by the earliest English printers, Caxton, Wynkyn de Worde and Richard Pynson in the fifteenth and early sixteenth centuries. Similarly, when he speaks of Lydgate's *Churl and the Bird*, and claims 'the pamflete sheweth it expressely' (line 1356), he is probably alluding to the numerous small quarto editions ('pamphlets') of this poem produced by these three early printers between around 1477 and 1510.

By the end of the fifteenth century printing from movable type had established itself within London and occasional outposts had been set up elsewhere. But it was not necessarily the case, as will already be apparent, that the new technology of print swiftly displaced the existing manuscript culture. Certainly it made possible the rapid reproduction of multiple copies of a work. And it also became linked to networks of distribution that ensured such printed copies could be widely and relatively swiftly disseminated even to areas as relatively remote as Bradshaw's Cheshire and beyond (Dodgson 1960; see further Edwards and Meale 1993). But printers were slow to see contemporary verse as a possible market. In its earliest phase, printing of verse was limited to disseminating verse of the past. Caxton and his chief successors initially printed Middle English verse by Chaucer, Gower and Lydgate, and some verse romances and saint's lives. Their preoccupation with markets established by the circulation of medieval manuscripts meant that by 1500 only three works of contemporary verse had been printed. The earliest of these was the elegy on the death of Jasper, Duke of Bedford by one 'Smert' printed by Pynson ([1496]; *STC* 14477); William of Tours', *Contemplation of sinners* was printed by de Worde ([1499]; *STC* 5643); while John Skelton's *Bouge of Court* ([1498]; *STC* 22597), also printed by de Worde, was the first contemporary work of courtly, secular verse to circulate in printed form.

It is unclear whether poets or printers were initially resistant to the medium of print. But at the start of the sixteenth century the emphasis began to change, as the poems of Hawes, Barclay and Skelton all demonstrate in different ways.

Hawes was the first contemporary poet whose works survive primarily in printed form. He clearly had a close relationship with Wynkyn de Worde, who issued his *Example of Virtue* ([1504?]; *STC* 12945), *Pastime of Pleasure* (1509; *STC* 12948), *Conversion of Swearers* (1509; *STC* 12943) and *Joyful Medytacyon* ([1509]; *STC* 12953) all in the first decade of the century, and followed them with his *Comfort of Lovers* ([1515]; *STC* 12942.5). He also subsequently reprinted most of these poems.

Hawes' relationship with de Worde seems to have been an unusually close one. It was not limited simply to the fact that de Worde was his only publisher during his lifetime. Their relation found expression in distinctive aspects of the forms in which his works were published. De Worde prepared series of wood-cuts specifically for some of his poems, most notably his *Pastime of Pleasure*. These woodcuts clearly draw very closely on verbal details in parts of his poem (see Edwards 1980) to establish an extremely unusual correlation between text and image in ways that would not normally have been feasible in a manuscript culture.

The relationship between poet and printer was also one that had more complex, less definable dimensions, which seem to have involved a shared role in the nurturing of a verse print culture at the beginning of the sixteenth century. A number of other contemporary poets printed by de Worde make allusion in various ways to Hawes' poetic achievement; these figures include William Neville, Thomas Feylde and William Walter (see Edwards 1991; Gillespie 2006), but extend into much smaller borrowings: the contemporary epilogue to de Worde's 1517 edition of Chaucer's *Troilus and Criseyde* incorporates a single line (line 3570) from the *Pastime of Pleasure*. It seems that Hawes may have been both a shaping presence and a key model in de Worde's willingness to disseminate contemporary verse.

The career of Alexander Barclay offers a parallel to Hawes' own. The majority of his verse works were first published by Richard Pynson (for details see Carlson 1995). At times, Barclay indicates a clear sense of his relationship with his printer/publisher in the printed forms of such verse. For example, at the end of his translation of Sebastian Brandt's *Ship of Fools* (1509; *STC* 3545) he adds this reminder to his audience as to where they can get copies of his book:

> Our shyp here leuyth the sees brode
> By helpe of God almyght and quyetlye
> At Anker we lye within the rode
> But who that lysteth of them to bye
> In Flete strete shall hem fynde truly
> At the George: in Richade [*sic*] Pynsonnes place
> Prynter vnto the Kynges noble grece
> Deo gratias (fol. cclxxiiii)

Here and elsewhere Barclay shows an awareness of the implications of the circulation of his works in printed form.

John Skelton was to use print to disseminate his verse throughout his poetic career. But he never had an exclusive relationship with a single printer; nor was print the only medium in which his writings circulated. His changing connec-

tions with both printers and media probably reflect the changing circumstances
of his literary career and the different subject matter of his verse, ranging from
eulogy to satire, from celebration to condemnation (see further Edwards 2008).
For Skelton, the medium he used depended on the nature of his message. His
satires on Wolsey in the 1520s seem to have been addressed to a very specific
coterie audience and hence circulated in manuscript. Other topics, forms of celebration, or institutional assertion, invited the more public form of representation
through print. Only one major work, his *Garland of Laurel*, survives in both manuscript and print. In contrast, the works of Hawes and Barclay did not have any
significant manuscript tradition.

With different media come different forms of poetic interaction. Wyatt and
Surrey suggest, as I have noted, social, perhaps even collaborative, dimensions
to the circulation of their verse. In the early printed verse it is possible to glimpse
levels of tension and enmity in the verse of the period. Perhaps unsurprisingly,
John Skelton is involved in a number of the indications of conflict between fellow
poets. He evidently excited Barclay's antipathy. He seems to speak dismissively
of Skelton in his *Ship of Fools* (1509), when he asserts

> I write no Iest ne tale of Robyn hode
> Nor sawe no sparkles ne sede of vyciousnes
> Wyse men loue vertue, wylde men wantones
> It longeth nat to my scyence nor cunnynge
> For Phylyp the Sparowe the Dirige to synge. (Edwards, ed., 1981: 46)

The allusion is clearly to Skelton's poem *Philip Sparrow*. And the tone of his
comment on it, linking it to 'vyciousnes ' and 'wantones' indicates the terms of
his disapproval. Elsewhere, in the same poem, Barclay seems to attack Skelton
even more vehemently not by name but under his title of 'poet laureate'. He
speaks of him in his Fourth Eclogue as 'poete laureate,/ When stinking Thais
made him her graduate' (Barclay, ed. White 1928: 165, lines 685–6) and when he
asserts '[…] he which is lawreat/ Ought not his name with vyce to violate' (ibid.:
xxvii).

Barclay found other targets for his disapproval, sometimes ones shared with
Skelton. In his First Eclogue he complains: 'Godfrey Gormand lately did me
blame' (ibid.: 29, line 838). This seems an oblique reference to Stephen Hawes,
who, in his *Pastime of Pleasure* includes the uncouth dwarf, Godfrey Gobelive.
In his flyting *Against Garnesche* Skelton speaks of himself as 'Skelton Lauryate
Defender Agenst Master Garnesche Chalangar, with Gresy, Gorbellyd Godfrey *et
cetera*' (Skelton, ed. Scattergood 1983: line 122), seemingly linking Hawes' poem
to another literary adversary, Christopher Garnesche. Hawes himself seems to
make some complaint about Skelton in his extremely cryptic work *The Comfort of
Lovers*, but the context is very hard to recover (see Hawes, ed. Gluck and Morgan
1974: 160–1, for tentative analysis of the possibly autobiographical aspects of the
poem).

These apparent conflicts and tensions between fellow poets seem paradoxical
in the contrast in their verse between the apparent desire for a public mode of
expression, through print, and the level of cryptic allusiveness in that expression.
Such a paradox seems to imply an audience sufficiently attuned to nuance as

to be capable of grasping the points of reference in such poems. This may be an aspect of the new literary court culture of the early sixteenth century that I have already mentioned. Such a culture, or cultures, may have sharpened the literary tensions between poets competing for patronage. Both Skelton and Hawes, for example, experienced the insecurities that followed from court life (see Burrow 1999: 796–8). The acrimony that can be seen in some of the literary exchanges of Skelton, Hawes and Barclay is an aspect of wider forms of literary, social and political criticism of new kinds that found expression in contemporary verse. Much of this is linked to invective, complaint and satire. One obvious manifestation in such terms is the flyting, a series of abusive exchanges in verse (on the tradition see Gray 1984). It is a form that seems to have enjoyed a vogue in the early sixteenth century, most extensively in William Dunbar's flyting with Andrew Kennedy (a work that Skelton may have known) and Skelton's *Against Garnesche*, a series of verse attacks on one of Henry VIII's courtiers, Sir Christopher Garnesche, probably composed around 1513.

For Skelton, satire was his most characteristic mode throughout much of his career, one that varies only in its targets, as it moves from courtly allegory in *The Bouge of Court* in the late fifteenth century, to his attacks on Wolsey in the 1520s in which the *ad hominem* and the political become indistinguishable, to his attacks on the Cambridge scholars Thomas Arthur and Thomas Bilney, as the voice of political orthodoxy, at the very end of his life. Satire was a mode that allowed Skelton full range to his verbal inventiveness, in which sense is at times subsumed by sound, in which multilingual expression creates its own virtuoso euphony whereby sound dominates at the expense of meaning:

> Parott *saves habeler Castylyano*,
> With *fidasso de cosso* in Turke and in Trace;
> *Vis consilii expers*, as techythe me Orace,
> *Mole ruit sua*, whose dictes are pregnaunte
> *Souentez foyz*, Parot, *en sovenaunte*.
> (*Speke Parrot*, in Skelton, ed. Scattergood 1983: lines 38–42)

The combination of Spanish, Latin, French and English here can scarcely be intelligibly linked to any occasion, let along the ostensible satiric object. Something of the same effect is achieved by other forms of polysyllabic unintelligibility:

> Some make epylogacyon
> Of hygh predestynacyon
> And of resydevacyon
> They make enterpretacyon
> Of auquarde facyon,
> And of the prescyence
> Of dyuine assence (*Colyn Clout*, in ibid.: lines 519–25)

In such passages, in which such dissonance reflects the discord of the satiric subject, lexis turns satire into poetic noise.

Skelton's use of such satiric modes is a further indication of a new sense in the early sixteenth century of an interpersonal poetic in which the poet's feelings are grounded in the contemporaneous and the immediate, where expression gains its energy from a heightened sense of specific grievance. In such circumstances, satiric engagement is particularised through a focus on the individual character or event rather than through a preoccupation with type, the general satiric mode in the fourteenth and fifteenth century and one employed in Skelton's early dream vision, *The Bouge of Court*.

If Skelton's approach to contemporary satire pushes technique to linguistic extremities at times, he was scarcely alone among his contemporaries in being preoccupied with the mode. Indeed, it is clearly a dominant one, possibly *the* dominant one in early sixteenth-century verse. It is enacted in Barclay's translations of Sebastian Brandt's *Narrenschiff, The Ship of Fools* (1509) and of the Eclogues of Aeneas Sylvius Piccolomini, and in a number of the longer poems of Wyatt and Surrey.

Such satire becomes a way of commenting on specifically courtly social and political circumstances related to the poet's own personal circumstances. Thomas Wyatt's three Epistolary Satires are one reflection of this tendency. The first two are addressed directly to John Poyntz (c.1485–1544), the last to Francis Brian (d.1550), both members, as was Wyatt, of Henry VIII's court circle. Their directness of address and their conversational yet urgent tone, as enacted in their shifting syntactical rhythms, give their own kind of authenticating authority to the critiques of court life Wyatt presents in these poems, ones drawn from his own experience:

> I cannot, I – no, no, it will not be!
> This is the cause that I could never yet
> Hang on their sleeves that weigh as thou mayst see
> A chip of chance more than a pound of wit.
> This maketh me at home to hunt and to hawk,
> And in foul weather at my book to sit.
>   (Wyatt, ed. Daalder 1975: 103, lines 76–81)

In both mode and manner such satires point to a kind of poetic in which such personal experience becomes a synecdoche for the discontents of a larger political construct.

The texture of personal antipathy that informs such verse shades into more oblique forms of personal reference that are coloured by other dimensions of an immediate awareness of their larger implications. This is apparent in Wyatt's verse most strikingly in the ways in which his love sonnets (themselves a formal innovation) set amatory complaint within wider courtly and more potentially hazardous contexts. One sees this most clearly perhaps in 'Who so list to hounte' (Wyatt, ed. Daalder 1975: 7), where the metaphor of the hunt becomes finally one that signifies personal danger: *'noli me tangere*, for Caesar's I am' (line 14), provides a plausible reference to both Wyatt's and Henry VIII's ('Caesar') relationships with Anne Boleyn.

Henry Howard, Earl of Surrey, at times draws on more traditional sources for his critiques of his world. His poem on London, for example ('London hast thow accused me', in Surrey, ed. Jones 1964: 30–1), attacks the 'dissolute lief' (line 4) of the city, which is compared to Babylon (lines 53, 67) and defined in terms of the seven deadly sins (lines 28–40), both medieval homiletic commonplaces. His occasional emphatic use of the medieval alliterative line similarly looks to the past: 'That secret synn hath secret spight' (line 14); 'Whose scourge for synn the Screptures shew' (line 22). Here, however, what seems innovative is the way such earlier satiric models become a new reformist voice; the voice of the courtier becomes 'a fygure of the Lordes behest' (line 21). Surrey's poem has been seen as a reflection of Protestant sympathies (see Surrey, ed. Jones 1964: 127), in its accusation of injustice in the city's conduct and the promise of divine judgement. Certainly the apocalyptic vision here has some parallels with such Protestant projects as Crowley's several editions of *Piers Plowman*, published in 1550, not long after Surrey's death. More generally, one might register here the embedded sense of the consequences of the political, and of the ways that the political is perceived as an agent of moral corruption: 'Thy dredfull dome drawes fast uppon./ Thy martyres bloode, by swoord and fyre,/ In Heaven and earth for justice call' (lines 55–7), occasionally echoing *Piers Plowman*, that crucial repository of Middle English satire, still being copied and read in the sixteenth century, even within court circles. (The phrase 'dredfull dome' occurs in Langland's poem, for example; see B, 7: 188). Here the courtier becomes preacher, the new Jonah; Surrey's rhetoric is informed, not by Wyatt's finely wrought moral distaste, but by a fervent energy 'with a reckles brest,/ To wake thy sluggards with my bowe' (lines 19–20), that sees the city as the embodiment of the corrupt patterns of society, to be rebuked by a public, righteous voice.

If such poetic stances are distinct from what has gone before, so are the forms in which they are expressed. The skeltonic, the sonnet, strambotto, blank verse and poulter's measure are among the verse forms, some derived from Italian verse, that appear for the first time in English in the early sixteenth century. Such formal innovation, represented most extensively in Surrey's corpus, is one aspect of a far wider influence that can be subsumed in the amorphous category 'humanism', a term that, very loosely, signifies the emergence of kinds of preoccupation with classical or Italian subjects and influences in the early sixteenth century. Such concerns were already adumbrated in the fifteenth century (as Wakelin shows in his chapter). But English verse of the early sixteenth century saw a broadening of them. Alexander Barclay, for example, composed the first eclogues in English. Surrey made the first translation into English verse of Virgil's *Aeneid*. Both Wyatt and Surrey translated Petrarch's sonnets (previously only accessible in English through Chaucer's rendering of one of them – not presented in sonnet form – in Book I of *Troilus*). Henry Morley, Baron Morley (1480/81–1556) translated Petrarch's *Trionfi*, a work whose influence can be seen in the verse of Hawes and Thomas More. And Skelton's recurrent concern with his own poetic self-representation and the nature of fame, expressed most extensively in his *Garland of Laurel*, draws on related Renaissance humanist preoccupations with the nature of fame.

Such intimations of wider cultural sensibility in English poetry should not be underemphasised. Nor, on the other hand, should they be seen as a very pronounced aspect of verse of the early sixteenth century. It is possible to view much of the verse of this period as primarily insular in its preoccupations. For example, one of the most extended translations of a classical text, Surrey's blank verse translation of Books II and IV of Virgil's *Aeneid*, probably composed around

1540, demonstrates an extensive debt to Gavin Douglas's earlier full verse couplet rendering of Virgil's poem, completed in 1513, which it seems to have used in some measure as a crib (Bawcutt: 298). And Skelton's concerns about the nature of fame draw obviously on Chaucer's own *House of Fame*. Such a filtering of emerging humanist attitudes through antecedent native traditions is perhaps unsurprising. But it means that the direct 'literary' impact of humanism on vernacular poetry is not always clear or even evident.

If this suggests that the poetic manifestations of the influence of humanism in earlier sixteenth-century English verse is rather circumscribed, it is worth recalling that the shadow of the literary past remained a long one. Chaucer continued to be printed in ever more compendious forms during the century, by Pynson in 1526 (*STC* 5086), in the various issues of William Thynne's edition of *The Works*, first published in 1532 and then again in 1542 (*STC* 5069) and [1550?] (*STC* 5070), in John Stow's edition of 1561 (*STC* 5075) and in the first edition by Thomas Speght in 1598 (*STC* 5077). John Lydgate's *Troy Book* was first published in 1513 (*STC* 5579) and reprinted in 1555 (*STC* 5580); and his *Fall of Princes*, published first in 1494 (*STC* 3175), was reprinted in 1527 (*STC* 3176) and in several editions in and around 1554 (*STC* 3177, 3177–5, 3178). Lesser works by both Chaucer and Lydgate were also printed during the century. John Gower's *Confessio Amantis* was reprinted in 1532 (*STC* 12143) and again in 1554 (*STC* 12144). And Langland's *Piers Plowman* first published in three editions in 1550 (*STC* 19906, 19907, 19907a) was reprinted in 1563 (*STC* 19908). Apart from Chaucer, none of these were to be reprinted until the nineteenth and twentieth centuries.

The 1550s and 1560s saw the last extensive evidence of interest in the maintaining of Middle English literary traditions and of those poets earlier in the century who in various ways still drew upon those traditions. Elizabethan poets and Jacobean poets largely repudiated or ignored their own literary history. They looked less to their own poetic past and in different ways more to European literary culture than did the earlier sixteenth century poets discussed here. For Ben Jonson writing in the early seventeenth century, the traditions that these earlier poets drew on were dangerous to young readers. He counsels: 'beware of letting them taste *Gower* or *Chaucer* at first, lest falling too much in love with Antiquity, and not apprehending the weight, they grow rough and barren in language onely' (Spurgeon 1925: I, 193). The poetic gaze looked forward; the past had become a country best ignored.

Works cited

Barclay, Alexander, *The Eclogues of Alexander Barclay*, ed. Beatrice White, EETS, o. s. 175 (London, 1928)

Bawcutt, Priscilla, *Gavin Douglas: A Critical Study* (Edinburgh, 1976)

Burrow, Colin, 'Literature and Politics in the Reigns of Henry VII and Henry VIII', in *The Cambridge History of Medieval English Literature*, ed. David Wallace (Cambridge, 1999), pp. 793–820

Carlson, David, 'Alexander Barclay and Richard Pynson: A Tudor Printer and his Writer', *Anglia*, 113 (1995), 283–302

Dodgson, John McNeal, 'A Library at Pott Chapel, Pott Shrigley, Cheshire, c. 1493', *The Library*, 5th ser. 15 (1960), 47–53

Edwards, A. S. G., 'Poet and Printer in Sixteenth Century England: Stephen Hawes and Wynkyn de Worde', *Gutenberg Jahrbuch* (1980), 82–8

——, ed., *John Skelton: The Critical Heritage* (London, 1981)

——, 'From Manuscript to Print: Wynkyn de Worde and the Printing of Contemporary Poetry', *Gutenberg Jahrbuch* (1991), 143–8

——, 'Surrey's Martial Epigram: Scribes and Transmission', in *Scribes and Transmission in English Manuscripts 1400–1700*, eds Peter Beal and A. S. G. Edwards (London, 2005), pp. 74–82

——, 'Skelton's English Poems in Manuscript and Print', in *John Skelton and Early Modern Culture: Papers Honoring Robert S. Kinsman*, ed. David R. Carlson (Tempe, AZ, 2008), pp. 85–98

——, 'The Circulation of English Verse in Manuscript after the Advent of Print in England', *Studia Neophilologica*, 83 (2011), 67–77

——, 'Print and Manuscript: The Text and Canon of Surrey's Lyric Verse', in *'In the prayse of writing': Early Modern Manuscript Studies*, eds S. P. Cerasano and Steven W. May (London, 2012), pp. 25–43

——, and Carol M. Meale, 'The Marketing of Printed Books in Late Medieval England', *The Library*, 6th ser., 15 (1993), 95–124

Gillespie, Alexandra, *Print Culture and the Medieval Author: Chaucer, Lydgate, and their Books, 1473–1557* (Oxford, 2006)

Gray, Douglas, 'Rough Music: Some Early Invectives and Flytings', *Yearbook of English Studies*, 14 (1984), 21–43

Hawes, Stephen, *The Pastime of Pleasure*, ed. William Edward Mead, EETS, o. s. 173 (London, 1928)

——, *The Minor Poems*, eds Florence W. Gluck and Alice B. Morgan, EETS, o. s. 271 (London, 1974)

Heale, Elizabeth, 'Women and the Courtly Love Lyric: The Devonshire MS (BL Additional 17492)', *Modern Language Review*, 90 (1995), 296–313

Saunders, J. W., 'The Stigma of Print: A Note on the Social Bases of Tudor Poetry', *Essays in Criticism*, 1 (1951), 139–64

Skelton, John, *John Skelton: The Complete English Poems*, ed. John Scattergood (Harmondsworth, 1983)

Spurgeon, Caroline, ed., *Five Hundred Years of Chaucer Criticism and Allusion, 1357–1900*, 3 vols (Cambridge, 1925)

Stevens, John, *Music and Poetry in the Early Tudor Court* (London, 1961)

Surrey, Henry Howard, *Henry Howard Earl of Surrey: Poems*, ed. Emrys Jones (Oxford, 1964)

Wyatt, Sir Thomas, *Sir Thomas Wyatt: Collected Poems*, ed. Joost Daalder (London, 1975)

Chronology

1399–1400 deposition and death of Richard II; accession of Henry IV
October 1400: death of Chaucer
1408: death of Gower
1411–12: Hoccleve's *Regiment of Princes*
1412–20: Lydgate's *Troy Book*
   1413: death of Henry IV
   1415: battle of Agincourt
   1422: death of Henry V
1426: death of Hoccleve
c.1426: death of John Audelay
1431–38: Lydgate's *Fall of Princes*
1449: death of Lydgate; John Metham's *Amoryus & Cleopes*
c.1450: Henry Lovelich's *Merlin*
   1455: end of Hundred Years' War
   1461: deposition of Henry VI; Edward IV becomes King
1464: death of John Capgrave
1465: death of John Hardyng
c.1467: death of Osbern Bokenham
   1470: Henry VI regains throne
   1471: murder of Henry VI; restoration of Edward IV
c. 1474: death of Peter Idley
1475: death of George Ashby
c.1476/77: William Caxton sets up first printing house in England at Westminster; first printing by Caxton of Chaucer's *Canterbury Tales*
   1483: death of Edward IV; accession of Richard III
   1485: Battle of Bosworth Field; death of Richard III; accession of Henry VII
1491: death of Caxton
1499: John Skelton's *Bouge of Court* printed
   1509: death of Henry VII; accession of Henry VIII
1529: death of Skelton
1542: death of Sir Thomas Wyatt
1547: death of Henry Howard, earl of Surrey
   1547: death of Henry VIII; accession of Edward VI
   1555: death of Edward VI; accession of Mary Tudor
1557: first publication of Tottel's *Songs & Sonnets*
   1558: death of Mary Tudor; accession of Elizabeth I

Index of Manuscripts

Index

This is primarily an index of names of primary authors, titles and places. There is a separate index of manuscripts. Items from the bibliographies to each chapter have not been included here, nor have citations of modern critics in the text.

Lightning Source UK Ltd.
Milton Keynes UK
UKOW04f1221190716

278734UK00005B/141/P

9 781843 844303